ENVIRONMENTAL LIFE-CYCLE ASSESSMENT

Environmental Engineering Books

ENVIRONMENTAL LIFE-CYCLE ASSESSMENT

Mary Ann Curran

McGraw-Hill

New York   San Francisco   Washington, D.C.   Auckland   Bogotá
Caracas   Lisbon   London   Madrid   Mexico City   Milan
Montreal   New Delhi   San Juan   Singapore
Sydney   Tokyo   Toronto

Library of Congress Cataloging-in-Publication Data

Curran, Mary .*.nn.
    Environmental life-cycle assessment / Mary Ann Curran.
       p.   cm.
    Includes bibliographical references and index.
    ISBN 0-07-015063-X (acid-free paper)
    1. Environmental risk assessment.   2. Environmental engineering.
    I. Title.
    GE145.C87   1996
    363.7'05—dc20   96-11633
                                                              CIP

McGraw-Hill

A Division of The **McGraw·Hill** Companies

1 2 3 4 5 6 7 8 9 0   DOC/DOC   9 0 1 0 9 8 7 6

ISBN 0-07-015063-X

The sponsoring editor for this book was Zoe G. Foundotos, the editing supervisor was Bernard Onken, and the production supervisor was Suzanne W. B. Rapcavage. It was set in Times Roman by Estelita F. Green of McGraw-Hill's Professional Book Group composition unit.

Printed and bound by R. R. Donnelley & Sons Company.

McGraw-Hill books are available at special quantity discounts to use as premiums and sales promotions, or for use in corporate training programs. For more information, please write to the Director of Special Sales, McGraw-Hill, 11 West 19th Street, New York, NY 10011. Or contact your local bookstore.

This book is printed on recycled, acid-free paper containing a minimum of 50% recycled, de-inked fiber.

CONTENTS

v

Chapter 4. Streamlining   **4.1**

Chapter 5. Applications of Life-Cycle Assessment   **5.1**

Chapter 6. Life-Cycle Design   6.1

Chapter 7. Life-Cycle Costing: Concepts and Applications   7.1

Chapter 8. Public Policy Applications of Life-Cycle Assessment   8.1

Chapter 9. European Perspective   9.1

Chapter 10. Materials in LCA   10.1

Chapter 11. Application of Life-Cycle Assessment to Business Performance   11.1

Chapter 12. Life-Cycle Assessment: A System Analysis   12.1

Chapter 13. Valuation as a Step in Impact Assessment: Methods and Case Study   13.1

Chapter 17. Beginning LCA: A Dutch Guide to Environmental Life-Cycle Assessment   **17.1**

Chapter 18. Future Perspective   **18.1**

Appendix. Life-Cycle Assessment Case Studies and Related Studies Table   **A.1**

CONTRIBUTORS

David Allen   *Henry Beckman Professor in Chemical Engineering, University of Texas at Austin, Austin, Texas* (CHAP. 5)

Nico W. van den Berg, Ir.   *Centre of Environmental Science (CML), University of Leiden, Leiden, The Netherlands* (CHAP. 17)

Jacques Besnainou   *President, Ecobalance, Rockville, Maryland* (CHAP. 12)

Terrie K. Boguski   *Senior Chemical Engineer, Franklin Associates, Ltd., Prairie Village, Kansas* (CHAP. 2)

James M. Cholakis, Ph.D.   *Principal Toxicologist, Cholakis Associates, Prairie Village, Kansas* (CHAP. 2)

Frank J. Consoli   *President, Consoli Consulting Company, Media, Pennsylvania* (CHAP. 11)

Remi Coulon   *Technical Manager, Ecobalance, Rockville, Maryland* (CHAP. 12)

Mary Ann Curran   *LCA Research Program Manager, U.S. Environmental Protection Agency, National Risk Management Research Laboratory, Cincinnati, Ohio* (CHAP. 1)

Dr. Chris Dutilh   *Unilever (Van den Bergh Nederland), Rotterdam, The Netherlands* (CHAP. 17)

James A. Fava, Ph.D.   *Director, Product Stewardship and Management System, Roy F. Weston, Inc., West Chester, Pennsylvania* (CHAP. 11)

Thomas D. Foust   *Team Leader, U.S. Department of Energy, Office of Industrial Technology, Washington, DC* (CHAP. 18)

William E. Franklin   *Chairman and Principal, Franklin Associates, Ltd., Prairie Village, Kansas* (CHAP. 2)

Jürgen Giegrich   *Researcher, ifeu—Institute for Energy and Environmental Research, Heidelberg, Germany* (CHAP. 13)

Douglas D. Gish   *Senior Consultant, Systems Research and Applications International, Washington, DC* (CHAP. 18)

Eun-Sook Goidel   *Environmental Protection Specialist, Environmental Protection Agency, Office of Pollution Prevention and Toxic Substances, Washington, DC* (CHAP. 8)

Ole Jørgen Hanssen   *Director, Østfold Research Foundation (STØ), Fredrikstad, Norway* (CHAP. 14)

Robert G. Hunt   *Adviser for Science and Technology, Franklin Associates, Ltd., Prairie Village, Kansas* (CHAP. 2)

Dr. Gjalt Huppes   *Centre of Environmental Science (CML), University of Leiden, Leiden, The Netherlands* (CHAP. 17)

Gregory A. Keoleian, Ph.D.   *Research Director, National Pollution Prevention Center, Assistant Research Scientist, School of Natural Resources and Environment, University of Michigan, Ann Arbor, Michigan* (CHAP. 6)

Neil Kirkpatrick   *Director, Ecobalance UK, Arundel, West Sussex, United Kingdom* (CHAP. 15)

Mary McKiel *EPA Voluntary Standards Network Manager, Environmental Protection Agency, Office of Pollution Prevention and Toxic Substances, Washington, DC* (CHAP. 8)

Nico T. de Oude *Executive Director, SETAC-Europe, Brussels, Belgium* (CHAP. 9)

Dr. J. W. Owens *Senior Environmental Scientist, The Procter & Gamble Company, Cincinnati, Ohio* (CHAP. 16)

Dennis Postlethwaite *Life Cycle Analysis Manager, Unilever Research Port Sunlight Laboratory, Bebington, Wirral, United Kingdom* (CHAP. 9)

Anne Rønning *Research Manager, Østfold Research Foundation (STØ), Fredrikstad, Norway* (CHAP. 14)

Brian F. Russo *Project Manager & Senior Researcher, Reynolds Research, Inc., Washington, DC* (APPENDIX)

Tomas Rydberg *Product Ecologist, Chalmers Industriteknik, Göteborg, Sweden* (CHAP. 14)

Deborah Savage, Ph.D. *Research Associate, Tellus Institute, Boston, Massachusetts* (CHAP. 7)

Stefan Schmitz *Federal Environmental Agency, Berlin, Germany* (CHAP. 13)

Karen Shapiro *Associate Scientist, Tellus Institute, Boston, Massachusetts* (CHAP. 7)

Bea de Smet *Environmental Quality Manager, The Procter & Gamble Company, European Technical Center, Brussels, Belgium* (CHAP. 16)

Joel Ann Todd *Vice President, The Scientific Consulting Group, Inc., Gaithersburg, Maryland* (CHAP. 4)

Bruce W. Vigon *Research Leader, Battelle Memorial Institute, Columbus, Ohio* (CHAP. 3)

Allen White *Vice President, Tellus Institute, Boston, Massachusetts* (CHAP. 7)

Dr. P. R. White *Senior Environmental Scientist, The Procter & Gamble Company, Ltd., Forest Hall, Newcastle upon Tyne, United Kingdom* (CHAP. 16)

Steven B. Young *University of Toronto, Department of Metallurgy and Materials Science, Toronto, Ontario, Canada* (CHAP. 10)

PREFACE

The environmental movement is on a fast track. Just when we become somewhat comfortable with terms such as *waste minimization* and *pollution prevention*, new terms such as *sustainability, environmental justice, industrial ecology*, and *life-cycle assessment* are added to the list. The result is a lot of enthusiastic people running around using these terms without clear definitions. The main intent of this book is to offer insight into the term *life-cycle assessment* (LCA) as viewed by several prominent players in the development and application of LCA worldwide.

The following chapters cover all facets of LCA in order to help the reader thoroughly understand the subject. The discussions range from the full, robust LCA model (inventory, impact assessment, and improvement analysis) to issues surrounding the development of a streamlined approach. Applications in life-cycle design and ecolabeling are presented, as well as initial attempts to include life-cycle thinking in the development of public policy in the United States and abroad. Of course, no discussion of industrial applications would be complete without consideration of life-cycle costing and its importance as a factor in decision making.

Since LCA is as much a concept as it is a tool, it can be viewed in different ways and through different applications. While much has been achieved in order to define life-cycle assessment, consensus has not been reached at all levels. As you progress through the book, you may notice the coauthors presenting differing viewpoints. This reflects the dynamic situation of the practice called LCA.

The goal of this book is to bring perspective to the practical application of LCA to products, processes, and activities. The chapters address how LCA is being applied by industry and government and assess its potential as it evolves both as an environmental tool and as an ethic, much as pollution prevention has. As with any new field that is in the developmental stage as LCA is, some of the information presented here may be outdated by the time of publication. The case studies presented here are offered as examples to product manufacturers and their suppliers of how the use of LCA can lead to beneficial results.

I encourage you to begin thinking about your operations and activities in the context of life-cycle thinking, to achieve true reduced environmental impacts.

Mary Ann Curran

ACKNOWLEDGMENTS

I wish to thank the contributing authors who showed unwavering enthusiasm in making this book a reality. Their work in the environmental field, of which LCA is only a part, is demanding enough; I appreciate their willingness to take time out of their busy schedules to help with this effort. It's a huge effort to put together a publication of this scale. I hope that seeing this book materialize encourages these authors, all experts in their respective fields, to continue writing and publishing. We have only begun to explore the potential of LCA. I look forward to our continued journey together. Thanks to all of you. And a special thank you to the super folks at McGraw-Hill for their support and the opportunity they made possible.

CHAPTER 1
THE HISTORY OF LCA

Mary Ann Curran
LCA RESEARCH PROGRAM MANAGER
U.S. ENVIRONMENTAL PROTECTION AGENCY
NATIONAL RISK MANAGEMENT RESEARCH LABORATORY
CINCINNATI, OH

1.1   OVERVIEW

Every year, more and more companies are becoming concerned with the environmental impacts of their activities. These companies span the entire spectrum of industries, from energy producers to product manufacturers and service-oriented companies. They want to be able to understand the environmental impacts they cause, in order to control or, better yet, avoid them. They do so in a time of increasingly strict environmental regulations in an effort to stay within compliance and meet customer needs, all the while staying financially healthy. Currently, the main driving force is understandably the need for companies to stay competitive in the marketplace. Corporate managers see the systematic reduction of environmental impacts as one way to help them accomplish this goal. There is also a general growing desire by companies to simply do the "right thing" for the environment.

Many companies have undertaken environmental audits or assessments to measure their own environmental performance. A facility assessment involves a systematic procedure to quantify and balance inputs and outputs around the facility or around a specific operation within a facility. Many guidance manuals are available which instruct operators on how to conduct such an assessment (see, e.g., the Environmental Protection Agency's *Facility Pollution Prevention Guide*[1]). However, these assessments typically focus on a particular facility or site and do not consider the entire industrial system of which they are only one part. Industrial processes and activities do not work in a vacuum but instead are interlinked, through their suppliers and customers, with other processes and activities. Outputs in the form of products and by-products transfer from one operation to another, and perhaps on to another, making them all interdependent. This systemic approach is the basis of the *life-cycle assessment* (LCA) concept.

1.2   THE SYSTEMIC NATURE OF INDUSTRY

A *system* is a collection of operations that together perform some defined function. Any industrial system can be represented by a system boundary that encloses all the opera-

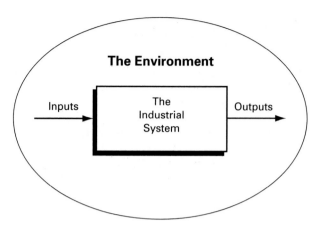

FIGURE 1.1   The industrial system. (*Source: SETAC, 1991.*)

tions of interest. The region surrounding this boundary is known as the *system environment* (Figure 1.1). The inputs to the system are all raw materials taken from the environment, and the outputs are waste materials released back into the environment.

An environmental LCA evaluates the environmental effects associated with any given activity from the initial gathering of raw materials from the earth (petroleum, crops, ores, etc.) to the point at which all materials are returned to the earth (Figure 1.2.) This evaluation includes all sidestream releases to the air, water, and soil. LCA is an attempt to comprehensively describe all these activities and the resulting environmental releases and impacts. How this is done is described in detail in later chapters.

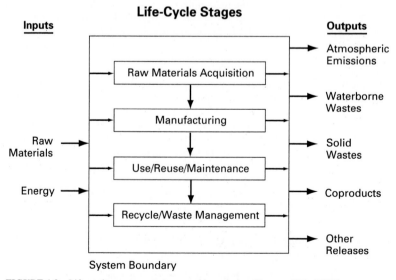

FIGURE 1.2   Life-cycle assessment stages and boundaries. (*Source: EPA, 1993.*)

1.3   EARLY APPLICATIONS OF LCA

Although LCA has been receiving a lot of attention by individuals in the environmental field since 1990, the first attempt to look at extended product systems can be traced back to as early as the 1960s. This work mainly focused on calculating energy requirements. Several such "fuel cycle" studies were conducted in the United States by the Department of Energy. Although they focused on energy characteristics, these studies also included limited estimates of environmental releases. With the oil shortages in the early 1970s, both the U.S. and British governments commissioned extensive studies of industrial studies to conduct detailed energy analyses.

As the oil crises faded, so did interest in the product system, or LCA, approach for evaluating energy use. Then in the mid-1970s, landmark studies which focused on environmental issues were performed by Arthur D. Little and Midwest Research Institute (MRI). The main investigators who conducted the studies at MRI later left to form Franklin Associates, Ltd. Activity in the United States on environmental LCAs continued at a slow, but steady, pace of around two or three studies per year. The exact number is not certain because most studies were (and still are) performed for private clients and not released for public consumption.

Similarly, extended system studies were conducted in Europe during this period; they looked mainly at packaging systems, such as beverage containers. But the 1980s found a renewed interest in LCA as the Green Movement in Europe brought the subject to public attention on issues related to recycling. As a result, environmental releases were routinely added to energy, raw materials, and solid waste considerations.

Interest in LCA was initially expressed by industry leaders (product manufacturers) as they took a defensive position in trying to demonstrate the environmental superiority of their product over a competitor's product. Similarly, consumer interest groups wanted to use LCA to compare products, in order to prove which ones were environmentally preferable. This information was intended to help guide consumers in making better purchasing decisions. While product comparison is still the goal of many groups, especially in ecolabeling programs, identifying opportunities to alter a product, or process, to improve its environmental profile (or make it "greener") is now often the motivation behind conducting an LCA. The last few years have seen a significant increase in research activity in this area by both government and private industry. The Appendix lists publicly available LCA case studies, along with other related studies, conducted mostly in the United States. Unfortunately, a similar list does not yet exist for other countries.

1.4   THE LCA MODEL

The Society of Environmental Toxicology and Chemistry (SETAC) has been instrumental in increasing the awareness and understanding of the LCA concept. The proceedings for a workshop held by SETAC in 1990 helped define terms to describe LCA. Those discussions laid the framework for how we view LCA today.[2]

The key finding of the 1990 workshop was the consensus to define LCA as a phased approach (Figure 1.3). LCA was defined as comprising three interrelated components.

Inventory: An objective, data-based process of quantifying energy and raw material requirements, air emissions, waterborne effluents, solid waste, and other environmental releases throughout the life cycle of a product, process, or activity.[3]

Impact assessment: A technical, quantitative or semiquantitative process to characterize and assess the effects of the environmental loadings identified in the inventory

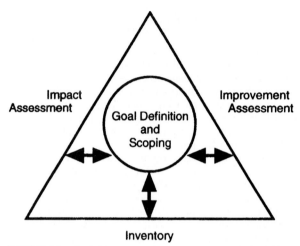

Impact Assessment

Improvement Assessment

Goal Definition and Scoping

Inventory

FIGURE 1.3   The LCA conceptual model. (*Source: SETAC, 1993.*)

component. The assessment should address both ecological and human health considerations, as well as other effects such as habitat modification or noise pollution.

Improvement assessment: A systematic evaluation of the needs and opportunities to reduce the environmental burden associated with energy and raw materials use and environmental releases throughout the whole life cycle of the product, process, or activity. This assessment may include both quantitative and qualitative measures of improvement, such as changes in product, process, and activity design; raw material use; industrial processing; consumer use; and waste management.

Subsequent LCA workshops in Europe added a fourth component, called *initiation* or *scoping.* Scoping, which precedes the inventory activity, defines the purpose of the study.[4] All subsequent activity in the assessment, including defining the boundaries, collecting data, and presenting results, must be consistent with the intended purpose.

1.5 TERMINOLOGY

Although the term *life-cycle assessment,* or *analysis,* is used most frequently to describe the cradle-to-grave approach being discussed here, *ecobalance* has also been used. The term *resource and environmental profile analysis* (REPA) is used by Franklin Associates, Ltd., to describe a life-cycle inventory.

SOMEWHAT SYNONYMOUS TERMS FOR LIFE-CYCLE ASSESSMENT

Product life-cycle assessment
Life-cycle analysis
Ecobalance
Resource and environmental profile analysis (REPA)—refers to life-cycle inventory
Product line analysis (Produktlinienanalyse)
Integrated chain management

1.6   WHY IS LCA IMPORTANT?

In most cases, LCA is used to gather information to make comparisons either between competing products performing the same function or in evaluating modifications to a product to make it more "environmentally friendly." LCA is important for identifying when the selection of one product over another or when modifications made to any part of the system have the desired end result of decreasing environmental impacts from all the life-cycle stages, from cradle to grave. Too many times, it seems, apparent improvements are made to operations or activities without any thought being given to possible secondary effects. Potentially, any change to any part of the product or process system can result in an unwanted shifting of burdens to another part of the system, unless a life-cycle framework is employed. Identifying these unwanted shifts between life-cycle stages, as well as between media (air, water, solid waste), is the key concept behind LCA.

For example, in studying effluents from industrial laundries, the Environmental Protection Agency's (EPA's) Office of Water identified hazardous solvents that were being released when shop towels were washed. These towels are used in cleaning and degreasing in auto repair shops, print shops, etc. It was suggested to the Office of Water staff that they fashion the regulations for this industry so that disposable shop towels are specified. Fortunately, the EPA realized that this would result in simply transferring the pollutant loading to the landfill (the waste management stage) and that a different approach should be used so that a broader field of information is considered when the regulation is written. The Office of Water is now evaluating the life-cycle inventory data for different shop towel systems as it writes the new guideline for industrial laundries.

Other instances of burden shift may not be so apparent. It is obviously not in a product manufacturer's best interest to change a product's design to one that places an increased burden on suppliers or customers; however, this can happen if the entire system is not considered. Specifying the use of postconsumer recycled material is done for one reason—to reduce the impact on landfills. Along with this goal, the broader environmental impacts that are created in carrying out recycling must be factored in by considering the entire life cycle of the product or process. These include increased energy use for reprocessing the material and increased transportation. The environmental loading associated with increased energy use, i.e., the emissions and discharges from electric power generation facilities, is often overlooked.

1.7   POLLUTION PREVENTION

Pollution prevention is another area which should be viewed with life-cycle impacts in mind. Many positive stories have been reported in the field of pollution prevention in which source reduction of hazardous waste streams and increased recycling opportunities have been achieved. In a pollution prevention assessment, the system boundaries are drawn very narrowly around the facility. In life-cycle terms, these boundaries would then only include one stage, usually manufacturing. Figure 1.4 shows how boundaries for pollution prevention assessments compare with boundaries that identify the entire system. Pollution prevention opportunities identified in this way will benefit the facility but may not always achieve reduced impacts on the environment.

As an example, the EPA developed a preliminary framework for using LCA to assess pollution prevention activities. The framework was demonstrated by taking as an example the lithographic printing industry.[5] The print shops that were studied elected to use solvents which would help their indoor air quality problems, i.e., low-VOC (volatile organic compounds) emission solvents. However, the findings of the EPA study indi-

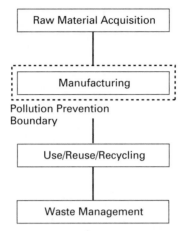

FIGURE 1.4 Pollution prevention assessment boundaries in the context of LCA.

cate that the overall life-cycle impacts may have increased as a result. Although the method is only preliminary and is in need of further development, it indicates that a broader scope is required in some cases when pollution prevention is being considered.

1.8 LIFE-CYCLE ASSESSMENT AS A TOOL

As already mentioned, the renewed interest in LCA in 1990 led to an increase in research activity by government, academia, and private industry. This was followed by increased interest by companies to assess the life-cycle impacts of their products and processes. The 1990 SETAC workshop resulted in the realization that the life-cycle inventory (LCI) methodology is more developed than impact assessment methodology and, therefore, the most often used approach. Most LCA practitioners use the same basic system analysis approach to conducting an inventory, with only slight variations. These differences in practices are discussed in greater detail in Chap. 2. The reason for this consistency is that LCI is essentially a large material and energy balance around the industrial system that has been identified. The goal is to account for all the materials going in and coming out.

LCAs are very data-intensive, and the success of any given study is driven by the availability of good data. While easily stated, achieving the balance is not so easy. The lack of readily accessible and credible data has limited the number of studies that have been conducted. Several efforts are under way to develop databases which will be useful to LCA practitioners. More of these types of databases or other inventory studies are expected to be developed in the near term, making LCAs easier to perform. Data needs and databases are explored further in Chap. 3.

Another obstacle to performing LCAs which researchers continue to investigate is the need to develop a generally accepted impact assessment methodology. Remember, LCA is defined to include all three components—inventory, impact assessment, and improvement analysis. Impact assessment translates inventory release data to impacts on human health, plant and animal life, and the environment. Many attempts have been made to develop a comprehensive impact assessment method, but more research is needed in this area.

1.9   STREAMLINING

Because of the large amount of data required by a full LCA, a lot of attention has been directed toward developing a streamlined LCA approach. The goal of streamlining LCA is to reduce the time and cost of doing an LCA without sacrificing the credibility of the results. A streamlined approach would make LCA more applicable by more users, especially smaller companies that may be limited in resources and unable to conduct LCAs. Streamlining would also benefit manufacturers of multiple products that are only able to study a few products at a time using full LCAs.

Streamlining in these applications refers to some method of shortcutting the LCA method. Such a shortcut method may require the user to make decisions about what to exclude from the study in order to "shrink" the boundaries and minimize the amount of data that must be gathered. Of course, this must be done with extreme caution and without jeopardizing the accuracy of the results. Depending on the goal of the study, omission of life-cycle stages may be valid if it has been confirmed that these stages are "static" and will not be affected by changes to the rest of the system being studied. Some shortcuts have focused on environmental impacts first, such as looking at releases of interest, e.g., particular air emissions. Keep in mind that these approaches are only presented as possibilities. Their validity has not yet been established. More research is needed on this type of streamlining.

Another way to view streamlining is through the application of the cradle-to-grave nature of LCA to look at products, processes, and activities in a more qualitative manner. This approach is also called *using the life-cycle concept* or *life-cycle thinking*. Life-cycle thinking requires the user to look upstream and downstream of the operation being studied, perhaps in an approach that combines quantitative and qualitative information. These issues surrounding streamlining of LCA are discussed in greater detail in Chap. 4.

1.10   LIFE-CYCLE DESIGN

Another area in which the application of the life-cycle concept is valid is in the design of products before they are manufactured. Life-cycle design integrates environmental concerns with factors that are typical in product development, such as product performance, cost, and cultural and legal requirements. Chapter 6 describes the goals and principles of life-cycle design. Case studies are presented to demonstrate design solutions for two products, a telephone and an oil filter.

1.11   COSTING

As seen through life-cycle design, environmental impact information generated through an LCA, while useful, is not a sufficient basis for making a sound decision about design, production, or operational changes. In attempts to broaden decision making, discussions on economics and the environment are being addressed more often in interrelated terms. However, more typically in the available literature, and especially in textbooks, the attention given to the environment is in the form of how economic theory can be applied to environmental issues, almost as an afterthought. Unfortunately, this approach does not emphasize how the consideration of environmental matters affects our economic thinking and, conversely, how economic decisions affect the environment.

Chapter 7 is dedicated to the ever-important topic of costing and how models can integrate costs with environmental considerations. Costs are what business managers understand best, and costs are an integral part of the decision-making process when one is identifying potential improvements to a product, a process, or an activity. Chapter 7 gives a useful perspective to often-used terms such as *total cost assessment, full cost accounting,* and *life-cycle costing.* While these terms refer to approaches that combine differing elements of conventional, direct costs with hidden, indirect costs, they are not interchangeable, and correctly understanding each term is essential for users of the information.

1.12   DEVELOPMENT OF PUBLIC POLICY

So far, the discussion has centered on the use of LCA in product design and manufacture. Another arena into which the life-cycle concept is slowly, but steadily, progressing is the development of public policy. European countries have perhaps been quicker than the United States in developing LCA-based policy. The most widely publicized use of LCA is in ecolabeling. Another highly visible area which is taking a dominant role in North America and abroad is the development of the International Standards Organization (ISO) standard on Environmental Management Systems, known as *ISO 14000.*

Substantial activity is occurring in the United States at the federal level in integrating a life-cycle approach with the formation of new policies, including solid waste management strategies, the regulatory development process (EPA rule making), and federal government acquisition policies (spurred on by Executive Order 12873 on federal acquisition of environmentally preferable products). Chapters 8 and 9 give an international perspective on how governments are beginning to adopt life-cycle thinking in the development of public policy.

1.13   INTERNATIONAL VIEWS OF LCA APPLICATIONS

Development of the basic LCA concept, leading to the current approaches being used by industry, consultants, and government organizations, has occurred at an international level. A network of information sharing and exchanges of experience has expedited the development process. Mainly, several North American and western European countries have led these efforts. Chapters 10 through 18 describe different approaches being taken by these countries. Material has been provided by representatives of Belgium, Canada, France, Germany, The Netherlands, Norway, Sweden, the United Kingdom, and the United States. These chapters, while certainly not comprehensive of all LCA-related work being conducted worldwide, are offered as examples of how LCA has been and is being used in practical applications in different countries.

1.14   THE FUTURE OF LCA

LCA is fast becoming an important tool for product designers and production managers. Until now, LCA has been used mostly by experts because of the complex nature of the analysis. Gradually, LCA is being used in more general applications as understanding of the approach grows and data become more readily available. Common sense suggests that companies that take a systemic approach to assessing environmental effects will gain a competitive advantage through cost savings, an improved image, and a more effective, holistic management style. Although interest in the systemic approach to viewing environmental consequences has fluctuated over the years, continuing concern for the environment and the new drivers of pollution prevention and sustainability are reemphasizing the need to look at products, processes, and activities holistically with a life-cycle approach. Since LCA techniques continue to evolve, information collected today can quickly become outdated. However, in the following chapters, examples are given of how government offices and private companies are viewing and using LCA now.

REFERENCES

1. Environmental Protection Agency, *Facility Pollution Prevention Guide* (EPA/600/R-92/088), Risk Reduction Engineering Laboratory, Office of Research and Development, Cincinnati, OH, 1992.

2. J. A. Fava, R. Denison, B. Jones, M. A. Curran, B. W. Vigon, S. Selke, and J. Barnum (eds.), *A Technical Framework for Life Cycle Assessments,* Society of Environmental Toxicology and Chemistry, Pensacola, FL, 1991.

3. Environmental Protection Agency, *Life-Cycle Assessment: Inventory Guidelines and Principles* (EPA/600/R-92/245), prepared by Battelle and Franklin Associates, Ltd., for the Risk Reduction Engineering Laboratory, Office of Research and Development, Cincinnati, OH, February 1993.

4. F. Consoli, D. Allen, I. Boustead, N. de Oude, J. Fava, W. Franklin, R. Parrish, R. Perriman, D. Postlethwaite, B. Quay, J. Séguin, and B. Vigon (eds.), *Guidelines for Life Cycle Assessments: A 'Code of Practice,'* Society of Environmental Toxicology and Chemistry, Pensacola, FL, 1993.

5. EPA, *Pollution Prevention Factors Methodology Based on Life-Cycle Assessment: A Lithographic Printing Industry Case Study* (EPA/600/R-94/157), prepared by Battelle for the Risk Reduction Engineering Laboratory, Office of Research and Development, Cincinnati, OH, 1994.

CHAPTER 2
LCA METHODOLOGY

Terrie K. Boguski
SENIOR CHEMICAL ENGINEER
FRANKLIN ASSOCIATES, LTD.
PRAIRIE VILLAGE, KS

Robert G. Hunt
ADVISER FOR SCIENCE AND TECHNOLOGY
FRANKLIN ASSOCIATES, LTD.
PRAIRIE VILLAGE, KS

James M. Cholakis, Ph.D.
PRINCIPAL TOXICOLOGIST
CHOLAKIS ASSOCIATES
PRAIRIE VILLAGE, KS

William E. Franklin
CHAIRMAN AND PRINCIPAL
FRANKLIN ASSOCIATES, LTD.
PRAIRIE VILLAGE, KS

2.1 OVERVIEW

Life-cycle assessment (LCA) is a tool that can be used to evaluate the environmental effects of a product, process, or activity. The LCA methodology has four components: goal definition and scoping, *life-cycle inventory* (LCI), impact assessment, and improvement assessment. A full life-cycle assessment includes each of these four components.[1]

The goal definition and scoping stage of LCA defines the purpose of the study, the expected product of the study, the boundary conditions, and the assumptions.[2] This stage has always been a part of LCI and LCA studies because the process of setting boundaries and of defining the specific life-cycle systems being studied is an essential first step for any LCI or LCA study. Increased interest in LCA over the past 5 years has been a catalyst for practitioners to more clearly address this stage of LCA.

The second stage of the LCA process is the life-cycle inventory. The LCI quantifies the resource use, energy use, and environmental releases associated with the system being evaluated. For a product life cycle, the analysis involves all steps in the life cycle of each component of the product being studied. This includes the acquisition of raw materials from the earth, the acquisition of energy resources from the earth, processing of raw materials into usable components, manufacturing products and intermediates, transportation of materials to each processing step, manufacture of the product being studied, distribution of the product, use of the product, and final disposition (which may include recycling, reuse, incineration, or landfill).[3–5]

LCI has been practiced in the United States and in Europe for more than 20 years, and the basic methodology for LCI is widely accepted and used. Practitioners generally agree upon a common system analysis approach for performing LCI studies. Most environmental life-cycle studies to date have been LCIs. This stage of LCA is critical because the LCI results are needed to perform any type of quantitative impact assessment. If impact assessment is not performed, then LCI results can be used directly to perform improvement assessments based on energy and emission results, not on effects on health or the environment.

Once the inputs and outputs of a system have been quantified by the LCI, *impact assessment* (IA), the third stage of LCA, can be performed. Conceptually, impact assessment consists of three stages: classification, characterization, and valuation.[2,6,7] Classification is the assignment of LCI inputs and outputs to impact groupings. For example, the use of fossil fuels may be assigned to the impact group "depletion of finite resources." Characterization is the process of developing conversion models to translate LCI and supplemental data to impact descriptors. For example, carbon dioxide and methane LCI outputs may be converted to units of global warming potential. *Valuation* is the assignment of relative values or weights to different impacts, allowing integration across all impact categories.

The methodology for impact assessment is still in the developmental stage. The few life-cycle IAs that have been performed in recent years have generated much interest in the scientific community. However, there is still no impact assessment methodology that is widely accepted. Conceptual guidelines for impact assessment have been published by the Society of Environmental Toxicology and Chemistry (SETAC), the United States Environmental Protection Agency (EPA), and the Canadian Standards Association. Besides the conceptual guidelines, many proposed methods for doing impact assessment have been developed. The EPA report *Life-Cycle Impact Assessment* (draft 1994) summarizes 36 different methods for performing the characterization and/or valuation steps of impact assessment. None of these methods is widely accepted by the scientific community.

Improvement assessment, like goal definition and scoping, has always been a part of LCI and LCA studies. The desire to reduce burdens on the environment by altering a product or process is often the driver for a given study. Another driver for LCA studies has been the desire to benchmark a product against competitive products or to prove that one product is environmentally preferable to another. This is also a type of improvement assessment. It falls into the area of assisting individuals or companies in making more environmentally sound choices.

Each of the four stages of LCA is discussed in greater detail in this chapter. Practices that are widely accepted among LCA practitioners are identified, and practices that vary among practitioners are discussed.

2.2 GOAL DEFINITION AND SCOPING

2.2.1 Defining the Purpose

Before an LCI or LCA is begun, the purpose for the activity must be defined. Typically LCI and LCA studies are performed in response to specific questions. The nature of the questions determines the goals and scope of the study.

LCI and LCA studies are comparative by nature. Usually someone is seeking information to use in making a decision. A company may be deciding whether to fund or promote a new process, a new product, or a different type of package for the product. Consumers may be faced with a choice that industry or the government wants to influence in an environmentally positive way. A legislative body may be trying to determine whether to encourage or discourage use of certain materials or products in favor of alternative materials or products.

Determining what choices are available helps determine what the purpose and scope of the LCI and LCA should be. Complex choices lead to more in-depth analysis and may require a full LCA. Simpler choices can perhaps be made with the information provided by an LCI of the competing systems.

The following four examples show how the purpose of an LCA or LCI study may be determined.

Example 1   Company A is developing a new product. It wants to compare the product to several competitive products already on the market. The purpose is to discover any potentially negative environmental aspects of the new product before it is marketed. The company hopes to use the information to make environmental improvements in the product so that it has an environmental profile similar to or better than those of competitive products. Company A is concerned with all aspects of the environment: resource use, energy use, and releases to the land, air, and water.

The purpose of the study is to perform an LCI of the new product and the competitive products. The LCI results will be evaluated and areas of concern identified. Improvement opportunities for the areas of concern need to be evaluated for the new product. To do this, very detailed information about the manufacture of the new product is required. Impact assessment will not be done unless certain areas of concern identified by the LCI require further analysis.

Example 2   A product that company B produces is being criticized because of environmental concerns. Public criticism has caused the market share for this product to drop. Company B believes that the criticism is unwarranted and that a comparison of its product to the most popular alternative will prove its point. Packaging for company B's product is identical to the packaging for the alternative product.

The purpose of the study is to perform a comparative LCI and impact assessment on company B's product and on the alternative product. Packaging will not be studied since it is the same for both products. The study will be independently reviewed by a peer review group because it is intended for public use.

Example 3   Company C is changing the packaging for one of its products because of marketing needs. Several options exist that would be acceptable to consumers. Company C wants more information about each packaging option in order to choose the most *environmentally friendly* packaging option. Company C is interested in obtaining more information, but not in funding the development of impact assessment methodology.

The purpose of the study is to perform an LCI of the different packaging options. A comparative analysis of the LCI results, in addition to marketing and cost information, will be used to make packaging choices for company C's product. The product itself will not be studied because the type of packaging does not affect the product formulation, in this case.

Example 4   An environmental group is considering undertaking a campaign to discourage the public from buying a certain consumer product in favor of using common household ingredients to serve the same function. The group wants to develop scientific evidence which will show that its homemade alternative to the consumer product is actually the environmentally preferable choice.

The purpose of the study is to perform an LCI and selective impact assessment of the two different alternatives. Both the products and the associated packaging must be studied because the consumer product and the ingredients for the homemade product are packaged differently. The results of the LCI will determine the focus of the impact assessment.

2.2.2 Defining Boundary Conditions

Once the general goals and purpose of the LCI or LCA study are understood, the boundaries of the study must be determined. It is common practice to define the life cycle of the product, process, or activity being studied as a system.[8] *All* operations that contribute to the life cycle of the product, process, or activity of interest fall within the system boundaries. The environment is the surrounding for the system. Inputs to the system are natural resources, including energy resources. Outputs of the system are ultimately a collection of releases to the environment (air, water, or land). If the system represents the manufacture and use of a product, then outputs include the postconsumer or discarded product. This system concept is illustrated in Fig. 2.1.

The system boundaries for an LCI or LCA of a product system are often illustrated by a general (cradle-to-grave) materials flow diagram, as shown in Fig. 2.2. The boundaries for the LCI or LCA encompass the acquisition of raw materials, manufacture of intermediate materials, manufacture of the product being studied, use of the product, and final disposition. Recycling or reuse of the product is part of the LCI or LCA analysis. The use

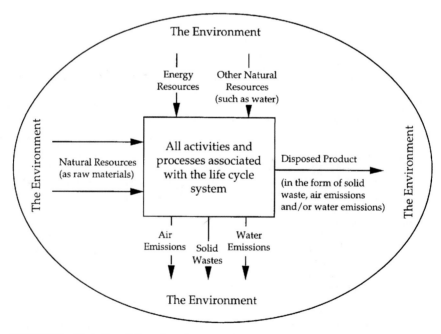

FIGURE 2.1   Illustration of life-cycle system concept.

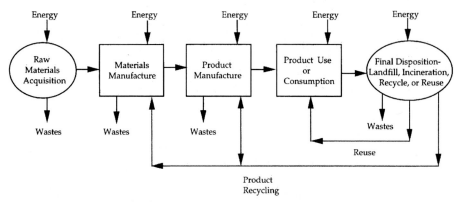

FIGURE 2.2   General materials flow diagram for a product life cycle.

of energy, as shown for each step in Fig. 2.2, carries with it the input of energy resources as well as the inputs and outputs for processing these energy resources into usable fuels. The inputs and outputs for transportation of materials between process steps are implied by the arrows showing the flow of materials between steps.

By definition, LCI and LCA systems are complex. For example, an LCA of a simple hairpin involves many different processes. Processes that fall within the system boundaries include mining and processing of iron ore; transportation of iron ore; mining and processing of limestone; transportation of limestone; steel manufacture; acquisition, processing, and transportation of other materials, such as limestone and coke, needed to manufacture steel; transportation of steel; manufacture of hairpins; acquisition and processing of fossil fuels; generation of electricity; manufacture of the lacquer used to coat the hairpin; manufacture and transportation of the raw materials needed to make the lacquer; manufacture of packaging materials used to ship the hairpins to the point of sale; use of hairpins; disposal of hairpins. This list of processes that must be evaluated for this example is not all-inclusive, but it does illustrate the point that an LCA of even a simple product is a complex activity. Forty to fifty separate processes must be studied in a typical project.

Practitioners have historically handled the complexity of LCI and LCA studies by developing "cradle-to-gate" subsystems that are complete and self-standing. The term *cradle-to-gate* means from the acquisition of raw materials to the manufacture of a usable product. For example, the life-cycle steps from iron ore mining through steel wire manufacture represent the cradle-to-gate segment for the manufacture of steel wire. This subsystem can then be linked to other subsystems to form a complete life-cycle system for hairpins. The concept of linked subsystems is illustrated for hairpins in the materials flow diagram shown in Fig. 2.3.

Although it was previously stated that all operations that contribute to the life cycle of the product fall within the system boundaries, the LCI and LCA system boundaries are not "endless." In some cases, iterative calculations are used to resolve circular links. For example, fuels and electricity are needed to produce and refine fuel resources, such as coal, crude oil, natural gas, and uranium. This creates a "chicken or egg" situation that can only be resolved through iteration. In other cases, inputs to the system become negligible as the outer boundaries of the system are reached.

Excluding Steps from the LCI or LCA.   After all the steps that fall within the system boundaries are identified, the practitioner may choose to simplify the LCI or LCA by

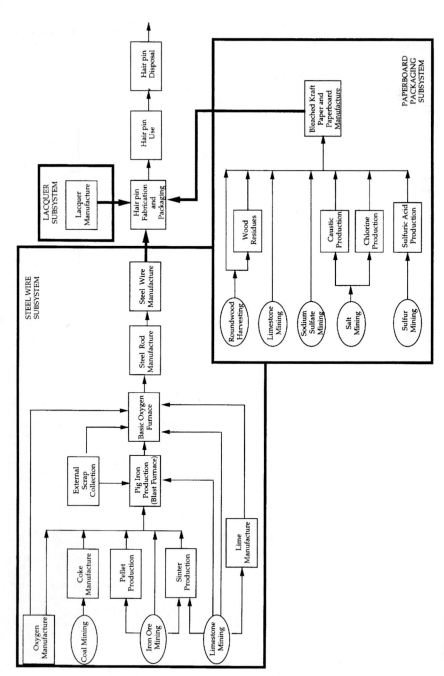

FIGURE 2.3 Linked systems.

excluding some steps from the study. This must be done with extreme caution and only after the entire system has been examined. The general rule for excluding steps from the study is that a step may be excluded only if doing so does not change the conclusions of the study. To determine whether a step affects the conclusions of a given study, the practitioner must do enough preliminary research to understand the potential contribution of each step or subsystem to the total system. For example, preliminary calculations usually show that inputs and outputs from the manufacture of capital equipment and buildings do not affect the LCI results for manufactured products. This is because the manufacture of a great number of products is usually associated with the capital equipment and buildings. Therefore, the manufacture of capital equipment is often excluded from LCI studies. This exclusion is only allowable in cases where the conclusions of the study do not change by either including or excluding this step.

The purpose and scope of the study are a factor when one is considering the exclusion of specific operations from the system. In a comparative LCI or LCA study, it may be logical to exclude operations that are common to the products being studied. For example, consider a comparison of refrigerated beverage packaging. If the refrigerated storage of each package is identical, then a valid comparison can be made without studying the refrigerated storage step. However, the decision to exclude the refrigerated storage step may preclude the use of the study for any purpose other than the stated comparison. That is, an impact assessment could not be performed because a very important step in the life cycle of each system has been omitted.

The purpose and scope of an LCI study can be substantially different from those of an impact assessment. The inclusion of impact assessment brings additional data needs to the study. Therefore, while it may be possible to exclude certain steps from an LCI study and not affect the conclusions of the study, this option may not exist for an impact assessment.

Sometimes the purpose and scope of an environmental study are such that only a partial LCI or LCA study is planned. For example, consider a study with the purpose of measuring the environmental effects of different solid waste management options. The different options may be landfill, combustion, and recycling. One may decide, at first, that only the steps for collecting and processing solid waste for each option need to be evaluated. However, it soon becomes apparent that recycling, as a solid waste management option, has impacts on entire production systems. The use of recycled materials reduces the need for virgin raw materials. Recycling may also reduce the need for certain processing steps associated with the use of virgin raw materials. A comparison of only the solid waste management steps for each option will not yield sufficient information and could lead to erroneous conclusions about which option has less environmental impact.

There is currently interest in the LCA community in developing ways to streamline LCI and LCA studies. Streamlining for LCI and LCA studies means to shortcut the LCI or LCA analysis by some preset method. For example, attempts have been made to truncate LCAs at either or both "ends." Raw material acquisition, product disposal, or both have not been included in these truncated LCAs. Streamlining is desirable for various reasons including the desire to control costs or to finish a study within a shorter time, or because of the lack of available data. Streamlining an LCI or LCA without substantial up-front research has the potential of producing erroneous conclusions. LCI and LCA studies are complex and usually require several study-specific decisions to be made in the course of performing a study. These difficulties do not lend themselves to the development of a streamlined methodology. Streamlining by omitting life-cycle stages is not an acceptable approach (unless it has been determined that doing so will not affect the assessment, as discussed above).

It is good practice, when one is reporting the results of the assessment, to discuss any steps that have been excluded from an LCI or LCA study and to explain the reasoning for exclusion of these specific steps. This allows the user of the LCI or LCA report to better understand the meaning of the conclusions of the study. It also helps ensure that information from the study will be used in the proper context.

Selecting Time and Spatial Boundaries.   In addition to determining what operations fall within the LCI or LCA system boundaries, the practitioner must choose time and spatial boundaries for specific LCI or LCA studies. Data for each operation and sub-system within an LCI or LCA system should be representative of the stated time and spatial boundaries.

Spatial boundaries are important because industrial practices, legislative requirements, and consumer habits vary for different cities, states, and countries. Also physical realities are different in different locations. For example, the Gulf Coast area has plenty of rainfall. California is subject to intense droughts, and Arizona is subject to high winds. The effect of these variations on LCI or LCA results can be significant. In some cases, it may be possible to use data collected for operations in one location to represent operations in another location. In other cases, this could lead to erroneous conclusions. Sometimes it is necessary to aggregate data from operations in several locations in order to better model the actual flow of materials in the marketplace. The goal of the LCI and LCA is to model, as closely as possible, what is actually occurring in the life cycle of the product, process, or activity being studied. Spatial boundaries need to be evaluated in this context.

Time boundaries are also important because industrial practices, legislative requirements, and consumer habits vary over time. Since LCI and LCA studies require large amounts of diverse data, it is unlikely that all data for each operation will have been collected within the relevant time period. When this is the case, the practitioner must evaluate whether data that have been collected for a different time period are still representative. If additional research shows that basic operational changes have been made since the LCI data were originally collected, then new data that are representative of the current time boundaries must be collected. Energy conservation programs, new technology, and new regulatory requirements for environmental releases are examples of activities that cause LCI or LCA data to become out of date.

2.3   INVENTORY METHODOLOGY

2.3.1   Introduction

An historical review of a few LCI studies shows that the basic systems approach to LCI methodology has remained consistent for the past 20 years.[9–15] This consistency was seen even before SETAC and other organizations became interested in standardizing LCI and LCA studies. Science dictates a large portion of the LCI methodology. Independent practitioners, following the basic laws of science and engineering, have largely developed the same techniques for performing LCI studies. The LCI methodology centers on material and energy balances for each operation within the system and for the whole life-cycle system itself.

Although a large portion of the LCI methodology is dictated by science, some LCI decisions are not. It is these decisions which are not dictated by science that cause variations in the LCI methodology used by various practitioners. These variations in methodology are a cause of concern for people who are trying to use LCI studies performed by different practitioners.

Practitioners must make three major types of LCI decisions: (1) allocation of inputs and outputs from an industrial operation to the various products that are produced, (2) analysis of recycling systems, and (3) reporting of energy that is embodied in products entering or exiting the LCI system.

Following is a discussion of the basic steps of an LCI, of the widely accepted components of LCI methodology, and of the three areas where LCI practices tend to vary. Examples showing how LCI results are affected by decisions in these three areas are given, and recommendations for standardized practice are made.

2.3.2 Steps to Perform an LCI

There are five basic steps in an LCI study: (1) Define the scope and boundaries; (2) gather data; (3) create a computer model; (4) analyze and report the study results; and (5) interpret the results and draw conclusions.

Define the Scope and Boundaries. This part of the LCI is a continuation of the goal definition and scoping stage of LCA discussed previously in this chapter. In the goal definition and scoping stage, the purpose of the study was stated. The systems to be evaluated were determined, and various geographic, spatial, and time parameters were set. In addition to these activities, specific information about the systems to be studied is needed. For example, if a product is being studied, the weight of each component of the product must be determined. The weight of any associated packaging must also be determined. The functional unit(s) (i.e., unit of output for which results will be presented) must be determined. For a comparative study, the equivalent-use ratio must also be decided.

To illustrate this step in performing an LCI, consider the comparative study of product A and product B. First, samples of each product and the associated packaging are obtained. Product A has two components (i.e., two different ingredients in the product formulation), and the product is packaged in a paperboard box. Weighing each component of product A shows that component 1 weighs 0.5 lb. Component 2 weighs 0.4 lb. The packaging weighs 0.2 lb.

Product B has three components (i.e., three different ingredients in the product formulation) which are all different from the components of product A. Product B is packaged in a high-density polyethylene (HDPE) bag. For product B, component 1 weighs 0.1 lb, component 2 weighs 0.4 lb, and component 3 weights 0.6 lb. The HDPE packaging weighs 0.05 lb. Additional research has determined that consumers use 1.5 units of product A to perform the same function as 1 unit of product B.

With this information, it is decided that results for product A will be presented on the basis of 15,000 units of product A. Results for product B will be presented on the basis of 10,000 units of product B. The functional unit for product A is thus 15,000 packaged units. Likewise, the functional unit for product B is 10,000 packaged units. The *equivalent-use ratio* of product A to product B is 1.5:1.0, or 15,000:10,000. Results are presented based on 15,000 packaged units of product A and 10,000 packaged units of product B, because these values are convenient quantities in which to present numerical results. Also, the results for each system will be presented on an equivalent basis and, therefore, can be directly compared when presented in a report format.

It is always important to specifically define the product, process, or activity for which an LCI is to be performed. This definition needs to be made in measurable terms, such as the weights of materials that make up the product. The comparative LCI study described above will evaluate two specific product systems:

Product A		**Product B**	
Component 1	7500 lb	Component 1	1000 lb
Component 2	6000 lb	Component 2	4000 lb
		Component 3	6000 lb
Paperboard boxes	3000 lb	HDPE bags	500 lb

Each of these product systems is made up of specific amounts of certain components. Specific amounts of packaging are used for each system. The LCI results for this study are applicable only to the specific systems described for the study. Any changes to either system would change the LCI results for that system.

Once the components of the system to be evaluated are defined, further research is usually needed to set the remaining boundaries for the study. The guideline for setting boundaries is that all operations that contribute significantly to the life cycle of the product, process, or activity of interest fall within the system boundaries. Beginning with each component of each product system, the steps needed to manufacture each component are determined. This process continues until all the system steps, from raw material acquisition to final disposal of the product and all associated materials, are defined and quantified.

Gather Data.   Data gathering begins with the research that is necessary to set the scope and boundaries for an LCI study. Usually a review of the literature will identify the cradle-to-gate process steps necessary to manufacture each component of a product. (The term *cradle-to-gate* is used to mean all life-cycle steps from raw material acquisition through the manufacture of the component or material of interest. This cradle-to-gate system representing the manufacture of a certain component is then a part or branch of a larger product system.) Identifying all the process steps within the system being studied is the first step in gathering data for an LCI. Beyond this, large amounts of process data are necessary to complete a typical LCI. Raw materials use, energy use, the ratio of product to coproduct(s), and environmental releases must all be quantified for each process step of the system. Often these data are not available from the literature. When this is the case, the practitioner must rely upon industry to supply the data needed to complete the study. This will occur if industry representatives have an interest in seeing the study completed. If a certain company is funding an LCI of its product, then data from this company and from their suppliers will generally be available.

Sometimes, site-specific data are needed for an LCI, such as data for the manufacture of a specific product using materials from a limited number of suppliers. Data for the manufacture of the product and for the manufacture of the materials used to make the product are site-specific data. At other times, average or commodity data are needed for an LCI. For example, an LCI of plastic grocery bags in the marketplace would require average or commodity data representative of the average plastic grocery bag in the marketplace. Data from only one bag manufacturer or one specific plastic resin manufacturer would not be representative of the plastic bags available in the marketplace.

Other examples of commodity data needed for an LCI are the data for the manufacture of fuels, data for the generation of electricity, and data for the mining of certain minerals. In these cases, the consumer is generally buying materials on the open market and does not know exactly where production is occurring.

Electricity generation presents a unique challenge for the LCI practitioner. Electricity is supplied regionally in North America with some transfer across regions. The consumer of electricity usually purchases electricity from the nearest public utility. However, the electricity actually used by the consumer may have been generated at any of several regional power plants, or it may have been transferred into the regional power grid from a different region. Different power plants use different fuels or energy sources to generate electricity and release different types and quantities of environmental pollutants. The way that electricity generation is represented by the practitioner affects the results of the LCI. For some studies it may be acceptable to use a national average or North American average fuel mix for electricity generation. Where production facilities are sufficiently spread throughout the chosen geographic scope, one average fuel mix is usually representative of overall electricity generation for the system being studied. For studies where this is not the case, production sites need to be identified, and regional fuel mixes for electricity generation should be used. If an impact assessment is to be done following the LCI, more details about power plant sites may be needed.

It is helpful if data collection for an LCI follows a consistent format. It is recommended that the practitioner use a data collection questionnaire and a template to guide the collection and organization of data. A sample data questionnaire is shown in Fig. 2.4, and the template is shown in Fig. 2.5. The use of a template for data collection by LCI practitioners is documented in the EPA document *Life-Cycle Assessment: Inventory Guidelines and Principles* (EPA/600/R-92/245) and in the Canadian Standards Association document *Standard Z760-94 Life Cycle Assessment*. In addition to these data collection aids, it is recommended that data quality documentation be completed at the time the data are collected.[16] This information will be useful later in assessing the quality of the LCI results.

Once data are collected for each step in the system being analyzed, certain calculations are necessary to put the data into the desired format for entry into a computer model. First, raw materials and energy data for production facilities are often expressed in terms of annual or monthly production. Air emissions are often expressed in terms of output per year, and waterborne emissions are often expressed in units of pollutant per unit of discharge water. These different ways of expressing data need to be translated to units (usually pounds or kilograms) per quantity of product. The quantity of product chosen is sometimes called the *functional unit*. In preparation for modeling, the data for each step in a system are expressed in terms of a common functional unit, such as 1000 lb of output. A materials flow diagram, as discussed in Sec. 2.2, then provides the amount of material from each step that contributes to the system being evaluated.

Second, production facilities often produce more than one useful product. Typically, only one of the coproducts enters the system being analyzed. When this occurs, a method must be developed to disaggregate the inputs and outputs of the production facility. This disaggregation must be done in such a manner that raw materials, energy use, and environmental releases are allocated between all the useful coproducts being produced by the facility. This process is called *coproduct allocation* (or *partitioning*). Coproduct allocation is most commonly done on the basis of the mass of the coproducts, as illustrated in Fig. 2.6. Other methods of coproduct allocation are discussed later in this chapter.

In summary, data collection for an LCI is driven by the goal to model, as closely as possible, what is actually occurring in the life cycle of the product, process, or activity. Data collection decisions should be made within this context.

Create a Computer Model.   Early LCI studies were completed without the aid of computers. However, the large number of complex calculations makes the use of a computer model ideal for LCI studies. Computer modeling can be done by using spreadsheets or more sophisticated software. The objective of the computer model is to combine and compile the input and output data for each step of the system. Results can be displayed in greater or lesser detail, depending on the purpose and goals of the study. A spreadsheet model for total air emissions for an LCI of product A is shown in Fig. 2.7. (Chapter 3 discusses computer software in greater detail.)

DATA FOR THE PRODUCTION OF
1,000 POUNDS OF

1) General Information   Page 1 of 2
Product: _____   Prepared by:_____
Quantity:_____ (if not 1,000 lb)   Company Name:_____
Date:_____   Phone Number:_____
Production Period Begining: _____   Production Period Ending: _____

System Inputs

2) Raw Material Inputs

Material	Weight	Units	Comments
1)		lb	
2)		lb	
3)		lb	
4)		lb	
5)		lb	

3) Other Inputs

Material	Amount	Units	Comments
Process Water		gallons	
Oxygen From Air		lb	
Others			
1)			
2)			

4) Purchased Energy

Energy Source	Amount	Units	Comments
Purchased Electricity		kwh	
Natural Gas		cu ft	
LPG		gallons	
Coal		lb	
Distillate Oil		gallons	
Residual Oil		gallons	
Gasoline		gallons	
Diesel		gallons	
Wood		lb	

5) Self Generated Electricity

Energy Source	Amount	Units	Comments
Amount Used		kwh	
Fuels used to generate			
1)			
2)			
3)			

6) Transportation (average shipping distance to customer)

Transportation Mode	Distance	Units	Comments
Combination Truck-Diesel		miles	
Combination Truck-Gasoline		miles	
Single unit Truck-Diesel		miles	
Single-unit Truck-Gasoline		miles	
Rail-Diesel		miles	
Rail-Electricity		miles	
Barge-Diesel		miles	
Barge-Residual		miles	
Ocean Freighter-Diesel		miles	
Ocean Freighter-Residual		miles	
Natural Gas pipeline		miles	
Petrochemical Pipeline		miles	

FIGURE 2.4   Data collection form.

DATA FOR THE PRODUCTION OF
1,000 POUNDS OF

System Outputs

7) Coproduct/Byproduct/Recycled Material Outputs

Material	Weight	Units	Comments
Recovered heat		Btu	
Steam		lb @ bar	
Other	////////////	/////////////	/////////////////////////////
1)			
2)			
3)			

8) Solid Waste (discarded material only, list recycled materials above)

Material	Weight	Units	Comments
Wastewater Sludge		lb	Percent moisture %
Process Waste		lb	
Off-spec. Product		lb	
Trim or Scrap		lb	
Packaging Material		lb	
Other	////////////	/////////////	/////////////////////////////
1)			
2)			
3)			

9) Atmospheric Emissions (process only)

Material	Weight	Units
Particulates		lb
Sulfur Oxides		lb
Nitrogen Oxides		lb
Carbon Monoxide		lb
Carbon Dioxide (fossil)		lb
Carbon Dioxide (non-fossil)		lb
Aldehydes		lb
Methane		lb
Kerosene		lb
Ethylene Oxide		lb
Benzene		lb
Ethylbenzene		lb
Naphthalene		lb
Coke Oven Emissions		lb
Chloroform		lb
Other Hydrocarbons(specify)	///////	////////
1)		lb
2)		lb
Ammonia		lb
Lead		lb
Mercury		lb
Chlorine		lb
Nitrogen		lb
Phosphorus		lb
Other Atmospheric Emissions	///////	////////
1)		lb
2)		lb
3)		lb
4)		lb

10) Waterborne Emissions

Material	Weight	Units
Dissolved Solids		lb
Suspended Solids		lb
COD		lb
BOD		lb
Phenol		lb
Oil and grease		lb
Other Hydrocarbons(specify)	///////	////////
1)		lb
2)		lb
Sulfuric Acid		lb
Hydrochloric Acid		lb
Other Acids (specify)	///////	////////
1)		lb
2)		lb
Phosphorus		lb
Phosphates		lb
Sulfates		lb
Fluorides		lb
Cyanide		lb
Chloride		lb
Chromium		lb
Iron		lb
Aluminum		lb
Nickel		lb
Mercury		lb
Lead		lb
Nitrogen		lb
Zinc		lb
Tin		lb
Other Metal Ions		lb
Ferrous Sulfate		lb
Alkalinity		lb
Ammonia		lb
Nitrates		lb
Pesticides		lb
Other Waterborne Emissions	///////	////////
1)		lb
2)		lb

11) Other Outputs

Material	Amount	Units	Comments
Discharged Water		gallons	
Evaporative Loss		lb	
Others	////////////	/////////////	/////////////////////////////
1)			
2)			

FIGURE 2.4   (*Continued*) Data collection form.

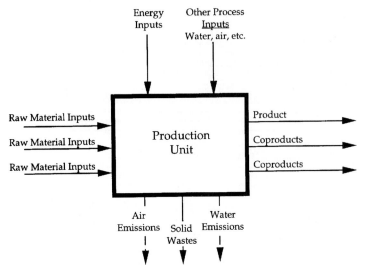

FIGURE 2.5 Data collection template.

Analyze and Report the Study Results. Once the computer model is completed, the results of the LCI must be analyzed and reported in a meaningful way that conveys all the LCI information. Planning for the presentation of LCI results is an important up-front exercise. It aids in the collection of LCI data and in setting up the computer model, so that all the necessary information is gathered and conveyed.

The purpose and goals of the study help determine the most beneficial presentation of LCI results. For example, a consumer products company trying to choose among several types of packaging may want a bottom-line presentation of results. A company considering different process options may require a very detailed presentation of results, showing the contribution of each step of the system to the environmental profile. An environmental group or government agency deciding whether to encourage the use of one product over another may want a detailed presentation to help with its decision making, as well as an overview of the results to present to the public. In all cases, however, reports must be accompanied by input and output data for each step of the life-cycle system(s) being evaluated.

In addition to meeting the purpose and goals of the study, the presentation of LCI results should be made so that important information is not inadvertently left out. Decisions made by looking only at total LCI results potentially could be different from decisions made by looking at more detailed LCI results. For example, consider the LCI energy results for product A and product B.

	Total energy, 10^6 Btu
Product A	70
Product B	90

The fact that product B requires almost 30 percent more energy than product A may cause decision makers to favor product A over product B. However, a look at the types of energy sources used for both systems may change this decision.

ACTUAL PROCESS

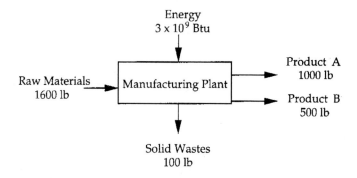

ALLOCATED PROCESSES

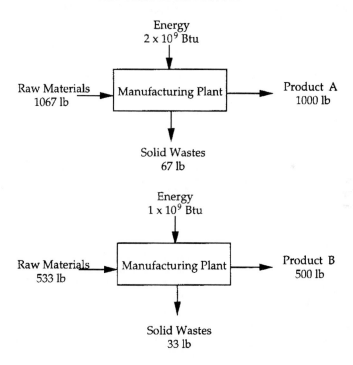

Using mass based coproduct allocation, product A , would be allocated two-thirds of the raw materials and energy inputs and two-thirds of the solid waste outputs from the manufacturing plant.

FIGURE 2.6 Illustration of coproduct allocation based on the mass of coproducts.

File Name: _____ Prepared by: _____
Date: _____ Time: _____

Component	Weight Factor	Weight (lb)	Carbon Monoxide (lb)	Hydro-carbons (lb)	Parti-culates (lb)	Nitrogen Oxides (lb)	Sulfur Oxides (lb)
STEPS IN THE PRODUCTION OF PRODUCT A							
Crude oil prod		1000			4.7		
Refinery operations		1000	0.06		0.3	0.2	
Chemical A		1000	0.04	1.335	0.48	0.003	0.255
Chemical B		1000	56.8	1.78	3.97	16.38	95.59
Chemical C		1000			0.125		
Product A		1000	0.01	1.04	2.66		0.57
REQUIREMENTS FOR MANUFACTURE OF 1000 LBS OF PRODUCT A							
Crude oil prod	0.23		0.00	0.00	1.06	0.00	0.00
Refinery operations	0.22		0.01	0.00	0.07	0.04	0.00
Chemical A	0.89		0.04	1.18	0.43	0.00	0.23
Chemical B	0.001		0.06	0.00	0.00	0.02	0.10
Chemical C	0.004		0.00	0.00	0.00	0.00	0.00
Product A	1.00		0.01	1.04	2.66		0.57
Product A Total			0.12	2.23	4.22	0.06	0.89

FIGURE 2.7 Spreadsheet model of air emissions for product A.

	Fossil fuels (10^6 Btu)							
	Petroleum	Natural gas	Coal	Nuclear	Hydropower	Wood	Other	Total
Product A	25	20	10	5	5	3	2	70
Product B	5	5	15	5	8	50	2	90

If the decision makers are primarily concerned with the conservation of fossil fuels, they may favor product B over product A because product B uses fewer fossil fuels than product A.

Total energy for products A and B includes process energy, transportation energy, and the energy of material resource. *Process energy* is the energy used to acquire and process the materials and fuels used within the system. *Transportation energy* is the energy used to transport materials between each step of the system. Transportation of materials usually occurs by truck, rail, barge, ship, or pipeline.

The *energy of material resource,* as defined by Franklin Associates, is the energy content of fuel resources that are used as raw materials. An example of energy of material resource is the energy content of petroleum and natural gas liquids used as raw materials for hydrocarbon-based chemicals or plastics. Using these fuel resources as raw materials removes them from our finite fossil fuel reserves. Therefore, the energy content of raw materials that are also common energy resources is included in the total energy use for a system. The energy content of raw materials that are not fuel resources is not included in the total energy use for a system. Wood that is used as a raw material is not assigned an energy of material resource by Franklin Associates. Wood used for process energy, such as in paper mills, is included in the total energy for a system.

A further look at the energy categories of process energy, transportation energy, and energy of material resource for product A and product B may help the decision makers in evaluating improvement options for the product A and product B systems.

	(10^6 Btu)		
	Process energy	Transportation energy	Energy of material resource
Product A	30	10	30
Product B	70	15	5

Different options for handling postconsumer materials may affect the total energy required by each system. For example, recovering the packaging for product A by recycling or recovering the energy content of product A by waste-to-energy combustion may reduce the impact of product A on fossil fuel reserves.

When LCI results are reported for environmental releases, it should be recognized that the listing of emissions to the air or water is in some ways an implied impact assessment. The presentation of lists of releases to the air or water implies that the substances listed have a detrimental effect on the environment. Even though no attempt has been made to determine the environmental effects of the listed pollutants, the implication is that release of smaller amounts of any of the pollutants will have a potentially positive effect on the environment.

Atmospheric Emissions. LCI results typically list 30 to 40 different air emissions, including carbon dioxide as well as substances classified as pollutants. It is important that actual discharges into the atmosphere after existing emission control devices (if used) are reported, and not uncontrolled emissions. The emissions associated with the combustion of fuel for process or transportation energy as well as process emissions are included in the inventory results. Some of the most commonly reported atmospheric emissions are particulates, nitrogen oxides, hydrocarbons, sulfur oxides, and carbon monoxide.

Carbon dioxide emissions have historically not been reported in LCI studies. However, they are now being reported in many studies because of the growing concern about the contribution of carbon dioxide to global warming. Distinction between carbon dioxide emissions from fossil sources and carbon dioxide emissions from nonfossil sources is important. Fossil carbon dioxide emissions are those resulting from the combustion of fossil fuels. Nonfossil carbon dioxide emissions are those emissions resulting from the combustion or decomposition of nonfossil materials. For example, the burning of wood as fuel produces nonfossil carbon dioxide emissions.

The reason for segregating carbon dioxide emissions into fossil and nonfossil categories is related to the recognition of the natural carbon cycle. The nonfossil carbon dioxide emissions are believed to be part of a natural carbon cycle and may not represent long-term releases of carbon dioxide to the environment. Distinguishing between these two types of carbon dioxide emissions is also helpful if an impact assessment is to be done.

Waterborne Emissions. Typically LCI results list more than 20 different waterborne releases. As with atmospheric emissions, waterborne wastes include substances classified as pollutants. The values reported by the LCI results should be the quantity of pollutants still present in the wastewater stream *after* wastewater treatment (if performed) and should represent discharges into receiving waters. The emissions associated with the combustion of fuel for process energy and for the acquisition of fuels, as well as process emissions, are included in the inventory results. Some of the most commonly reported waterborne wastes are *biochemical oxygen demand* (BOD), *chemical oxygen demand* (COD), suspended solids, dissolved solids, iron, chromium, acid, and ammonia.

Analyzing air and waterborne emissions in a comparative LCI is complex and rarely results in one product emitting more of each type of air or waterborne pollutant. This is a real difficulty with LCI studies and makes impact assessment a desirable goal.

Solid Wastes.   For solid waste results, an LCI reports the solid wastes generated from all sources. Solid wastes are any solid outputs from the system that are sent to landfills or disposed in some way that has a potentially detrimental effect on the environment. Solid wastes include the ash from the combustion of postconsumer materials at waste-to-energy facilities. They do not include postconsumer materials that are recycled or composted. When a product is evaluated on an environmental basis, attention is often focused on postconsumer wastes. Industrial wastes generated during the manufacture of the product are sometimes overlooked. It is important to examine industrial wastes. Industrial solid wastes include wastewater treatment sludge; solids collected in air pollution control devices; trim or waste materials from manufacturing operations, which are not recycled; fuel combustion residues such as the ash generated by burning coal or wood; and mineral extraction wastes.

In a few cases, solid outputs from a system may be defined as *neutral outputs* instead of as solid wastes. For example, animal manure that is applied to land may, in some cases, be defined as a neutral substance. Also, overburden from mining operations may be considered as a neutral substance, if eventually it is to be put back into the mine. This is done so that the results of the LCI are meaningful. If the reason to track solid waste is because of the burden of landfilling or incinerating these wastes, then a material that is applied to land in a responsible way does not contribute to our landfill or solid waste disposal problems. Likewise, a material that is piled and stored to eventually be returned to its original site does not contribute to our landfill problems. Other environmental outputs associated with disposal by land application or open storage, such as waterborne pollutants in runoff, should be evaluated within the boundaries of the LCI.

It is desirable to report solid wastes in terms of the volume that they will occupy in the landfill as well as by weight. Sometimes, very dense and heavy products take up less landfill space than less compressible, lighter alternatives. One way to determine the volume that materials will occupy in a landfill is to sample the volume of materials extracted from landfills. Another method is to simulate landfill conditions and then measure the volume occupied by specific types of materials and products. Very few studies of landfill volume have been completed. One document that does report landfill volume for selected materials is the EPA report *Characterization of Municipal Solid Waste in the United States, 1992 Update* (530/R-92/019).

Interpret the Results and Draw Conclusions.   Once the results of the LCI are presented in the desired format, they can be interpreted and conclusions can be drawn. Conclusions for LCI studies are specific to the product, process, or activity being analyzed. They are valid only for the specific situation described by the scope and boundaries of the study.

There is sometimes a tendency to extrapolate LCI conclusions beyond what is supported by the study results. One common example of this occurs because of the desire to use an LCI to compare basic materials instead of products. Consider an LCI comparing a steel auto part to an aluminum auto part on an equivalent-use basis. The study may show that the steel part uses less energy, creates less solid waste, and emits lower levels of air and waterborne emissions for most pollutant categories. This does not mean that steel as a material is environmentally preferable to aluminum. The results are applicable only to the specific parts studied. A study of different steel and aluminum parts may yield the opposite results, depending on the nature of the application.

LCI results list resource use, energy use, and environmental releases to the air, water, and land. At this stage of the LCA, no attempt is made to determine the relative impact of each of these on the environment or on human health. Therefore, conclusions and improvement analysis are limited to seeking less resource use, less energy use, and lower levels of emissions to the environment. The value of tradeoffs within result categories (e.g., fossil energy sources versus nonfossil energy sources, or greater air emissions versus greater waterborne emissions) is a question left for the next stage of the LCA—impact assessment.

2.3.3 Variable Practices for Performing LCI Studies

The discussion of LCI methodology, thus far, covers LCI methodology as practiced by the authors. This methodology is standard practice in the United States and Europe, for the most part. Much of the LCI methodology is dictated by science. Material balances, material flow diagrams, and energy balances are key to the systems analysis approach used by the LCI methodology. Some decisions in the LCI methodology, however, are not dictated by science. When these decisions are made, variability in the methodology occurs as different practitioners perform different LCI studies. The main areas where variability occurs are coproduct allocation, recycling, and reporting the inherent or embodied energy of raw materials (energy of material resource). Each of these areas is discussed below.

Coproduct Allocation. *Coproduct allocation* is the allocation of the inputs and outputs of a manufacturing facility to the various coproducts being produced. As discussed earlier in this chapter and illustrated in Fig. 2.6, coproduct allocation is most commonly done on a mass basis. That is, inputs and outputs are allocated to all useful coproducts based on the relative mass of each produced. Other methods of disaggregating a production process and allocating inputs and outputs to the various coproducts can also be used. Science does not dictate a method of coproduct allocation.

Other methods of coproduct allocation include use of the mass of dry solids, stoichiometry, and heat of reaction. For certain specific systems, one of these methods of coproduct allocation may be more reasonable than allocating on a mass basis. The mass of dry solids is useful when one is analyzing systems that use or produce agricultural products. For these systems, one or more coproducts may be diluted with large quantities of water. Performing coproduct allocation on a dry-solids basis avoids the problem of allocating most of the inputs and outputs to a very dilute coproduct.

Coproduct allocation based on the stoichiometry of a chemical equation allows for a more accurate allocation of resources to the coproducts of complex chemical reactions. If the molecules of one raw material in a chemical reaction contribute solely to one of several coproducts, then allocation of that raw material to only one coproduct may make more sense than coproduct allocation on a total-mass basis.

Coproduct allocation based on the heat of reaction may be used for the manufacture of hydrocarbons, such as the manufacture of ethylene, propylene, and mixed butenes in an olefins unit.

Allocation on the basis of economic value is generally discouraged because the LCI methodology is based on the measurement of physical parameters, and economic value is not a physical parameter.

"The aim, of coproduct allocation, is to find a partitioning parameter that in some way reflects, as closely as possible, the physical behavior of the system itself" (Ref. 8, p. 11).

Recycling. If a product is recycled or made from recycled material, then the collection and recycling processes are a part of the product life cycle. Ideally the entire system, including both the manufacture of the virgin product and the manufacture of the recycled product, is evaluated in an LCI study. This seldom happens because LCI studies are commonly set up to evaluate either the virgin product being recycled or the product made from recycled material, but not both. As with coproduct allocation, it is desirable to disaggregate the inputs and outputs of the total system and to allocate them between the virgin and recycled products. Again, this allocation process is not dictated by science. It is an arbitrary decision made by the practitioner.

There are basically two types of recycling that must be analyzed: industrial scrap and trim recycling and postconsumer materials recycling. In the first case, the material being recycled has never been used. Industrial scrap or trim is commonly recycled internally or sold to a producer of a lower-grade product. Often there is an economic incentive for the recycling process. For some industries, trim or scrap is a valuable and desirable raw material. In the second case (postconsumer material), the material being recycled has fulfilled its intended purpose. It has been used and discarded by a consumer. There may be an economic incentive for recycling, as in the case of aluminum cans, or recycling may be solely an attempt to manage a solid waste problem.

Industrial Scrap and Trim. The treatment of industrial scrap and trim recycling is an important issue. There are two major conceptual options, as illustrated in Fig. 2.8, concerning the way in which industrial scrap is viewed. These different options are labeled *incremental recycling* and *allocated recycling* in this chapter. In the incremental systems shown at the top of Fig. 2.8, industrial scrap is viewed as a waste which is recovered by recyclers. This waste is free of any allocation of energy or environmental emissions needed to produce it, but carries with it natural resource requirements and emissions in the process of collecting it and making a recycled product. In the allocated system shown at the bottom of Fig. 2.8, the material that makes up the industrial scrap is considered a coproduct of the system manufacturing the primary product. With this approach, the scrap carries with it the resource requirements and emissions that were associated with its initial production (except for any allocation from the fabrication step for the virgin product). The scrap is viewed just as any other intermediate raw material within the boundaries of an LCI.

Incremental System Approach. The incremental approach produces results which correspond to actual conditions in manufacturing operations. The amounts of raw materials shown for the virgin product and for the recycled product correspond to the measured amounts of resources required for each type of facility. The energy and pollutants reported for each product (virgin or recycled) correspond to meter readings and other actual measurements made in the operations.

This scenario assumes that industrial scrap or trim is a waste. If the scrap is considered a waste, then all the inputs and outputs associated with the manufacture of the virgin product are allocated to the virgin product, as shown at the top of the incremental system in Fig. 2.8. Product from the recycling operation, then, is shown to require very little incremental energy and produces only small amounts of environmental emissions because none of the original inputs and outputs required to make the scrap (used as the raw material) are included in the LCI results for the product made from scrap. One would conclude from this that purchasing products made by recycling industrial scrap or trim is more desirable than buying the virgin product.

This conclusion will not lead to environmental improvement. Recycling of certain types of scrap or trim is already at virtually 100 percent and has been occurring for a very long time. If a company seeks to improve its environmental profile by increasing the use of scrap, it will reduce its own energy and emissions by using the incremental

INCREMENTAL SYSTEMS

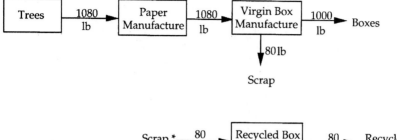

* For the incremental systems, the scrap is not allocated any of the inputs or outputs associated with manufacturing the virgin paper from which the scrap is made.

ALLOCATED SYSTEMS

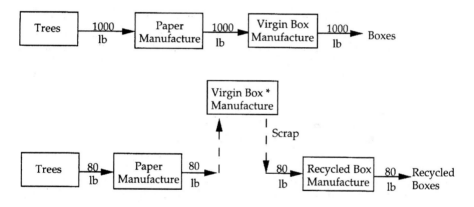

* The inputs and outputs for the process step, virgin box manufacture, are allocated only to the virgin box, not to the scrap used to make the recycled box.

FIGURE 2.8   Incremental and allocated systems for recycling industrial scrap.

analysis approach. However, the planet, and society in general, will not benefit. The increased use of industrial scrap or trim by one company simply takes the scrap or trim away from another company because the supply of scrap or trim is not expandable. From a narrow, individual company's point of view, recycling of industrial scrap is good and may reduce the energy and wastes allocated to its operations, but from the larger point of view, no environmental value accrues to society. One possible exception is that increased demand for industrial scrap may force marginal users to replace industrial scrap with postconsumer scrap. However, use of postconsumer scrap is a separate issue, and it should be analyzed within the framework of the products for which this change is a viable option.

Allocated System Approach.   The allocated system shown at the bottom of Fig. 2.8 more appropriately portrays industrial scrap or trim recycling. In that view, the material which makes up the scrap that is recycled is considered a coproduct of product manufacturing. Resource use and emissions for all the steps leading to the fabrication of the virgin product (and scrap) are allocated between the virgin product and the industrial scrap. In support of this view, one can observe that box plant clippings from corrugated container operations are considered a high-quality source of recovered paper, almost as a substitute for virgin pulp. Except when contaminated, it is recycled at nearly 100 percent, and historically it has been. The income to the plants from the sale of clippings to the recovered-paper market is significant. Similar situations exist for other materials as well.

In the allocated system approach, the natural resources and environmental emissions associated with manufacturing the industrial scrap or trim remain associated with the scrap or trim. The scrap must then be transported, reprocessed, and made into a product. In this view, if products are made from clippings, the products may use more energy and produce more emissions than a simple virgin product because of the extra steps needed to reprocess the scrap. This scenario is very similar to what occurs in situations where recycling is not an issue. Consider the use of market pulp in a nonintegrated paper mill. Market pulp is manufactured very much like a paperboard product that is dried, baled, and shipped to a recycling mill where it is repulped and manufactured into a product.

Some products cannot be made without generating scrap or trim. Because of its value, the scrap or trim may not be discarded as waste. But the use of the scrap or trim requires additional natural resources and produces additional environmental emissions. These events are all tied together. The question here is a matter of allocation. Should the natural resources required and the environmental emissions from the production of the virgin material be assigned only to the virgin product or allocated between the virgin product and the scrap?

If the scrap or trim is used to make more of the same product, the solution may be to consider the industry as a whole system, from which products are produced by using a combination of virgin materials and scrap. There would be no distinction made between virgin product and products made with scrap or trim. In this view, scrap would be viewed as being reused internally. The extra energy and emissions associated with the reprocessing of the scrap would be part of the LCI results for the industry product.

A more complex issue arises when industrial scrap or trim leaves the original industry. For example, suppose corrugated box clippings go to a recycled paperboard mill to make folding cartons. Or, suppose *expanded polystyrene* (EPS) scrap is recycled into EPS packing shapes. The two options, once again, are to consider the scrap as a waste or to consider it as a coproduct of the virgin product. Industrial scrap is conceptually more like a lower-value coproduct than a waste, so to it should be allocated the natural resource and environmental burden associated with its production.

When an individual company uses industrial scrap or trim to make a product, the resources and emissions associated with the manufacture of the scrap or trim are brought into the LCI results for the product system. The resources and emissions associated with the virgin product from which the industrial scrap is generated are decreased because of the allocation of a portion of the system inputs and outputs to the industrial scrap.

Postconsumer Recycling.   As stated earlier, recycling of postconsumer materials is different from recycling of industrial scrap or trim. There are two common methods of analyzing postconsumer recycling, called *closed-loop recycling* and *open-loop recy-*

cling.[5,17] Both closed-loop and open-loop recycling are means to divert postconsumer materials from the municipal solid waste stream. The nature of the recycling system, as well as the nature of the material (i.e., whether the material degrades with repeated recycling and use), determines whether the system is closed-loop recycling or open-loop recycling.

Closed-Loop Recycling.   In a closed-loop system, material is diverted from disposal by its unlimited recycling or reuse. For example, glass from glass bottles is recycled and fabricated into bottles again. Since recycling of the same material can occur many times, the material may be permanently diverted from disposal. Figure 2.9 presents a graphical description of how individual processes can be viewed in a closed-loop system. This figure illustrates that, at the ideal recycling rate of 100 percent, the energy requirements and environmental emissions from the virgin raw material acquisition, processing, and disposal steps become negligible. In contrast, if closed-loop recycling does not occur, then virgin raw materials must be acquired and processed and postconsumer wastes must be disposed of each time a product is produced. In practice, 100 percent of a product cannot be recovered for recycling, and there is also a loss of material in the remanufacture process.

Open-Loop Recycling (Allocated System Approach).   In an open-loop system, a product made from virgin material is manufactured, recovered for recycling, and manufactured into a new product which is not recycled. This extends the life of the initial material, but only for a limited time. Figure 2.10 illustrates an open-loop recycling system.

The significant difference between the open-loop and closed-loop recycling systems is the way in which recycling benefits are incorporated in or allocated to the system under examination. In a closed-loop system, since the material is recycled many times, the energy and emissions of the initial virgin material manufacture are divided between the first product and all subsequent products made from that original material. Consequently, these initial impacts become insignificant, and the only energy and emissions associated with closed-loop recycled material are those which result from the recycling process and any processes that follow, such as fabrication.

For an open-loop system, typically the same material is used to make two products. Initially, virgin material is used to make a product which is recycled into a second product that is not recycled. Thus, for the open-loop recycled material, the energy and emissions of virgin material manufacture, collection, recycling, and eventual disposal of the recycled material are divided proportionately on a mass basis between the first and second products. The analysis assumes that the recycled material replaces virgin material when the second product is produced.

Open-loop recycling sometimes occurs more than once, creating a third, fourth, or fifth product before the material is finally disposed. The same allocation method, by mass, can be used to allocate life-cycle inputs and outputs for these systems as is used for the two-product system described above.[17]

Open-Loop Recycling (Incremental System Approach).   Similar issues arise for postconsumer materials in an open-loop recycling scenario as for industrial scrap recycling. The method of allocating total system inputs and outputs to the first (virgin) product and the second (recycled) product is not dictated by science. An alternative method of allocating the system inputs and outputs is the incremental approach. From the recycler's point of view, an incremental approach may seem more reasonable. In this scenario, the virgin product is manufactured, used, and disposed of, with all the inputs and outputs for these activities allocated to it. The recycled product then incurs incremental inputs and outputs associated with collection, recycling, and fabricating of the recycled product.

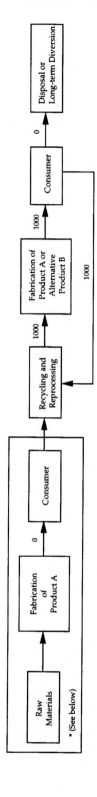

Independent view of the systems at 0 percent recycling

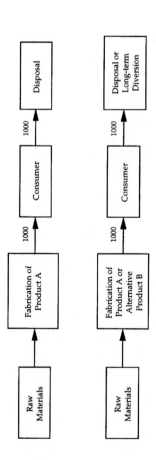

* Note: In a closed-loop system, since the material is recycled many times, the impacts of the initial virgin system manufaturing steps are divided between the mass of all of the many products made from that original material. Consequently, these inital impacts become negligible and the only impacts associated with closed-loop recycled material are those which result form the recycling process and any subsequent processes such as fabrication.

FIGURE 2.9 Illustration of closed-loop recycling system at steady state in comparison to each system operating independently.

Open-loop system at 100 percent recycling

Independent view of the systems at 0 percent recycling

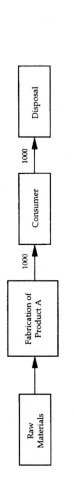

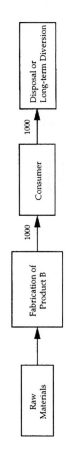

FIGURE 2.10 Illustration of open-loop recycling system in comparison to each system operating independently.

The incremental approach more closely matches the meter readings and other measurements made at the recycling plants. Also, it is much simpler to evaluate only the virgin product or only the recycled product. Less research is required to evaluate only one product or only the other. However, the incremental approach is deficient. It ignores the linked relationship between the virgin product and the recycled product. The recycled product is not possible if the virgin product is not produced first. Often the manufacturer of the virgin product is called upon to facilitate recovery and recycling. The incremental approach to open-loop recycling does not show any benefit for this effort. The allocation method described above ascribes a mutual benefit to both the manufacturer of the virgin product and the recycler, providing an incentive for both.

Both the allocated approach and the incremental approach are arbitrary, and the choice of one over the other is subjective. The 50:50 allocation method is recommended in the SETAC document *A Technical Framework for Life-Cycle Analysis.*[3]

Embodied Energy.   Embodied energy, energy of material resource, or inherent energy can be defined two different ways for LCI studies. Franklin Associates defines *energy of material resource* as the energy content (higher heating value) of raw materials entering the system that are also commercial fuel sources for the geographic region being studied. Other practitioners may define *embodied energy, energy of material resource,* or *inherent energy* as the energy content (higher heating value) of raw materials entering the system, regardless of whether the materials are commercial fuel sources.

The difference between the two different definitions stems from the different uses for LCI studies. Care must be taken with studies that are used for comparative purposes. A comparison of total energy use for two different systems would not be very meaningful if the total energy for one system included energy values that did not represent withdrawals from available fuel reserves. For example, consider an LCI comparing leather garments to plastic garments. The major raw materials for the leather garment are grass and grain eaten by cattle. These raw materials have an energy content, just as the petroleum raw material for plastic garments does. If the energy content of the feed for cattle is included in the total energy for leather, then a comparison of the total energy for the leather and plastic garments is not very meaningful.

An understanding of the purpose of the LCI study and the conventions followed in the presentation of results is essential for the users of LCI studies. Without this understanding, misconceptions can easily occur.

2.4   IMPACT METHODOLOGY

Environmental life-cycle inventories produce large quantities of complex information on natural resource use and releases to the environment. This is especially true in the areas of atmospheric and waterborne emissions, where a typical result consists of long lists of 20 to 30 different chemicals for each product, process, or packaging scenario. An example is shown in Fig. 2.11, which lists the atmospheric emissions of a hypothetical product A. These data are difficult to interpret; that is, it is difficult to conclude whether product A or its functional equivalent, product B, is better or worse for the environment. For example, 1 lb of one type of airborne or waterborne pollutant can cause vastly different health and environmental effects from 1 lb of another type of atmospheric or waterborne pollutant. Also, with varying site-specific conditions, 1 lb of a single pollutant can cause different effects under different conditions. For example, 1 lb of sulfur oxides creates very different acid rain problems depending on rainfall, temperature, regional wind conditions, and the presence or absence of carbonate rocks on the surface.

Atmospheric Emissions	Pounds
Aldehydes	0.0074
Ammonia	0.050
Carbon Monoxide	0.93
Carbon Dioxide	80.6
Chlorine	0.087
Hydrogen Fluoride	0
Kerosene	0.0001
Lead	0.0019
Mercury	2.1E-06
Methane	0.023
Nitrogen Oxides	0.71
Odorous Sulfur	0.0075
Particulates	0.41
Phosphorus	0
Sulfur Oxides	0.89
Volatile organic compounds (VOCs)	0.37

FIGURE 2.11 Example of typical atmospheric emissions reported for LCAs.

The development of measures of actual impact on human health, ecological quality, and natural resource depletion enables impact assessments (IAs). In theory, IA converts the results from an LCI to a set of common impact measures such as excess mortality, habitat disruption, etc., that allows interpretation of the total environmental effects of the system being evaluated.[2,6,7]

IA requires some way of combining complex LCI data outputs into a small number of impact categories. This requires a conversion mechanism, such as a number that could serve as a multiplier. For example, factors for acid rain potential could be developed for the various air emission categories. Pounds of sulfur oxides could be multiplied by one factor, and particulate emissions could be multiplied by another factor. The results could be summed to form an IA score for acid rain potential. The same could be done with other atmospheric wastes or with wastewater discharges and other impact areas. Being able to accomplish this would enable a relatively straightforward comparison of various product systems based upon each impact category.

It would be still more helpful to be able to generate numerical scores to weight the various impact categories First, individual pollutant data would be combined into impact categories, as discussed above. Then diverse impact categories, such as energy resource depletion and toxic discharges, would be combined into a single quality-of-life category. This would require the ability to compare and to weight accurately the impacts of various emission and impact categories on human health, ecological quality, and natural resources.

In 1969, on the very first LCA study performed, it was realized that an impact assessment would be quite desirable. In that first work, a set of subjective factors was developed and applied. However, because of the subjective nature of the analysis, it was not accepted. The IA was discontinued after a few years because there were insufficient data to develop a scientifically based set of factors. Today in the United States there is still a high level of interest in IA, but no widely accepted methodology has been developed. The problem remains the lack of adequate data to support IA activity.

In Europe, IA has been driven by the desire of public policy advocates to obtain a single numerical descriptor so that results can be readily interpreted. This has given rise to a large number of proposed IA methodologies in the last 10 years. While many of them have merit, none has been embraced by the scientific community. As in the United States, the problem is data availability and data quality. Thus, IA is still an emerging scientific analysis. While some IAs are presently performed, they yield only qualitative and subjective results.

There are two documents that provide excellent background on IA in the United States and Europe. The Society of Environmental Toxicology and Chemistry published *A Conceptual Framework for Life-Cycle Impact Assessment* in 1993 that outlines conceptual approaches.[2] The Environmental Protection Agency has developed a document entitled *Life-Cycle Impact Assessment* (draft 1994) that summarizes 36 potential methods for performing the characterization and/or valuation steps of impact assessment.

In this chapter, the current status of IA is described. A conceptual framework is presented, which is followed by a discussion of issues and difficulties.

2.4.1 Conceptual Framework

Following the lead of SETAC and the EPA, the LCA community generally accepts a three-phase conceptual model of LCA impact assessment, consisting of the following:

- *Classification*—the process of assignment and initial aggregation of LCI data into relatively homogeneous impact groups.
- *Characterization*—the process of identifying impacts of concern and selecting actual or surrogate characteristics to describe impacts. It is a goal of characterization methodologies to develop conversion models that are used to translate LCI and supplemental data to impact descriptors. For example, BOD data for wastewater discharges may be translated to fish mortality.
- *Valuation*—the assignment of relative values or weights to different impacts. This allows integration across all impact categories. When valuation is completed, the decision makers can directly compare the overall potential impacts of each product. Although it is a highly desirable goal, the valuation step is also highly subjective. The assignment of relative weights to various potential impacts is inherently value-laden, and there is no scientific method for accurately completing the valuation step of impact assessment.

2.4.2 Classification

The first step of the impact assessment is classification. This is the process of assigning and aggregating results from the inventory into relatively homogeneous impact categories. Impact categories are chosen to represent the issues of interest for a specific study. SETAC lists four general impact categories: (1) environmental or ecosystem quality, (2) quality of human life (including health), (3) natural resource utilization, and (4) social welfare.[2] There is no agreement yet on how to conduct an IA of social welfare issues.

For this chapter, work from a previous IA for Union Carbide is used to illustrate the classification step.[18] Examples of impact categories are drawn from the two major impact classifications of ecosystem quality and human health. Within these two major categories, subcategories are identified based on an extensive analysis of the environmental literature.

Some of the typical LCI listings are actually complex derived measurements. For example, the waterborne emissions labeled suspended solids, dissolved solids, chemical oxygen demand (COD), biochemical oxygen demand (BOD), and alkalinity are interrelated. Suspended and dissolved solids affect the COD, BOD, and alkalinity measurements. All these pollutant categories impact water quality, which in turn impacts the ecosystem quality. Thus, individual LCI data points may be entered into more than one impact category.

The survey of scientific literature results in the following list of *ecological stressors.* These stressors are described by outputs from an LCI. They are the apparent cause of environmental impact.

Acid (air)	Dissolved solids	Nitrogen oxides
Acid (water)	Ethylene oxide	Odorous sulfur
Aldehyde	Fluorides	Oil
Aluminum	Herbicides	Other organics
Ammonia	Hydrocarbons	Particulates
Arsenic	Hydrogen fluoride	Pesticides
Biochemical oxygen demand	Iron	Phenol
	Kerosene	Phosphates
Carbon dioxide	Lead	Phosphorus
Carbon monoxide	Mercury	Sulfides
Chemical oxygen demand	Metal ion (water)	Sulfuric acid
Chlorine	Methane	Sulfur oxides
Chromium	Nickel	Suspended solids
Cyanide	Nitrogen (water)	Zinc

Each of these stressors must be classified into a relatively homogeneous group of ecosystem impact. For the Union Carbide study, the following list of categories was developed:

- Greenhouse gas—global warming
- Ozone-depleting gas—ozone depletion
- Acid rain precursor—acid rain
- Smog precursor—photochemical smog
- Air dispersion, aging, transport
- Aquatic life
- Eutrophication, plant life
- Visibility alterations (air or water)
- Weather alterations
- Thermal changes
- pH alterations
- Chemical and biological content alteration
- Oxygen depletion
- Aquifer contamination

For the major classification of human health, potential impact categories were defined as follows:

- Human carcinogen (class A)
- Irritant (eye, lung, skin, GI tract), corrosive
- Respiratory system effects
- Central nervous system effects
- Allergenicity, sensitization
- Methemoglobinemia, blood diseases
- Odors
- Cardiovascular system effects
- Reproductive system effects
- Behavioral effects
- Bone or renal effects

It is important to realize that when exposure data are lacking, the classification of a chemical to a potential ecological impact category or human health target site is at best semiquantitative. Occupational exposures cannot be considered directly relevant to the classification analysis unless exposure or concentration data are available. Exposure data are not typically available in LCI results. Moreover, there are many workplaces (industrial and nonindustrial) with varying conditions, and an overall impact analysis is not practical because of variable or unknown concentration levels.

Similarly, animal toxicology data cannot be directly incorporated into the classification analysis since experimental design criteria (i.e., high-dose studies, inbred animal strains) in toxicity studies, particularly carcinogenesis studies, may not be relevant to very low-level general population exposure.

2.4.3 Characterization

The second step of the impact assessment is characterization. *Characterization* is the assessment of the magnitude of potential impacts on the chosen major categories (human health or ecosystem quality) for each of the subcategories evaluated.

For example, carbon monoxide, carbon dioxide, chlorine, and methane are all classified under the category of greenhouse gas and global warming. Each chemical has a potential impact on ecosystem quality through this subcategory. Models for the potential impact of each substance are used to equate the quantities of each pollutant to units of potential global warming.

To develop a characterization system to assess the contribution of each emission, various models were reviewed. The goal of each of these models is to assess the magnitude of environmental harm from the product systems being studied. For example, if one manufacturing system produces 15 lb of airborne particulates and another system produces 30 lb, some mechanism is desired to assess whether this is a matter for concern. Some proposed characterization models follow.

- *Loading.*   These models assess inventory chemical data on quantity alone, with the assumption that less quantity produces less potential impact.
- *Equivalency.*   These models use derived equivalency factors to aggregate inventory data with the assumption that aggregated equivalency factors measure potential impacts.

- *Inherent chemical properties.* These models pool inventory data based on chemical properties, toxicity, persistence, and bioaccumulation with the assumption that these criteria would normalize the inventory data to provide measures of potential impacts.

- *Generic exposure and effects.* These models estimate potential impact based on generic environmental and human health information.

- *Site-specific exposure and effects.* These models determine the actual impacts of product systems based on site-specific fate, transport, and impact information for the relevant area or site.

Loading. The loading models are the simplest to execute. The inventory data provide quantities of physical measures, such as kilograms, pounds, and cubic meters, of the various pollutants. However, physical measures alone are not a measure of environmental impact. This means that loading models are best used in a comparative analysis for two or more systems or two or more process steps within one system. In that application, the quantities of a specific emission category are compared for each product system, and the system that generates the least is considered to cause the least harm to ecosystem quality or to human health. For example, one manufacturing system may release 35 lb of atmospheric sulfur oxides, while another system manufacturing an equivalent product may release 90 lb of the same chemical. In this case, one might be tempted to conclude that the first system creates less potential environmental impact from atmospheric sulfur oxides.

There are several problems with these types of conclusions. One problem is that it is not known if either quantity poses a significant threat or what the severity of that threat may be. This depends, in part, upon the exposure rate. The exposure rate varies depending upon, among other factors, whether the chemical is emitted to the environment in a large amount or is released slowly over time.

Another problem with the loading characterization model is that many emission categories are poorly defined. An example is hydrocarbon emissions. Analytical tests performed to measure this pollutant category do not reveal chemical composition detail. One system may release considerable quantities of hydrocarbons with significant potential environmental impacts, while the other system may release equivalent quantities of more benign hydrocarbons. If hydrocarbon emissions are reported only as a generic total, the product systems will appear to have equal potential impact, using the loading model.

Another disadvantage of loading models is that emission categories cannot be intercompared. For example, suppose one manufacturing system produces more suspended solids in wastewater but another produces more acid. The loading model provides no guidance on how to conclude which produces the greater potential impact or if there even is an impact.

Given all these caveats and problems, there is still potential utility in loading models. In some cases, one product system produces more emissions in virtually every category when compared to other equivalent product systems. In addition, if the product systems are similar, the hydrocarbon and other combined emission categories may have quite similar compositions. Under these conditions, limited conclusions can be drawn with some level of certainty.

Equivalency. Some of the problems of the loading models could be solved if equivalency factors could be found. For example, if one could determine the potential impact on human health and ecosystem quality of 1 lb of sulfur oxides compared to the potential impacts of 1 lb of nitrogen oxides, it might be possible to construct a system that would allow intercomparison.

The following is a list of possible bases for equivalency factors found in a survey of recent documents. This list is illustrative and is not meant to be complete, but it shows a number of possible options.

- Cancer potency index
- Molecular weight or other molar basis
- Reference dose values (Rfd)
- Hydrogen-ion or acid equivalents
- Carbon equivalents
- Oxygen equivalents
- Halogen-ion equivalents
- Acute toxicity values (LD_{50})
- Sensory irritation index (RD_{50})
- Chemical "potentials" (e.g., ozone-depleting potentials, global warming)
- Environmental or ecotoxicity data (e.g., genetic toxicity values, Ames' mutagenicity test, chromosomal aberration, aquatic toxicity values)
- Other physical or chemical data (e.g., partition coefficients)
- Quantitative risk assessment

None of these techniques is considered to be routinely acceptable. The main reason for rejection is lack of information. To use equivalency modeling, an LCI must be available to provide quantitative data in sufficient detail for each emission produced by a product system. One difficulty lies in identifying what chemicals compose the inventory items designated as particulates, hydrocarbons, other organics, aldehydes, nitrogen oxides, sulfur oxides, pesticides, herbicides, and metal ions. The chemical diversity that could exist within each pollutant label makes quantitative risk assessment and other quantitative techniques difficult to use for equivalency modeling. Unfortunately, more detailed information on individual manufacturing processes is usually not available. Data are reported from results of analytical tests completed on waste streams. The data are typically reported in the level of detail obtained during this testing, which follows standards set by manufacturers to respond to government reporting agencies. Also, the detail of the data reported does not include information on the exposure rate to the ecosystem or humans.

As an illustration of this problem, particulates in the acid rain impact category could be normalized based on molecular weight, reference dose, or acid equivalents. What values would the researcher use? To what fraction of particulates should the impact apply (i.e., respirable suspended particulates or others)? The required information is usually not available.

Another example occurs with the degradation of water quality, called *eutrophication*. Does the researcher assume the nitrogen water pollutant listed by the LCI is nitrates, nitrites, or possibly even nitrosamines? Most likely, it is a combination of several nitrogen-containing chemical compounds, but testing would report only total nitrogen, and this is what is reported in inventories. Another problem with eutrophication demonstrates the need for site-specific data. Specific bodies of water can be phosphate-limited or nitrogen-limited. In nitrogen-limited water, phosphate would not create a negative impact on the environment as it would in other bodies of water which are phosphate-limited.

Use of the cancer potency index illustrates similar problems with health effect measures. For example, does the researcher use the cancer potency index for benzene as a surrogate measure for the hydrocarbon inventory item? Use of this potency index or other potency estimates (e.g., reference doses, acute toxicity values) is also limited in accuracy by differences in the experimental design and execution of animal studies, as well as by any assumptions (safety factors, animal-to-human extrapolation) used or errors made during estimate calculations.

Generalized attempts at equivalency modeling are very common in Europe, and to a lesser extent in the United States. Some of the common names include *critical-volume approaches, environmental priority strategies,* and *environmental indicators.* A set of dimensionless equivalency impact factors is frequently derived, by which inventory data are multiplied or summed, or to which some combination of mathematical operations is applied. The problem is that there is *no* widely accepted single method for doing this that is endorsed by the scientific community. In fact, in the May 1994 issue of *LCA-News* (a SETAC-Europe publication), it is reported that, at the 1994 Annual SETAC-Europe Congress, it was generally agreed that "...single result systems (e.g., eco-points) are not viable."

One subset of equivalency models, however, has met with some success. These are impact potentials. An example is the global warming set of chemicals. These include carbon dioxide, methane, and chlorofluorocarbons (CFCs). There are widely accepted equivalency factors for the various chemicals. One factor is that each pound of methane is considered to cause 69 times as much global warming as each pound of carbon dioxide. Factors such as these can be used in the isolated cases where there is general scientific agreement that valid equivalencies exist and specific exposure and fate data are not needed. These could include global warming, ozone depletion, and perhaps acid rain.

Inherent Chemical Properties. These models take into account specific properties of various chemicals emitted. Properties may include toxicity, ignitability, carcinogenicity, bioaccumulation, and so on. Impact-ranking systems require appropriate data on the property selected that are relevant to the inventory data. For example, a list of air pollutants emitted during the course of product manufacture and transport can be evaluated for toxicity. In that case, some uniform set of values is needed. An example might be the LD_{50} values for each chemical. These values could be multiplied by the amount of each chemical released to arrive at a ranking score for the various pollutants emitted, and subsequently products could be ranked.

This approach suffers from some of the same serious problems as equivalency models. The use of LD_{50} does not take into account that one chemical may biodegrade at a much faster rate than another chemical. With a quicker biodegradation, the potential for exposure would be lowered.

Another fundamental problem is that some pollutants are not reported in terms of chemical composition. Primary examples of nonspecific air pollutants are particulate emissions and hydrocarbon emissions. These are among the dominant pollutants generated, so this problem is quite serious.

The lack of any knowledge of chemical composition makes an appropriate choice of properties to study impossible. This problem is not unique to air pollution, but is a characteristic common to all environmental emission categories.

The third major problem is data quality. Many types of specific emissions are included in an inventory, and accurate measures of all kinds of pollutants are not always available. Thus, while quite good data may exist for one emission, such as carbon monoxide, the data for highly toxic materials released in very small quantities may be quite poor. In many cases, reported data on toxic emissions are only very rough estimates, and they may be in error by factors of 10, 100, or more.

While these chemical property models exist, they need to be used with great care, and with a realization of the potential errors. Typically, use of these models eventually requires an abandonment of purely analytical modeling in favor of subjective weighting factors or other opinion-based measures. The historical record is clear that use of models by governments has sometimes been quite effective at protecting human health and the environment. In these cases, the model is applied to a specific site where exposure is known, and the chemicals have similar properties. In other cases, however, the use of models has resulted in unnecessary remediation, and in some cases possibly greater damage to health and the environment than no action at all.

Generic Exposure and Effects.   These models seek to use general or generic information to build hypothetical models of the environment in order to assess the complex interaction of emissions and the environment. These are generally very large computer models. These models are only as good as the data available and the ability to accurately model complex environmental and health situations. This requires knowledge of atmospheric dynamics, hydrological dynamics, and the complex ways that stressors interact with ecosystems and human health.

Two examples of models that attempt to quantify the fate of chemicals primarily in an aquatic ecosystem are the Mackay unit-world approach and the use of *canonical environments*. These models are described in the SETAC document *A Conceptual Framework for Life-Cycle Impact Assessment* (1993). They use a specific site approach with the Mackay model defining a *site* as a unit world of 1 km^3 and the canonical model defining a generalized stream, lake, or other ecosystem as a site. The Mackay model relies on fugacity coefficients to determine how the chemical will partition between the different environments. The canonical model requires knowledge of several environmental factors such as stream flow and soil organic matter content.

While some computer models exist, there is no general agreement in the scientific community that the accuracy and reliability of these models are anywhere near what is needed for an LCA impact assessment. The data quality in many cases is a substantial problem, and there is a large degree of subjective content. In addition, application of these models to life-cycle inventory data would not be feasible, given the lack of information on specific chemicals within broad categories and lack of exposure data.

Site-Specific Exposure and Effects.   These models are potentially much more successful at this time than generic approaches or the approaches that are geographically "global" in scope. The site-specific data are frequently more accurate, and the specific effects on a local environment can be modeled more effectively than in broader-based analyses. In fact, many of the identified ecosystem and environmental health problems can be adequately studied only at the local level.

However, LCI is inherently a global approach. The whole point of life-cycle assessment is to include indirect effects that go beyond plant boundaries of a single company. A site-specific approach would require site-specific data for each site in the entire production system. This would typically require 40 or more sets of comprehensive site-specific studies, with each set examining the many different emissions identified from the process. This in itself is so expensive and extensive that it precludes the effort because of practical considerations.

There are also other problems. In any production system, there comes a point where specific plants can no longer be tied to the system. For example, if a company is buying fuels on the open market from a pipeline, it is buying a commodity product. The specific sources of the fuel may not be known, and in fact they may change from day to day. This makes the site-specific approach impossible for most LCIs. An unpublished EPA document suggests that site-specific models be limited to LCAs of limited scope or used as a supplement to generic methods. In any event, the precise role of site-specific methods for LCAs needs to be carefully analyzed.

One suggestion is to follow the same general characterization and assessment determinations as discussed above. However, it may be necessary to select representative sites in order to carry out the analyses. For example, one might select an arid area subject to atmospheric inversion, such as Los Angeles; a midcontinental region with moderate rainfall and well-mixed atmosphere, such as Topeka, Kansas; and an area that might be more intermediate and more typical of the eastern one-third of the United States, such as Cincinnati. Results would then be reported in ranges of possible values.

2.4.4 Application Issues

Now comes the critical question: What does a user require to produce a useful IA result? One problem is that the analyses described above do not, in most cases, yield an actual environmental impact. They yield impact surrogates, such as pounds of CO_2 equivalents. This means that the true effect on the environment is not revealed. These results are useful only for a relative analysis. For example, the results of one manufacturing system can be compared to those of another. Another possible application is to evaluate proposed process changes and see which one produces less CO_2 equivalents. Still another application might be to conduct a temporal analysis on a company or on some sector. A 1995 baseline could be established, and each year an environmental score card could be calculated to see if the company was producing greater or less impact on the environment. This could be accomplished by completing an IA for major product lines.

Another problem is the diversity of the reported results. It is not clear how to compare acid rain results with global warming, yet these must be combined to determine some overall environmental impact. This would occur only in a valuation step, and there is no general agreement among scientists on a valid analytical approach. All methods contain a high degree of subjectivity. Analysts must take careful notice of the fact that no matter how sophisticated a quantitative analysis may be, if it has a subjective basis or uses subjective data, it still gives subjective results. All too often these impact analysis schemes try to hide their subjectivity in complicated mathematics or complicated arguments.

Most companies and public policy agencies are accustomed to making decisions based upon judgments, because in most complicated real-life systems there is no adequate analytical model. However, any valuation of relative impacts is considered premature. Rather, any project should focus on developing the classification and characterization methodologies and securing peer review acceptance for those efforts. When that is completed, the more complex task of valuing impacts can be addressed.

2.4.5 Implications for LCI Data Development

Revised Data Needs for LCI. Impact assessments are intended to use data developed in the LCI stage. As described in this chapter, existing LCIs already contain many of the data needed to conduct a full LCA, but there are many gaps, and the data are often not as complete as desired. In some cases, additional data are needed, such as acres of land disturbed during mining or rate of release for air emissions. In other cases, it is simply a matter of chemical specificity. For example, the air pollution category of particulates may contain very small particles of sulfur compounds that can contribute to acid rain. At present, regulatory authorities require only that total particulates be reported in most cases, so that chemical specificity does not exist.

This may or may not be a serious problem. If the particulates are primarily uncombusted and incombustible inert materials, this is not an obstacle. At this time it is unknown whether this is the case. To find out, it may require additional and expensive work by manufacturing and processing facilities' personnel to determine chemical composition of their airborne particulates. However, this issue does need attention.

Apart from health issues, the following air emission data categories that are routinely collected by LCI practitioners are in need of chemical specificity: particulates, nitrogen oxides, hydrocarbons, and sulfur oxides. If health issues or even ecotoxicity is considered, the list gets much longer. The category of hydrocarbons does need chemical specificity, while the other categories may or may not be critical. This cannot be determined without more chemical information on those composite categories.

In addition to the need for chemical specificity for certain categories of air emissions, the source of certain air emissions may be important. For example, carbon dioxide released from the combustion of fossil fuels may contribute more to global warming than carbon dioxide released from the combustion of biomass. This is because carbon dioxide releases from the combustion of biomass may be viewed as part of the natural carbon cycle. Carbon dioxide is taken up by growing plants or trees and is released when the by-products from the harvested trees or plants are burned for energy. The time needed for this cycle to repeat itself may be the critical factor in the fossil versus non-fossil carbon dioxide issue.

There are similar chemical specificity concerns about waterborne emissions as there are for air emissions. For example, in the case of eutrophication, chemical specificity for phosphorus and nitrogen compounds is needed. Some will yield available nutrients much more readily than others. Categories such as dissolved solids and suspended solids need to be chemically analyzed for possible nutrient content. Also, temperature and the presence of acidity or alkalinity may be important variables for analyzing eutrophication potential.

The chemical composition of dissolved or suspended solids in wastewater is not generally measured, so that requests for this information would almost certainly require unwelcome extra effort by plant personnel.

Site-Specific and Generic Data Issues. The data categories discussed above are routinely collected in an LCI project from specific sites. The additional specificity could be added to that routine data collection if an IA is desired. Additional analyses not presently done would be required.

As discussed previously, some inputs to a process do not come from an identifiable source. This means that additional information will need to be accumulated for generic material impact assessments. Not all the data changes can be specifically determined until a generic material methodology is fully developed. However, it is likely that model or typical sites would have to be analyzed to provide the generic environmental impact assessment. In order for this to faithfully represent the sampled population of sites, information on the distribution of sites would need to be collected. For example, for generic fuel oils, it is necessary to determine the location and production level of facilities in the potential target population of fuel oil producers. If there are geographic concentrations (such as perhaps the Gulf Coast), this could provide guidance for selection of model site characteristics for the impact assessment. In any event, additional data are needed to characterize generic materials.

Additional Data Issues. There are other data requirements. For example, climatic data are required if atmospheric dispersion models are needed. Complete data are also required for receiving waters in order to conduct conversion models for eutrophication and oxygen depletion. This may include not only physical parameters, but also biological diversity or other biological data.

These data needs cannot be completely specified in general terms at this time. However, they become apparent when decisions are made on the specific conversion models.

2.4.6 Conclusion

IA is still in its infancy. Even after 25 years of development, it is hampered by a lack of data of sufficient quality and a lack of scientifically accepted methodologies. However, significant progress is being made. We can look forward to resolution of some issues in the near future. However, some parts of IA will remain subjective for many years to come.

REFERENCES

1. SETAC, *Guidelines for Life-Cycle Assessment: A "Code of Practice,"* Workshop (31 March–3 April 1993) report, The Society of Environmental Toxicology and Chemistry, Pensacola, FL, 1993.

2. SETAC, *A Conceptual Framework for Life-Cycle Impact Assessment,* Workshop (February 1–7, 1992) report, The Society of Environmental Toxicology and Chemistry, Pensacola, FL, 1993.

3. SETAC, *A Technical Framework for Life-Cycle Assessment,* Workshop (August 18–23, 1990) report, The Society of Environmental Toxicology and Chemistry, Pensacola, FL, 1991.

4. Robert G. Hunt, Jere D. Sellers, and William E. Franklin, "Resource and Environmental Profile Analysis: A Life Cycle Environmental Assessment for Products and Procedures," *Environmental Impact Assessment Review,* 12: 245–269 (1992).

5. Environmental Protection Agency, *Life-Cycle Assessment: Inventory Guidelines and Principles,* EPA/600/R-92/245, report to the EPA by Battelle Memorial Institute and Franklin Associates, Ltd., February 1993.

6. Canadian Standards Association, Standard Z760-94, Life Cycle Assessment, Etobicoke, Ontario, Canada, 1994.

7. Environmental Protection Agency, *Life-Cycle Impact Assessment,* report to the EPA by Research Triangle Institute, draft 1994.

8. Ian Boustead, *Eco-balance Methodology for Commodity Thermoplastics,* The European Centre for Plastics in the Environment (PWMI), Brussels, December 1992.

9. Environmental Protection Agency, *Resource and Environmental Profile Analysis of Nine Beverage Container Alternatives,* EPA/530/SW-91c/245, report to the EPA by Robert G. Hunt and William E. Franklin, 1974.

10. Environmental Protection Agency, *Resource and Environmental Profile Analysis of Five Milk Container Systems,* report to the EPA by Midwest Research Institute and Franklin Associates, Ltd., August 17, 1977.

11. Gary R. Nuss, Richard Welch, Robert Hunt, and James Cross, *Resource and Environmental Profile Analysis of Plastics and Competitive Materials,* The Society of the Plastics Industry, Inc., Washington, D.C., 1974.

12. Alan F. Ferguson, John Moberly, Fred Weil, and Robert Smith, *Description of Beverage Container Systems and Their Environmental Impact Measurements,* Stanford Research Institute, Menlo Park, CA, 1973.

13. Ian Boustead, *The Milk Bottle,* The Open University Press, Milton Keynes, West Sussex, U.K., 1972.

14. M. P. Lundholm and G. Sundström, *Tetra Brik Environmental Profile,* G. Sundström AB, Malmö, Sweden, 1986.

15. Elliot H. Barber, Karl Fagans, and Henry Martin, *Resource and Environmental Profile Analysis of Selected Disposable versus Reusable Diapers, Napkins and Towels,* Arthur D. Little, Inc., report to the Tissue Division, American Paper Institute, Inc., March 1977.

16. SETAC, *Life-Cycle Assessment Data Quality: A Conceptual Framework,* Workshop (October 4–9, 1992) report, The Society of Environmental Toxicology and Chemistry, Pensacola, FL, 1994.

17. Terrie K. Boguski, Robert G. Hunt, and William E. Franklin, "General Mathematical Models for LCI Recycling," *Resources, Conservation and Recycling,* 12: 147–163 (1994).

18. Keri K. Hoffsommer, William E. Franklin, and Robert G. Hunt, *Life Cycle Assessment of Ethylene Glycol and Propylene Glycol Based Antifreeze* (final report and peer review), a report to Union Carbide Corporation by Franklin Associates, Ltd., August 1994.

CHAPTER 3
SOFTWARE SYSTEMS AND DATABASES

Bruce W. Vigon
RESEARCH LEADER
BATTELLE MEMORIAL INSTITUTE
COLUMBUS, OHIO

The conduct of life-cycle assessments demands considerable effort on the part of the investigator if accepted professional guidelines for study quality are to be met. Software and public databases can facilitate defining the system under investigation, supporting the identification and collection of data of appropriate quality, and performing the extensive computations. As aptly noted by Heijungs and Guinée,[1] "The development of methodology for life-cycle assessment (LCA) is highly theoretical, whereas the collection of data has a direct connection with practice. Software takes a position in between: it contains the formalized methodology in a way that is accessible to the data, with its practical limitations. The development of software increases the practical usability of the methodology and the suitability of the data within the theoretical framework. Software may thus act as a bridge between theory and practice."

To facilitate data collection and characterization as well as the performance of myriad computations required in LCA, the personal computer has been incorporated as a readily accessible tool on the practitioner's desktop. The utility of the computer (or engineering workstation) is only as good as the software tools used. This chapter will describe the evolving relationship between LCA and software and the well-documented need for comprehensive yet easy-to-use software tools. It further will explore the types and structure of LCA software tools for filling existing needs and will, one hopes, provide a useful guide to evaluating features of software that may be critical to effectively supporting LCA projects. Also addressed are a number of public data sets and databases which can furnish a portion of the information required for the inventory or impact assessment. Finally, some thoughts will be given to both inspire and direct next-generation software product development that will provide even higher levels of convenience and capability for investigators and results users alike.

In the early days of the science of LCA, the personal computer was a dim gleam in the eyes of developers. In the late 1960s, those organizations fortunate to have computers at all were saddled with huge mainframes lacking even the semblance of user convenience. Computer users were expected to be literate in one or more arcane programming languages. Programs were written and data were input through the use of punched cards. Changing a program line or a data point meant the investigator had to punch a new card and rerun the program deck. Finding and correcting errors could be such a time-consuming and tedious task that the relationship of LCA to "software" as such was a tenuous one. In fact, much of the early effort to conduct the inventory portion of LCAs was done by hand, checking the computations with a hand calculator as necessary. Small wonder that the number of studies conducted during the late 1960s and early 1970s was limited.

Later in the 1970s, several practitioners developed mainframe-based software packages able to describe and perform calculations on quite complex systems. The general user accessibility to these programs, however, was still negligible. The programs were designed to be used by the developer for conducting the analyses. In a sense, this reinforced the notion that life-cycle inventories (LCIs) were an expert tool for use by specialized practitioners in support of business decision making. Only in the 1990s have the needs of general as well as expert users meshed with the increased capability of personal computers to provide an enhanced menu of software choices for supporting LCA.

3.1 USER NEEDS AND REQUIREMENTS FOR LCA SOFTWARE

Today's typical LCA users are a mixture of LCA experts and individuals with skills in other disciplines who want to be able to evaluate their products, processes, or activities in a life-cycle context. Because LCA is being used more as a support tool in application of methods such as Design for the Environment (DFE) or Pollution Prevention (P2) engineering, LCA software must mesh at some level with the tools typically used by these disciplines. For all these users, three main considerations apply. The first is computational support. Although it is possible to conduct an LCA by using the "stubby pencil" approach, for most users the primary requirement of software is to organize the data and minimize the effort necessary to conduct an inventory analysis or impact assessment. This is especially true of those for whom LCA is a means of supporting enhanced decision making within their technical or policy sphere. Computational support includes not only helping to relieve the burden of performing the systems analysis calculations necessary for determining the overall or stage-specific inputs and outputs, but also ensuring that data quality goals are met and that professional practices guidelines promulgated or under development by various national or international bodies are adhered to.[2-4]

Documentation is the second major user requirement. Documentation issues have been identified in numerous forums as a critical element in the conduct of successful LCAs, particularly those intended for use in external applications.[5,6] Computer programs are particularly useful in organizing the large amounts of data used in an LCA, in recording the decisions made by the investigator during the course of conducting the study, and in presenting the information in a coherent manner. Not all these capabilities are fully realized in current-generation software packages. Details on information management in software are discussed more fully in a subsequent section.

Because LCA is generally used as a decision support tool, it is rarely used alone. Whether the decision to be made is a strategic one demanding the integration of LCA information with market and sales data or a tactical one where LCA results would be used in conjunction with performance and cost measures, the compatibility of LCA software with other information system components and software tools is also an issue for most users. Here as well, current-generation software does not fully exploit the capabilities of the technology.

3.2 DEFINITION OF LCA SOFTWARE CLASSES

LCA software can be classified into three generic categories: strict LCA tools, product design tools, and engineering tools. The selection of a particular category by a prospective user depends on the intended use setting and the expected level of investment in LCA and environmental expertise. Strict LCA tools are intended to supply information to support LCA as a stand-alone activity. Levels of sophistication in the implementation of the concepts can vary, but the basic idea is to help conduct inventory analyses and less frequently impact assessments. Users generally must interpret the information themselves in order for it to be useful in a given application. Software products typically comprise a user interface (graphic-based systems now challenge text-driven interfaces in commercial or near commercial products), a database, a computational engine, and a report processor, as illustrated in Fig. 3.1. This type of LCA model, as distinguished

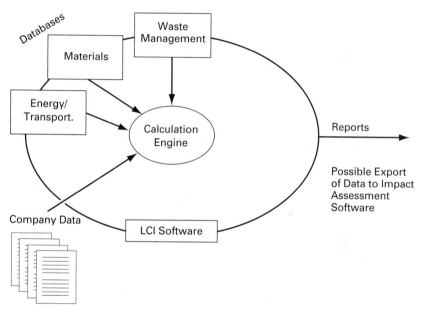

FIGURE 3.1   Typical structure of integrated LCA software.

from design or engineering LCA modeling tools, will be referred to as an *input/output model*. The intent is to capture the materials and energy balance at the system level and not to focus on the process details.

Product design-oriented LCA tools make an explicit attempt to reach a user audience who is not and probably will not become expert in LCA and who has little or no knowledge or technical expertise in environmental issues. Product design software tends to embed LCA computations within a shell that more nearly assumes the appearance and character of software within the domain expertise of the intended user. Product design-oriented software also includes software intended primarily for packaging design. Product design software users can include mechanical design engineers, packaging designers, product concept specialists, and graphic designers whose primary interface with software is through a computer-aided design (CAD) or mechanical and structural design package, e.g., solid modeling.

LCA software products developed for these users typically result in a kind of "green adviser" who provides recommendations on materials and process choices based on LCA considerations. The user is prompted for information about the physical form and/or layout of the components or product and is given choices regarding materials that may be used in a given application.[7] Some software also provides the capability to select alternative processes for manufacture of the item. Within the software a database and an expert system have been incorporated to translate the designer's choices to the necessary inventory and impact assessment computations. Choices of the depth and breadth of the LCA may have been preselected by the developer in order to balance complexity and the multidimensional nature of the decision process.[8] One such multidimensional decision space is illustrated in Fig. 3.2. It can be seen that detailed incorporation of all

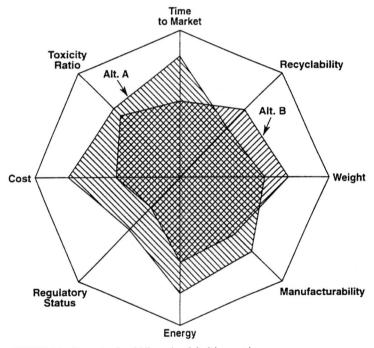

FIGURE 3.2 Example of multidimensional decision metric.

the unit operations throughout the life cycle of a complex product could result in a software system that is cumbersome to use and slow. The tradeoff for acceptable convenience and speed is that some LCA practice guidelines may not be fully realized. In addition, a considerable effort must be made to incorporate process and materials information in the system before it can be usable by designers.

Within the third class are LCA software models oriented to engineering tools. Although LCA is itself an embodiment of systems engineering concepts, software in the third category represents engineering analysis tools that have been adapted for use in LCA. These generally fall into two subcategories: general systems (activity) models and process simulators. General systems models as a class typically require the user to specify for each process or activity (specification must represent a verb of some type) the inputs, outputs, constraints (descriptions of physical, financial, or temporal limits where the activity can take place), and mechanisms (resources that make the activity occur which may include machines, individuals, organizations, and so on).[9] Activities may be hierarchical, sequential, or networked such that an entire product system can be described. Varying levels of detail in data or activity description can be used to tailor the model to the study scope and goal definition. Activity models usually do not incorporate databases, spreadsheets, or extensive text editing, but can be linked with these tools. Activity models can be used in conjunction with management information tools, such as activity-based costing models. As with the design models, general systems models may not fully incorporate all the standard LCA practices. In this case the potential deficiency is not due to prior choices made by the software designer, but rather is due to the flexibility afforded the user in describing and analyzing the system.

Engineering process simulators comprise a group of models where the inputs and detailed transformation function are described for each process. Outputs in the form of products, coproducts, and residuals are predicted from the operating conditions and process rules. Models may simulate either mechanical assembly-type operations or chemical engineering operations. Based on the system depicted by the interconnected processes, the model simulates the details of the activity going on in each operation and the movement of materials, parts, etc., among the operation steps. Fundamental physical and chemical properties, standardized unit operations modules, and other primary data are required in the databases of such models. The basic premise behind this type of model is quite different from that of the typical strict LCA model and allows for results to be generated under circumstances that would be difficult to model by using an input/output LCA model. For example, most simulators treat time as an explicit variable. Time trends of resource consumption and residuals generation can be output and are sometimes useful in targeting improvements opportunities. Simulators also can embody default rules for handling incomplete or minimally specified data sets. During the early stages of product development in an improvements assessment mode, such models may be able to provide general indications of production efficiencies and environmental burdens, even when operational details are sketchy and no facility yet exists for which actual data might be collected.

On the other hand, simulation of complex product systems by using this type of model is more difficult than with strict LCA models because of the details involved and the need for considerable domain expertise in chemical or mechanical engineering. It has been proposed to utilize engineering-type models as a second tier below the primary-level input/output LCA model (Fig. 3.3).[10] Instances are common where manage-

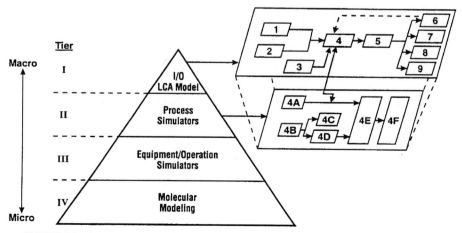

FIGURE 3.3   Tiered concept for interrelated LCA and design software tools.

rial tier users may not be interested in the detailed landscape depicted in the engineering model, but have subsidiary staff whose success depends on understanding details at the facility level. Thus, the two types of models complement one another. Actual linking of the models at the software level has not yet occurred.

The following sections will focus on a more complete analysis of software systems with an emphasis on the dedicated input/output type of LCA models. Many of the principles can be applied to the other classes of LCA models with the appropriate consideration of the intended user groups and the model architecture.

3.3 GENERAL STRUCTURE AND FUNCTION OF LCA SOFTWARE

Stand-alone LCA software has evolved rapidly over the past several years from largely spreadsheet-based systems to graphically oriented systems employing standard Windows features and appearance. The following section provides a description of the operating modes, general feature sets, and functional capability of LCA software.

3.3.1 Inventory Analysis Software

Most of the current-generation inventory software is based on commercial spreadsheet programs.[11] Microsoft Excel and Lotus 1-2-3 are two of the more popular systems. The most basic execution of this level of LCA inventory software uses the unadorned spreadsheet as the input data template, computational engine, and output form. A simple database on materials and processes may be included in a section of the spreadsheet so that users are not required to input anything more than basic functional unit and product descriptions. The database is modified or augmented only with difficulty. Printing of tabular or graphical results is dependent on the internal capability of the spreadsheet used or the ability to download the output to a graphic or text postprocessor.

Some advanced features of contemporary spreadsheets have been used to advantage in recent incarnations of software of this type. These features include a multisheet capability so that input, intermediate calculation, and output sections can be separated. Separation of certain common operational elements, such as electric power generation and transportation systems, also is facilitated. Many of the internal computational tools of practitioners as well as industry commodity data sets are maintained in spreadsheet format. Graphical capabilities of spreadsheets have been improving to the point where for many uses it may not be necessary to use a separate stand-alone graphics package to present the results in a meaningful manner, particularly if the study goal is an internal one.

Advantages of this format are that the development costs of the software are low and that the software packages themselves are readily available. The fact that managers and technical staff routinely use spreadsheets also makes them able to mesh with other analytical tools (e.g., financial spreadsheets) that may be used conjunctively to reach a decision. Also, depending on the industry and the purpose of the study, it is relatively easy to modify the format of the output to meet various needs. The data and computational algorithms in a spreadsheet are accessible, and it is possible to trace the computational sequence through the model.

Few external, commercial models use the basic spreadsheet format directly. Upgrades of the basic model include macrosets within and shells constructed around the spreadsheet to facilitate user interaction. These may range in sophistication from simple information organizational devices to quite complex, help and computational and data input support capability. Commercial baler software is available to assist in turn-

ing common spreadsheets to compiled systems with limited user modification (read-only) capability and for providing semiautomated data inputs to embedded data sets.[12]
Drawbacks to this type of software implementation are significant:

- Properly formatted and easily reusable (modular) databases are generally incompatible with the existing spreadsheet structure.
- The probability of making an error is high.
- Data entry and calculations are time-consuming, as are scenario development, sensitivity analysis, report formatting, and so on.[13]

A step beyond these basic inventory models are models that have been developed with extended interfaces between the program and the user. The software does not look like a spreadsheet, and the user has no direct interaction with the underlying computational engine or database, even though some of the programs do in fact use a spreadsheet to perform the calculations and/or hold the data. These programs may be divided into product and package design models (developed for use by nonexpert users) and general-purpose LCI models.

In the most elaborate versions of design models, the user is prompted by the input screen(s) for some basic information about the product or package. This usually entails providing a unique product name and description, specifying the calculation (functional) unit for presentation of the results, and describing the components (materials and/or processes) comprising the product or package. Users will generally be able to select these options from a list. An example of a typical system specification process is shown in Table 3.1. In some models, the processes associated with the manufacturing of certain materials or components are prelinked to the material specification. To fully describe the product, the user only has to identify the type and amount of materials. All the input raw materials and energy and output products and residuals are automatically attached and carried along in the calculations, once this specification is completed. Assuming that the permanent database contains all the materials and processes, the user can proceed to the results generation.

In some software, the user can also exercise limited control over how the calculations are handled. This is normally associated with allocation or nonserial types of systems, such as those involving recycling loops. Different software treats the recycling issue in different ways, with the user specifying a recycling percentage or determining

TABLE 3.1 Example of Product Specification Procedure

Product name: My Product (Version 1)				
	Materials list			
Description:	Category	Description		
Functional analysis basis:	AD	Hot-melt glue		
	AD	Starch-based glue		
Component name:	MT	Unbleached kraft linerboard		
	MT	Sheet steel		
	MT	Aluminum stamp		
Recycle percentage:	<F1>	Description		
	<Enter>	Select	<Esc>	Cancel
Component weight: kg	<F3>	Find	<Home>	Top
	<F4>	Next	<End>	Bottom
	<F5>	Scroll materials list		

the type of recycling (open- or closed-loop). The software then applies a predetermined set of decision rules to complete the calculations. Typically, several formats for tabular or graphical data are offered, and some flexibility on how the results are shown is afforded. For example, the user can placed several alternative designs side by side to compare their overall life-cycle environmental burdens. Or a single system may be dissected to identify where the greatest-quantity contributions to the overall total arise.

In the general-purpose models, the process is similar, but the user has a great deal more control over the system specification, the manner in which the processes are linked, the application of coproduct allocation rules, the algorithms for input/output transformations (i.e., assigning input and output quantities to a process), and the data format. The system boundaries may be specified by displaying and linking graphical objects on a screen instead of providing text references. In addition, the data templates are more extensive but at the same time support a greater variety of data types and units. The embedded databases themselves are much more sophisticated, often incorporating a commercial database software system in the model. Popular choices for embedded database software are dBase IV, FoxPro, and Access. When the permanent database lacks certain information, the software allows for augmentation of the permanent database records. The user is presented with input data templates for materials or processes, and when the information is inserted, the new information can be linked to describe a system in the same manner as that resident in the permanent database.

The ultimate in user-controlled data capability is embodied in models that can import information from external databases, either those created expressly for LCA or more general-purpose data in public databases (see Sec. 3.5). Efforts to create harmonized specifications for importable LCA data sets are underway. To ensure compatibility among data sets, it is necessary to define a certain format for the reporting of external data sets and to incorporate in the software the ability to translate the specification to process or segment (multiple linked processes) definitions. Categories of specification elements include the following:

Identification of the Data Set

- *General descriptors,* e.g., reference code, record date, and abbreviated ID; generator name and address; and reference identification (title, editor, and date)
- *Function specification,* e.g., category, subcategory, name, reference unit, time period, geographic relevance, technology type, technology level, and representativeness
- *Data characteristics,* e.g., sources, measurement type (measured, calculated, or estimated), aggregation and averaging information (number of locations, location areas, and weighting process), and verification procedure

System Model Description

- Boundaries and cutoff rules
- Coproducts and allocation rules
- Energy model and efficiencies
- Transportation, recycling, and waste models used
- Other assumptions, data parameterizations, and subsystems code

System Structure

- Boundaries
- Major process steps

- Functional flow and recycling loops
- Coproducts

Data Fields

- Inputs
- Outputs
- Transportation

Most LCA software currently supports one or more data interchange formats. Although the details of data importing vary from package to package, the general idea is that commercial databases, such as dBase files, can be read and matched to the corresponding internal format for data. Unfortunately, there are no standards presently set for this operation. Typically, the user creates the necessary fields internally (to the LCA software) and then exports a dummy data set to the external database to "calibrate" the setting up of the needed file structure in the database software.[14] When the user loads this data set in the database software, the true data values can be loaded into the appropriate fields via a manual or semiautomated procedure (controlled by a macro) and imported back into the LCA software.

The most advanced general-purpose models run under graphical interfaces that let the user define the system through pictorial representation and linking of processes. Few limitations are encountered with these models in handling loops and interconnections, such as the need for electricity to make plastic and the need for plastics in electricity generation infrastructure. The current state-of-the-art models also provide few or no limits on the number of inputs or outputs that are able to be connected to a process, allow for varying levels of aggregation in the data (at either the unit operation or higher level), and permit annotation of data sets for descriptive or data quality assessment purposes.

3.3.2 Impact Assessment Software

As yet, there are few examples of stand-alone *life-cycle impact assessment* (LCIA) software. The spreadsheet and extended spreadsheet type of model does support impact assessment in some of the software packages. These ordinarily consist of the inventory results data resident in some part of the spreadsheet or database being further processed through some additional steps. Tabular and graphical output of both the impact metrics and the inventory data are possible.

Two primary impact assessment methodologies are used in the software: the *critical-volumes approach* and the *conversion of inventory values* (per functional unit) to monetized or quasi-monetized units. In the former case, the relevant values for the regulatory levels are embedded in the software with or without user control or specification. The printouts provide automatic compilation and summing of the values for air, water, and solids based on the contained substances and the location for the analysis. No software examples of this type relevant to North American locations or environmental standards are presently available.

In the case of value-based impact assessment, the current modeling approach is to take the results of an inventory analysis performed with other software and transfer the functional unit value-based data to a spreadsheet set up to convert the mass values to impact metrics.[15] The most developed software package provides in the spreadsheet a long list of substances (for example, CO_2), activities (e.g., emission to air), impact categories, and types (e.g., decreased crop production due to temperature rise) for which a time frame, spatial extent, frequency and intensity, duration, and normalization factor (contribution of a given environmental burden to the total effect in a given area) are already assigned. These factors are used to modify literature-derived values for the willingness to pay to avoid a *unit effect.* Thus, if the user accepts all the default values, the calculation of the aggregated impacts (measured in load units) requires only the insertion of appropriate inventory data. When used to support improvement assessment, the software also assists in conducting sensitivity and error analysis through plotting the difference between the environmental loads of alternatives and, using the variance measures in the spreadsheet assigned to the various factors, computing the likelihood that the difference is less than the expected value (i.e., that the alternatives are in fact less differentiable than the mean value would indicate). One therefore has the means to judge the degree of confidence that the observed differences are real.

3.3.3 Improvement Assessment Software

It can be argued (probably with some validity) that LCI and LCIA software that allow the user to perform side-by-side comparisons of alternative systems fit the definition of improvement assessment software. Further, a more limited definition of the boundaries of life-cycle improvement assessment encompasses only the identification of improvement possibilities through the application of a systematic evaluation process. The software component of improvement assessment then becomes the electronic embodiment of the algorithm(s) for the systematic analysis of the inventory and/or impact assessment information and the methods for presenting the results. Implementation is outside the scope of LCA.

The improvement assessment process has been divided into two supplementary analysis techniques—dominance analysis and marginal analysis—followed by an interpretive component that creates the iterative loop back to the inventory and or impact assessment phase for the identified alternatives.[16] *Dominance analysis,* in a conceptual sense, refers to a means of identifying those substances and processes responsible for the greatest portion of the environmental burdens, measured as either inventory loadings or impact units. Dominance analysis, in a mathematical sense, refers to a set of matrix algebra operations on the inventory or the environmental effects data that identifies the operations or activities that contribute a specified amount to the overall effect, e.g., the relative contribution from electricity generation for aluminum manufacturing for a product package to acidic precipitation.

The causal relationships analyzed in a dominance analysis may be very complex. *Marginal analysis,* which is a type of sensitivity analysis, identifies the parameters for which the results (dependent variables) change most dramatically for a given change in an input parameter (an independent variable). Geometrically speaking, marginal analysis represents a measure of the slope of a tangent line to the curve describing the relationship between the process or activity parameter (or even the controlling processes relating an input to a process, e.g., combustion temperature) and the resulting inventory (say, NO_x emissions) or impact parameter (acid precipitation equivalents). The steeper the slope (larger values in the marginal analysis matrix), the more sensitive the parameter. This method also lends itself to incorporation in computer software, but because there are no constraints placed on the physical reality of the analysis, not all suggestions for improvement will be realizable. These improvement analysis operations can be formally incorporated into the LCA software to generate output tables or lists which can be analyzed by the user to identify possible new scenarios for the LCI or LCIA. However, the nature of the mathematical operations necessitates that careful evaluation of the improvements opportunities be made by a knowledgeable user in order to validate the suggestions. In fact, the multistakeholder nature of this process suggests that a network version of the software would facilitate identifying an optimum, practical set of improvement alternatives.

A more integrated improvements assessment software system would permit this phase to be done within a design context. There are no commercial software systems meeting this stricter definition at present. However, prototypes are in the development stage. To allow for the improvement assessment to be done without the user having to be an LCA, materials, or process expert, some decisions may have to be made which limit the degree to which the software implements a "full" LCA methodology. In particular, the assumed span of control of the intended user (i.e., a product designer) within the manufacturing stage of the life cycle precludes a full LCA process. The inventory analysis considers only materials entering and leaving the manufacturing operations and assigns impact attributes to them. The impact assessment portion of the model in effect covers the full life cycle because of the partitioning of the impact attributes across the life cycle. That is, some criteria apply to extraction of the raw material, others to intermediate processing, still others to the actual product manufacturing, and some to use and disposal or recycling. The comprehensiveness of the approach and hence its ability to capture the significant impacts depend on the definition and scoring of the magnitude of the attributes by the software developer. The attributes are weighted according to several ethical perspectives, allowing for an environmental quality value to be assigned to a design according to each perspective. All this is transparent to the ultimate user who only has to describe the part or product and provide certain design measurements. However, to allow the system to be used in this way, a considerable effort is necessary in process characterization, data acquisition, and expert system scoring of the alternatives. The model, therefore, would normally be set up to serve a very narrow user community.

3.4 EVALUATING LCA SOFTWARE

This section describes in greater detail the features of an "ideal" software system and analyzes them from the perspective of an individual or organization considering purchase, lease, or other means of acquisition. The descriptions are specifically not referenced to a particular commercial LCA software package. This deliberate choice was made because the software is changing very quickly and because the entire suite of attributes described may not be available in any one package. Obviously, not all the capabilities will be equally important to all users. Some features may be considered uncritical or potentially useful but not necessarily frequently used. A checklist for reviewing software is provided in Table 3.2.

3.4.1 Overall Structure and System Representation

There are a variety of ways that a software engineer can choose to construct a software system. *Object-oriented programming* (OOP) and databases are generally considered to be the preferred system to provide users with the maximum ease of use.[17] Without being too technical, an object-oriented program manipulates objects rather than data or text per se. Objects represent collections of items (both data and the functions that operate on those data) and can have information associated with them through address pointers that refer to other objects. For example, a screen object, say, a process box, can itself be an information icon on a screen, but it also may be linked to other sets of information in the database or in other locations. When a user clicks on the object with a mouse, the

TABLE 3.2 Checklist for LCA Software Evaluation

Overall structure and system representation
- Object-based with data linked to screen objects
- Graphical user interface for intuitive and flexible system assembly and manipulation
- Ability to view a variety of levels of detail in system diagram
- No practical limits on number of resource or process linkages
- Flexible specification of input/output relationships
- Automatic units checking and rectification
- Ability to set system for different levels of user expertise

Embedded data and databases
- Contains database which is independently accessible
- Straightforward input of new data to templates
- Easy copying or export of data modules
- Incorporation of basic materials data sets
- Data accessible and at a disaggregated level

Data and methodology quality assessment
- Provides mechanism for quality assessment of data and higher aggregation units
- User-definable data quality indicators
- Provides traceable documentation of user decisions

Reports, results analysis, and archiving
- Flexibility to tailor reports for various audiences
- Sophisticated graphical presentation of results
- Extensive sensitivity analysis capability
- System optimization capability
- Parametric variability in system specifications capability

Hardware and operating system choices
- Runs with acceptable efficiency on locally available system(s)
- Reasonable memory and disk storage requirements

Financial considerations
- Reasonable price and acquisition terms

---

software automatically links the screen object with the related information. The advantages to the user from this type of program structure are obvious. From a practical standpoint, it makes OOP-based software intuitive and easy to use and permits modular software design.

The LCA practitioner thinks about systems as collections of operations or modules (industrial operations, transport, power production, etc.) that perform some intended function when linked in a defined way.[17] Systems can be quite complex, especially when describing the function of producing products consisting of many parts, each of which may in turn comprise many materials. In such cases a graphical representation of the system is very useful. The screen diagram should not simply be a picture on the screen, but should actually function to build the inventory. Further, one should not have to start constructing the system at the beginning (raw materials) and move sequentially through to disposal (end of life). One should be able to start anywhere, link processes through their associated input/output resources in any fashion desired (subject to consistent application of mass and energy balance constraints), and remove or replace individual processes or process groups (segments) by manipulating graphical objects without having to reconfigure the system in any way. It should be possible to vary the detail in the display of the system on the screen from panoramic (the entire product network) to microscopic (individual process data).

A process module should be capable of (within reason) unlimited resource connections. One should not have to prespecify products, coproducts, raw materials, and wastes. In one application, an output resource could be a waste while in another (or in a variation for the same product system) it could be an input resource for a subsequent process. There should be flexibility in choosing the transformation relationship between inputs and outputs. Presently, most software fixes the relationship as linear proportionate. The user should be able to select other representations such as linear offset (i.e., nonzero resource requirements for no product output), quadratic, other nonlinear, and/or user-specified equation. The input/output relationship should not have to be the same for each resource or resource group. The user should not have to be concerned about the units in which the resources are specified, and there should be no requirement that the units in the model match those in the database. Given some basic properties information, the software should rectify all inconsistencies in the units.

The software should strike a balance between ease of use, on one hand, and completeness, flexibility, and applicability, on the other. Multiple versions might be made available for different classes of users, or certain features may be able to be turned off or access-restricted.

3.4.2   Embedded Data and Databases

The software should be coupled with a database. The database should be accessible independently of the rest of the software and should be able to import data from the more common commercial database software products. Input of new data sets for either resources or processes should be straightforward. Either the user should be queried through the process, or there should be ample pull-down menus, buttons, or other graphical devices so that the entry of data is efficient and the potential for erroneous entry minimized. One should be able to create, store, transfer, or copy modules or segments from one analysis to another quickly and easily. The database architecture should be open to allow third-party vendors to create and market data sets.

Modules and/or segments should be hierarchical if desired. For example, a user should be able to create or have available, if needed, the national electric generation grid, the individual regional grids, the eastern U.S. coal-based generation average, and a peaking plant representing the technological marginal plant that would be put on-line for a unit increase in power demand, all with similar-appearing structure and function. The software should permit searching of the database to identify modules meeting defined group criteria. The user should be able to easily substitute one module for another to facilitate improvement assessments.

Basic commodity material and process data sets required for most LCAs should be included in the database. Boundaries and other characteristics of these data sets should be compatible and clearly described. These data sets should be accessible to the individual process and material level whenever possible, subject to appropriate considerations of proprietary data sourcing.

3.4.3   Data and Methodology Quality Assessment

The software should provide for data quality assessment support. The quality of individual data and data sets should be discernible through the selection and application of descriptive or quantitative *data quality indicators* (DQIs).[18] At a minimum, the software should provide either quality indicators or narrative fields to identify the source, applicability, and relevancy of the data. The user should have the capability to create additional DQIs for data sets input as new items. The quality assessment of data and data sets should be incorporated into a higher-level data quality assessment for individual life-cycle stages, scenarios, and entire LCAs. To enhance uniformity and allow for comparability with regard to data quality among data sets from various sources, there should be a set of discrete data quality attributes that translates to an overall level of data quality. Once the user or data developer specifies a minimum required set of these lower-tier attributes, the software should assign a data quality level. Some graphical or otherwise easy-to-grasp means of viewing the data quality designations should be provided.

The methodology used in the computations should be transparent. Decisions made during the course of system definition, data input, scenario execution, and results analysis should be accessible for review in a trace log by users and third parties, e.g., during peer reviews. The integrity of the trace log should be ensured by its establishment as a read-only file. The trace log should record any decisions made that affect the compliance of the assessment with organizational policy or international LCA guidelines, with the ability for user audiences to interpret the results, or where alternative, acceptable methods coexist in the current methodology. At a minimum, documentation of choices made for system boundaries, coproduct allocation, precombustion energy factors, and inherent energy definition should be included. Additional documentation that would be useful includes flagging of processes for which mass or energy balance has not been achieved within defined tolerances, resources that are not traced to earth-sourced materials (so-called primary or elementary flows),[19,20] and decisions regarding the use of secondary data sources.

3.4.4 Reports, Results Analysis, and Archiving

The reporting function of LCA software is a critical one if clear communication to targeted audiences is to be achieved. It should be possible for the software user to tailor reports for a variety of audiences. In one instance, the information may be presented to a group of senior managers at a strategic planning meeting where excessive details presented in endless tables only serve to confound the decision-making process. In another instance, the same study may be presented to manufacturing facility engineers deciding on pollution prevention project alternatives. For them the details of where in individual processes the contributions are derived and the comparison with the overall stage inputs and outputs are all-important. Software should permit selecting, rearranging, and graphically presenting results in a variety of ways. The graphical representation of the system flow diagram developed interactively should be printable at a high level of quality.

The user should be able to conduct a sensitivity analysis of the results. This should be supported either by manual specification of certain parameters to vary (e.g., change the input electricity requirements of process X by 50 percent) or by a search capability (e.g., find all processes that contribute more than x percent to the solid waste generation of the system). System optimization under specified constraints has been noted as a desirable software feature.[13,21] This corresponds to having the system automatically search for combinations of modules and resources that meet certain constraints (e.g., minimize solid waste generation while not allowing energy consumption to increase by more than x percent). Such constraint-based optimization can be extended to include parameter sets other than environmental loadings, such as costs.

The user also should be able to vary certain product specifications to test the effect of material use on the outcome. The specifications could entail modifying the functional definition (i.e., changing the efficiency of use of the product) or the composition (e.g., using a thinner gage of plastic to reduce material use). Unless the input/output LCA model is coupled to other models which check the performance of the system when such changes are specified, the user must ensure that the analysis still remains valid. Software prompts to indicate that this should be done would be beneficial.

3.4.5 Hardware and Operating System Choices

The existing base of installed computers includes a wide variety of platforms and operating systems. The ideal environment from a software systems development standpoint may not coincide with the needs of users. The majority of potential users of current LCA software are using IBM-compatible PC-based systems employing the Intel 486 or Pentium processor or the equivalent. Most of the commercial or prototype LCA software will run quite well on such machines. However, a number of models that are capable of execution on a personal computer (PC) were not developed for this type of platform. Software originally developed on a mainframe and later converted for use on the PC may require considerable RAM (up to 32 Mbits) and hard disk capability (up to 50 Mbits) which may be beyond the capacity of some machines. Software designed to be used on engineering workstations based on the UNIX operating system can be made to run on PCs, but will not necessarily be optimized for such an environment. Execution speeds may be slow, and the full range of capability of the software may not be available.

Some of the earlier LCA software runs under the Microsoft MS-DOS (Disk Operating System) and does not feature a graphical user interface or the conveniences of state-of-the-art screen objects. Newer software runs under graphical interfaces, such as Windows, but prospective users should determine the extent to which the software implements the linking of screen objects with underlying data and other graphical features. MacIntosh users will have difficulty finding any software written for their machines. Limited capability exists at present to run LCA software in a networked configuration (multiple users), but this limitation is changing. At least two of the commercial packages are available in a network configuration for work-group applications, albeit at an increased cost from the single-user version.

3.4.6 Financial Considerations

Commercial LCA software acquisition arrangements include both outright purchase and various leasing options. Purchase agreements may or may not include a certain number of upgrades or revised data sets. As with other PC software, upgrades are usually less than the retail price of the original package. Lease agreements can be tailored somewhat to the needs and requirements of the user. Typically, leases are for a restricted period (normally 1 year), and no options for purchase are available. The second and subsequent years' lease prices are often lower than the first-year price. Software that is leased generally is not available for purchase, and vice versa.

The price (either purchase or lease) of LCA software varies from zero (freeware) to upward of $25,000. Although there is some correlation between the price and the capability of the program, the relationship is not linear. The higher-priced programs generally provide more flexibility, a better user interface, or a more extensive database, but not necessarily all three. The prices of commercial LCA software describe a bimodal distribution. One group of programs has a median price of about $2000, the other about $10,000. In either case, an investment in LCA software will not be of the same magnitude as purchasing a spreadsheet program. *Caveat emptor* (let the buyer beware)!

3.5 PUBLIC DATABASES

The conduct of LCAs is a data-intensive endeavor. The use of databases, either public or private, can markedly increase the efficiency of performing an LCA. Databases may be divided into three types:

- Nonbibliographic databases containing on-line information covering resource use; energy consumption; environmental emissions; and chemical, biological, or toxicological effects
- Database clearinghouses, which are on-line services, both government-run and private, that facilitate the retrieval of information from a variety of databases and bibliographies
- Bibliographic databases, which are on-line databases containing bibliographic references to the actual data which must be extracted from the referenced sources

External databases are those that are available as distinct information products separate from LCA software systems. Very few databases sold with LCA software packages are available as external databases. Although a significant fraction of LCA data comes from product, material production (cradle-to-gate), or study-specific data collection efforts, the remainder is derived from so-called secondary data sources. *Secondary data* are defined as publicly available data which have not been collected specifically for the purpose of conducting LCAs and for which the LCA practitioner has no input into the data collection process.[22]

A number of databases have been and continue to be developed specifically for LCA. These are sometimes, but not always, available independent of the computational software that they are associated with. In North America, several notable efforts either have been completed or are underway to provide stand-alone, public database support for LCA:

- *Life-Cycle Inventory (phase 1: cradle-to-pellet) of the North American Plastics Industry* is sponsored by the American Plastics Council (APC) and the Environment and Plastics Institute of Canada (EPIC). It provides peer-reviewed, summary-level inventory data for five commodity polymers (polyethylene in high-density, linear low-density, and low-density forms; polypropylene; polystyrene; polyvinyl chloride; and polyethylene terphthalate), three engineering polymers [acrylonitrile butadiene styrene copolymer, polycarbonate, and nylon (both 6 and 6/6 forms)], and polyurethane feedstocks (methyldiisocyanate, toluene diisocyanate, and various polyols). Future phases will provide data on other life-cycle stages.

  The data represent primary information compiled from a representative set of producers for the polymers and their primary feedstock producers. For the upstream products and processes (primarily petroleum and natural gas processing and petrochemical operations) and raw materials, data were derived from public sources, and practitioner data were cross-checked for accuracy and reasonableness. Data quality indicators are applied to the various data sets, weighted by the production of the individual producer. The highest quality was assigned to the measured, unallocated data and the lowest quality to estimated information.

- *Canadian Raw Materials Database* (*CRMD*) provides a peer-reviewed and -arbitrated set of inventory data for a selected set of commonly used materials including paper, aluminum, steel, glass, wood, and various thermoplastics. The data are collected and processed according to a rigorous, consensus-based procedure with the intent to publish a single, best set of data representing the national average. Quality metrics will be applied to screen data for inclusion in the database.

- *Environmental Resource Guide* is sponsored by the American Institute of Architects and the Environmental Protection Agency. Although not an electronic database, ERG contains a structured presentation of quantitative and qualitative information across the life cycle of various building and interior decorating materials. Materials reports include concrete, brick and mortar, concrete masonry, aluminum, steel, wood, plywood, particleboard, plastic laminates, thermal insulation, sealants, glass, plaster and lath, gypsum board, ceramic tile, ceiling panels and tiles, floor coverings (linoleum, vinyl, and carpet), paint, and wall coverings.

Other North American database developments have occurred and are occurring in the context of LCA software commercialization. These include

- *Life-Cycle Computer-Aided Data* (*LCAD*) is sponsored by the Department of Energy, Office of Industrial Technologies. It provides data modules from raw material extraction to intermediate materials (cradle to gate) for major commodity materials including paper, various plastics (derived from the APC/EPIC database described above), commodity chemicals, steel, aluminum, and electricity. The data are for U.S. average conditions except where a regional or an international perspective is needed to appropriately describe the operations. Data will be quality-assessed and the characteristics included as part of the database. The database is intended for distribution as part of an LCA modeling software package. (Availability is anticipated in mid-1996.)
- *Various databases from North American LCA practitioners.* As part of the lease or purchase agreements for LCI software, several packages provide data sets as part of the arrangement. Typically the users can access the data themselves either not at all or only with some difficulty. A list of the available software is included at the end of the chapter.

Several foreign LCA databases also exist which may contain some pertinent information. In most cases these databases are not stand-alone entities but are associated with spreadsheet or other more sophisticated LCA models:

- *BUWAL '84, '90, and '95.* The BUWAL (Swiss Office of Environmental Protection) database was originally developed to support ecoprofile analysis within Switzerland. In 1990 and again in 1995, the Swiss Federal Technical Institute (ETH) updated and expanded the database. The stand-alone data are available in hardcopy and generally are applicable to western European conditions, although portions are limited to Switzerland. Most of the data pertain to packaging materials.
- *EMPA.* This database has been developed by the Swiss Federal Laboratory for Testing and Materials and is associated with an LCA model. In addition to containing the energy, resource input, and environmental emissions data for a wide variety of processes, there is information on transportation and electricity production. In some cases the data are derived from secondary sources. The impact concept of critical volumes is incorporated in the system. Most of the data are specific to Swiss conditions, although the secondary data are more broadly applicable.
- *Packaging Industry Research Association (PIRA).* This database has been created by PIRA International with data derived from a study commissioned by the U.K. government. The data are contained in an Excel spreadsheet and include a computational model for inventory analysis. Standard materials covered include virgin and recycled paper and board, steel tinplate, glass, and aluminum, as well as the plastics data from the PWMI database listed below.
- *Plastic Waste Management Institute (PWMI).* This database (phase I) contains plastic resin information from raw materials acquisition through the pellet stage for eight commodity thermoplastics. It is similar in content and approach to the APC/EPIC database for North America described above. Data represent European average and in some cases country-specific conditions.

Secondary data sources can be very useful in the conduct of LCAs when they are used with appropriate understanding of their limitations. Secondary data sources include

- Reference books, such as *The Encyclopedia of Chemical Technology*
- Industry reports, such as SRI International studies on economic and production statistics
- Open literature, including journal articles and patent summaries
- Environmental Protection Agency databases covering chemical emissions and disposition
- Department of Energy databases, especially those of the Energy Information Administration
- Department of the Interior data on natural resources

Given that secondary data sources are those which have been developed for purposes other than LCA, these data sources are all likely to contain substantial data gaps in relation to any particular LCA. Specific examples of current database gaps are transportation energy in the nonbibliographic databases and the general lack of coverage of individual manufacturing processes. Many databases listed in Table 3.3 have not been tested in LCA applications. Practitioners will need to review which of them would be the most useful for their purposes.

3.6 FUTURE DEVELOPMENTS

As difficult as it is to describe an "ideal" LCA software package, it is even more of a challenge to prognosticate the future direction of software development. With the rapid advances in both hardware (especially processor speed, memory, and storage) and the programming tools available, software developers are quick to incorporate features that they believe will add to the capability of the program and make it easier and more logical to use.

Several trends are almost givens. One is the use of even more graphical features than are available in current systems. This is true for both the user interface and the report formats. More multidimensional approaches will be tried in order to better deal with the complexity of LCA data. Incorporation of more advanced impact assessment and data quality assessment schemes will challenge developers to present results in interesting and novel ways. A second trend is the incorporation of more expert systems capability in the software. Nonexpert users of LCA software are anticipated to grow in number. Keeping them from making fundamentally wrong decisions or from drawing incorrect conclusions is important if LCA tools are to be put into the hands of a broader user community.

Despite the expansion of embedded databases, developers will need to enable users to link with external databases through on-line systems. Broad-based use of the Internet and the identification of locations (both physical and organizational) will make it possible to have data sets built, maintained, and augmented at remote locations and downloaded to the LCA software. Similarly, users will be able to use LCA software in an environment that is familiar to them, whether an engineering design program, a process simulator, or a strategic decision support program. Users will be highly interconnected with one another. Product designers at company locations around the world will be able to contribute to, integrate, and use the results of independent efforts. Consultants, external stakeholders, and others will have controlled access so that peer and stakeholder reviews can be conducted on-line.

TABLE 3.3 Categories of Information Available from Selected Nonbibliographic Databases

Database name*	LCA application†	Media covered‡	Data specificity§	Data age	Update frequency
304(l)	Inventory (2)	W	na	Current	Biannually
AIRS	Inventory (2, 3, 4) Impact (10)	A	F	1957–present	Daily
AQUIRE	Impact (5, 7, 8)	W	C	1972–present	Quarterly
ARIP	Inventory (2) Impact (5)	A, W	I	1988–present	Monthly
ASHDISPOS	Inventory (4) Impact (10)	W, L, SW	F	1989 only	na
BLIS	Inventory (2, 4)	A	F	Current	Monthly
BRS	Inventory (1, 2, 3, 4)	A, W, L, SW	F	1981–present	Biannually
CAIR	Inventory (1, 2) Impact (5, 7, 8)	A, W, L, SW	PC, I, F	1991–present	na
CCRIS	Impact (5)	A, L, W	C	Current	Monthly
CESARS	Inventory (2) Impact (5, 7)	A, W	C	1992	na
CHEM4NTELL	Inventory (1, 2)	na	PD, C	1973–present	Monthly
CUS	Inventory (1, 2)	A, W, L, SW	C	1990	Once in 4 yr
"DSOSS"	Impact (5, 7)	L	PD, C	na	Biannually
EDB	Inventory (1, 3)	A, W, L, SW	PC	1992	Continually
EFDB	Impact (5, 7)	W, SW	C	na	Periodically
EFG	Inventory (1, 2) Impact (10)	W	F	Current	na
"GTOM/YR"	Inventory (1, 2)	na	PC	Current	Annually
HSDB	Inventory (2) Impact (5, 7, 10)	A, W, L, SW	C	Current	Monthly
IRIS	Impact (5, 7, 8)	A, W	C	Current	Monthly
IRPTC	Inventory (1, 2, 3, 4) Impact (5, 6, 7, 8)	A, W, L, SW	C	1989–present	na
"MCDB"	Inventory (1, 2)	L, SW	PD, PC, I, F	Current	Continually
MINES	Inventory (1) Impact (9)	A, W, L	PD, I	na	na
NATICH	Inventory (2) Impact (5, 10)	A	PD, I, F	1984–present	Annually
ODES	Inventory (2, 3, 4) Impact (6, 7, 8, 10)	W	F	Current	Biweekly
PADS	Inventory (4)	SW	F	Current	Weekly
PCS	Inventory (2, 4) Impact (5)	W	PC, F	Current	Biweekly
PHYTOTOX	Impact (5)	L, SW	C	1986	Periodically
PISCES	Inventory (2) Impact (7, 8)	A, W, L, SW	PC, F	Current	Regularly
PPIS	Inventory (2)	A, W, L, SW	PD	Current	Regularly
RCRIS	Inventory (3, 4) Impact (10)	A, W, L, SW	F	Current	Quarterly
REPROTOX	Impact (5)	na	C	Current	Weekly
RTECS	Impact (5,7)	A, W, L	C	Current	Quarterly
SIMAPRO	Inventory (1, 2, 4)	A, W, SW	PD, PC, I, F	Current	Annually

TABLE 3.3 Categories of Information Available from Selected Nonbibliographic Databases (*Continued*)

Database name*	LCA application†	Media covered‡	Data specificity§	Data age	Update frequency
STORET	Inventory (4) Impact (10)	W	F	1980–present	Weekly
TERRE-TOX	Impact (5)	L	C	1989	na
TRI	Inventory (2, 4)	A, W, L, SW	PD, I, F	1987–present	Continually
WATSTORE	Impact (10)	W	F	Current	na
WBS	Impact (10)	W	C	Current	Biannually
WHOWMO	Impact (6, 10)	A, W	na	1972–present	Weekly

*Database acronyms and information contacts are defined in Ref. 18, appendix A.
†Key to LCA applications is as follows:

Inventory:	1—raw materials acquisition
	2—manufacturing
	3—use/reuse/maintenance
	4—recycle/waste management
Impact:	5—biological effects
	6—ecosystem effects
	7—chemical properties
	8—chemical modeling
	9—resource depletion
	10—background concentration

‡A = air, W = water, L = land, SW = solid waste, na = not available
§PD = production, PC = process, I = industry, F = facility, C = chemical
Current data include those equal to or less than 1 year old.

LCA software is still very much in its infancy. Programs being developed today are far better than those commercialized even 2 years ago. It is a sure bet that those introduced in the near future will be even more capable, easy to use, and, one hopes, not more expensive.

REFERENCES

1. R. Heijungs and J. Guinée, "Software as a Bridge between Theory and Practice in Life-Cycle Assessments," *Journal of Cleaner Production,* 1(3–4): 185 (1993).

2. J. A. Fava, R. Denison, B. Jones, M. A. Curran, B. W. Vigon, S. Selke, and J. Barnum (eds.), *A Technical Framework for Life-Cycle Assessments,* Society of Environmental Toxicology and Chemistry, Pensacola, FL, 1991.

3. F. Consoli, D. Allen, I. Boustead, N. de Oude, J. Fava, W. Franklin, R. Parrish, R. Perriman, D. Postlethwaite, B. Quay, J. Séguin, and B. Vigon (eds.), *Guidelines for Life-cycle Assessment: A "Code of Practice,"* Society of Environmental Toxicology and Chemistry, Pensacola, FL, 1993.

4. Environmental Protection Agency, *Life-Cycle Assessment: Inventory Guidelines and Principles,* EPA/600/R-92/245, ISBN: 1-55670-015-9, NTIS PB93-139681, prepared by Battelle and Franklin Associates, Ltd., for the Risk Reduction Engineering Laboratory, Office of Research and Development, 1993.

5. R. Heijungs, J. B. Guinée, G. Huppes, R. M Lankreijer, A. M. M. Ansems, P. G. Eggles, R. van Duin, and H. P. de Goede, *Manual for the Environmental Life Cycle Assessment of*

Products, Second Interim Version, Centre of Environmental Science, Leiden University; Dutch Organization for Applied Scientific Research; and the Fuels and Raw Materials Bureau, 1991.

6. R. G. Hunt, J. D. Sellers, and W. E. Franklin, "Resource and Environmental Profile Analysis: A Life Cycle Environmental Assessment for Products and Procedures," *Environmental Impact Assessment Review,* 12: 245–269 (1992).

7. R. Watkins, S. Kleban, R. Hall, L. Claussen, B. Gockel, G. Luger, and G. Gershanok, "EcoSys—A Life Cycle Information System and Expert System," Briefing Notes, Meeting of DOE/DOD LCA Modeling Teams, December 1994, unpublished.

8. M. R. Wixom, "The NCMS Green Design Advisor: A CAE Tool for Environmentally Conscious Design," *Proceedings of International Symposium on Electronics and the Environment,* May 2–4, 1994, San Francisco, Institute of Electrical and Electronic Engineers, pp. 179–182.

9. V. J. Tipnis, "Towards a Comprehensive Methodology for Competing on Ecology: How to Integrate Competitive Strategy and Corporate Financial Objectives with Life Cycle Environmental Impact and Improvement Analyses," *Proceedings of International Symposium on Electronics and the Environment,* May 2–4, 1994, San Francisco, Institute of Electrical and Electronic Engineers, pp. 139–145.

10. L. R. Laibson, "Overview of Recent Government and Commercial LCA Initiatives: Policy or Guide?" *Proceedings of Life Cycles of Energetic Materials Conference,* Los Alamos National Laboratory, December 11–14, 1994, LA-UR-95-1090, pp. 105–126.

11. B. W. Vigon, "Life-Cycle Assessment," in H. Freeman (ed.), *Industrial Pollution Prevention Handbook,* McGraw-Hill, New York, 1994, chap. 19, pp. 310–311.

12. D. F. Bari, "The North American Plastics Industry: Life-Cycle Inventory Methodology," *Proceedings of APME Eco-Balance Review Conference,* Association of Plastics Manufacturers in Europe, Brussels, Belgium, October 1993.

13. P. F. Baisnée and B. Heintz, "Some Requirements of an Interactive Software Tool for Life Cycle Analysis," *Journal of Cleaner Production,* 1(3–4), 181–184 (1993).

14. U. Fritsche and L. Rausch, "Total Emission Model for Integrated Systems (TEMIS): User's Guide for TEMIS Version 2.0," Öko-Institute (Institute for Applied Ecology), Energy Division, Freiburg, Germany, pp. 78–82.

15. S.-O. Ryding, B. Steen, A. Wenblad, and R. Karlsson, "The EPS System—A Life Cycle Assessment Concept for Cleaner Technology and Product Development Strategies, and Design for the Environment," *Proceedings of EPA Workshop on Identifying a Framework for Human Health and Environmental Risk Ranking,* EPA 744-S-93-001, Environmental Protection Agency, Washington, 1994, pp. 21–24 and appendix G.

16. R. Heijungs, J. B. Guinée, G. Huppes, R. M. Lankreijer, H. A. Udo de Haes, A. W. Sleeswijk, A. M. M. Anselms, P. G. Eggles, R. van Duin, and H. P. de Goede, "Environmental Life Cycle Assessment of Products," Centre of Environmental Science, Leiden University, Leiden, The Netherlands, 1992, vol. 1, *Guide,* pp. 57–62 and vol. 2, *Backgrounds,* pp. 115–122.

17. J. B. Guinée, H. A. Udo de Haes, and G. Huppes, "Quantitative Life Cycle Assessments of Products: Goal Definition and Inventory," *Journal of Cleaner Production,* 1(1): 1–13 (1993).

18. Environmental Protection Agency, *Guidelines for Assessing the Quality of Life-Cycle Inventory Analysis,* EPA/530/R-95/010, NTIS PB95-191235, prepared by Research Triangle Institute for the Office of Solid Waste, 1995.

19. B. Heintz and P. F. Baisnée, "System Boundaries," *Proceedings of SETAC-Europe Workshop on Environmental Life Cycle Analysis of Products,* December 1991, Leiden, The Netherlands, pp. 35–52.

20. A.-M. Tillman, T. Ekvall, H. Baumann, and T. Rydberg, "Choice of System Boundaries in Life Cycle Assessment," *Journal of Cleaner Production,* 2(1): 21–29 (1994).

21. G. Stephanopoulos and A. Linninger, "Batch Design Kit (BDK)—An Update," Briefing Notes, Meeting of the Emission Reduction Research Center (ERRC) AI Steering Group, Cambridge, MA, July 1994, unpublished.

22. Environmental Protection Agency, *Life-Cycle Assessment: Public Data Sources for the LCA Practitioner,* EPA 530/R-95/009, NTIS PB95-191227, prepared by Battelle for the Office of Solid Waste, 1995.

FURTHER INFORMATION

Further information about specific software packages is available from the following sources:

Boustead Model

Contact: Dr. Ian Boustead, 2 Black Cottages, West Grinstead, Horsham, West Sussex GB-RH-13 7BD. Phone 44-403-864-561, fax 44-403-865-284.

EcoManager

Contact: Franklin Associates, Ltd., 4121 W. 83d Street, Suite 108, Prairie Village, KS 66208; phone (913) 649-2225, fax (913) 649-6494. Or PIRA International at Randall Road, Leatherhead, KT22 7RU Surrey, United Kingdom. Phone 03-72-376161, fax 03-72-377526.

ECOPACK 2000

Contact: Dipl. Chemiker Max Bolliger, Esslenstrasse 26, CH-8280, Kreuzlingen, Switzerland.

EcoPro

Contact: EMPA (Eidgenössiche Materialprüfungs- und Forschungsanstalt), Unterstrasse 11, Postfach CH-9001, St. Gallen, Switzerland. Phone 71-30-0101, fax 71-30-0199.

EcoSys

Contact: Randall Watkins, Sandia National Laboratories, MS 0730, Albuquerque, NM 87185-0730. Phone (505) 844-3387, fax (505) 844-1723.

EPRI CLEAN (Comprehensive Least Emissions ANalysis)

Contact: Dwight Agan, Science Applications International Corporation, 5150 El Camino Real, Suite c-31, Los Altos, CA 94022. Phone (415) 960-5918, fax (415) 960-5965.

EPS (Environmental Priorities Strategies) System

Contact: Sven-Olof Ryding, Swedish Environmental Research Institute (IVL), Box 21060, S-10031 Stockholm, Sweden. Phone 46-8-729-1500, fax 46-8-318-516.

IDEA (International Database for Ecoprofile Analysis)

Contact: International Institute for Applied Systems Analysis (IIASA), 1220 Wien, Bernoullistrasse 4/5/6/19, Laxenburg, Austria. Phone 43-22-36-715521, fax 43-22-36-71313.

LCI 1 Spreadsheet

Contact: Procter & Gamble, European Technical Center, Boechoutlaan 107, 1820 Strombeek Bever, Belgium. Phone 32-2-456-4257.

LCA Inventory Tool (LCAiT)

Contact: PRe' Consultants, Bergstraat 6, 3811 NH Amersfoort, The Netherlands. Phone 31-33-611046, fax 31-33-652853. Or Chalmers Industriteknik, Chalmers Teknikpark, S-412 88, Göteborg, Sweden. Phone 46-31-772-4020, fax 46-31-827421.

Life-cycle Computer-Aided Data (LCAD)

Contact: Kenneth Humphreys, Battelle Pacific Northwest Laboratories, Battelle Boulevard, P.O. Box 999, Richland, WA 99352. Phone (509) 372-4379, fax (509) 372-4378.

Life-cycle Interactive Modeling System (LIMS)

Contact: Adel Hakki, Chem Systems Inc., 303 So. Broadway, Tarrytown, NY 10591-5487. Phone (914) 631-2828, fax (914) 631-8851.

PEMS (PIRA Environmental Management System)

Contact: PIRA International at Randall Road, Leatherhead, KT22 7RU Surrey, United Kingdom. Phone 03-72-376161, fax 03-72-377526.

Product and Process Software

Contact: ir. B. Mazijn, V.I.T.O., Boeretang 200, 2400 Mol, Belgium. Phone 32-14-333-111, fax 32-14-320-310.

Product Improvement Assessment (PIA)

Contact: TME, Grote Marktstraat 24, 25 11 BJ 's-Gravenhage, The Netherlands. Phone 31-70-346-4422, fax 31-70-362-3469.

REPAQ (Resource and Environmental Profile Analysis Query)

Contact: Franklin Associates, Ltd., 4121 W. 83d Street, Suite 108, Prairie Village, KS 66208. Phone (913) 649-2225, fax (913) 649-6494.

SimaPro 3.0

Contact: PRe' Consultants, Bergstraat 6, 3811 NH Amersfoort, The Netherlands. Phone 31-33-611046, fax 31-33-652853.

TEMIS (Total Emission Model for Integrated Systems)

Contact: Uwe Fritsche, Öko-Institute (Institute for Applied Ecology), Energy Division, Central Office, Binzengrün 34 a, 79114 Freiburg, Germany. Phone 49-761-473130, fax 49-761-475437.

Tools for Environmental Analysis and Management (TEAM)

Contact: Ecobalance Inc., 1 Church Street, Suite 700, Rockville, MD 20850. Phone (301) 309-0800, fax (301) 309-1579.

For further information about stand-alone databases:

BUWAL

Contact: ETH, Institute for Energy and Cryoprocesses, ETH Zentrum, CH-8092, Zurich, Switzerland. Phone 41-1-256-4978, fax 41-1-262-5141.

Canadian Raw Materials Database

Contact: Kevin Brady, Environment Canada, Solid Waste Management Division, PUM 12, Ottawa, Ontario K1A 0H3, Canada. Phone (819) 953-1112, fax (819) 953-6887.

EMPA

Contact: Swiss Federal Laboratories for Materials Testing and Research, Unterstrasse 11, CH-9001 St. Gallen, Switzerland. Phone 71-20-9141, fax 71-22-7220.

Environmental Resource Guide (ERG)

Contact: American Institute of Architects, ERG Project, 1735 New York Avenue, NW, Washington, DC 20006. Phone (202) 626-7300, fax (202) 626-7518.

Plastic Waste Management Institute (PWMI)

Contact: Dr. Vincent Matthews, European Centre for Plastics in the Environment, Avenue E. Van Nieuwenhuyse 4, Box 5, B-1160, Brussels, Belgium. Phone 32-2-675-3258, fax 32-2-675-4002.

CHAPTER 4
STREAMLINING

Joel Ann Todd
VICE PRESIDENT
THE SCIENTIFIC CONSULTING GROUP, INC.
GAITHERSBURG, MD

4.1 WHY STREAMLINE?

A great deal of effort is being directed toward developing consensus on methodology for life-cycle assessment (LCA)—why are some researchers now trying to devise short-cuts for these studies? Why are some researchers beginning to define their work as "using a life-cycle concept" or as "life-cycle thinking" rather than as full-scale life-cycle assessment?

The most obvious answer is cost. A full-scale life-cycle assessment that uses the SETAC and EPA model for inventory can require from $10,000 to several hundred thousand dollars for each product studied. This investment is beyond the means of many smaller companies or larger companies with many varied product lines. A second answer involves time—full-scale life-cycle assessments can take time and may not be able to provide rapid answers to immediate questions. A third answer revolves on aggravation—a company that chooses to perform the studies in-house will find that gathering information from vendors and suppliers can be very difficult.

The Office of Technology Assessment (OTA) in *Green Products by Design*[1] suggests that LCA information can get out of hand and that, for complex products, LCAs will be impossible. OTA contends that "(l)ess information will probably be required, not more. LCAs may have to be streamlined to focus on a few critical dimensions of a product's environmental impact, rather than all dimensions. One possibility might be to limit the analysis to three dimensions: a product's contribution to catastrophic or irreversible environmental impacts (e.g., ozone destruction or species extinction), acute hazards to human health, and life-cycle energy consumption. Any such 'partial' LCA can be criticized as being incomplete...(b)ut some such simplification seems essential if LCAs are to be widely used" (pp. 61–62).

Some who seek to streamline LCA hope to learn all they need to know from these studies. Others plan to use the streamlined studies as screening devices, pointing the user toward the most fruitful areas for further study. Sponsors of streamlined LCA studies report that they have found the results useful in prioritizing improvements, achieving environmental goals, making design decisions during the R&D process, determining whether the cost is justified for conducting a more extensive LCA, and responding to requests for LCA information. Some have noted that simply drawing the life-cycle material flow was useful in understanding the product environmental profile.[2]

Users of streamlined LCAs remind us that most decisions are based on a variety of factors, with environmental considerations being one of these factors. Therefore, they are looking for important and generally large differences between alternatives that can often be detected by a streamlined study. Further, they are looking for surprises—those elements in the life cycle that are unanticipated and yet noteworthy; many of these unanticipated elements can be detected by a streamlined study.

The notion of developing consensus on acceptable practices for streamlining LCA is in its infancy—a work group on streamlined LCA was formed in April 1994 by the Society for Environmental Toxicology and Chemistry (SETAC). An EPA-sponsored conference on streamlining was held in June 1995 to initiate discussion among practitioners about the state of the practice. Those who consider this a valid field of study will be working over the next few years to explore the possibility of reaching consensus on standards for streamlining LCA, just as researchers worldwide are working on developing consensus on standards for inventory analysis, impact assessment, data quality, a code of practice, and other LCA issues. These efforts will also describe the alternative approaches to streamlining and the most appropriate uses of each.

Many observers would contend that the practice of LCA is best represented by a continuum (see Fig. 4.1) rather than two discrete categories of full-scale versus streamlined LCA. The continuum is perceived to be a more accurate representation because few, if any, LCAs are truly full-scale in every aspect. If EPA and SETAC reports on LCA methods[3,4] represent the definition of a full-scale LCA, most studies take some shortcuts or abridge the process in some fashion in the interest of feasibility. The issue, then, is the *extent* of the streamlining and the point at which the study should no longer be called an LCA.

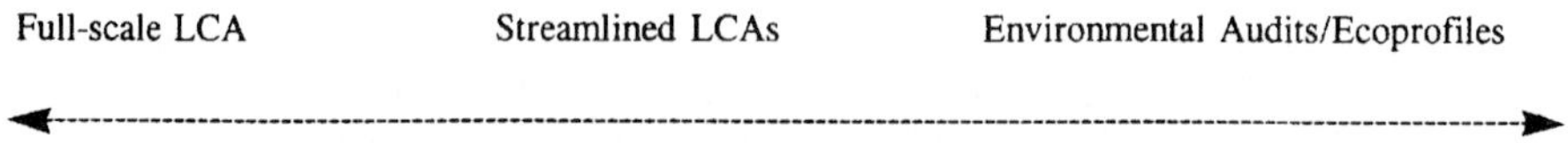

Full-scale LCA   Streamlined LCAs   Environmental Audits/Ecoprofiles

◄--►

FIGURE 4.1   LCA continuum.

Streamlining LCA methods requires that the researcher make difficult choices as to what to include and what to omit from a study. These choices can relate to the level of specificity, the study's boundaries, and other conditions. These choices must be made within certain limits, however, if the study is to be considered an LCA at all; streamlined LCAs should meet certain criteria just as full-scale LCAs do, if they are to remain in the LCA portion of the continuum. Although there is no consensus on these criteria to date, the following might be among those finally selected:

• The study should address all the stages of the life cycle, including raw material extraction, acquisition, and processing; product manufacture, fabrication, and distribution; use and maintenance; and final recovery for reuse or recycling and disposal.

• The study should include some form of inventory; it may also include impact assessment and improvement assessment.

• The study should describe clearly the boundaries defined for the study and the methods used to streamline accepted LCA methodology; ideally, the study should include a complete description of its deviations from accepted LCA methods.

• The study should yield results that are consistent with those produced by a full-scale LCA of the product; while the streamlined study might not yield all the conclusions that the full-scale study does, it should not result in contradictory conclusions.

4.2 WHAT IS STREAMLINING?

Streamlining refers to various approaches that have been developed to reduce the cost and effort required for studies using an LCA framework. There are two perspectives on how to accomplish this objective.

- The first involves modifying the *method* used for the study. Researchers are currently testing various approaches for making these modifications.

- The second involves making the *process* of doing an LCA easier, primarily through the establishment of databases that contain basic information needed for LCA studies and can be accessed by the public at a reasonable cost. This could reduce the data collection effort substantially. Several projects that are designed to result in publicly accessible databases of LCA information are underway in the United States and Canada.

This chapter will focus on streamlining of methods; discussion of improving access to data and data needs is covered elsewhere.

In this chapter *streamlining* is not synonymous with *screening*. *Screening* is a *use or application* of study results, primarily to determine whether additional study is needed and where that study should focus. Screening can be accomplished through a variety of methods, including streamlined LCA. *Streamlining* is an *approach* to conducting LCAs. Streamlined LCAs can be used for purposes of screening, but they can also be used as stand-alone studies.

4.3 APPROACHES TO STREAMLINING LCA METHODS

Several approaches have been suggested for streamlining LCA methods and procedures, although the validity and applicability of these approaches have not been determined. Most of these approaches involve narrowing the boundaries of the study, particularly during the inventory stage; targeting the study on issues of greatest interest; and using more readily available data, including qualitative data.

A recent study by Research Triangle Institute provided insight into the approaches that have been developed by practitioners in industry, academia, consulting firms, and government to streamline LCA methods.[2,5] This study suggested that practitioners are using several very different methods for streamlining and that more than one approach is often applied in a study. Approaches that are currently used by practitioners include

- Limiting or eliminating life-cycle stages
- Focusing on specific environmental impacts or issues
- Eliminating specific inventory parameters
- Limiting or eliminating impact assessment
- Using qualitative as well as quantitative data
- Using surrogate data
- Establishing criteria to be used as "show stoppers" or "knockouts"
- Limiting the constituents studied to those meeting a threshold quantity
- Combining streamlining approaches

Each of these approaches is discussed in the sections that follow.

4.3.1 Limiting or Eliminating Life-Cycle Stages

Under this broad category, there are three variations that are called *streamlined LCA* by their practitioners: limiting or eliminating *upstream* stages, limiting or eliminating *downstream* stages, and limiting or eliminating *both* upstream and downstream stages.

Limiting or Eliminating Upstream Stages.   In some studies, it seems that the tracing of materials upstream, or back to the ground, can go back through an infinite number of steps. In the manufacture of bar soap, for example, tracing the constituent *tallow* back through meat packing and rendering, cattle raising and feedlot management, harvesting and processing of feed, and soil preparation, seeds, fertilizers, and pesticides leads to another major effort to trace the fertilizers and pesticides back to their chemical constituents, and so forth. This research begins to feel very distant from the product that is the target of study.

All LCAs must set upstream boundaries. One approach to streamlining, then, sets the study boundaries within a prescribed number of stages, such those processes that are within one or two steps of the primary manufacturing process or process. In the example of the manufacture of a bar of soap, this could limit the upstream steps to be studied to cattle raising and feedlot management. The stages of harvesting and processing of feed, soil preparation, seeding, fertilizing, and pesticide application, as well as analysis of the fertilizers and pesticides themselves, could be omitted.

In some cases, all upstream stages are eliminated so that the study looks at only the manufacturing stage and the downstream stages (use and disposal). Some companies with product stewardship programs have chosen this approach, focusing on maintenance requirements and reducing downstream environmental considerations of their products, building in recyclability or reusability, and "take-back" programs in which the user can return the product to the manufacturer at the end of its useful life. They may become concerned with upstream stages of the life cycle only insofar as these stages affect downstream stages. For example, the use of hazardous constituents in the manufacture of a feedstock may complicate efforts to recycle or take back a used product.

The benefit of this approach is that it sets clear boundaries and includes all the products and processes that are immediately involved in producing the item under study. From the manufacturer's perspective, it focuses on those issues that are most under his or her control—feedstocks and processes within the plant gates and immediate vendors or suppliers. It also eliminates the issue of proprietary vendor data, one of the more difficult data collection problems in LCA.

The disadvantage of this approach is that important environmental consequences of raw material extraction or production may be eliminated from consideration, and thus a skewed picture may emerge. This could lead to conclusions that are erroneous and would contradict those of a full-scale LCA. Unfortunately, the researcher has no information on which to estimate whether the streamlined study fairly represents the entire life cycle—before it can be determined whether the omission of stages will affect the validity of the study, those stages must be evaluated.

Limiting or Eliminating Downstream Stages.   Some practitioners limit or eliminate the downstream stages and focus on the materials coming into the plant and the processes within the plant gates. These users might be looking for alternative materials or processes that have improved environmental profiles.

The advantage of this approach is that it captures some of the important environmental concerns within the life cycle that can be used in product improvement. Another benefit is that it can be used to encourage vendors and suppliers to provide materials that have improved environmental profiles.

As with the previous approach, the disadvantage of this method is that it ignores important stages in the life cycle. In particular, the use stage for some products is the most critical (e.g., given the long lifetime of many building materials, their effects on building performance can overshadow environmental effects during other stages). For others, final disposal is an important issue.

Limiting or Eliminating Upstream and Downstream Stages. In a few cases, manufacturers have applied the LCA template to only their own operation. This *gate-to-gate* approach uses the LCA template to assist in organizing and analyzing data gathered within the facility. While several practitioners called this approach streamlined LCA, many would consider that it is more appropriately called *environmental accounting* or *auditing*.

The advantage of this approach is that the data can be gathered and the processes under study can be affected directly by the user. The results of the study are likely to be useful to the sponsor. The disadvantage is that the benefits of looking at the life cycle of the material are lost.

4.3.2 Focusing on Specific Environmental Impacts or Issues

In this approach, the study sponsor or the researcher selects high-priority issues as the focus of the study and follows these issues throughout the life cycle. These could include issues of particular importance to the environment or to the study sponsors, such as a contribution to catastrophic or irreversible environmental impacts, acute hazards to human health, depletion of endangered resources or species, generation of one or more highly toxic pollutants, or life-cycle energy consumption. Some practitioners use a group of in-house and/or external experts to identify these issues.

The advantage of this approach is that it focuses on the issues of importance to the user and is likely to produce information that the user will find helpful. This approach can be particularly useful when regional considerations are critical. This approach also addresses one of the problems involved in using the results of LCA studies to compare alternative processes or products—it is likely that no single product or process will be superior on all environmental parameters. If the user has decided in advance which parameters are most important, the decision-making process will be facilitated.

The obvious disadvantage of this approach is that important environmental considerations will be excluded and the decisions made as a result of the study may not be the best overall for the environment or human health.

In a variation on this approach, some studies limit their focus to those issues for which data are available and quantifiable and which are of interest to the study sponsors. For example, environmental factors that are difficult to quantify, such as habitat loss and loss of biodiversity, may be explicitly excluded. Energy-related factors and air emissions are elements that are more readily quantifiable and are more likely to be included.[6]

The advantages of this approach are feasibility and quality of data. The results are less vulnerable to attack on grounds of subjectivity. The disadvantages are similar to those cited in the previous example—important environmental factors may be excluded.

4.3.3 Eliminating Specific Inventory Parameters

Since gathering data for the inventory is a major portion of the LCA effort, reducing the scope of the inventory will reduce the effort. The scope of the inventory can be reduced if specific impact categories or environmental issues have been selected as the focus of the study. In these cases, the impact categories drive the inventory, and the study needs to investigate only inventory items that relate to the impacts of concern.

The advantage of this approach is that it can reduce scope and yet allow for in-depth data collection in areas of particular interest.

A disadvantage is that important concerns may not be explored. The likelihood of overlooking important environmental issues will be greatly reduced if the initial scoping and selection of issues or impact areas are thorough and accurate.

4.3.4 Limiting or Eliminating Impact Assessment

Many LCAs do not address impacts and are more accurately termed *life-cycle inventories* (LCIs). This could be considered streamlining since the inventory is just one part of the picture. Those studies that address impacts often limit their assessment to "less is better." This could be considered a streamlined approach to impact assessment since it does not proceed through the process outlined by SETAC, EPA, and other leaders in methodology development in their reports on impact assessment frameworks.[7]

In addition, there have been a few efforts to streamline the impact assessment stage. These efforts have included the development of broad impact categories and indices. These approaches classify the impacts without attempting to quantify them or quantify one type of impact as an indicator of many others.

4.3.5 Using Qualitative as Well as Quantitative Data

A major expense in conducting a full-scale LCA is the collection of reliable quantitative data. Obtaining these data for the inventory can be an enormous task; preparing a quantitative impact assessment or improvement assessment at this point goes beyond the current state of the art. There are several problems that the researcher encounters in collecting quantitative data for an LCA. Many manufacturing facilities produce more than one product line—it may be difficult to assign energy consumption or waste generation values to separate products. Further, many companies consider the data needed for LCA to be proprietary and are reluctant to divulge this information to outside researchers.

In this approach, qualitative information is gathered when quantitative data are not available. The material flow diagrams that are constructed for the studies include processes and materials, but are not true mass balances since they do not include quantities at each step.

The benefit of using this approach is that all potential environmental issues are detected at each stage of the life cycle. Another benefit of using qualitative as well as quantitative data is that some environmental factors are not readily amenable to quantification, such as biodiversity and habitat issues. If the study design requires quantification, these issues may be simply eliminated from consideration because they are not quantifiable, resulting in a distorted picture.

The major drawback of this approach is the difficulty in assessing the importance of each environmental concern in the overall life cycle and in comparison to other products. This approach may not allow the user to compare two alternative products, e.g., in terms of their contribution to ozone depletion or release of a particular carcinogen. It may not provide enough information to enable manufacturers to choose one process or feedstock over another.

4.3.6 Using Surrogate Data

Sometimes it is impossible or very difficult to obtain data on a particular product or process, but data on a similar product or process are more readily available. Similarly, data on a material in one application may be more available than data on the material in another application. The more readily available data can be used as a surrogate for other information if the differences between the products, materials, or processes are minor and if these differences do not have significant environmental consequences. It is crucial in selecting a surrogate product, material, or process to analyze all key elements to ensure comparability.

The advantage of this approach is that estimates can be developed for data that would otherwise be unavailable. The caution is that the surrogates must be chosen very carefully to ensure that the surrogate truly represents the product, material, or process under study.

4.3.7 Establishing Criteria to Be Used as "Show Stoppers" or "Knockouts"

This approach is related to the focus on specific issues of importance. In this approach, however, criteria are established that, if encountered during the study, can result in an immediate decision. Proponents of this approach believe that because these criteria are so important, other elements of the life cycle pale in comparison and become irrelevant. These criteria must be based on the values of the researcher or client. The criteria can include any of the issues listed under the previous approach—a product's contribution to catastrophic or irreversible environmental impacts, acute hazards to human health, depletion of endangered resources or species, generation of one or more highly toxic pollutants, or life-cycle energy consumption—or others. Under this approach, the inventory shifts from a methodical exploration of all constituents to an examination of questions such as, During the life cycle of product A, are any endangered species threatened? or, During the life cycle of product B, are any ozone-depleting substances released? If the answer to the relevant question is negative, the inventory proceeds according to established guidelines.

4.3.8 Limiting the Constituents Studied to Those Meeting a Threshold Quantity

Some LCA studies eliminate those constituents that comprise less than a specified percentage of the product or process. A threshold of 1 percent is sometimes used in full-scale LCAs; a larger percentage could result in a "streamlined" LCA.

This approach has the advantage of limiting the number of items that must be studied and focuses on those that are likely to be most important for the product under study, since they represent the largest proportion or volume. This approach is also easy to define clearly and does not have an inherent bias.

The disadvantage is that by focusing only on volume and not on hazard or on toxicity, important environmental effects can be overlooked.

4.3.9 Combining Streamlining Approaches

Practitioners may combine several of these approaches in designing a study that will meet specific information needs. For example, a manufacturer might conduct a quantitative study of operations within the facility gates and a qualitative or semiquantitative study of the upstream and downstream stages. This type of study is intended to focus on the sponsor's own processes and materials choices but also to alert the sponsor to potentially important environmental considerations throughout the life cycle. In another example, a manufacturer might select specific impact categories of interest and conduct a qualitative or semiquantitative study of those categories over the entire life cycle.

The key advantage in combining streamlined approaches is the ability of the study designer to tailor the study to provide the information needed in the most efficient and timely manner. In such a custom-tailored study, only the information needed is gathered, and all extraneous elements are eliminated.

4.4 SELECTING AN APPROACH

The type of approach selected should relate to the goals of the study and the intended use of the results. The results then must be evaluated within the context of the study limitations and should not be used to imply something broader than intended. Potential uses of an LCA include in-house strategic planning and product development, marketing and public relations, education (both in-house and public), labeling and certification, public policy, and screening to determine whether further study is needed and where that research should focus. In some cases, companies conduct LCAs in response to requests for information from their customers or the public.

A study sponsor seeking to narrow or streamline an LCA study should consider a series of questions to determine whether streamlining is appropriate or feasible and will enable the study to meet its goals and be useful to its target audience. Issues to be considered include the following:

4.4.1 How Will the Study Be Used?

The anticipated use of the study is, of course, one of the key factors that determines its scope and boundaries. The more clearly the purpose can be defined, the more likely it is that certain streamlining steps will be possible. Will the study be used for internal purposes, or will its results be distributed to the public? Will the study stand alone, or is it a prelude to a more in-depth LCA? Is the sponsor seeking answers to very specific questions, or is the study a more general investigation? In general, studies that are to be distributed to the public demand far more documentation and precision than those used for internal purposes. Studies that serve as scoping or screening exercises can be less precise and quantitative, since the follow-up in-depth study will provide the precision. Studies that seek to answer specific questions can be targeted toward the information required to answer those questions.

4.4.2 What Alternatives or Actions Will Be Considered as a Result of the Study?

If the study will lead to the consideration of alternative materials (feedstocks) or processes, these elements should be included in the study. If no viable alternative exists for a particular component of the product life cycle, a company conducting a study for its internal use might eliminate that component from the study since it would not be able to act on the information produced. However, a study conducted for external distribution should include these components.

4.4.3 What Information Is Needed to Support the Uses of the Study?

If the study will focus on specific questions, such as reducing energy consumption during the life cycle, reducing pollutant emissions, or some other topic, the study can be designed to provide information keyed to these questions. For example, in a study that focuses on energy consumption, the pollutants generated at each step of the life cycle may not need to be quantified except insofar as their treatment or disposal uses energy.

4.4.4 What Level of Specificity Is Required?

This question encompasses several related questions. Does the study require information from a particular facility or industry, or can industry averages or generic estimates be used? A company wishing to improve its own production systems would require information specific to its operation. A company wishing to compare the environmental performance of several vendors would also need data specific to those vendors. But a study user who is comparing two alternative types of products for a given application might be better served by industry averages or generic estimates.

A second element of this question is the amount of quantification needed. Are the study users trying to identify potential environmental concerns or to weigh the performance of various products in terms of those concerns? In the first instance, qualitative data will suffice; but in the second instance, quantification will be needed.

4.4.5 What Data Quality Objectives Must Be Met?

Streamlining an LCA is not an excuse for using poor-quality data. Streamlined LCAs should include data quality objectives and analyses of data quality. The data quality objectives established for the study might provide opportunities for streamlining or might rule out the possibility.

Data quality objectives specify the requirements that data must meet to be used in the study. These requirements include documentation, precision, bias, completeness, representativeness, comparability, and compatibility. The study users and designers must determine the appropriate level for each of these factors. How much documentation will be required? If the data are from secondary sources, will confirmation from more than one source be required? How precise must the data be? Are estimates permitted? What are the points of potential bias in the study, and how will they be addressed? What will the researcher do if the data are incomplete? Will estimates or models be used? How many data points must be collected to ensure representativeness? How will the study handle secondary data that do not permit aggregation or comparison due to differences in the studies from which they are gathered?

4.4.6 How Much Is Already Known?

The more the study designers know about the product or process under study, the more confidence they can have in making decisions to streamline the study. If, e.g., designers of an internal company study know that two alternatives use the same raw materials for certain processes, they could omit those processes from the study since the processes will have equal effects on each of the alternatives. In another example, if the designers are using the streamlined study in a scoping process, they can eliminate those components of the life cycle that they know will require full-scale LCA and can focus the streamlined LCA on those portions of the life cycle that may or may not require follow-up study.

On the basis of their existing understanding of the product or process under study, the study designers may also be able to identify in advance the elements of the life cycle for which data are not available or are not available in the form needed. When this is the case, the study can be streamlined to use proxies or to substitute qualitative information for quantitative data.

4.4.7 How Well-Defined and Specific Is the Product or Process under Study?

Is the subject of the study a specific product made by a particular manufacturer, or is it a generic category of products or materials? Studies of generic categories of products can often be streamlined because they are not amenable to precise quantification. Instead, the study will investigate various types of constituents and formulations to identify a range of potential environmental issues associated with the category of products. This information could be useful in comparing categories (should these walls be painted, paneled, or wallpapered?) but would be less useful in comparing specific manufacturers' products within a given type.

4.5 CASE STUDIES

Five case studies illustrate the approaches outlined above.

- The first case study uses qualitative as well as quantitative information to examine all life-cycle stages. Impact assessment and improvement analysis are based on expert judgment.
- The second identifies relevant impact areas for each life-cycle stage during the scoping phase and focuses the study on these areas.
- The third uses a qualitative approach to impact assessment and improvement analysis, with little or no inventory phase. It explores all life-cycle stages and assesses impacts in five broad categories arrayed on a matrix.
- The fourth approach uses qualitative information to construct an index of human health and environmental concerns for selected stages of the life cycle.
- The fifth approach includes a full-scale inventory and a streamlined impact assessment that focuses on summary indices in a few key impact categories.

The case studies also describe the intended uses of the approaches and, when the information is available, the extent to which the studies met the intended objectives.

4.5.1 Qualitative and Quantitative Approach for Studies of Building Materials

A streamlined method that used qualitative as well as quantitative data to focus studies on issues of most concern to users was developed by The Scientific Consulting Group, Inc., for the American Institute of Architects' (AIA) *Environmental Resource Guide*

(ERG) project. This project, funded in part through a cooperative agreement with the Environmental Protection Agency, was designed to encourage architects to consider environmental factors in their designs and to select materials that carry less of an environmental burden. The methodology was developed to conduct studies of building materials for publication in the *ERG*.[5,8]

AIA and EPA wanted the studies of building materials to use an LCA framework to encourage architects and manufacturers of building materials to broaden their perspectives on environmental considerations, but modifications to accepted LCA methods were needed due to lack of resources to support full-scale LCA inventories. The key to streamlining for this project was the need to focus on environmental issues of importance. Since architects take into account many factors as they select materials for each job, if the environmental aspects of several alternative materials differ only slightly, the architect is likely to base her or his selection on other factors, such as cost, aesthetics, or durability. As a result, the streamlined methodology enabled the *ERG* studies to focus on the environmental issues that seem to be most important, in terms of volume, potential toxicity, or potential environmental damage, within the life cycle of the materials under study.

In this approach, a complete materials flow diagram and qualitative inventory are prepared. This includes identification of all constituents in the life cycle and descriptions of the processes that occur at each step of the life cycle. The associated material, energy, and water inputs as well as the waste outputs are identified. Where quantitative data are available, they are added to the inventory. Where quantitative data are not available, qualitative information is gathered.

Once the inventory is complete, each of the processes is examined to identify potential environmental stressors—those factors that can cause adverse impacts on the environment or human health. For each stressor, potential impacts are identified. It is not possible to determine actual impacts since the studies are not site-specific. Examples of these potential impacts include potential contribution to global warming, ozone depletion, and acidification and acid deposition; potential effects on aquatic communities; and potential impacts on human health due to the inherent properties of the emissions, such as carcinogenicity.

The impact assessment is performed by a group of experts, assembled from industry, academia, government, and environmental groups. The impact assessment involves examining the relative environmental performance of alternative materials in a given application. Performance is assessed in impact categories that address the environment, human health, energy, and issues specific to building materials. The broad impact categories, such as air quality and availability, are broken into more specific subcategories, such as ozone-depleting potential. Criteria are provided for considering each of the specific impact categories. These criteria include both quantitative and qualitative indicators. In some cases, the performance of a material will depend on steps taken by the architect; in these cases, the performance is given a split rating, and notes are provided so that the architect can take the steps that improve performance.

The streamlined method developed for the *ERG* also includes recommendations for the architect to improve the environmental profiles of materials in specific applications. These improvements could include choosing the most appropriate materials for specific uses, using materials wisely, designing for recovery and reuse or recycling, and reducing overall materials use.

An important constraint influencing the development of this approach is that the studies for the *ERG* address generic materials, such as paint, rather than specific products manufactured at particular facilities. AIA adopted this approach to avoid the appearance of endorsing or criticizing individual manufacturers' products. Therefore, the *ERG* enables an architect to compare, in this example, broad categories of paint with other wall-covering options, such as paneling, paper and vinyl wall coverings, tile, or cork; but it does not provide information on the differences between various manufacturers' paints within each category. The major environmental considerations are identified along with steps that can be taken by the architect to address these considerations. For example, in comparing steel and wood framing systems, the reports do not advocate one system over the other but instead discuss the advantages and disadvantages of each from an environmental perspective, note the applications in which steel or wood is preferable, and suggest steps that can be taken in specifying one or the other to reduce the environmental impact.

This approach has been used and refined over a 4-year period. Thirty-two reports have been prepared on building materials, with 20 using the approach described above and 12 using a more abbreviated approach. (Reports prepared during the first year of the project used a slightly different approach that was modified for the second and third years.) The 20 reports demonstrating the use of this approach cover the following materials: gypsum wallboard systems, plaster and lath, plastic laminate, wall coverings, wood framing, steel framing, glass, acoustical ceiling tiles, brick, concrete masonry units, stone (for curtain wall), composite wood members, asphalt shingles, ceramic tile, workstation fabric, and stains and varnishes. A less extensive version of the approach was used to prepare reports on aluminum, particleboard, vinyl flooring, sealants, plywood, linoleum, tropical wood, steel, paint, concrete, insulation, and carpet. The reports have been published in the AIA's *Environmental Resource Guide* and are also available from the EPA.

This approach had several advantages. First, qualitative information is often more readily available and, therefore, could be obtained within the resource constraints of the project. Second, it allowed the researchers to use generic information on industrial processes and did not require that industry provide data which individual companies consider proprietary. Third, it allowed the studies to address impacts in the absence of agreed-upon methodology and to report potential impacts that are not amenable to quantification.

There are, however, several drawbacks to the approach. The primary drawback is that comparisons among alternative materials remain subjective—the approach does not yield a single number or series of numbers by which the user can say, "This material has a greater environmental impact than another." It relies on expert judgment to assess the relative performance and impact of alternative materials rather than on some quantitative score.

The methodology developed for the *ERG* could also be useful in other applications. It could serve as a scoping tool for sponsors considering a full-scale LCA, providing useful information to assist in targeting more in-depth studies toward the more potentially serious problems. Companies could also use this approach to begin discussions with their suppliers in an effort to identify and obtain the most environmentally preferable materials. Since this approach does not require that proprietary information be divulged, it is less threatening. Further, since it is less expensive than full-scale LCA, smaller vendors might be more likely to cooperate.

4.5.2 Pollution Prevention Factors Approach

A pollution prevention factors methodology was developed by Battelle for the EPA that uses a streamlined LCA approach.[9] The methodology was tested in a study of the lithographic printing industry. The study compares two pollution prevention options available to this industry: (1) solvent substitution in blanket and press wash and (2) waterless versus conventional dampening fountain system printing. Environmental impact criteria were developed with a range of scores from 1 to 9. The criteria were selected from all possible impacts by examining stressor-impact chains to identify the impacts that might be affected by the pollution prevention activities under study. Criteria were identified for each stage of the life cycle. These criteria included habitat alteration and resource renewability for the raw material acquisition stage; energy use, toxic and hazardous airborne emissions, and waterborne effluents for the manufacture stage; and energy use, photochemical oxidant creation potential, ozone-depleting potential, global warming potential, a surrogate for transportation energy and emissions, and inhalation toxicity for the fabrication (printing) stage.

This approach enabled researchers to assign values for each of the impact criteria before and after implementation of the pollution prevention measures. The criteria were weighted equally, and a total score was calculated. A pollution prevention factor was then calculated; it was defined as the total score after implementation of the pollution prevention measure divided by the total score before implementation. The authors noted that improvement on one or a few impact criteria should be considered as well as the total score.

A major advantage of this approach is that it provides a quantitative scoring system that permits clear comparison of alternatives. It is applicable to individual companies, and results can be averaged across several companies. It can serve as a screening tool for selection of pollution prevention alternatives as well as the basis for further study, if needed.

Drawbacks of the approach include the fact that the accuracy of the scores depends on better data collection than many companies generally perform. The authors note that further development and testing of the methodology are needed to (1) evaluate the impact on the score that may occur if more than one pollution prevention activity is implemented simultaneously, (2) determine whether the methodology is applicable to other industries, and (3) evaluate how much improvement in the pollution prevention factor score is needed to indicate that the activity is worthwhile from an environmental standpoint. The authors also note that criteria need to be added that give credit for reduction in the quantity of hazardous materials used.

The authors stress that the pollution prevention factors are used for making comparisons among alternatives rather than as the basis for absolute claims as to whether one alternative is good or bad for the environment. In other words, one factor can be compared with other such factors to assess which pollution prevention activities offer the greatest environmental improvement.

4.5.3 Matrix Approaches to Abridged Life-Cycle Assessment

Thomas Graedel, Brad Allenby, and their colleagues at AT&T have developed a streamlined or *abridged* approach to LCA that is used by AT&T for in-house evaluations of products. The approach is semiquantitative and uses matrices to facilitate assessment and scoring by a group of experts drawn from various departments within the company. The objectives of this approach are to perform a study rapidly and to identify the principal environmental effects that occur throughout the life cycle. It does not include a structured inventory but focuses instead on impact assessment and the analysis of improvements.[10,11]

This approach is designed to have several characteristics that the developers believe are crucial elements of a useful assessment tool: It should "enable direct comparisons among rated products, be usable and consistent across different assessment teams, encompass all stages of product life cycles and all relevant environmental concerns, and be simple enough to permit relatively quick and inexpensive assessments."[10]

All stages of the life cycle are addressed in the approach, including all premanufacturing activities such as raw material extraction and production of intermediate products, manufacturing operations, packaging and shipping, customer use, and termination of the product's life. Several of these stages are under the direct control of the manufacturer while others can be influenced by how products are designed and through continued manufacturer involvement in the use and termination stages.

The foundation of the abridged system is a 5×5 matrix, called the *environmentally responsible product assessment matrix* by the developers. The matrix arrays the life-cycle stages against five categories of environmental concern—materials choice, energy use, solid residues, liquid residues, and gaseous residues. This matrix is used by an assessment team to assign scores for each category at each life-cycle stage. The scores range from 0 (the worst, indicating greatest impact) to 4 (the best, indicating lowest impact). Assessors are given checklists and protocols to guide their assessment. While this process appears to be quite subjective, interrater reliability has been found to be high, with ratings differing by less than 15 percent among assessors.[10] Once the scores are assigned in each category, they are summed and an overall rating is obtained. This method assumes that all cells of the matrix are of equal importance. Alternatively, weights can be applied to the matrix to give some cells greater importance, if these values are known.

This approach also includes a streamlined method for presenting results. In addition to the matrix and its cell-by-cell explanation of scores, a target plot is constructed. The target plot contains 25 spokes, representing the 25 matrix cells, radiating out from a central point or bull's-eye. Concentric circles represent the possible scores, from 4 in the center of the target to 0 on the outer rim. The score for each cell is plotted on the appropriate spoke. The more closely the points are gathered in the center of the target, the better the overall environmental score. In addition to graphically depicting the overall score, the target clearly shows those areas that are farthest from the bull's-eye and might warrant attention.

4.5.4 Application of Life-Cycle Concepts to Product Stewardship

Roy F. Weston, Inc., has developed streamlined approaches that focus on identifying impacts that are most important for the particular product under study. These impact areas can then drive the study, whether it involves an LCA inventory or other form of analysis. In one example of the use of relevant impacts in a project, Weston developed an approach to product stewardship that incorporates life-cycle concepts and risk assessment. This approach was designed to bring health and environmental concerns into decisions related to product growth and product development.[12]

The approach is based on a conceptual model consisting of a two-dimensional graph that reflects health and environmental vulnerability from a life-cycle perspective on the Y axis and a measure of the product's competitive advantage on the X axis. The Y axis score is derived from a *health and environmental ranking* (HER) scheme. For the pilot test of the system, the HER index included three stages of the life cycle: manufacturing, distribution, and use by primary customers. For each stage, qualitative criteria were developed that reflected the key variables that affect the potential for human health risk at that stage. These included areas such as routine air emissions, hazardous waste volume, presence of carcinogens and other hazardous chemicals, and concentration of the population surrounding the manufacturing facility, among others. Products were then assigned a score for each variable. A multidisciplinary team of experts, including environmental, health, and safety specialists as well as business, marketing, and manufacturing managers, was involved in the project.

The scores on the HER index were then plotted against an assessment of the products' competitive advantage. This yielded a *product strategy matrix* that provided useful information for decision making. The matrix contained four sectors:

- *Low HER score, low competitive advantage.*   Products falling into this sector have lower health and environmental vulnerability and should be able to improve their market position. Investment in these products should focus on marketing and communication with potential buyers.

- *High HER score, high competitive advantage.*   These products are performing well in the market but are vulnerable from the health and environmental standpoint. Given their strength in the market, they might warrant investment to improve their health and environmental performance.

- *High HER score, low competitive advantage.*   Products falling into this sector would require investment in both areas to reduce environmental and human health vulnerability and to improve competitive position. These products might be candidates for phase-out if investment required is sufficiently high.

- *Low HER score, high competitive advantage.*   These products are the clear winners.

4.5.5   ATHENA—Environmental Assessment Model for the Building and Design Community

In 1992, an alliance organized by Forintek Canada began working on the Sustainable Construction Materials Project and a computer model called ATHENA.[13] ATHENA will allow building designers, researchers, and others to readily assess the relative life-cycle impacts of various building materials in specific applications.

The database for ATHENA contains data on specific materials in vertical and horizontal structural assemblies for light industrial and low-rise commercial, industrial, and residential buildings. The database includes a full life-cycle inventory for these materials and a streamlined impact assessment.

The impact assessment has been streamlined to focus on four measures: (1) greenhouse gas index, (2) air pollution index, (3) water pollution index, and (4) ecological carrying capacity index.

The *greenhouse gas index* is a calculation of CO_2 equivalents. The index is calculated for a 20-year and a 100-year horizon.

The *air pollution index* is also based on equivalencies. In this index, the inventory data for atmospheric emissions are reduced to a single index using relative environmental impact factors. The air pollution index estimates the total volume of ambient air necessary to dilute all releases to recommended or acceptable levels. The worst pollutant becomes the index key.

The *water pollution index* is calculated in a similar fashion. Inventory data for liquid effluents are reduced to a single index figure by estimating the total volume of water that would be required to dilute all releases to the recommended or acceptable levels. As with the air pollution index, the worst pollutant becomes the index key.

The *ecological carrying capacity index* includes effects on biodiversity, ground and surface water quality, soil stability and regenerative capacity, wildlife habitat, and other factors. The project surveyed a group of experts to develop a relative ranking for six resource extraction activities along four dimensions. The six resource extraction activities are timber harvesting (British Columbia coast), timber harvesting (boreal forest), iron ore mining, coal mining, limestone quarrying, and aggregates quarrying. The four dimensions that are used to define ecological carrying capacity impacts are the intensity of the impacts, the extent of the areas typically affected, the duration of the impacts, and the ecological significance of the areas affected.

4.6 THE FUTURE OF STREAMLINING EFFORTS

Until recently, most leaders in the development of LCA methodology believed that streamlining LCA was impossible; a researcher must follow the prescribed methods, or the results could not be considered LCA. While many still adhere to this belief, others recognize that full-scale LCA is beyond the reach of many companies and potential users of the information. Some of these companies and users are modifying LCA methods to meet their needs and budgets.[14]

As a result, there is growing acknowledgment that a more rigorous examination of possible approaches to streamlining LCA would be beneficial. This effort could assist companies in identifying streamlined methods that would provide needed information and yet meet minimum criteria for reliability and validity.

REFERENCES

1. U.S. Congress, Office of Technology Assessment, *Green Products by Design: Choices for a Cleaner Environment,* OTA-E-541, Government Printing Office, Washington, 1992.

2. K. A. Weitz, "Keynote Address: Summary of Streamlining Interviews," presented at the Streamlining Life Cycle Assessment Conference and Workshop, Cincinnati, OH, June 12–13, 1995.

3. Environmental Protection Agency, *Life Cycle Assessment Inventory Guidelines and Principles,* EPA/600/R-92/245, prepared by Battelle and Franklin Associates, Ltd., for the Risk Reduction Engineering Laboratory, Office of Research and Development, Cincinnati, OH, February 1993.

4. SETAC, Foundation for Environmental Education, *A Technical Framework for Life-Cycle Assessment,* Society of Environmental Toxicology and Chemistry, Pensacola, FL, 1991.

5. J. A. Todd, "Streamlining LCA," presented at the Streamlining Life Cycle Assessment Conference and Workshop, held by EPA, Cincinnati, OH, June 12–13, 1995.

6. R. J. Cole, D. Rousseau, and S. Taylor, "Environmental Audits of Alternative Structural Systems for Warehouse Buildings," *Canadian Journal of Civil Engineering,* 19: 886–895 (1992).

7. SETAC, Foundation for Environmental Education, *A Conceptual Framework for Life-Cycle Impact Assessment,* Society of Environmental Toxicology and Chemistry, Pensacola, FL, 1993.

8. J. A. Todd, "Pollution Prevention in Architecture: The Application of Life Cycle Assessment to Building Materials," *Proceedings of the Annual Air Force Pollution Prevention Conference,* Air Force Center for Environmental Excellence, San Antonio, TX, June 1993.

9. Environmental Protection Agency, *Development of a Pollution Prevention Factors Methodology Based on Life-Cycle Assessment: Lithographic Printing Case Study,* EPA/600/R-94/157, prepared by Battelle for the Risk Reduction Engineering Laboratory, Office of Research and Development, Cincinnati, OH, 1994.

10. T. A. Graedel, B. R. Allenby, and P. R. Comrie, "Matrix Approaches to Abridged Life Cycle Assessment," *Environmental Science and Technology,* 29 (3): 134–139A (1995).

11. T. A. Graedel and B. R. Allenby, *Industrial Ecology,* Prentice-Hall, Englewood Cliffs, NJ, 1995.

12. J. A. Fava, E. D. Weiler, and K. H. Reinert, "Product Life-Cycle Assessment: A Tool to Implement Product Stewardship," *The Weston Way,* September 1993.

13. Jamie Meil, "Environmental Measures as Substitution Criteria for Wood and Non-Wood Building Products," *Evergreen Magazine,* December 1994.

14. M. Breville, T. Gloria, M. O'Connell, and T. Saad, *Life Cycle Assessment, Trends, Methodologies, and Current Implications,* Tufts University Department of Civil and Environmental Engineering, Medford, MA, August 5, 1994.

CHAPTER 5
APPLICATIONS OF
LIFE-CYCLE ASSESSMENT

David Allen
HENRY BECKMAN
PROFESSOR IN CHEMICAL ENGINEERING
UNIVERSITY OF TEXAS
AUSTIN, TX

5.1 INTRODUCTION

Life-cycle assessment (LCA) has been used in a variety of applications in both the public and private sectors. Many of these assessments have been well publicized. Among the applications of LCA that are particularly well known are comparisons between cloth and disposable diapers (Franklin Associates, Ltd., 1990b), comparisons between plastic and paper cups (Franklin Associates, Ltd., 1990a; Hocking, 1991), and comparisons between polystyrene clamshells and coated paper wrappers for hamburgers (see Svoboda and Hart, 1993). These studies have done much to raise awareness about LCA as an analytical tool; however, they have also generated a significant amount of confusion and skepticism about the value of LCA.

The confusion and skepticism generated by a few highly publicized studies, focused on identifying environmentally preferable products, have diverted attention from many of the other applications of life-cycle assessments and life-cycle concepts that are less controversial. The goal of this chapter is to outline the spectrum of uses to which LCA has been applied, illustrating the applications with case studies. To begin, consider the data in Fig. 5.1, which report some of the common motivations for performing an LCA, as identified by product manufacturers. Figure 5.2 provides similar data from the viewpoint of public policymakers. These data were assembled by the Swedish Waste Research Council (Ryding, 1994) and were based on an international survey of over 40 organizations actively involved in LCA. The data indicate that the most common reasons for performing an LCA are to improve the environmental performance of products and to inform long-term policy decisions. Product comparisons are a less common motivation. Figure 5.3 expands on the information needs that drive LCAs, and Fig. 5.4 indicates that the feature of an LCA that is one of its most valued is its emphasis on multi-attribute interdisciplinary analysis.

These data indicate that many information needs are driving the growing use of LCA. This chapter organizes current uses of LCA and life-cycle concepts into a number of public and private sector application categories. In private sector applications, case studies address product improvement, product comparisons, and strategic planning.

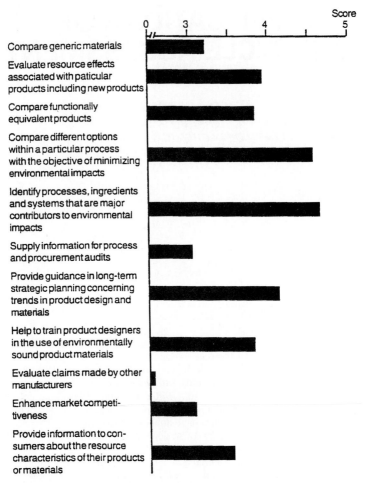

FIGURE 5.1   Relative importance (5 = high) of various applications of life-cycle assessment as assigned by product manufacturers surveyed by the Swedish Waste Research Council (Ryding, 1994).

Ecolabeling and the use of life-cycle assessments in drafting regulations are among the public sector applications that are illustrated through case studies.

The Appendix lists publicly available LCA studies that have been conducted in the United States. This list includes studies which are not considered to be life-cycle inventories or LCAs, but are related, such as fuel cycle assessments.

5.2   CASE STUDIES OF PRODUCT IMPROVEMENT

As noted in the last section, one of the most common uses of life-cycle assessments is to identify critical areas in which the environmental performance of a product can be improved. Often a life-cycle assessment will only confirm conventional wisdom. For

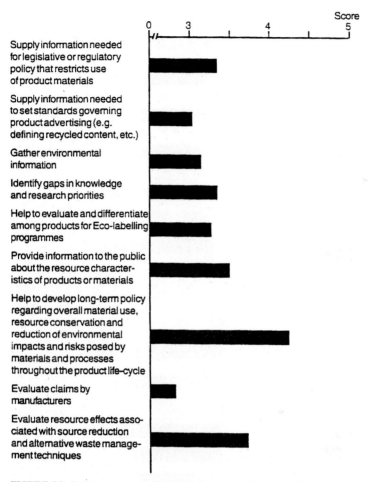

FIGURE 5.2 Relative importance (5 = high) of various applications of life-cycle assessment as assigned by product manufacturers surveyed by the Swedish Waste Research Council (Ryding, 1994).

example, the data in Table 5.1 indicate that the vast majority of the fuel required to produce 1 kg of polyethylene is the oil, coal, or other hydrocarbon that is diverted from fuel use in order to make ethylene and polyethylene. Thus, improvements in the energy efficiency of polyethylene products are most effectively made by reducing the mass of polyethylene. This is not a surprising result to anyone familiar with chemical manufacturing processes. Some life-cycle assessments, however, do yield surprises. Consider the data presented in Fig. 5.5, which report the results of a life-cycle inventory done by Franklin Associates for the American Fiber Manufacturers Association. This study examined the life cycle of a woman's blouse made of 100 percent knitted filament polyester (Franklin Associates, 1993). The study found that 86 percent of the energy consumed during the life cycle of a blouse (50 wearings with 2 wears between washings) is associated with hot water cleaning and machine drying. As shown in Fig. 5.5*b,* this energy demand associated with cleaning could be reduced by 90 percent if the garment

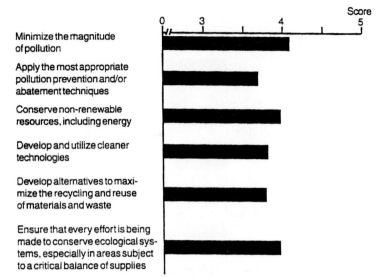

FIGURE 5.3 Relative importance (5 = high) of goals defined for life-cycle assessments (Ryding, 1994).

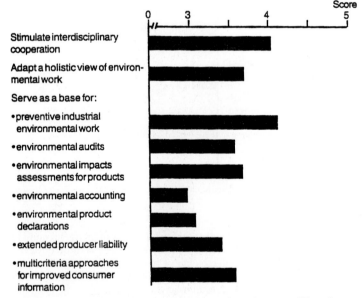

FIGURE 5.4 Relative importance (5 = high) of the various advantages of life-cycle assessments.

is washed in cold water and dried on a line rather than in a machine. This life-cycle assessment demonstrated that the greatest opportunities for improved energy efficiency for garments lie in the development of fabrics, dyes, and detergents that are compatible with cold water washing.

Another life-cycle inventory that yielded a surprising result was done by UCLA for Patagonia, Inc. (Hopkins et. al., 1994). Patagonia is a privately held company known

TABLE 5.1   Average Gross Energy Required to Produce 1 kg of Polyethylene (All Grades) in Europe (Boustead, 1993)

Fuel type	Fuel production and delivery, MJ	Delivered energy, MJ	Feedstock* energy, MJ	Total energy, MJ
Electricity	5.31	2.58	0.00	7.89
Oil fuels	0.53	2.05	32.76	35.34
Other fuels	0.47	8.54	33.59	42.60
Totals	6.31	13.17	66.35	85.83

Feedstock energy is the calorific value of materials that are input to the processes required to produce polyethylene.

primarily for the high-performance outdoor clothing and travel-related products that it designs and markets. Sales and distribution are handled through dealers, Patagonia-owned retail outlets, and mail order. The study focused on the transportation and distribution of one of Patagonia's garments, throughout its life cycle. The rationale for focusing on environmental improvements in the transportation and distribution of a garment may not be immediately apparent. Previous studies of garment life cycles have not found transportation and distribution to have significant impacts. Such studies generally assume, however, that transport of products and material is done exclusively by truck and rail. These modes of transport are efficient, but they are often not rapid enough for Patagonia's customer demands. Limited space in retail outlets and highly seasonal sales necessitate small but frequent product deliveries. For example, during the Christmas season, the urgency of keeping store shelves stocked often means that products are shipped by air. The use of air transport dramatically changes the relative importance of transportation and distribution in the life-cycle inventory for a garment. Shown in Fig. 5.6 are estimates of the energy burdens associated with air deliveries and combined truck and rail (intermodal) deliveries, compared to manufacturing energy burdens. Patagonia intends to respond to this study with a customer information campaign.

Another group of applications in which life-cycle assessments can lead to new insights is composed of those that involve products with multiple components. Consider the *life-cycle inventory* (LCI) of a computer workstation, performed by an industry team coordinated by the Microelectronics and Computer Technology Corporation (MCC, 1993). Workstations contain a variety of major and minor components, including the cathode-ray tube (display), plastic housings, semiconductors, and printed wiring boards. The life-cycle inventory conducted by MCC was able to identify, for a variety of environmental inventory categories, which components were of primary concern. For example, product disposal was dominated by issues related to cathode-ray tubes. Hazardous waste generation was dominated by semiconductor manufacturing. Energy use was dominated by the consumer use stage of the life cycle. Somewhat surprisingly, semiconductor manufacturing was a significant component of material use. Results are shown in Fig. 5.7. This study was used to prioritize research and technology needs for the microcomputer industry.

A final type of application in which LCA can be useful in product improvement is the evaluation of product design options. Table 5.2 illustrates this use of LCA. A variety of product reformulations and packaging alternatives for a liquid fabric conditioner are presented. The energy and solid waste burdens associated with each of these options are compared, revealing some of the tradeoffs associated with each design.

The examples cited above demonstrate that life-cycle assessments of products can be valuable from a variety of perspectives. They can help to identify areas for environmental improvement that, at times, can be surprising. They can help identify processes, components, ingredients, and systems that are major contributors to environmental impacts, and they can be used to compare options for minimizing environmental impacts.

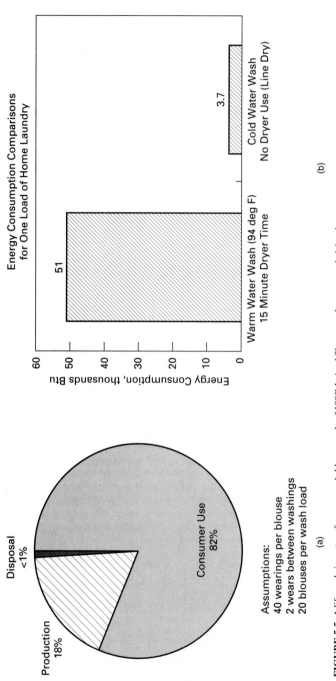

FIGURE 5.5 A life-cycle inventory for a woman's blouse made of 100% knitted filament polyester revealed that the greatest improvements in the energy efficiency of the life cycle could be obtained by changing washing and drying methods (Franklin Associates, Limited, 1993).

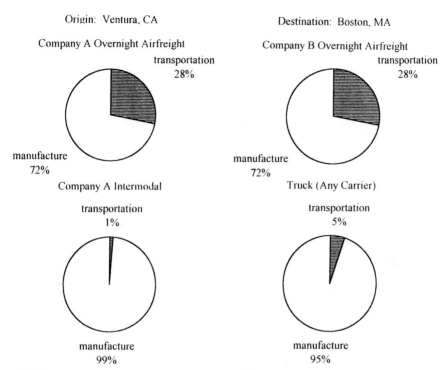

FIGURE 5.6 A study for Patagonia revealed that the energy required to deliver a garment to a customer or a retail outlet by overnight air freight can make the transportation component of a garment life cycle significant. Use of intermodal transport substantially reduces this burden (Hopkins *et al.*, 1994).

5.3   CASE STUDIES OF PRODUCT COMPARISONS

There is a general consensus supporting the use of life-cycle inventories and life-cycle assessments in targeting areas and identifying methods for the environmental improvement of a product. Far more controversial, however, is the use of LCAs and LCIs to compare products that serve similar functions. Three notable case studies are presented in this section to illustrate some of the controversies: a comparison of cloth and disposable diapers, a comparison of beverage packaging systems, and a comparison of sandwich packaging products.

A comparison of cloth and disposable diapering systems illustrates several critical features of product comparisons. First, it highlights the ambiguity associated with picking winners and losers. As shown by the data in Table 5.3 (Franklin Associates, 1990b), the use of cloth diapers lowers the generation of solid waste but increases water use relative to disposable diapers. Energy requirements may or may not be significantly different between the two systems, depending on whether the cloth diapers are laundered at home or commercially. Thus, there is no clearly environmentally superior product unless the relative importance of energy demand, water demand, and solid waste generation can be explicitly evaluated. A second point illustrated by the comparison of diapering systems is related to product reuse. Cloth that has been retired from diapering finds many applications, including use as rags where the cloth diaper may replace the

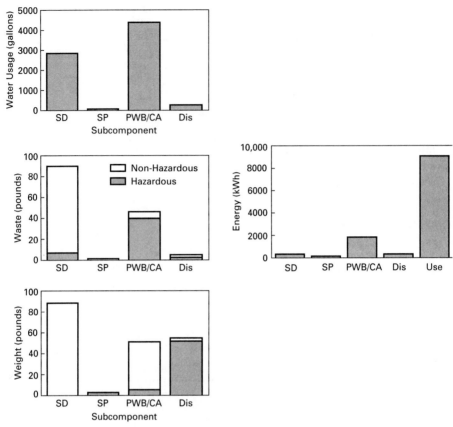

FIGURE 5.7 Energy use, material use, water use, and waste generation in computer workstation manufacturing (MCC, 1993). Note that different subcomponents of the workstation (SD = semiconductor, SP = semiconductor packaging; PWB/CA = printed wiring board and computer assemblies; DIS = display) dominate different inventory categories.

TABLE 5.2 Summary of a Life-Cycle Inventory of Packaging Alternatives for a Liquid Fabric Conditioner

Strategies for packaging improvement	Decrease in energy needs, %			Decrease in emissions, %		
	Process	Transport	Feedstock	Solid	Aqueous	Air borne
1. Incorporate 25% recycled plastic	3	0	9	9	(+4)	4
2. Encourage 25% consumer recycling	3	2	11	11	(+4)	5
3. Triple-concentrate (3X) product	55	53	56	55	54	55
4. Market product soft pouch	3	18	67	85	(+12)	24
5. Market 3X product in soft pouch	68	73	89	95	63	75
6. Market 3X product in paper carton	53	58	94	91	40	62
7. Encourage 25% composting for strategy 6	53	58	94	92	40	62

Source: Procter & Gamble, personal communication, 1993.

TABLE 5.3 Relative Environmental Burdens for Cloth and Disposable Diapers (Based on Data from Franklin Associates, 1990b)

Impact	Disposable	Cloth Commercially laundered	Cloth Home-laundered
Energy requirements	0.50	0.55	1.0
Solid waste	4.1	1.0	1.0
Waterborne wastes	0.14	0.95	1.0
Water volume requirements	0.27	1.3	1.0

use of a paper towel. The methods used for assigning material, energy, and waste credits for these end-of-life uses influence the overall burdens associated with the cloth diaper, but not the disposable diaper. Thus, it is virtually impossible to treat the cloth and disposable products in a consistent manner in the comparison. Finally, the comparison of diapering systems illustrates the importance of the functional unit. To effectively compare any two product systems, the material use, energy use, and waste generation must be defined on an equivalent basis. In the case of comparing diapering systems, the functional unit might be the diapering of a baby for a week. With this as the functional unit, it is, in principle, possible to determine how many cloth and disposable diapers would be required by an average child. In practice, the exercise is not simple because cloth diapers generally require more frequent changes, some consumers use multiple cloth diapers for a single change, and diapering is not the only use of cloth diapers in a home containing children.

The comparison of beverage containers reinforces the importance of the choice of functional unit. The data in Table 5.4 are from a comparison of 12-oz aluminum cans, 16-ounce nonrefillable glass bottles, and 64-oz polyethylene terephthalate (PET) plas-

TABLE 5.4 Energy and Environmental Impacts for Three Soft Drink Container Groups Using Two Different Functional Units (Based on Data from Franklin Associates, 1989)

Container group	Recycling rates, % 0	Recycling rates, % 50	Recycling rates, % 100	Container group	Recycling rates, % 0	Recycling rates, % 50	Recycling rates, % 100
Energy required per 1000 gal, TBtu				Energy required per container, Btu			
PET (64 fl oz bottles)	21.2	17.9	14.6	PET (64 fl oz bottles)	10,600	8,950	7,300
Aluminum (12 fl oz cans)	50.0	32.9	15.9	Aluminum (12 fl oz cans)	4,687	3,084	1,491
Glass (16 fl oz bottles)	49.0	35.0	20.9	Glass (16 fl oz bottles)	6,125	4,375	2,612
Atmospheric emissions per 1000 gal, lb				Atmospheric emissions per container, oz			
PET (64 fl oz bottles)	62.0	53.4	44.8	PET (64 fl oz bottles)	0.50	0.43	0.36
Aluminum (12 fl oz cans)	137.0	91.7	48.3	Aluminum (12 fl oz cans)	0.21	0.14	0.07
Glass (16 fl oz bottles)	217.4	145.4	73.5	Glass (16 fl oz bottles)	0.43	0.29	0.15
Solid waste per 1000 gal, lb				Solid waste per container, oz			
PET (64 fl oz bottles)	513.1	351.3	189.5	PET (64 fl oz bottles)	4.1	2.8	1.5
Aluminum (12 fl oz cans)	1,938	1,068	198.2	Aluminum (12 fl oz cans)	2.9	1.6	0.3
Glass (16 fl oz bottles)	7,000	3,881	762.3	Glass (16 fl oz bottles)	14.0	7.8	1.5

tic bottles (Franklin Associates, 1989). Two choices of functional unit are presented: 1000 gal of beverage delivered and a container delivered to the customer. Clearly, the choice of functional unit matters. The large PET bottle is efficient when the functional unit is defined as a fluid volume delivered to the customer, but is inefficient if it is assumed that the customer will consume a serving, whether it is 12, 16, or 64 ozs. In reality, it is probably inappropriate to compare the 64-oz bottle with 12- and 16-oz containers since the larger product is typically used for multiple servings and smaller containers are generally used for single servings. But, it is not at all clear what the appropriate functional unit should be in comparing 12-oz aluminum cans and 16-oz PET and glass bottles. This example, while somewhat artificial, dramatizes the importance and the difficulty associated with choosing a functional unit.

Despite all the challenges associated with fairly conducting product comparisons, life-cycle inventories are being used to discriminate between products. The decision by McDonald's to convert from polystyrene to paper-based quilt wrap containers for its food products is one of the best-known cases. In announcing its decision on November 2, 1990, McDonald's cited a 90 percent reduction in volume of packaging and reductions in energy consumption, air emissions, and water pollution as key factors in the decision. Data supporting these claims were drawn from a life-cycle inventory and are summarized in Table 5.5. In making this decision, McDonald's was effectively withdrawing as a major contributor to the effort to develop a recycling infrastructure for polystyrene, and it is unclear what the results of the product comparison would have been if aggressively recycled polystyrene were compared to the quilt wrap products which are difficult to recycle. As a result, the response to the decision was mixed. The Environmental Defense Fund's January 1991 newsletter called it a "major victory for environmentalists." *The New York Times* described the "Greening of the Golden Arch" by stating that "McDonald's is at last showing some McSense on the Environment." In contrast, the *Los Angeles Times* concluded that McDonald's "found itself doing the wrong thing for the wrong reason." A comprehensive examination of this case study has been performed by the National Pollution Prevention Center at the University of Michigan (Svoboda and Hart, 1993), highlighting the uncertainties in this complex decision.

TABLE 5.5   Energy Requirements and Environmental Emissions for the Production, Delivery, and Disposal of 10,000 Sandwich Packaging Products (Svoboda and Hart, 1993)

	Total energy requirement, TBtu	Energy credit from incineration, TBtu	Net energy requirement, TBtu	atmospheric emissions, lb	Waterborne wastes, lb	Total solid waste lb	Total solid waste ft³
Standard paper wrap	1.5	0.1	1.4	4.5	0.8	63.7	2.0
Layered paper wrap	3.5	0.2	3.3	9.7	1.4	129.5	4.1
Polystyrene foam container	6.5	0.4	6.1	13.8	2.5	159.8	16.5
Paperboard container	9.2	0.5	8.8	25.7	4.3	382.4	11.7
Paperboard collar (optional for use with either wrap)	2.7	0.1	2.5	8.3	1.4	117.1	3.5

5.4   CASE STUDIES IN STRATEGIC PLANNING

The McDonald's case study described above illustrates how life-cycle inventories have been used at a corporate level to select material suppliers. LCAs can play other roles in corporate decision making if the definition of life-cycle assessment is broadened to include qualitative and semiquantitative life-cycle concepts. "The life cycle concept is based on the recognition that a 'cradle to grave' perspective is critical to any evaluation" and that "an inherently integrated concept...is the best way to allow for the evaluation of economic, environmental and energy dimensions of a problem at the same time" (SETAC, 1994). This section examines case studies of the use of life-cycle analyses or life-cycle concepts in corporate decision making. The experiences of AT&T, Scott Paper Company, and Dow provide excellent case studies of how the information provided by LCAs can be used to inform corporate planning, decision making, and supplier relations.

AT&T has used life-cycle concepts in a variety of settings. Using the qualitative matrices shown in Fig. 5.8, AT&T evaluated a variety of substitutes for lead solder. As shown in the figure, the matrices attempt to qualitatively evaluate the environmental, manufacturing, toxicity, and political factors that affect the choice of a solder throughout the life cycle of the alternative materials. The information is then condensed into a summary matrix that helps the designer evaluate alternatives; in this case, the semiquantitative analysis using life-cycle concepts led AT&T to conclude that bismuth, indium, and epoxy solders were not preferable to the existing blend containing lead (Allenby, 1992). AT&T is also developing a semiquantitative, life-cycle-based approach to evaluating the environmental concerns associated with its facilities. The ecological impacts, energy use, solid wastes, liquid wastes, and gaseous wastes are evaluated for the life cycle of each facility, which includes siting, principal business activities, facility operations, and closure (Allenby, 1994).

Scott Paper Company, as well as Dow Chemical Company and AT&T, has employed analytical frameworks that utilize life-cycle concepts to strategically evaluate product lines or core businesses. The framework used by Scott Paper evaluates resource and environmental issues at each stage of the life cycle, including natural resources, raw materials, manufacture, product and packaging development, and product use and disposal. At each life-cycle stage, ecological and human health factors are evaluated. Examples of this scoring system for human health factors in the manufacturing stage are given in Fig. 5.9. A similar framework used by Dow is shown in Fig. 5.10. Each addresses a range of impacts and a variety of stages in the life cycles of the products. These comparisons between products and core businesses are quite different from the product comparisons described in the previous section. In this case, rather than comparing products with similar functions to determine which is environmentally preferable, the immediate goal is to compare the relative magnitudes of the environmental burdens of products with different functions and markets. The overall goal is to incorporate life-cycle environmental thinking into corporate decisions in strategic planning, research and development, product and process design, manufacturing, decommissioning, and closure or restoration.

5.5   CASE STUDIES OF PUBLIC SECTOR USES

The previous sections have focused on private sector uses of life-cycle concepts and life-cycle assessments. There are, however, a growing number of public sector applications of life-cycle concepts and life-cycle assessments, and some of these are summa-

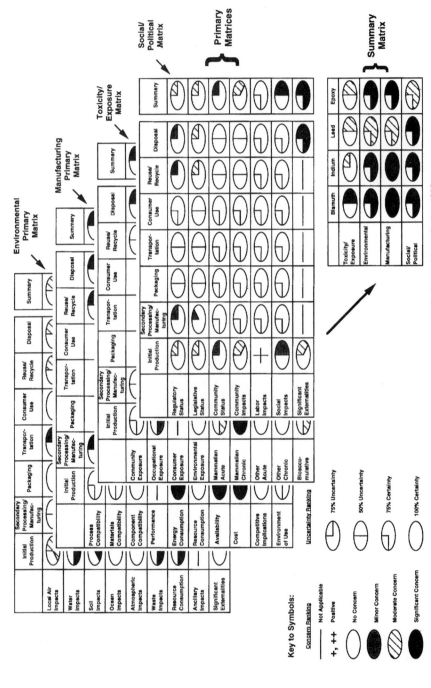

FIGURE 5.8 Qualitative matrix analysis used by AT&T in the analysis of substitutes for lead solder (Allenby, 1992; Richards and Frosch, 1994).

HUMAN HEALTH	SCORE		
Subsystem Manufacturing			
1. Number of manufacturing sites	Lower	Intermediate	Higher
2. Population surrounding manufacturing site locations	Sparse	Moderate	Dense
3. Status of manufacturing process			
a. Degree of automation	Higher	Intermediate	Lower
b. Complexity (number of process steps)	Lower	Intermediate	Higher
c. Age, upgrade status	New or upgrade	Moderate old and upgraded	Old and not upgraded
d. Process stability (susceptibility to upset)	Stable (low upset)	Moderate	More subject to excursions
4. Hazardous chemicals/ carcinogens present	No	Yes (either)	Yes (both)
5. Production volume	Lower	Intermediate	Higher
6. Routine air emissions	Lower	Intermediate	Higher
7. Hazardous waste volume	Lower	Intermediate	Higher
8. Wastewater releases	Lower	Intermediate	Higher
Manufacturing Score			

FIGURE 5.9 Human health evaluation criteria for the manufacturing stage. These criteria are one component of a life-cycle product evaluation framework used by Scott Paper Company (Consoli, 1993).

rized in Table 5.6 (U.S. Congress, Office of Technology Assessment, 1992). The range of applications includes environmental labeling, acquisition, procurement, and regulation. Examples of each of these public sector uses are given below.

Among the most visible government uses of life-cycle concepts and life-cycle assessments are environmental labels. Environmental labels are issued in a variety of countries, as shown in Fig. 5.11. In many countries (Austria, Canada, France, Germany, the Nordic countries, the Netherlands, and the European Community), life-cycle concepts are used to identify the criteria used in awarding the labels, and multiple criteria are used. This represents a significant shift away from single-attribute labels, focused on a single stage of the life cycle (e.g., recycled content labels). Some of the principles and practices underlying environmental labeling can be illustrated by examining the system employed in the Netherlands. The Netherlands has been awarding the Dutch ecolabel (*Stichting Milieukeur*) based on a qualitative matrix of environmental criteria. Label criteria are developed by a Board of Experts for product groups; once the criteria have been set, any manufacturer, importer, or licensee can submit an application for her or his product to be approved by a certification authority. The first such label was awarded in September 1993 to a writing paper product. The Dutch ecolabel is thus typical of many labeling programs. Multiple life-cycle-based criteria are set. Products are evaluated and labels are awarded, but the consumer seeing the label generally has no immediate access to the full range of data on environmental burdens and must accept the tradeoffs between burdens used in setting the criteria. The Netherlands is now defining a substantial expansion to this system that will provide more information to consumers and retailers. In the next

Environmental Dimensions	RME	RMP	MFG	DST	CNV	NDU	DSP	RCY
Safety Fire Explosion								
Human Health								
Residual Substances								
Statospheric Ozone Depletion								
Air Quality								
Climate Change								
Natural Resource Depletion								
Soil Contamination								
Waste Accumulation								
Water Contamination								
Public Perception Gap								
Competition								

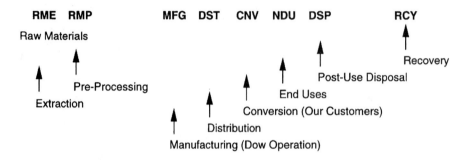

RATING SYSTEM

Hazard or Effect	Exposure (Volume, Frequency)		
	HIGH	MEDIUM	LOW
HIGH	-9	-9	-9
MEDIUM	-9	-3	-1
LOW	-3	-1	

9	Proven Implemented Solution
3	Project Initiated Resources Allocated
1	Project Identified

Vulnerabilities   *Opportunities*

FIGURE 5.10 Life-cycle product evaluation framework used by Dow Chemical Company (Noesen, 1993).

generation of labeling, a simplified description of five environmental indicators will be provided on the labels of all products. These indicators are energy, waste, resources, emissions, and nuisance. Background data for the labeling will be publicly available. The information will take into account "all the environmental considerations related to a product in each phase of its life cycle ('from the cradle to the grave')" (National

TABLE 5.6 Environmental Policies Relating to Products

Economic Commission for Europe (United Nations)
- A task force is developing guidelines for *environmental product profiles*—a qualitative description of the environmental impacts of a product for use by commercial and institutional buyers.

European Community (EC)
- Draft law requiring specific percentages of recovery (recycling, incineration, and composting) for product packaging.
- EC ecolabel.

Canada
- The National Packaging Protocol is a voluntary program with packaging reduction targets and dates.
- Environmental Choice ecolabel.

Denmark
- Ban on domestically produced nonrefillable bottles and aluminum cans.
- Fee imposed on waste delivered to landfills and incinerators as an incentive to recycling and to support clean technology.
- Clean Technology Action Plan.

Germany
- Packaging waste law, passed in 1991, gives manufacturers responsibility for collecting and recycling various kinds of packaging at specified rates by certain dates.
- Manufacturer take-back-and-recycle laws have been proposed by the government for automobiles, electronic goods, and other durables.
- Mandatory deposit refund on plastic beverage containers (except milk).
- Blue Angel product ecolabel.

Japan
- Recycling law, passed in 1991, sets target recycling rates of about 60 percent for most discarded materials by the mid-1990s. Includes product redesign strategies for packaging and durable goods.
- Eco-mark product ecolabel.

Netherlands
- National Environmental Policy Plan sets national targets and timetables for implementing clean technology, including redesign of products.
- Voluntary agreements reached with industry target 29 priority waste streams and reduction of packaging waste.

Norway
- Tax on nonreturnable beverage containers.
- Deposit refund on old car bodies.

Sweden
- Ban "in principle" on the use of cadmium.
- Voluntary deposit refunds for glass and aluminum beverage containers.

Source: Office of Technology Assessment, 1992.

Environmental Policy Plan Plus, 1994). Thus, ecolabels are evolving. Prior to government intervention, many single-attribute labels focusing on a single phase of the life cycle (e.g., recycled content) were used in the marketplace. These have been replaced in many markets with multiattribute labels that address the entire product life cycle, but the consumer was shielded from the complexity of the multiattribute decision-making process involved in awarding a label. Now, programs such as the Dutch product labeling system are attempting to communicate more information to the readers of ecolabels.

FIGURE 5.11 Environmental labels from around the world.

Many governments are themselves users of ecolabeling data. For example, in the United States, Executive Order 12873, issued by President Clinton, mandates the procurement of environmentally preferable goods and services by federal agencies. The Environmental Protection Agency (EPA) is using the life-cycle concept to establish guidelines for the procurement process. Governments can also use life-cycle concepts in setting research and development policy, stimulating markets, and setting regulations. As examples consider:

- The EPA is considering using life-cycle concepts in rule-making activities under the Clean Air Act Amendments. Life-cycle concepts would be used to assess materials cleaning options including the use of chlorinated solvents, aqueous degreasers, and semiaqueous degreasers.

- In developing effluent guidelines for industrial laundries under the Clean Water Act, the EPA became concerned that regulations on the laundries might cause a shift from the use of cloth wiping towels to disposable towels, resulting in a transfer of pollutant loadings from water to landfills. The EPA will use a life-cycle framework to examine the tradeoffs between laundry effluent levels, the use of disposable wipes, and other alternatives.

- The U.S. Department of Defense (DoD) now incorporates life-cycle environmental costs into procurement decisions. DoD 5000.2-M [part 4, section F] provides the following guidance: "During each phase of the acquisition process, identify and analyze the potential environmental consequences of each alternative being considered. This analysis includes environmental impacts of each alternative throughout the system's life cycle."

- Life-cycle assessments were performed by the Department of Energy to examine the effects of mandating the use of electric vehicles and to assess the environmental impacts of a variety of energy options, including renewables.

These are just a few of many emerging public policy applications of life-cycle concepts and life-cycle assessments.

5.6 SUMMARY

Life-cycle concepts and life-cycle assessments can be powerful frameworks for analysis in support of public and private sector decisions. Only a few of the case studies demonstrating the value of these tools could be presented in this review, but the diversity of the applications presented here provides a glimpse of the range and power of these emerging tools.

BIBLIOGRAPHY

Allenby, B. R.: "Design for Environment: Implementing Industrial Ecology," Ph.D. dissertation, Rutgers University, 1992.

Allenby, B. R.: Personal communication, 1994.

Boustead, Ian: "Ecoprofiles of the European Plastics Industry, Report 3: Polyethylene and Polypropylene," Plastics Waste Management Institute, European Centre for Plastics in the Environment, Brussels, Belgium, May 1993.

Consoli, Frank: Scott Paper Company, personal communication, 1993.

Federal Office of the Environment: *Comparison of the Effects on the Environment from Polyethylene and Paper Carrier Bags,* Bismarkplatz 1, 1000 Berlin 33, Federal Republic of Germany, August 1988.

Franklin Associates, Ltd.: "Comparative Energy and Environmental Impacts for Soft Drink Delivery Systems," report prepared for the National Association for Plastic Container Recovery, Prairie Village, KS, March 1989.

Franklin Associates, Ltd.: "Energy and Environmental Profile Analysis of Polyethylene and Unbleached Paper Grocery Sacks," report prepared for the Council for Solid Waste Solutions, Prairie Village, KS, June 1990a.

Franklin Associates, Ltd.: "Energy and Environmental Profile Analysis of Children's Disposable and Cloth Diapers," report prepared for the American Paper Institute's Diaper Manufacturers' Group, Prairie Village, KS, July 1990b.

Franklin Associates, Ltd.: "Summary of Life Cycle Analyses of Four Sandwich Packages," report prepared for McDonald's and Environmental Defense Fund Task Force, Prairie Village, KS, 1991.

Franklin Associates, Ltd.: "Resource and Environmental Profile Analysis of a Manufactured Apparel Product," report to the American Fiber Manufacturers' Association, Washington, June 1993.

Hocking, Martin B.: "Paper versus Polystyrene," *Science,* **251:** 504–505 (February 1991). See also letters commenting on this paper, *Science,* **253:** 1361–1363 (June 1991).

Hopkins, L., D. T. Allen, and M. Brown: "Quantifying and Reducing Environmental Impacts Resulting from Transportation of a Manufactured Garment," *Pollution Prevention Review,* **4**(4): 491–500 (1994).

Microelectronics and Computer Technology Corporation (MCC): "Environmental Consciousness: A Strategic Competitiveness Issue for the Electronics and Computer Industry," MCC, Austin, TX, March 1993.

National Environmental Policy Plan Plus (Netherlands): *Policy Document on Products and the Environment,* Ministry of Housing, Spatial Planning and the Environment, The Hague, 1994.

Noesen, Scott: Dow Chemical Company, personal communication, 1993.

Richards, D. J., and R. A. Frosch (eds.): *Corporate Environmental Practices: Climbing the Learning Curve,* National Academy Press, Washington, 1994.

Ryding, S.: *International Experiences of Environmentally Sound Product Development Based on Life Cycle Assessment,* Swedish Waste Research Council, AFR-Report 36, Stockholm, May 1994.

Society of Environmental Toxicology and Chemistry (SETAC): Executive Summary of Workshop on Public Policy Applications of Life Cycle Assessment, Pensacola, FL, 1994.

Svoboda, S., and S. Hart: "McDonald's Environmental Strategy," National Pollution Prevention Center for Higher Education, Ann Arbor, MI, doc. 93-3, December 1993.

U.S. Congress, Office of Technology Assessment, *Green Products by Design: Choices for a Cleaner Environment,* OTA-E-541, Government Printing Office, Washington, October 1992.

CHAPTER 6
LIFE-CYCLE DESIGN

Gregory A. Keoleian, Ph.D.
RESEARCH DIRECTOR
NATIONAL POLLUTION PREVENTION CENTER
ASSISTANT RESEARCH SCIENTIST
SCHOOL OF NATURAL RESOURCES AND ENVIRONMENT
UNIVERSITY OF MICHIGAN

6.1 INTRODUCTION

Design offers an excellent opportunity to reduce environmental burdens associated with products and processes, which ultimately can lead to a more sustainable relationship between economic and ecological systems. Guiding environment improvement and sustainable development through design requires framework(s), tools, and innovation. Decisions involving material selection, useful product life, packaging systems, manufacturing processes, and strategies for product service and retirement shape the environmental profile of a product. But even if a designer were unconstrained by performance and cost requirements, it is not obvious what an environmentally optimal design would represent. In addition to this challenge, design participants face pressing issues such as shortening development cycles, expanding global competitiveness, increasing and inconsistent regulations, and continually shifting market demand. Evaluating and improving environmental performance have become major challenges facing the design community.

Life-cycle design is beginning to emerge as a new field for addressing this challenge.[1] For example, the Environmental Protection Agency (EPA) has sponsored the development of the *Life Cycle Design Framework and Demonstration Projects: Profiles of AT&T and AlliedSignal.*[2] The basic theory of life-cycle design is that the product life-cycle system provides a logical framework for representing the diverse interests of multistakeholders in the development of sustainable products. The product life cycle which encompasses raw materials acquisition, manufacturing, use and service, and end-of-life management (e.g., remanufacturing, recycle, disposal) defines the boundaries of the system for addressing the full environmental consequences associated with a product.

Recognition of the life-cycle framework has been driven by a variety of reasons including public concern about municipal solid waste which represents the end of a product life cycle, environmental marketing claims to distinguish products, and product take-back regulations. The application of the life-cycle framework is still in its infancy. Many organizational and operational changes in corporate environmental management systems, the design process, and government policy and regulation are necessary to realize the benefits of life-cycle design and related approaches.

This chapter presents the key elements of life-cycle design and examines the role of life-cycle assessment and other tools in its application.

6.2 TERMINOLOGY

A wide assortment of terminology has been introduced in this field. The terminology, however, is often used without a clearly defined framework, objectives, and boundaries; hence its use may not be consistent. For example, the product life cycle may or may not be recognized as a system boundary. The following is a set of definitions of commonly used terms. Many other terms have been used in this field, but they do not necessarily represent a life-cycle approach. Such terms include *environmentally conscious design, environmentally conscious manufacturing, cleaner products, cleaner production,* and *ecodesign.*

Life-Cycle Assessment (LCA):   A comprehensive method for evaluating the full environmental consequences of a product system. LCA has four components: goal definition and scoping, inventory analysis, impact assessment, and improvement analysis. Life-cycle assessment represents the most comprehensive analytical tool for evaluating environmental burden, but unfortunately there are several practical barriers limiting its widespread application.[4]

Life-Cycle Costing: In the environmental field, this has come to mean all costs associated with a product system throughout its life cycle, from raw materials acquisition to disposal. Currently, *life-cycle costing,* also referred to as *full cost accounting or environmental accounting,* has limited practical applicability. Some environmental costs can be difficult to measure (future liabilities) and/or allocate (externalities). Traditionally the term is applied in military and engineering to mean estimating costs from acquisition of a product to disposal (includes operating and maintenance costs).

Life-Cycle Design: A systems-oriented approach for designing more ecologically and economically sustainable product systems. It couples the product development cycle used in business with the physical life cycle of a product. Life-cycle design integrates environmental requirements into the earliest stages of design so total impacts caused by product systems can be reduced. In life-cycle design, environmental, performance, cost, cultural, and legal requirements are balanced. Concepts such as concurrent design, total quality management, cross-disciplinary teams, and multiattribute decision making are essential elements of life-cycle design.

Design for Environment: This is another widely used term for incorporating environmental issues into a product system design process. DFE has been defined as "a practice by which environmental considerations are integrated into product and process engineering design procedures."[5] Life-cycle design and DFE are difficult to distinguish from each other; they are usually considered different names for the same approach. Yet, despite their similar goals, the genesis of DFE is quite different from that of life-cycle design. DFE evolved from the *design for X* (DFX) approach, where X can represent manufacturability, testability, reliability, or other downstream design considerations.

6.3 DEFINITION OF THE PRODUCT SYSTEM

6.3.1 Life-Cycle Stages

Figure 6.1 presents a general flow diagram of the product life cycle. As this figure shows, a product life cycle is circular, beginning with resource consumption and ending as residuals eventually accumulate in the earth and biosphere. A product life cycle can be organized into the following stages:

- Raw material acquisition
- Bulk material processing
- Engineered and specialty materials production
- Manufacturing and assembly

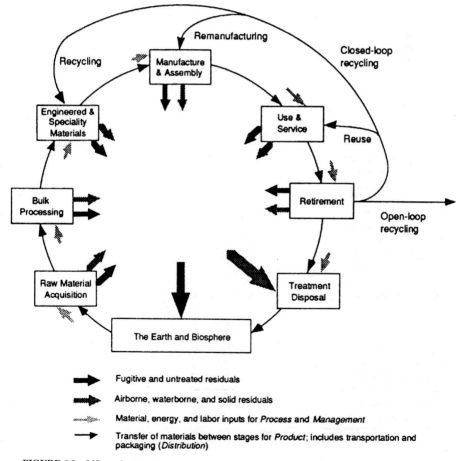

FIGURE 6.1 Life-cycle stages.

- Use and service
- Retirement
- Disposal

Raw materials acquisition includes mining nonrenewable material and harvesting biomass. These bulk materials are processed into base materials by separation and purification steps. Examples include flour milling and converting bauxite to aluminum. Some base materials are combined through physical and chemical means into engineered and specialty materials. Examples include polymerization of ethylene into polyethylene pellets and the production of high-strength steel. Base and engineered materials are then manufactured through various fabrication steps, and parts are assembled into the final product.

Products sold to customers are consumed or used for one or more functions. Throughout their use, products and processing equipment may be serviced to repair defects or maintain performance. Users eventually decide to retire a product. After retirement, a product can be reused or remanufactured. Material and energy can also be recovered through recycling, composting, incineration, or pyrolysis. Materials can be recycled into the same product many times (closed loop) or used to form other products before eventual discard (open loop).

Some residuals generated in all stages are released directly into the environment. Emissions from automobiles, wastewater discharges from processing facilities, and oil spills are examples of direct releases. Residuals may also undergo physical, chemical, or biological treatment. Treatment processes are usually designed to reduce volume and toxicity of waste. The remaining residuals, including those resulting from treatment, are then typically disposed in landfills. The ultimate form that the residuals take depends on how they degrade after being released into the environment.

The life-cycle system is complex due to its dynamic nature and its geographic scope. Activities within each stage of the life cycle change continuously, often independently of change in other stages. Life-cycle stages are also widely distributed on a geographic basis, and environmental consequences occur on global, regional, and local levels.

6.3.2 Product System Components

The product system is defined by the material, energy, and information flows and conversions associated with the life cycle of a product. This system can be organized into three basic components in all life-cycle stages: product, process, and distribution. As much as possible, life-cycle design seeks to integrate these components.

Product.   The product component consists of all materials constituting the final product. Included in this component are all the forms that these materials might take throughout the various life-cycle stages. For example, the product component for a wooden baseball bat consists of the tree, stumpage, and unused branches from raw material acquisition; lumber and waste wood from milling; the bat, wood chips, and sawdust from manufacturing; and the broken bat discarded in a municipal solid waste landfill. If this waste is incinerated, gases, water vapor, and ash are produced.

The product component of a complex product such as an automobile consists of a wide range of materials and parts. These may be a mix of primary (virgin) and secondary (recycled) materials. The materials contained in new or used replacement parts are also included in the product component.

Process.   Processing transforms materials and energy to a variety of intermediate and final products. The process component includes any direct and indirect material inputs used in making a product. Catalysts and solvents are examples of direct process materials that are not significantly incorporated into the final product. Plant and equipment are examples of indirect material inputs for processing. Resources consumed during research, development, testing, and product use are included in the process component.

Both the process and distribution components of the product system share the following subcomponents:

- Facility, plant, or offices
- Unit operations, process steps, or procedures (including administrative services and office management)
- Equipment and tools
- Human resources (labor, managers)
- Direct and indirect material inputs
- Energy

In the *Life Cycle Design Guidance Manual,* management was considered a separate component. Experience gained in life-cycle design demonstration projects resulted in a simplification of product system components to make it more intuitive. Management, including the entire information network that supports decision making, occurs throughout the process and distribution components in all life-cycle stages. It is thus best considered an element of process and distribution rather than a separate component. Within a corporation, management responsibilities include financial management, personnel, purchasing, marketing, customer services, legal services, and training and education programs. These activities may generate a substantial environmental burden and therefore should not be ignored.

Distribution.   Distribution consists of packaging systems and transportation networks used to contain, protect, and transport products and process materials. Both packaging and transportation result in significant adverse environmental impacts. In 1990, containers and packaging accounted for 32.9 percent (64.4 million tons) of municipal solid waste generated in the United States.[6] Rail, trucks, ships, airplanes, and pipelines constitute the major modes of transport; each consumes energy and causes environmental impacts. Material transfer devices such as pumps and valves, carts and wagons, and material handling equipment (forklifts, crib towers, etc.) are part of the distribution component, as are storage facilities such as tanks and warehouses.

Selling a product is also considered part of distribution. This includes both wholesale and retail activities.

Table 6.1 presents an example of product system elements across life-cycle stages. The distribution component is shown between connecting life-cycle stages to indicate that either transportation and/or packaging has been used to carry the product or process materials.

6.4 LIFE-CYCLE FRAMEWORK AND GOALS

The life-cycle framework provides a logical structure for guiding the management and design of sustainable product systems because it systematically considers the full range of environmental consequences associated with a product. By focusing on the entire product system, designers and managers can prevent the shifting of impacts between media (air, water, land) and between stages of the life cycle.

TABLE 6.1 Partial Example of Product System Elements for a Reusable Plastic Cup over Its Life Cycle

	Raw material extraction	Bulk processing or engineered material	Manufacturing	Use	Retirement or disposal
Product	Petroleum Natural gas	HDPE pellets Stabilizers, pigments	Cup	Cup	Cup or residuals from recycle, incineration
Process	Drilling equipment, labor, energy	Ethylene production, polymerization	Injection molding with SPI markings for recycling	Handling, filling, cleaning	Collect, process, recycle, burn, or landfill
Distribution	Pipeline and tankers	Rail, barge, truck, containers		Transport, wholesale, retail, packaging	Trucks, containers

The life-cycle framework encompasses information from multiple stakeholders whose involvement is critical to successful design improvement. The primary elements of the framework are goals, life-cycle management, and life-cycle development process.

6.4.1 Life-Cycle Design Goals

The fundamental goal of life-cycle design is to promote sustainable development at the global, regional, and local levels. Specifically, life-cycle design seeks to reduce the total environmental burden associated with product development by applying sustainable principles to the product system.

Achieve Sustainable Development. Sustainable development seeks to meet the needs of the present generation without compromising the ability of future generations to fulfill their needs. Translation of this broad goal to practical tools for design is a major challenge. The following general principles for achieving sustainable development, however, can be defined: sustainable resource use (conserve resources, minimize depletion of nonrenewable resources, use sustainable practices for managing renewable resources), pollution prevention, maintenance of ecosystem structure and function, and environmental equity. These principles, described in Table 6.2, are interrelated and highly complementary.

Life-cycle design seeks to minimize adverse environmental impacts and utilize resources efficiently to meet basic societal needs. Determination of what constitutes basic societal needs is based on individual value judgments and preferences, which is a topic outside the scope of this chapter. Achieving sustainable development goals, however, requires design innovation and in some cases forgoing the production of products that contribute large environmental burdens.

Specific Environmental Goal of Life-Cycle Design. The environmental goal of life-cycle design is to maximize resource efficiency and minimize the aggregate life-cycle environmental burden associated with product systems. Environmental burden can be classified into the following impact categories:

TABLE 6.2 Principles of Sustainable Development

Promote Sustainable Resource Use and Efficiency
- Conserve resources, minimize depletion of nonrenewable resources, and use sustainable practices for managing renewable resources.
- The amount and availability of resources are ultimately determined by geological and energy constraints, not human ingenuity.

Promote Pollution Prevention
- Proactive approach based on source reduction avoids the transfer of pollutants across media (air, water, land).
- Addressing environmental issues in the design stage is one of the most effective approaches to pollution prevention.

Protect Ecological and Human Health
- Healthy, functioning ecosystems are essential for the planet's life support system.
- Avoiding irreversible damage to the ecosystem such as loss of biodiversity is necessary to protect human health.

Promote Environmental Equity
- Address the distribution of resources and environmental risks.
- Intergenerational equity—meet current needs of society without compromising the ability of future generations to satisfy their needs.
- Intersocietal equity—change patterns of resource consumption and associated environmental risks within developed and less developed countries to achieve sustainable development and to address the disparity among socioeconomic groups within a country.

- Resource depletion
- Ecological and human health

These impacts are the result of resource use and environmental releases to air, water, and land. Conceptually, an environmental profile can be developed that characterizes the aggregate impacts for each life-cycle stage and the cumulative impacts for the entire life cycle.

ENVIRONMENTAL BURDEN

Environmental burdens are not distributed evenly over the product life cycle. For example, the major environmental burdens associated with automobiles are caused by the consumption of petroleum and resulting air pollutant emissions during use. By contrast, environmental burdens resulting from furniture use are minimal, but significant impacts occur from manufacture and disposal of these products.

Although there are no universal methods for precisely characterizing and aggregating environmental burdens, Fig. 6.2 shows a hypothetical example of an environmental profile. As illustrated, impacts are generally not uniformly distributed across the life cycle. This figure also shows how burdens in all life-cycle stages are aggregated to arrive at the full environmental consequences of a product system. It is important to recognize that human communities and ecosystems are also impacted by many product life-cycle systems at once.

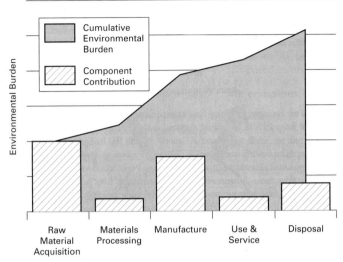

FIGURE 6.2   Environmental burden in hypothetical units of a product system.

6.5   LIFE-CYCLE MANAGEMENT

Life-cycle management includes all decisions and actions taken by multiple stakeholders which ultimately determine the environmental profile and sustainability of the product system. Each stakeholder has an important role in guiding improvement, as indicated in the following box. A major challenge for product manufacturers lies in coordinating the diverse interests of these stakeholder groups.

ROLES FOR KEY STAKEHOLDERS IN LIFE-CYCLE MANAGEMENT

Users and Public
- Advance understanding and values through education
- Modify behavior and demand toward more sustainable lifestyles

Policymakers and Regulators
- Develop policies to promote sustainable economies and ecological systems
- Apply new regulatory instruments or modify existing regulations
- Apply new economic instruments or modify existing ones

Suppliers, Manufacturers, End-of-Life Managers
- Research and develop more sustainable technologies
- Design cleaner products and processes
- Produce sustainable products
- Improve the effectiveness of environmental management systems

Investors and Shareholders
- Support cleaner product system development

Service Industry
- Maintain and repair products

Insurance Industry
- Assess risk and cover losses

A range of internal and external factors influence the product development team's ability to effectively address environmental considerations through design. These factors form the context for the design process.

6.5.1 Internal Elements

Environmental stewardship issues are increasingly addressed within corporations by formal environmental management systems.[7,8] Ideally, the environmental management system is interwoven within the corporate structure and not treated as a separate function.[8]

An integral relationship between a company's design management structure and its environmental management system is essential for implementing life-cycle design. Successful life-cycle design projects require commitment from all employees and all levels of management. A corporation's environmental management system supports environmental improvement through a number of key components including its environmental policy and goals, performance measures, and strategic plan. This system must also provide access to accurate information about environmental impacts. An effective environmental information system is critical to guiding the design process in the direction of environmental improvement. Three main attributes of a well-designed environmental management system are *vision, organization,* and *continuous improvement.*[9] Figure 6.3 summarizes these issues.

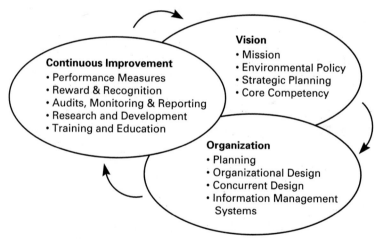

FIGURE 6.3 Internal elements of life-cycle management.

Figure 6.4 depicts the various members of the design team that could participate in product development and graphically shows how the cross-functional team translates the interests and needs of external stakeholders to product system requirements. The product system links these diverse groups.

6.5.2 External Factors

External factors that strongly influence life-cycle design, but may be beyond the firm's immediate control, include government regulations and policy, infrastructure, and mar-

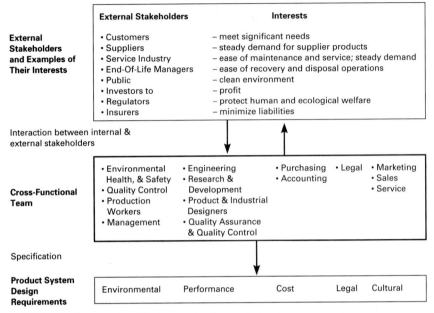

FIGURE 6.4   Cross-functional design team develops product system requirements.

ket demand, which depends on the state of the economy, state of the environment, scientific understanding of environmental risks, and public perception of these risks.

6.6 LIFE-CYCLE DEVELOPMENT PROCESS

The life-cycle development process, which occurs in the context of sustainable development and life-cycle management, is shown in Fig. 6.5. The development process varies widely depending on the type of product and company, the design management organization within a company, and many other factors. In general, however, most development processes begin with a needs analysis and then proceed through formulating requirements, employing various strategies, and performing evaluations of alternative designs. A design solution is then implemented, resulting in various environmental consequences. A simplified diagram of the development process is shown in Fig. 6.5.

During the needs analysis or initiation phase, the purpose and scope of the project are defined, and customer needs are clearly identified. Needs are then expanded into a full set of design criteria including environmental requirements. Various strategies that act as a lens for focusing knowledge and new ideas onto a feasible solution are then explored to meet these requirements. The development team continuously evaluates alternatives throughout the design process. Environmental analysis tools ranging from single environmental metrics to comprehensive life-cycle assessments (LCAs) may be used in addition to other analytical tools.

The development process is best characterized by an iterative process rather than a linear sequence of activities. Ideas, requirements, and solutions are continuously modi-

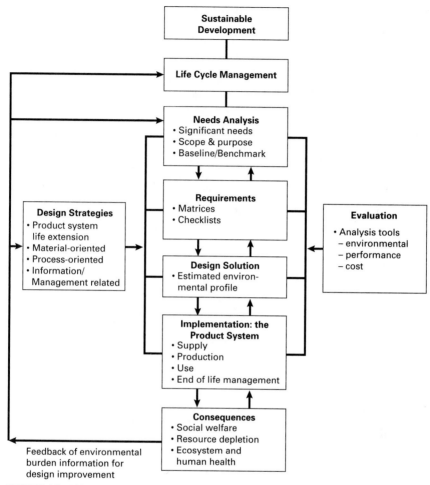

FIGURE 6.5 Life-cycle development process.

fied and refined until the detailed design is fixed or, in some instances, until the project is terminated or abandoned. Successful designs must ultimately balance environmental, performance, cost, cultural, and legal requirements.

Implementation of the design solution requires inputs of material and energy throughout all life-cycle stages and results in outputs of products, coproducts, and waste. Environmental consequences of these inputs and outputs include positive and negative social welfare effects, resource depletion, and ecological and human health effects. The actual environmental burden resulting from design implementation then feeds back into the process to guide future design improvements.

Product development is a dynamic, extremely complex process. Each step from needs analysis through implementation undergoes continuous change. Figure 6.5 shows the iterative nature and feedback mechanisms of the development process which includes multiple sequences of analysis, synthesis, and evaluation.

6.7   NEEDS ANALYSIS AND PROJECT INITIATION

Life-cycle development projects should focus on filling significant customer and societal needs in a sustainable manner. Unless life-cycle principles such as sustainable development shape the needs analysis, design projects may not create cleaner products. LCA can be used to identify cleaner substitutes and alert product managers to begin to phase out products of higher environmental burden.

Defining the system boundaries is necessary for both life-cycle design and LCA. Both begin with a clear definition of the need being addressed by the product system. Whenever possible, it is useful to express this "need" in terms of a functional unit which can serve as a basis for comparison of alternative designs. The basis for analysis should be *equivalent use,* defined as the delivery of equal amounts of product or service. It is useful to define a functional unit of the product whenever possible, but it is often difficult to express performance in a single measure. The functional unit, e.g., volume of beverage delivered (beverage containers), or surface area protected (paint), serves as a basis for comparative analysis of product or design alternatives. Incorporating primary functional attributes into a single parameter can be arbitrary and demonstrates the multigoal nature of design.

6.7.1   Define Project Scope and Purpose

The type of environmental assessment tools and design strategies explored in a design project will depend on the nature of the product system and the timeline and resources available. Conducting a comprehensive LCA of an entire automobile with over 25,000 parts is not feasible at this time, so the scope of initial activities must be limited. For example, life-cycle inventories have been conducted on alternative materials for a single component of the vehicle.

Practitioners of life-cycle design must also decide whether the project will address a current or future design. In addition, the life-cycle framework can be employed in strategic planning or in the conceptual design phase rather than in detailed design.

6.7.2   Set System Boundaries

Determine which stages of the product life cycle the design team will emphasize and what spatial and temporal scales will be used.

In choosing an appropriate system boundary, the development team should initially consider the full life cycle from raw material acquisition to the ultimate fate of residuals. More restricted system boundaries may be justified by the development team. Beginning with the most comprehensive system, design and analysis can focus on the

- Full life cycle
- Partial life cycle
- Individual stages or activities

Choice of the full life-cycle system will provide the greatest opportunities for overall adverse-impact reduction.

In some cases, the development team may confine analysis to a partial life cycle consisting of several stages or even a single stage. Stages can be omitted if they are static or not affected by a new design. As long as designers working on a more limited scale are aware of potential upstream and downstream impacts, environmental goals can still be reached. Even so, a more restricted scope will reduce possibilities for design improvement.

After life-cycle endpoints are chosen, the project team should define how analysis will proceed. Depth of analysis determines how far back indirect inputs and outputs will be traced. Materials, energy, and labor are generally traced in a first-level analysis. A second-level analysis accounts for facilities and equipment needed to produce items on the first level.

Spatial and temporal boundaries must also be determined prior to system evaluation. The time frame or conditions under which data were gathered should be clearly identified. Often performance of industrial systems varies over time; therefore, worst- and best-case scenarios should be used whenever possible. In regard to spatial conditions, the design team must recognize that the same activity may have quite different impacts in different places. For example, consumptive water use in arid regions has a greater resource depletion impact than in areas where water is abundant.

6.7.3 Evaluate Baseline and Benchmark Competitors

Baseline and benchmark activities assist practitioners of life-cycle design in developing environmentally conscious designs of new or existing products and processes. The purpose of evaluating the *baseline* condition of manufacture, use or service, and end-of-life management is to gain an understanding of the environmental profile of an existing product system. Baseline analysis of existing products may indicate opportunities for improving a product system's environmental performance.[10,11] Baseline analysis may consist of a life-cycle inventory analysis, audit team reports, or monitoring and reporting data. *Benchmarking* activities are designed to ascertain information that facilitates comparisons with other products that fulfill similar customer needs. While companies and trade publications have programs to compare product performance and cost against those of their competitors, environmental criteria are generally more difficult to benchmark due to lack of information, insufficient scientific understanding, and limited availability of resources.

6.7.4 Identify Opportunities and Vulnerabilities

The objective of this phase of the life-cycle design development process is to state explicitly the current and future design goals. Current and future design goals must reflect a company's strategic direction including its corporate goals, consumer market, competitive strategy, and image, among other fundamental business criteria. The results of the design team's baseline analysis and benchmarking activities can serve as a basis for developing short- and long-term goal horizons.

Dow Chemical Company has developed a matrix tool for assessing environmental opportunities and vulnerabilities across the major life-cycle stages of the product system. Opportunities and vulnerabilities are assessed for core environmental issues, including safety, human health, residual substances, ozone depletion, air quality, climate change, resource depletion, soil contamination, waste accumulation, and water contamination. Corporate resource commitments may then be changed to more closely match the assessed opportunities and vulnerabilities.

6.8 PRODUCT SYSTEM REQUIREMENTS

Formulating requirements may well be the most critical phase of design.[12] Requirements define the expected outcome and thus are crucial for translating needs and environmental goals to an effective design solution. Design usually proceeds more efficiently when the solution is clearly bounded by well-considered requirements. In later phases of design, alternatives are evaluated on how well they meet requirements.

Incorporating environmental requirements into the earliest stage of design can reduce the need for later corrective action. Pollution control, liability, and remedial action costs can be greatly reduced by developing environmental requirements that address the full life cycle at the outset of a project. Life-cycle design also seeks to integrate environmental requirements with traditional performance, cost, cultural, and legal requirements. All requirements must be properly balanced in a successful product. An environmentally preferable product that fails in the marketplace benefits no one.

Regardless of the project's nature, the expected design outcome should not be overly restrictive, nor should it be too broad. Requirements defined too narrowly eliminate potentially attractive designs from the solution space. But vague requirements (such as those arising from corporate environmental policies that are too broad to provide specific guidance) lead to misunderstandings between potential customers and designers while making the search process inefficient.

The majority (approximately 70 percent) of product system costs are fixed in the design stage. Activities through the requirements phase typically account for 10 to 15 percent of total product development costs, yet decisions made at this point can determine 50 to 70 percent of costs for the entire project.[13,14]

Requirements matrices, design checklists, and other methods are available to assist the design team in establishing requirements. Requirements can also be established by formal procedures such as the "house of quality" approach.

6.8.1 Design Checklists

Checklists are usually a series of questions formulated to help designers be systematic and thorough when addressing design topics. Environmental design checklists that accommodate quantitative, qualitative, and inferential information in different design stages have been offered for consideration. As an example, AT&T developed proprietary checklists for DFE that are similar to the familiar *design for manufacturability* (DFM) checklists. In the AT&T model, a toxic substance inventory checklist is used to identify whether a product contains a select group of toxic metals.

The Canadian Standards Association is currently developing a DFE standard which includes checklists of critical environmental core principles. A series of yes/no questions are being proposed for each major life-cycle stage (raw materials acquisition, manufacturing, use, and waste management).

Checklists are not difficult to use, but they must be compiled carefully so that they do not place excessive demands on designers' time. Generic checklists can also interfere with creativity if designers rely on them exclusively to address environmental issues, thereby failing to focus on the issues most important to the specific project.

6.8.2 Requirements Matrices

Matrices allow product development teams to study the interactions between life-cycle requirements. Figure 6.6 shows a multilayer matrix for developing requirements. The

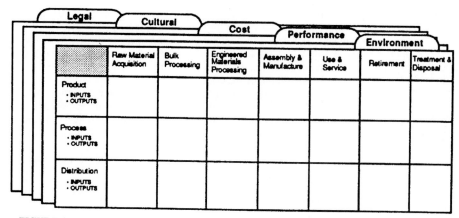

FIGURE 6.6 Conceptual multilayer matrix for developing requirements.

matrix for each type of requirement contains columns that represent life-cycle stages. Rows are formed by the product system components described under "Performance Requirements"—product, process, and distribution. Each row can be subdivided into inputs and outputs. Elements can then be described and tracked in as much detail as necessary. Table 6.3 shows how each row in the environmental matrix can be expanded to provide more details for developing requirements.

TABLE 6.3 Example of Subdivided Rows for Environmental Requirements Matrix

	Product	Process	Distribution
Inputs			
Materials	• Content of final product	• Direct: process materials • Indirect: First level (equipment and facilities, office supplies) Second level (capital and resources to produce first level)	• Packaging • Transportation Direct (e.g., oil and brake fluid) Indirect (e.g., vehicles and garages) • Office supplies • Equipment and facilities
Energy	• Embodied energy	• Process energy (direct and indirect)	• Embodied in packaging • Consumed by transportation [Btu/(ton•mi)] • Consumed as power for administrative services, etc.
Human resources		• Labor (workers, managers) • Users, consumers	• Labor (workers, managers)
Outputs	• Products • Coproducts • Residuals	• Residuals • Generated energy	• Residuals

The requirements matrices in Fig. 6.6 are strictly conceptual. Practical matrices can be formed for each class of requirements by further subdividing the rows and columns of the conceptual matrix. For example, the manufacturing stage could be subdivided into suppliers and the original equipment manufacturer. The distribution component of this stage might also include receiving, shipping, and wholesale activities. Retail sale of the final product might best fit in the distribution component of the use phase.

There are no absolute rules for organizing matrices. Information may be classified according to quantitative/qualitative, present/future, and must/want requirements. Development teams should choose a format that is appropriate for their project. The section entitled "AT&T Life-Cycle Design Project" describes the application of requirements matrices for a business telephone.

Following is a discussion of the environmental, performance, cost, legal, and cultural requirements that constitute the matrices.

Environmental Requirements.   Environmental requirements should be developed to minimize:

- The use of natural resources (particularly nonrenewables)
- Energy consumption
- Waste generation
- Health and safety risks
- Ecological degradation

By translating these goals to clear functions, environmental requirements help identify and constrain environmental impacts and health risks.

Table 6.4 lists issues that can help development teams define environmental requirements. This book cannot provide detailed guidance on environmental requirements for each business or industry. Although the lists in Table 6.4 are not complete, they introduce many important topics. Depending on the project, teams may express these requirements quantitatively or qualitatively. For example, it might be useful to state a requirement that limits solid waste generation for the entire product life cycle to a specific weight.

In addition to criteria uncovered through needs analysis or benchmarking, government policies can be used to set requirements. For example, the Integrated Solid Waste Management Plan developed by the EPA in 1989 targeted municipal solid waste disposal for a 25 percent reduction by 1995.[6] Other initiatives, such as the EPA's 33/50 program, are aimed at reducing toxic emissions. It may benefit companies to develop requirements that match the goals of these voluntary programs.

It may also be wise to set environmental requirements that exceed current government regulations. These requirements may have been identified during the investigation of opportunities and vulnerabilities early on in the needs analysis and project initiation phase of the design project. At this stage in the design process, goals are translated to specific requirements. Designs based on such proactive requirements offer many benefits. Major modifications dictated by regulation can be costly and time-consuming. In addition, such changes may not be consistent with a firm's own development cycles, creating even more problems that could have been avoided.

Performance Requirements.   Performance requirements define the functions of the product system. Functional requirements range from size tolerances of parts to time-and-motion specifications for equipment. Typical performance requirements for an automobile include fuel economy, maximum driving range, acceleration and braking capabilities, handling characteristics, passenger and storage capacity, and ability to pro-

TABLE 6.4 Issues to Consider in the Development of Environmental Requirements

Materials and energy			
Type	Character	Resource base	Impact caused by extraction and use
Renewable Nonrenewable	Virgin Reused and recycled Reusable and recyclable	Location—local vs. other Scarcity Quality Management and restoration practices	Material and energy use Residuals Ecosystem health Human health
Residuals			
Type	Characterization	Environmental fate	Treatment and disposal impact
Solid waste Air emissions Waterborne	Nonhazardous—constituents, amount Hazardous, radioactive—constituents, amount, concentration, toxicity	Containment Bioaccumulation Degradability Mobility and transport	
Ecological health			
Ecosystem stressors	Impact categories	Impacts	Scale
Physical Biological Chemical	Diversity Sustainability, resilience to stressors	System structure and function Sensitive species	Local Regional Global
Human health and safety			
Population at risk	Exposure routes	Toxic character	Accidents
Workers Users Community	Inhalation, skin contact, ingestion Duration and frequency	Acute effects Chronic effects Morbidity and mortality	Type and frequency Nuisance effects Noise and odors

tect passengers in a collision. Environmental requirements are closely linked to and often constrained by performance requirements.

Performance is limited by technical factors. Practical performance limits are usually defined by *best-available technology* or *best-affordable technology*. Absolute limits to performance are determined by thermodynamics or the laws of nature. Noting the technical limits on product system performance provides designers with a frame of reference for comparison.

Other limits on performance must also be considered. In many cases, process design is constrained by existing facilities and equipment. This partial constraint affects many aspects of process performance. It can also limit product performance by restricting the range of possible materials and features. In such cases, the success of a major design project may depend on upgrading or investing in new technology.

Designers should be aware that customer behavior and social trends affect real and perceived product performance. Innovative technology might increase performance and reduce impacts, but possible gains can be erased by increased consumption. For example, automobile manufacturers doubled average fleet fuel economy over the last 20 years, yet U.S. gasoline consumption remains nearly the same because more vehicles are being driven more miles.

Although better performance may not always result in environmental gain, poor performance usually produces more impacts. Inadequate products are retired quickly in favor of more capable ones. Development programs that fail to produce products with superior performance can therefore contribute to excess waste generation and resource use.

PERFORMANCE REQUIREMENTS LIMITING ENVIRONMENTAL IMPROVEMENTS

- Thermodynamic limits (e.g., first and second laws of thermodynamics)
- Best-available technology
- Best-affordable technology

Cost Requirements.   Meeting all performance and environmental requirements does not ensure project success. Regardless of how environmentally responsible a product may be, many customers will choose another if it cannot be offered at a competitive price. In some cases, a premium can be charged for significantly superior environmental or functional performance, but such premiums are usually limited.

Modified accounting systems that better reflect environmental costs and benefits are important to life-cycle design. With more complete accounting, many low-impact designs may show financial advantages. Methods of life-cycle accounting that can help companies make better decisions in developing requirements are discussed later in this section.

Cost requirements should guide designers in adding value to the product system. These requirements can be most useful when they include a time frame (such as total user costs from purchase until final retirement) and clearly stated life-cycle boundaries. Parties who will accrue these costs, such as suppliers, manufacturers, and customers, should also be identified.

Cost requirements need to reflect market possibilities. Value can be conveyed to customers through estimates of a product's total cost over its expected useful life. Total customer costs include purchase price, consumables, service, and retirement costs. By providing an estimate of costs for the entire product life, quality products may be judged on more than least first cost, which addresses only the initial purchase price or financing charges. Table 6.5 lists some cost requirements over the product life cycle.

Cultural Requirements.   Cultural requirements define the shape, form, color, texture, and image that a product projects. Material selection, product finish, colors, and size are guided by consumer preferences. In order to be successful, a product must meet customer cultural requirements.

Decisions concerning physical attributes and style have direct environmental consequences. However, because customers usually do not know about the full environmental consequences of their preferences, to create pleasing, environmentally superior products is a major design challenge. Successful cultural requirements enable the design itself to promote an awareness of how it reduces impacts.

Cultural requirements may overlap with other types of requirements. Convenience is usually considered part of performance, but it is strongly influenced by culture. In some cultures, convenience is elevated above many other functions. Cultural factors therefore

TABLE 6.5 Example of General Cost Requirements over Product Life Cycle

	Stakeholders	
	Manufacturers	Consumers

Raw materials and supplies
Manufacturing
	• Minimize unit cost of materials or parts
	• Minimize unit cost of production
	   Waste management costs
	   Cost of packaging
	• Administrative	

Use	• Product and environmental liability	• Purchase price
		• Operating cost
		   Energy
		   Maintenance
		   Repair

Service	• Minimize warranty costs	
End-of-life management	• Environmental liabilities	• Disposal cost

may determine whether demand for perceived convenience and environmental requirements conflict.

Legal Requirements. Local, state, and federal environmental, health, and safety regulations are mandatory requirements. Violation of these requirements leads to fines, revoked permits, criminal prosecution, and other penalties. Both companies and individuals within a firm can be held responsible for violating statutes. Firms may also be liable for punitive damages.

Paying attention to legal requirements is clearly an important part of design requirements. Environmental professionals, health and safety staff, legal advisers, and government regulators can identify legal issues for life-cycle design. Local, state, federal, and international regulations that apply to the product system provide a framework for legal requirements.

Federal regulations are administered and enforced by agencies such as the Environmental Protection Agency (EPA), Food and Drug Administration (FDA), and the Consumer Product Safety Commission (CPSC). In addition to such federal authorities, many other political jurisdictions enforce environmental regulations. For example, some cities have imposed bans on certain materials and products. Regulations also vary dramatically among countries. The take-back legislation in Germany is beginning to draw more attention to end-of-life issues in product design.

Whenever possible, legal requirements should take into consideration the implications of pending and proposed regulations that are likely to be enacted. Such forward thinking can prevent costly problems during manufacture or use while providing a competitive advantage.

LEGAL AND QUASI-LEGAL REQUIREMENTS

- International regulations
- National regulations (U.S.)
- State
- Local (municipalities)
- Voluntary standards

Assigning Requirements Priority. Ranking and weighting design requirements help to distinguish between critical and merely desirable requirements. After requirements are assigned a weighted value, they should be ranked and separated into several groups. An example of a useful classification scheme (after Ref. 12) follows:

* *Must requirements* are conditions that designs have to meet. No design is acceptable unless it satisfies all these must requirements.

* *Want requirements* are less important, but are still desirable traits. Want requirements help designers seek the best solution, not just the first alternative that satisfies mandatory conditions. These criteria play a critical role in customer acceptance and perceptions of quality.

* *Ancillary functions* are low-ranked in terms of relative importance. They are relegated to a wish list. Designers should be aware that such desires exist, but ancillary functions can be expressed in design only when they do not compromise more critical functions. Customers or clients should not expect designs to reflect many ancillary requirements.

Once the must requirements are set, want and ancillary requirements can be assigned priority. There are no simple rules for weighting requirements. Assigning priority to requirements is always a difficult task, because different classes of requirements are stated and measured in different units. Judgments based on the values and experience of the design team must be used to arrive at priorities.

The process of making tradeoffs between types of requirements is familiar to every designer. Asking, How important is this function to the design? or What is this function worth (to society, customers, suppliers, etc.)? is a necessary exercise in every successful development project.

Organizing Requirements. Various approaches can be taken to organize requirements. The must versus want distinction can be a useful guide. Table 6.6 provides some additional methods for organizing the requirements in each component of the matrix.

Resolving Conflicts. Development teams can expect conflicts between requirements. If conflicts between must requirements cannot be resolved, there is no solution space for design. When a solution space exists but is so restricted that little choice is possible, the must requirements may have been defined too narrowly. The absence of conflicts usually indicates that requirements are defined too loosely. This produces cavernous solution spaces in which virtually any alternative seems desirable. Under such conditions, there is no practical method of choosing the best design.

In all these cases, design teams need to redefine or assign new priorities to requirements. If careful study still reveals no solution space or a very restricted one, the pro-

TABLE 6.6 Organizing Frames for Requirements

Must	Compliance with existing environmental laws
Want	Beyond compliance
Qualitative	Reduce the use of toxic constituents
Quantitative	Specify a 25 percent reduction in use of lead
Present	Current regulations
Future	Future regulations (promulgated phaseout of CFC or take-back legislation)
General criteria	Component recyclable
Environmental metric	Energy efficiency and energy used per unit of operation

ject should be abandoned. It is also risky to proceed with overly broad requirements. Only projects with practical, well-considered requirements should be pursued. Successful requirements usually ensue from resolving conflicts and developing new priorities that more accurately reflect customer needs.

AT&T Life-Cycle Design Project. The matrix method of formulating requirements was recently applied to designing a business telephone in a demonstration project conducted between the authors and AT&T.[15] Radical departures from previous designs were not deemed feasible for this next-generation product. Given this and other constraints, the project concentrated on a partial, consolidated life cycle consisting of manufacturing, use, and end-of-life management stages. Examples of some environmental and legal must and want design requirements formulated by the project team are listed in Tables 6.7 and 6.8. These matrices resulted from seven "green product realization" team meetings attended by representatives from product line management, marketing, research design, product engineering, and environmental health and safety engineering. Tables 6.7 and 6.8 contain some examples of the critical requirements relevant to this particular design and certain considerations for the future.

The environmental requirements in Table 6.7 contain both elements defined in terms of results and elements specifying how a desired result is to be achieved. Results-oriented requirements address quantitative corporate goals for reducing CFC emissions, toxic air emissions, process wastes, and paper consumption as well as increasing the use of recycled paper. Other requirements specify mechanisms to facilitate parts and components reuse and material recycling, especially of plastic housings.

Local, state, federal, and international regulations and standards provide a framework for the legal requirements outlined in Table 6.8. Legal requirements relevant to this design range from EPA regulations, FTC guidelines, and Germany's packaging ordinance to International Standards Organization (ISO) marking codes for plastics and Underwriters Laboratories (UL) requirements. Such diversity in legal requirements for widely sold products can be a barrier to realizing environmental improvements.

As an example of the conflicts that arise between requirements, one environmental want requirement for this project states that recycled materials must be used for new products. However, a legal *must* requirement calls for housings of telephone equipment to comply with UL specification UL 746, Standard for Polymeric Materials—Fabricated Parts. Recycled resins that meet the material testing and certification procedures required for this standard are not now available, from either internal recycling programs or commercial vendors. Even if this conflict did not exist, use of recycled materials for housings might still be impeded by other types of want requirements. To be marketable, a desktop product must also comply with perceived cultural requirements for flawless surface quality and perfectly matched colors. These attributes may not be possible to achieve with recycled materials because they have experienced additional heat cycles and typically contain at least trace amounts of contaminants.

6.9 DESIGN STRATEGIES AND SOLUTION

6.9.1 Design Strategies

Selecting and synthesizing design strategies for meeting the full spectrum of requirements are a major challenge of life-cycle design. Presented by themselves, strategies may seem to define the goals of a design project. Although it may be tempting to pursue an intriguing strategy for reducing environmental impacts at the outset of a project, deciding on a course of action before the destination is known can be an invitation to disaster. Strategies flow from requirements, not the reverse.

TABLE 6.7 Environmental Requirements for Business Phone[3]

Product		
Manufacture	Use or service	End-of-life management
Materials should be recyclable on-site Engineering plastics production can reuse scrap Use recyclable materials Choose ozone depleting substance (ODS)-free components Eliminate the use of toxic materials (e.g., lead) Minimize defective products		Reuse parts Standardize parts to facilitate remanufacture Product components recyclable (after consumer use) Open-loop recycling into fiber cables, spools, and reels Easy to disassemble: no rivets, glues, ultrasonic welding, and minimal use of composites Components easy to sort by marking and minimal use of materials
Process		
Minimize process wastes including air emissions, liquid effluents, and hazardous and nonhazardous solid wastes Minimize resource consumption Minimize power consumption Meet corporate environmental goals (list five goals) Use greener R&D processes: engineering research center (ERC) developing environmental technology Design guidelines, checklists, other DFE initiatives Green index Purchasing records to monitor ODS Suppliers encouraged to discontinue use of ODS in parts manufacturing	Energy-efficient operation (operates on line power only)	Service or reconditioning operations should minimize use of solvents
Distribution		
Minimize supplier packaging Nonhazardous Packaging containing recycled material (postconsumer content specified) Reusable trays for parts in factory	Minimize product packaging Use electronic packaging guidelines Nonhazardous Optimize number of phones per package Specify packaging containing recycled material (postconsumer content specified) Use recycled paper for manual (list environmental features)	Recyclable packaging

TABLE 6.8 Legal Requirements for Business Phone[3]

Product		
Manufacture	Use or service	End-of-life management
U.S. regulations and product safety standards	Underwriter Laboratories UL 1459-product safety	Product should meet applicable statutory requirements
Clean Air Act Amendments: CFC labeling requirement (Apr. 15, 1993)	UL 94-flammability test (must meet UL94-HB at minimum)	Product should not contain hazardous materials under RCRA
Underwriter Laboratories UL 746D fabricated parts: use of regrind and recycled materials	FCC requirements Limits on polybrominated fire retardants (EC)	Pigments and other plastic additives should not contain heavy metals
Green Seal	Canadian Safety Specifications CSA C22.2	Electronic Waste Ordinance (Germany, Jan. 1, 1994) and Packaging Ordinance
Foreign regulations and product safety standards	European Safety Specifications	UL flammability test: approval of recycled resins difficult
Blue Angel and other relevant standards	EN 60 950 (IEC950; safety, network capability, EMC, susceptibility)	Previous flame retardant banned in Europe which prohibits recycling of old terminals
	EN 41003	
	EN 71 (lead pigments and stabilizers in plastic parts)	
Process		
Clean Air Act	FTC guidelines: definitions for labeling	Easy to disassemble
Clean Water Act		Sherman Anti-Trust Act responsible for developing market for remanufactured phones
CERCLA (SARA-313)		
RCRA		Recycled content
EPCRA		ISO marking codes for plastics
OSHA		
ISO marking codes for plastics		
Distribution		
DOT (transportation of hazardous materials)		Specific claims on packaging Green Dot program

General strategies for fulfilling environmental requirements are shown in Table 6.9. An explanation of each strategy is given in the *Life Cycle Design Guidance Manual* published by the EPA. Most of these strategies reach across product system boundaries; life extension, e.g., can be applied to various elements in all three product system components.

In most cases, a single strategy will not be best for meeting all environmental requirements. Recycling illustrates this point. Many designers, policymakers, and consumers believe recycling is the best solution for a wide range of environmental problems. Even though recycling can conserve virgin materials and divert discarded material from landfills, it also causes other impacts and thus may not always be the best way to minimize waste and conserve resources.

Single strategies are unlikely to improve environmental performance in all life-cycle stages; they are even less likely to satisfy the full set of cost, legal, performance, and cultural requirements. In most cases, successful development teams adopt a range of strategies to meet design requirements. As an example, design responses to an initiative such as extended producer responsibility[16,17] are likely to include waste reduction, reuse, recycling, and aspects of product life extension.

TABLE 6.9 Summary of Design Strategies

General categories	Specific strategies
Product life extension	• Extend useful life • Increase durability • Ensure adaptability • Increase reliability • Expand service options • Simplify maintenance • Facilitate repairability • Enable remanufacture of products • Accommodate reuse of product
Material life extension	• Develop recycling infrastructure • Examine recycling pathways • Use recyclable materials
Material selection	• Use substitute materials • Devise reformulations
Reduced material intensiveness	• Conserve resources
Process management	• Substitute better processes • Increase process energy efficiency • Increase process material efficiency • Improve process control • Improve process layout • Control inventory and material handling • Plan facilities to reduce impacts • Ensure proper treatment and disposal
Efficient distribution	• Optimize transportation systems • Reduce packaging • Use alternative packaging materials
Improved management practices	• Use office materials and equipment efficiently • Phase out high-impact products • Choose environmentally responsible suppliers or contractors • Encourage ecolabeling and advertise environmental claims

Appropriate strategies need to satisfy the entire set of design requirements, as shown in Fig. 6.6, thus promoting integration of environmental requirements into design. For example, essential product performance must be preserved when design teams choose a strategy for reducing environmental impacts. If performance is so degraded that the product fails in the marketplace, then the benefits of environmentally responsible design are only illusory.

AT&T Life-Cycle Design Project.   The AT&T life-cycle design demonstration project also offers a practical example of applying several environmental strategies to satisfy requirements. Only a few strategies pertaining to a single product component, the housing, will be discussed here. Environmental requirements for the manufacturing stage state that material for the housing must be recycled and recyclable, with toxics eliminated and waste reduced. End-of-life requirements state that the housing must be reusable or at least recyclable.

Material recyclability and toxics reduction during manufacturing were achieved by using a thermoplastic resin with good recyclability (ABS, or acrylonitrile butadiene styrene) that contained no stabilizers or colors formulated with heavy metals. The chosen resin also does not rely on polybrominated fire retardants, which are the subject of proposed bans in Europe. Manufacturing scrap was reduced by specifying a textured housing. A textured surface for external plastic parts, such as the housing, hides minor molding flaws better than a high-gloss, smooth surface, thus increasing molding yield and reducing waste from this process.

Other features were intended to ensure that at end of life, the housing can be turned into an uncontaminated and readily recyclable or reusable material by means of low-cost automatic processes. The design accomplished this by avoiding glue joints and incorporation of foreign material such as metal inserts, paints, and stick-on labels which cannot be practically separated from the base polymer.

In addition, AT&T has a network of reclamation and service centers which receives both leased telephones and trade-ins for new purchases. Depending on their condition, either the phones are refurbished and sold or leased again, or they are scrapped and recycled. Because the centers can return still-serviceable phones to another tour of duty as well as properly recycle those beyond repair, the company controls aspects of product and material life extension. Designs focusing on these strategies thus benefit the company and are easier to implement.

6.9.2 Design Solution

Needs analysis and requirements specification provide the ideas, objectives, and criteria that eventually define the design *solution space,* which then shapes the development process from the conceptual design phase through detailed design. The solution space is the intersection of all potential design solutions that meet each of the criteria specified, including environmental, performance, cost, legal, and cultural criteria. Figure 6.7 illustrates this point graphically. The space in the diagram where all criteria overlap is the solution space. Strategies for satisfying design criteria are implemented after the solution space is known. At this point in development, designers select and synthesize strategies, keeping in mind concerns outlined in Table 6.9, that fulfill multicriteria design requirements.

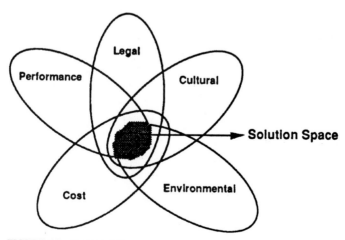

FIGURE 6.7 Design solution space.

TABLE 6.10   Difficulties and Limitations of the Current LCA Methodology[4]

Goal definition and scoping	Costs to conduct an LCA may be prohibitive to small firms; time required to conduct LCA may exceed product development constraints especially for short development cycles; temporal and spatial dimensions of a dynamic product system are difficult to address; definition of functional units for comparison of design alternatives can be problematic; allocation methods used in defining system boundaries have inherent weaknesses; complex products (e.g., automobiles) require tremendous resources to analyze.
Data collection	Data availability and access can be limiting (e.g., proprietary data); data quality including bias, accuracy, precision, and completeness is often not well addressed.
Data evaluation	Sophisticated models and model parameters for evaluating resource depletion and human and ecosystem health may not be available, or their ability to represent the product system may be grossly inaccurate. Uncertainty analyses of the results are often not conducted.
Information transfer	Design decision makers often lack knowledge about environmental effects, and aggregation and simplification techniques may distort results. Synthesis of environmental effect categories is limited because they are incommensurable.

6.10   DESIGN EVALUATION

Analysis and evaluation are required throughout the product development process. If environmental requirements for the product system are well specified, design alternatives can be checked directly against these requirements. Tools for design evaluation range from comprehensive analysis tools such as life-cycle assessment (LCA) to the use of single environmental metrics. In each case, design solutions are evaluated with respect to the full spectrum of requirements.

DESIGN EVALUATION

Life-cycle assessment
  EPA/SETAC framework (inventory analysis, impact and improvement assessment)
  DFEIS matrix (Allenby)
  Dow matrix
  EPS system (Federation of Swedish Industries)

General environmental metrics
  Resource productivity index (Sony)
  Waste per unit product

Specific metrics
  Energy consumed in use stage per unit product
  Percentage recycled; weight of recyclable components or weight of product

Cost assessment
  Life-cycle costing
  Environmental accounting

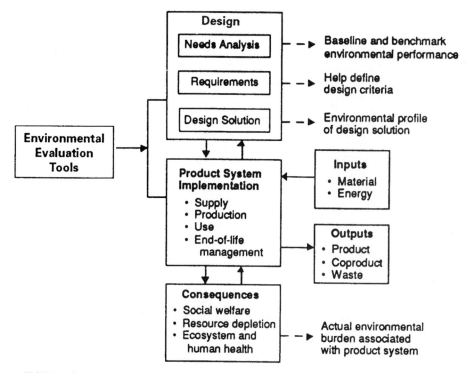

FIGURE 6.8   Environmental evaluation in the development process.

Figure 6.8 shows different applications of environmental evaluation tools through-out the development process. Note that the actual environmental burden associated with a product system may differ from the environmental profile estimated during design. Such variation is likely in a dynamic system.

6.10.1   LCA and Its Application to Design

LCA consists of several techniques for identifying and evaluating the adverse environ-mental effects associated with a product system.[18–23] The most widely recognized framework for LCA consists of inventory analysis, impact assessment, and improve-ment assessment components. At present, inventory analysis is the most established methodology of LCA.

LCA and more streamlined approaches can potentially be applied in needs analysis, requirements specification, and evaluation of conceptual through detailed design phases. Although numerous life-cycle inventories have been conducted for a variety of products,[24] only a small fraction have been used for product development. Procter & Gamble is one company that has used life-cycle inventory studies to guide environ-mental improvement for several products.[25] One of its case studies on hard surface cleaners revealed that heating water resulted in a significant percentage of total energy use and air emissions related to cleaning.[26] Based on this information, opportunities for reducing impacts were identified which include designing cold water and no-rinse for-mulas or educating consumers to use cold water.

The *Product Ecology Report* is another example where life-cycle inventory and a valuation procedure are used to support product development.[27] For this project, the environmental priority strategies in product design (the EPS system) evaluate the environmental impact of design alternatives with a single metric based on environmental load units. An inventory is conducted using the LCA inventory tool developed by Chalmers Industriteknik, and valuation is based on a willingness-to-pay model, which accounts for biodiversity, human health, production, resources, and aesthetic values. This system enables the designer to easily compare alternatives, but the reliability of the outcome will be heavily dependent on the valuation procedure.

Several LCA software tools and computerized databases may make it easier to apply LCA in design. Examples of early attempts in this area include SimaPro, developed by the Centre of Environmental Science (CML), Leiden University, Netherlands; LCA inventory tool, developed by Chalmers Industriteknik in Göteborg, Sweden; and PIA, developed by the Institute for Applied Environmental Economics (TME) in the Hague, Netherlands [available from the Dutch Ministry for Environment and Informatics (BMI)]. These tools can shorten analysis time when one is exploring design alternatives, particularly in simulation studies, but data availability and quality are still limiting. In addition to these tools, a general guide to LCA for European businesses has been compiled which provides background and a list of sources for further information.[28]

Difficulties.   General difficulties and limitations of the LCA methodology are summarized in Table 6.10. In principle, LCA represents the most accurate tool for design evaluation in life-cycle design and DFE. Many methodological problems, however, currently plague LCA, thus limiting its applicability to design.[4] Costs to conduct an LCA can be prohibitive, especially to small firms, and time requirements may not be compatible with short development cycles.[29,30] Although significant progress has been made toward standardizing life-cycle inventory analysis,[18–22] results can still vary significantly.[31,24] Such discrepancies can be attributed to differences in system boundaries, rules for allocation of inputs and outputs between product systems, and data availability and quality issues. LCA also generally lacks uncertainty analysis of results.

Incommensurable data present another major challenge to LCA and other environmental analysis tools. The problem of evaluating environmental data remains inherently complicated when impacts are expressed in different measuring units (e.g., kilojoules, cancer risks, or kilograms of solid waste). Furthermore, different conversion models for translating inventory items to impacts are required for each impact. These models vary widely in complexity and uncertainty. For example, risk assessment and fate and transport models are required to evaluate human and ecosystem health effects associated with toxic emissions. Model sophistication dictates whether additional data beyond inventory results are needed for proper evaluation. Simplified approaches for impact assessment, such as the *critical-volume or -mass method*[23] have fundamental limitations. These general models are usually much less accurate than more elaborate, site-specific assessment models, but full assessment based on site-specific models is not presently feasible.

Other simple conversion models, such as those translating emissions of various gases to a single number estimating global warming potential or ozone-depleting potential, are available for assessing global impacts.[32,33]

Even if much better assessment tools existed, LCA has inherent limitations in design, because the complete set of life-cycle environmental effects associated with a product system can be evaluated only after the design has been specified in detail. But at this stage, the opportunities for design change become drastically limited. This condition is represented graphically in Fig. 6.9. In the conceptual design phase, the design solution space is wide, whereas in detailed design, the solution space narrows. Thus the feasibility of a comprehensive LCA is inversely related to the opportunity to influence

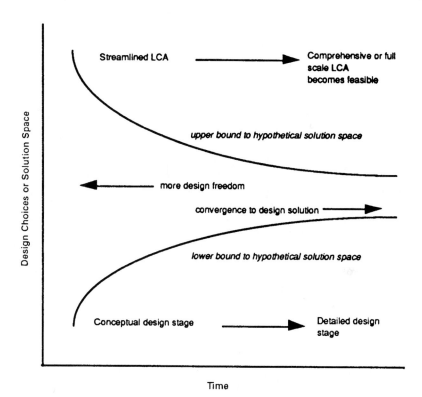

FIGURE 6.9 Design solution space as a function of time.[4]

product system design. In addition to these limitations, many of the secondary and tertiary inventory items of a life-cycle system that are often neglected in an LCA, such as facilities and equipment, are significant forces that greatly affect product development.

6.10.2 Other Design Evaluation Approaches

Environmental Indicators or Metrics. In contrast to a comprehensive life-cycle assessment, environmental performance parameters or metrics can be used to evaluate design alternatives. Navin-Chandra[34] introduced the following set of environmental indicators: percentage recycled, degradability, life, junk value, separability, life-cycle cost, potential recyclability, possible recyclability, useful life and utilization, total and net emissions, and total hazardous fugitives. Many of these indicators can be calculated relatively easily; the last two, however, require life-cycle inventory data to compute.

Watanabe[35] proposes a *resource productivity* measure for evaluating "industrial performance compatible with environmental preservation." The resource productivity is defined as:

$$\frac{\text{(Economic value added)} \times \text{(product lifetime)}}{\text{(Material consumed} - \text{recycled)} + \text{(energy consumed for production, recycling)} + \text{(lifetime energy used)}}$$

where the individual terms in the denominator are expressed in monetary units. Longer product life, higher material recycle, and lower material and energy consumption all contribute to a higher resource productivity. Watanabe has applied this metric in evaluating three rechargeable-battery alternatives. While resource productivity incorporates many environmental concerns, it is not comprehensive because costs associated with toxic emissions and human and ecosystem health are ignored. In addition, the *value-added* component of the numerator includes other factors besides environmental considerations. Despite these limitations, this metric is relatively simple to evaluate and accounts for resource depletion, which correlates with many other environmental impacts.

Matrix Approaches.   DFE methods developed by Allenby[5,36] use a semiquantitative matrix approach for evaluating life-cycle environmental impacts. A graphic scoring system weighs environmental effects based on available quantitative information for each life-cycle stage. In addition to an environmental matrix and toxicology/exposure matrix, manufacturing and social/political matrices are used to address both technical and nontechnical aspects of design alternatives.

Dow Chemical Company has also developed a matrix tool for assessing environmental issues across major life-cycle stages of the product system. Opportunities and vulnerabilities are assessed for core environmental issues, including safety, human health, residual substances, ozone depletion, air quality, climate change, resource depletion, soil contamination, waste accumulation, and water contamination. Corporate resource commitments may then be changed to more closely match the assessed opportunities and vulnerabilities.

Computer Tools.   ReStar is a design analysis tool for evaluating recovery operations such as recycling and disassembly.[37] A computer algorithm determines an optimal recovery plan based on tradeoffs between recovery costs and the value of secondary materials or parts.

6.11   SUMMARY

Numerous companies are beginning to apply life-cycle design principles and tools. Table 6.11 highlights several examples where life-cycle design and related tools have been implemented by industry. As this chapter has demonstrated, many difficulties still must be confronted before life-cycle design tools can be more fully incorporated into product development programs. All major stakeholders, including industry, the public, and government, have a role in designing, manufacturing, and using products which are more sustainable. The following life-cycle design principles are presented to aid these stakeholders in guiding environmental improvement of product systems.

6.11.1   Life-Cycle Design Principles

Use a Systems Approach.   A systems approach is essential to achieving sustainable development goals. The life-cycle system is the basis for a comprehensive framework for addressing environmental issues in design. Life-cycle design focuses on the product systems level in an industrial systems hierarchy. However, understanding the contribution of product systems to higher-order levels (i.e., global flows of materials and energy, economic sectors, corporations) as well as the influence of individual subsystems (specific

TABLE 6.11 Examples of Life-Cycle Design

Company	Project or Program	Activity
Xerox	Asset Recycle Management	This program has been successfully implemented for the design and manufacture of xerographic equipment. A hierarchy of strategies has been developed to optimize resource use including equipment and parts remanufacturing, repair and reuse, and materials recycling.
Dow	Life-cycle inventory	Conducted a life-cycle inventory of poultry packaging alternatives.
AT&T	Life-cycle design	Developed environmental, performance, cost, legal, and cultural requirements for a business telephone terminal. The multicriteria matrix was used to specify requirements for manufacturing, use, and end-of-life management. Various design strategies were implemented to reduce environmental burden.[15]
AlliedSignal	Life-cycle design	Developed environmental, performance, cost, legal, and cultural requirements for an engine oil filter design. A comparative analysis of cartridge and spin-on filter designs was conducted including a life-cycle cost analysis for the customer.
Volvo	EPS	Environmental priorities strategies (EPS) system uses a single metric (environmental load units) to evaluate environmental impacts. It is based on a willingness-to-pay model which accounts for biodiversity, human health, production, resources, and aesthetic values. Comparative assessments were made of alternative materials for the design of a hood and a front-end construction.
Digital	Pre-LCA	Digital applied a "pre-LCA" method to the evaluation of videodisplay shipping packaging. The pre-LCA tool consisted of a set of criteria and a numerical scoring system for evaluating environmental impacts for each criterion ranging from 1 to 9. The idea of this approach was to develop a tool for nonexperts.
Ford	Life-cycle design	Performed a comparative analysis of alternative designs, (two aluminum and a nylon composite) for an air intake manifold.[39]
Procter & Gamble	Life-cycle inventory and improvement analysis	Conducted several life-cycle inventories of various cleaners and detergents. Opportunities for design improvement were identified in several cases.
GM	Streamlined LCA	Participating in a streamlined LCA of autobody painting. This project is coordinated by the President's Council on Sustainable Development.
United Solar	Life-cycle design	Conducted a life-cycle energy analysis of an amorphous silicon photovoltaic module and studied alternative design parameters.

life-cycle stages, unit operations) is crucial to effective life-cycle design. Successfully reducing net environmental impacts from product systems while still meeting societal needs requires an awareness of the complex interactions among different hierarchical levels and between the various organizational categories (e.g., economic, ecological, and sociological structures).

Take Action Early.   Addressing environmental issues in the earliest stages of design is one of the most efficient ways to reduce environmental burdens.

Manage Internal and External Factors.   Both internal and external factors strongly influence design. Within a company, an environmental management system that includes goals and performance measures provides the organizational structure for implementing life-cycle design. Access to accurate information about environmental impacts is also critical in achieving environmental improvement. External factors that shape design include government regulations, market forces, infrastructure, the state of the environment, and scientific understanding of human and ecological health risks and public perception of these risks.

Implement Concurrent Design.   Concurrent design, a procedure based on simultaneous design of product features and manufacturing processes, includes product, process, and distribution components of the product system. Interdisciplinary participation is key to defining requirements that reflect the needs of multiple stakeholders such as suppliers, manufacturers, consumers, resource recovery and waste managers, the public, and regulators.

Specify Environmental Requirements.   Specification of requirements is one of the most critical design functions. Requirements guide designers in translating needs and environmental objectives to successful designs. Environmental requirements should focus on minimizing natural resource consumption, energy consumption, waste generation, and human health risks as well as promoting the sustainability of ecosystems.

Satisfy Multiple Objectives.   Environmental issues cannot be addressed in isolation. Life-cycle design seeks to meet environmental objectives while also best satisfying cost, performance, cultural, and legal requirements. The challenge is to apply design strategies that resolve conflicting requirements.

Establish Environmental Metrics and Other Design Evaluation Tools.   Metrics and other comparative methods of evaluation enable product designers to determine the advantages and disadvantages of design options. Comparisons across all stages of the product life cycle are necessary to accurately assess environmental burden and to develop priorities for improvement.

Educate and Train Employees, Customers, and Suppliers.   All members of a product realization team, including production workers and upper management, should be knowledgeable about environmental issues. Moreover, because environmental issues generally extend beyond the company boundary to customers and suppliers, attention should be given to helping all participants in the life cycle improve environmental performance.

REFERENCES

1. Gregory A. Keoleian and Dan Menerey, "Sustainable Development by Design: Review of Life Cycle Design and Related Approaches," *Journal of the Air and Waste Management Association,* **44**(5): 645–668 (1994).

2. EPA, "Life Cycle Design Framework and Demonstration Projects: Profiles of AT&T and AlliedSignal," EPA/600/R-95/107, Office of Research and Development, Risk Reduction Engineering Laboratory, Cincinnati, OH, 1995. This report is an update of EPA's "Life Cycle Design Manual: Environmental Requirements and the Product System" EPA/600/R-92/226, 1992.

3. W. Edwards Deming, "Transformation of Western Style of Management," *Interfaces,* **15**(3): 6–11 (1985).

4. Gregory A. Keoleian, "The Application of Life Cycle Assessment to Design," *Journal of Cleaner Production,* **1**(3–4): 143–149 (1994).

5. Braden R. Allenby, "Design for Environment: A Tool Whose Time Has Come," *SSA Journal,* pp. 6–9, September 1991.

6. *Characterization of Solid Waste in the United States: 1990 Update,* EPA 530-SW-90-042A, Environmental Protection Agency, Washington, 1990.

7. B. W. Marguglio, *Environmental Management Systems,* Marcel Dekker, New York, 1991.

8. Brian Rothery, *Implementing the Environment Management Standard and the EC Eco-Management Scheme,* Gower, Brookfield, VT, 1993.

9. John C. Newman and Kay M. Breeden, "Managing in the Environmental Era: Lessons from Environmental Leaders," *Columbia Journal of World Business,* **27**(3&4): 210–221 (1992).

10. Brenda Klafter, "Pollution Prevention Benchmarking: AT&T and Intel Work Together with the Best," *Total Quality Environmental Management,* **2**(1): 27–34 (1992).

11. Marcia E. Williams, "Why—and How—to Benchmark for Environmental Excellence," *Total Quality Environmental Management,* **2**(2): 177–185 (1992).

12. Donald G. Gause and Gerald M. Weinberg, *Requirements: Quality before Design,* Dorset House, New York, 1989.

13. Bill Hollins and Stuart Pugh, *Successful Product Design: What to Do and When,* Butterworths, Boston, 1989.

14. Wolter J. Fabrycky, "Designing for the Life Cycle," *Mechanical Engineering,* **109**(1): 72–74 (1987).

15. Gregory A. Keoleian, Werner J. Glantschnig, and William McCann, "Life Cycle Design: AT&T Demonstration Project," *Proceedings of IEEE International Symposium on Electronics and the Environment,* San Francisco, 2 May, Institute of Electrical and Electronic Engineers Service Center, Piscataway, NJ, 1994.

16. Georg Kreuzberg and Hans Sas, "Shared Responsibility for Life-Cycle Management. Extended Producer Responsibility as a Strategy to Promote Cleaner Products, 22–26. Trolleholm Castle, Sweden, 4 May," Dept. of Industrial Environmental Economics, Lund University, Lund, Sweden: 1992.

17. Silvia Pizzocaro, "Learning from Undoing: An Industrial Strategy. Extended Producer Responsibility as a Strategy to Promote Cleaner Products," Dept. of Industrial Environmental Economics, Lund University, Lund, Sweden, 1992.

18. SETAC, *A Technical Framework for Life-Cycle Assessment—SETAC Workshop,* Smugglers Notch, VT, August 18, 1990, Society of Environmental Toxicologists and Chemists Foundation for Environmental Education, Washington, 1991.

19. R. Heijungs, J. B. Guinée, G. Huppes, R. M. Lankreijer, H. A. Udo de Haes, A. Wegener Sleeswijk, A. M. M. Ansems, P. G. Eggels, R. van Duin, and H. P. de Goede, *Environmental Life Cycle Assessment of Products—Guide,* Center of Environmental Science, Leiden, Netherlands, 1992.

20. R. Heijungs, J. B. Guinée, G. Huppes, R. M. Lankreijer, H. A. Udo de Haes, A. Wegener Sleeswijk, A. M. M. Ansems, P. G. Eggels, R. van Duin, and H. P. de Goede, *Environmental Life Cycle Assessment of Products—Backgrounds,* Center of Environmental Science, Leiden, Netherlands, 1992.

21. B. W. Vigon, D. A. Tolle, B. W. Cornary, H. C. Latham, C. L. Harrison, T. L. Boguski, R. G. Hunt, and J. D. Sellers, *Life Cycle Assessment: Inventory Guidelines and Principles,*

EPA/600/R-92/245, Environmental Protection Agency, Risk Reduction Engineering Laboratory, Cincinnati, OH, 1993.

22. SETAC, *Workshop on Guidelines for Life-Cycle Assessment: A Code of Practice,* Sesimbra, Portugal, Society of Environmental Toxicology and Chemistry, Pensacola, FL, March 31, 1993.

23. J. B. Guinée, H. A. Udo de Haes, and G. Huppes, "Quantitative Life Cycle Assessment of Products 1: Goal Definition and Inventory," *Journal of Cleaner Production,* **1**(1): 3–13 (1993).

24. Mary Ann Curran, "Broad-based Environmental Life Cycle Assessment," *Environmental Science and Technology,* **27**(3): 430–436 (1993).

25. C. C. Kuta, D. G. Koch, C. C. Hildebrandt, and D. C. Janzen, "Improvement of Products and Packaging through the Use of Life Cycle Analysis," in *Resources, Conservation and Recycling,* **14**: 185–198 (1995).

26. *Resource and Environmental Profile Analysis of Hard Surface Cleaners and Mix-Your-Own Cleaning Systems,* Franklin Associates, Prairie Village, KS, 1993.

27. *The Product Ecology Report: Environmentally-Sound Product Development Based on the EPS System,* Federation of Swedish Industries, Stockholm, 1993.

28. *The LCA Sourcebook,* SustainAbility, Society for the Promotion of LCA Development (SPOLD), and Business in the Environment, London, 1993.

29. Michael S. Sullivan and John R. Ehrenfeld. "Reducing Life-Cycle Environmental Impacts: An Industry Survey of Emerging Tools and Programs," *Total Quality Environmental Management,* **2**(2): 143–157 (1992).

30. Allen L. White and Karen Shapiro, "Life Cycle Assessment: A Second Opinion," *Environmental Science & Technology,* **27**(6): 1016–1017 (1993).

31. Göran Svensson, Experience from the Inventory Phase of LCA studies. First NOH European Conference: Design for the Environment, 1.1.1, 1-8. Nunspeet, Netherlands, 21 September 1992.

32. J. T. Houghton, G. J. Jenkins, and J. J. Eprhaums (eds.), *Climate Change. The IPCC Scientific Assessment,* Cambridge University Press, Cambridge, England, 1990.

33. Assessment Chairs for the Parties to the Montreal Protocol, *Synthesis of the Reports of the Ozone Scientific, Environmental Effects, and Technology and Economic Assessment Panels,* UNEP, New York, 1991.

34. D. Navin-Chandra, "Design for Environmentability," *ASME Design Theory and Methodology Conference,* Miami, 1991, School of Computer Science, Carnegie Mellon University, Pittsburgh, PA, 1991.

35. Seiichi Watanabe, *Resource Productivity as a New Measure for Industrial Performance,* Sony, 1993.

36. Braden R. Allenby and Ann Fullerton, "Design for Environment—A New Strategy for Environmental Management," *Pollution Prevention Review,* **2**(1): 51–61 (1991).

37. D. Navin-Chandra, "The Recovery Problem in Product Design," *Journal of Engineering Design,* **5**(1): 67–87 (1994).

38. Gregory A. Keoleian, "Life Cycle Design Criteria for Engine Oil Filters: AlliedSignal Case Study," SAE Technical Paper Series 951849. Reprinted from: *Proceedings of the 1995 Total Life Cycle Conference,* Vienna, Austria, October 16-19, 1995.

39. Krish Kar and Gregory A. Keoleian, "Application of Life Cycle Design to an Intake Manifold," SAE Technical Paper Series 960410, SAE International, Warrendale, PA, 1996.

40 Geoff Lewis and Gregory A. Keoleian, "Amorphous Silicon Photovoltaic Modules: A Life Cycle Design Case Study," *Proceedings of IEEE International Symposium on Electronics and Environment,* Dallas, 6-8 May 199.

CHAPTER 7
LIFE-CYCLE COSTING: CONCEPTS AND APPLICATIONS

Allen L. White, *Vice President*
Deborah Savage, *Research Associate*
Karen Shapiro, *Associate Scientist*
TELLUS INSTITUTE
BOSTON, MA

7.1 CONCEPTUAL FRAMEWORK

Costing of life-cycle impacts is integral to realizing the full potential of life-cycle assessment (LCA) as a decision support tool. The reason is straightforward—inventory and impact studies are most useful to industry when they are translated to a metric that business managers understand, namely, dollars and cents.

This is not to say that LCA impact studies which do not monetize impacts have no value. Moving from emissions inventory to estimates of ecological and health effects per se provides decision-relevant information by helping to pinpoint targets of opportunity for process and product improvement. Technology improvements which eliminate or drastically reduce waste streams may be—indeed, often are—undertaken without elaborate cost analysis. However, any organization's resources are finite, and for the majority of process and product improvement decisions, at least a rudimentary financial justification is prerequisite to approval of a proposed action. And financial justification requires a clear, unbiased, and comparable analysis of how much current (business-as-usual) practices cost now and will cost in the future versus what an alternative practice costs now and will cost in the future. It is this type of comparison that lies at the heart of modern project investment analysis.

Rigorous characterization and quantification of life-cycle costs are neither straightforward nor easy. In fact, even defining LCA "costs" and "costing" can be surprisingly elusive, with definitions ranging from narrow and restrictive to one in which cost boundaries are broad and inclusive. Use of terms such as *full cost accounting, total cost assessment, life-cycle costing,* and *total cost accounting* are frequently used interchangeably, a practice which introduces ample opportunity for confusion and ambiguity. Choosing the correct terminology and sticking with it throughout a costing exercise are essential for both internal company audiences and external stakeholders concerned with a company's environmental performance and improvement program.

Cost Boundaries

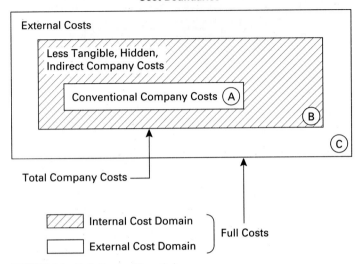

FIGURE 7.1 Definitions and boundaries.

Figure 7.1 presents a set of definitions and boundaries used in this chapter. It is based on the concept of *nested costs* in which life-cycle costs may be disaggregated into two categories: internal (or company) costs and external (sometimes called *social* or *societal*) costs. Internal company costs, in turn, fall into two major subcategories: (1) conventional and direct and (2) less tangible, hidden, and indirect.

Within area *A* are *conventional costs* which appear in typical company accounts for use in process control, product costing, investment analysis and capital budgeting, and performance evaluation. They include both annual operational costs such as labor, materials, and product transportation and one-time capital costs such as new equipment and buildings, engineering and design for new installations, and utility connections.

Beyond these conventional costs is a second set contained in area *B* termed *less tangible, hidden, and indirect costs.* As far as profitability is concerned, these subcategories of costs are no less real than area *A* costs. However, they tend to be less measurable and quantifiable, frequently are contingent or probabilistic in nature, and often are obscured by placement in an overhead account (instead of being allocated directly to a process or product). For these reasons, area *B* costs frequently are overlooked or miscalculated by industry managers in conducting control, costing, budgeting, and evaluation activities. Examples of area *B* costs include environmental permitting and licensing, reporting, waste handling, storage, and disposal. Also included are costs for waste cleanup, toxic tort actions, natural resource damages, and personal or property injury associated with the use and disposal of hazardous materials; worker productivity, employee health insurance, and worker compensation related to exposures to hazardous substances in the workplace; production losses due to hazardous materials incidents; and corporate image and market share effects of toxics use reduction or elimination.

Summing area *A* plus area *B* gives the *total company costs*—all costs for which a company is responsible (again, at a specified time) in light of prevailing or foreseeable market and regulatory conditions. The outer edge of area *B* forms the boundary delineating all costs which should enter management decisions. Collectively, they are the real costs of doing business.

Beyond area *B* lies area *C, external costs.* External costs are those for which a company, at a specified time, is not responsible, in the sense that neither the marketplace nor regulations assign such costs to the firm. In a life-cycle context, these can be understood in relation to the various stages of the life-cycle inventory.

Consider the case of automobile manufacturing. This industry relies on dozens of suppliers of various inputs, ranging from coatings, plastics, steel, rubber, glass, and aluminum. Even the largest, most vertically integrated automakers such as General Motors purchase materials and products from a large number of ancillary manufacturers. Making each of these materials and products requires some combination of raw material extraction, transport, and intermediate and final processing of materials before they reach GM for assembly into a final product—the motor vehicle.

From an analytical perspective, one should include the emissions and associated health and environmental impacts of each of these ancillary industries within an LCA of an automobile. Such a choice would mean, for example, that emissions from steel plants that supply the auto industry should be assigned to the final product, the vehicle, as part of a vehicle LCA. Then as more intensive use of aluminum and plastic displaces steel in automobile manufacturing, one might track changes in the emissions inventory to determine how various emissions types change in response to materials substitution.

For many of these ancillary industries, the pricing mechanism will capture environmental impacts. Control of air pollutants requires stack equipment; wastewater effluent may be handled by pretreatment facilities; and hazardous wastes must be properly labeled, transported, and disposed of. These activities incur capital and operating costs which, to some extent, are embodied in the prices that suppliers charge to the automaker. To the extent that this occurs, such costs find their way into vehicle prices, thereby signaling buyers that purchase of a particular vehicle causes certain environmental impacts in the upstream stages of product manufacture. Under these conditions, there are no external impacts and there is no area C. All costs are internal, and the auto manufacturer accounts for upstream costs either directly or indirectly through the pricing mechanism.[1]

Of course, the real world does not operate so smoothly and precisely. The pricing mechanism is less than perfect, and regulations do not cover all adverse impacts which result from materials extraction, transport, and manufacture. Impacts such as residual health effects, wetlands loss, and climate change owing to greenhouse gas emissions exemplify costs to society at large which fall into area C. They occur at all stages of the life cycle as a result of both direct activity (in our automobile example, final assembly of the vehicle) and ancillary activities (e.g., glass, aluminum, plastics manufacture) which supply the final product maker. To be consistent, when the LCA inventory encompasses such activities, so should the impact valuation stage, including its costing phase. Consistency aside, however, it is clear that many LCA proponents, despite their use of terms such as *full* and *total* costs, do *not* propose to include area C costs in the development of process or product LCAs.

What reason does a firm have to incorporate some or most of area C costs in performing its various business functions? At least three are identifiable:

Avoiding the "Regulatory Treadmill."   An external cost today may well be an internal cost tomorrow. While it is impossible to predict the exact direction of future regulations, the last decade clearly indicates that environmental policy is moving toward increasingly broader coverage in the materials and impacts it regulates. Impacts such as greenhouse gas emissions and wetlands loss may see more stringent regulations in the next decade. Thus, it behooves industry managers to consider such impacts and their associated costs in their planning and budgeting activities.

International Competitiveness.   An increasingly global economy means in many instances that the highest environmental standards for product content (e.g., solvent- and heavy-metal-free paper coating, disassemblable and recyclable automobiles) increasingly will dictate the global standard. To secure a place in an increasingly global marketplace, setting or exceeding the highest environmental standard is preferable to retrofitting designs and processes after they are put in place.

Accountability beyond Responsibility.   Business is under increasing pressure to protect the environment, regardless of whether formal regulatory mandates are in place. Environmentalists, investors, and the public at large are increasingly sensitive to a firm's willingness to subscribe to voluntary codes of conduct and regularly and completely disclose its environmental performance in annual reports and through other reporting mechanisms. For many stakeholders, the distinction between internal and external (boxes *A* and *B* versus box *C*) is an arbitrary one, and the firm ought to be held accountable for impacts even in the absence of regulation. This, many would argue, is the essence of environmental stewardship.

With this framework as background, we turn to a more detailed consideration of how managers can operationalize costing concepts in applying LCA as a decision support tool.

7.2   *TOTAL COST ASSESSMENT*

Total cost assessment (TCA) describes the long-term, comprehensive analysis of the full range of *internal* costs and savings resulting from pollution prevention projects and other environmental projects undertaken by the firm.[2] As such, TCA encompasses the two inner boxes in Fig. 7.1 and is a subset of life-cycle costs. It is a dynamic subset, however, subject to change and redefinition as the boundary between internal and external costs shifts with changing regulations and company policies.

The value of TCA as an alternative to conventional cost analyses stems from the failure of conventional practices to capture the full range of potential benefits of pollution prevention and other environmentally beneficial projects. These failures result from the misallocation of cost items, neglect of long-term costs and savings, and neglect of indirect (or second-order) costs or savings often omitted in conventional analyses. The application of TCA involves four key elements designed to correct these shortcomings: (1) a comprehensive costs and savings inventory, (2) more precise cost allocation, (3) use of time horizons long enough to capture long-term costs and savings, and (4) use of profitability indicators which account for the time value of money.

7.2.1   Comprehensive Cost Inventory

A comprehensive cost inventory should include all costs and savings relevant to the analysis at hand (Fig. 7.2). For brevity, the term *cost items* encompasses both costs and savings. Relevant cost items include both one-time capital costs and annual operating costs, direct project costs and indirect project support costs, easily quantifiable costs and more-difficult-to-quantify (less tangible) costs, known costs and probabilistic (contingency) costs, and short-term and long-term costs. For example, the cost of a piece of equipment necessary for project start-up is a capital, direct, quantifiable, one-time cost and, as such, is included in any conventional capital budgeting analysis. Direct annual operating costs such as those for direct labor and direct materials are also included in a typical company analysis.

In contrast, many indirect, less tangible, or probabilistic costs are often neglected in conventional company analyses. Environmental projects, which by nature often produce costs that are uncertain in character, magnitude, and timing, are particularly prone to an

Direct Conventional Costs

- Capital expenditures
- Buildings
- Equipment
- Utility connections
- Equipment installation
- Project engineering
- Operation and maintenance expenses/revenues
- Raw materials
- Labor
- Waste disposal
- Utilities: energy, water, sewerage
- Revenue from recovered material

Indirect or Hidden Costs

- Compliance costs
- Permitting
- Reporting
- Tracking
- Monitoring
- Manifesting
- Training
- Waste handling
- Recordkeeping
- Labeling
- Testing
- Emergency preparedness
- Medical surveillance
- Waste storage
- Operation of on-site pollution control equipment
- Raw materials costs linked to nonproduct output (NPO)
- Environmental insurance (acute events, gradual impairment)

Probabilistic and Less Tangible Costs

- Penalties and fines
- Personal injury and property damage
- Increased revenue from enhanced product quality
- Increased revenue from increased market share of "green products"
- Reduced worker compensation and absenteeism costs from improved employee health
- Increased productivity from improved employee relations
- Reduced staff burdens in dealing with community concerns

FIGURE 7.2   Cost inventory.

incomplete cost inventory. Examples of hidden costs which frequently are omitted from the project financial analysis include environmental insurance costs and labor costs for waste handling prior to off-site shipment. An example of a potential future cost which might be neglected due to its probabilistic nature is the likelihood of an increase in wastewater treatment fees from the local municipal treatment plant. Liability costs are often mentioned only in a qualitative fashion because they are both uncertain and difficult to quantify. This overlap between uncertainty and quantifiability also exists for cost items such as company image and green product revenues.

The following illustrates cost items which are more or less likely to be included in current practice:

More likely to be included:	*Less likely to be included:*
One-time, capital costs	Annual, recurring costs
Direct costs	Indirect, hidden costs
Certain costs	Uncertain, probabilistic costs
Short-term costs	Longer-term costs
Easily quantifiable costs	Difficult-to-quantify costs

A more detailed sample list of potential costs and savings appears in Fig. 7.2.

Once a comprehensive project cost inventory has been developed, the corresponding cost data must be developed for the analysis. Actual cost data, or the information necessary to develop such data, may be available from many different departments and personnel both within and outside the firm: purchasing, materials management and inventory, production, finance and accounting, environmental, research and development, equipment vendors, and outside consultants. Equipment vendors, for example, can provide estimates of purchased equipment cost, delivery and installation costs, and operation and maintenance costs. Purchasing or materials accounting records can provide data on the current annual cost of raw materials used for a process which will be affected by the environmental project under consideration. The annual amount and costs for off-site disposal of a current waste stream may be obtained from shipment manifest records or from the waste disposal contractor.

In some cases, costs attributable to a process or product under consideration may not be readily available from in-house or vendor records, but may have to be estimated by knowledgeable personnel; e.g., the environmental engineer can estimate the annual worker-hours devoted to monitoring, recordkeeping, and compliance reporting for a particular waste stream. The key point to note in obtaining data on cost items is that no cost item should be dismissed as negligible before at least a first-cut estimate has been made of its magnitude relative to other cost items in the analysis.

7.2.2 Appropriate Cost Allocation

Cost allocation procedures determine how production and other operating costs are assigned to specific process and product lines within a firm. Many cost data are first collected in overhead accounts and then, for product pricing purposes, attributed back to various company operations via some chosen allocation basis, such as product volume.

Costs related to environmental management, such as waste storage, handling, and treatment and environmental permitting, often are lumped into such overhead accounts. An illustration of this practice is a firm which has a single wastewater treatment system for aqueous wastes from multiple production lines, and has two environmental engineers on site to supervise all environmental activities related to production and waste management for all production lines and products. A facility overhead account might typically include not only all costs of operating the wastewater treatment system, i.e., materials and utilities, but also the salaries of the engineers who run the system and perform the environmental monitoring and permitting activities.

From a capital budgeting point of view, placing such costs in overhead accounts is problematic in two ways. First, costs placed in overhead accounts are often simply omitted from the project analysis cost inventory because the project analyst is not accustomed to viewing those costs as attributable and/or relevant to the specific process targeted by a proposed project. Second, even if overhead costs are identified as relevant, the lumped overhead costs are often misallocated to a process or product because the allocation basis chosen is inappropriate.

For example, one allocation basis commonly chosen is product volume, i.e., the number or quantity of product generated by a specific production line. However, the frequency of required environmental monitoring, the filing of related reports, and the resulting time commitment necessary on the part of the environmental engineer at the facility may be completely unrelated to product volume. For a facility with two different production lines, only one of which utilizes a hazardous raw material requiring formal environmental management, the allocation of environmental labor and operations costs on a total product volume basis will lead to inaccurate product costing. Allocating data for a capital budgeting analysis by the above method will lead to a false picture of project profitability. In turn, this undermines the ability of the firm to identify affordable and potentially profitable waste reduction opportunities.

For project financial analysis, the environmental management costs generated by a current process would be more accurate if the environmental engineer estimated worker-hours actually required by the process under review. To estimate project profitability, the same estimate must be generated for the alternative process under consideration. While these types of estimates might be developed on a project-by-project basis for capital budgeting purposes, a more formal adjustment to the firm's accounting and cost allocation system is preferable, ensuring that cost data are routinely allocated in a manner reflecting the way costs actually are incurred.

Activity-based costing (ABC) is a term often used to describe systems which track costs back to the products and processes whence they arose, rather than using simple, but often inaccurate, allocation bases such as product volume or manufacturing floor space.[3,4] Under an ABC approach, costs are generally divided into broad categories characterizing the type of activity driving the cost. Table 7.1 illustrates these activity categories.[5]

TABLE 7.1 Activity Categories for Cost Allocation

Activity category	Activity examples
Facility-sustaining activities	Plant management, building and grounds
Product-sustaining activities	Process engineering, product specifications
Batch-level activities	Setups, material movements, inspections
Unit-level activities	Materials, labor, energy

Within each broad category, an attempt is made to match each cost item with an activity driver directly related to the cost generated. Energy costs, for example, might be allocated according to machine hours run on each production line, while batch setup labor time is allocated according to the number of batches run on each production line.

Depending on the complexity of a firm's accounting system, operations, and product and process mix, comprehensive restructuring of materials and cost accounting systems can require significant commitments of human and financial resources. However, continued misallocation itself may incur substantial costs by directing the firm's limited capital resources to second- and third-best investment options, inappropriate product pricing, and misplaced incentives for managers. The potential value of converting to an ABC system can be generally assessed by reviewing the diversity of production volume, product size, and materials use within the firm, but can be specifically illustrated best by performing specific cost allocation case studies illustrating the magnitude of the problem.

7.2.3 Time Horizon

Another feature of TCA is a longer time horizon for project profitability analysis. A time horizon longer than the 2- to 5-year time frame used by many firms is necessary to capture the longer-term benefits characteristic of pollution prevention projects, particularly out-year avoided liability, recurrent savings due to waste avoidance, and revenue growth due to market development of environmentally green products. The willingness of a firm to select a longer time horizon of 10 to 15 years can depend on the particular project under consideration, the typical level of detail in project analysis, firm size, availability of funds for various projects, and competition for those funds by other projects.

7.2.4 Financial Indicators

Just as the time horizon chosen for project analysis should be long enough to capture the long-term costs and savings characteristic of pollution prevention projects, the financial indicator chosen should be capable of incorporating those same costs and savings into a measure of long-term project profitability. For example, indicators such as *net present value* (NPV) and *internal rate of return* (IRR) take into account all cash flows (positive and negative) over the life of a project and integrate the time value of money by discounting future cash flows. Simple payback, however, does not capture any costs, savings, or revenues which occur in the long term and does not consider the time value of money. As such, although payback in certain cases may be adequate for preliminary project assessment, it should not be selected as the sole indicator of profitability for the full project analysis.

7.3 CASE STUDY

The following case study illustrates the application of TCA to the analysis of an environmental project in the pulp and paper sector.[6,7] The manufacturing facility described is a specialty paper mill producing a variety of uncoated and coated papers. This example was chosen because it is a particularly powerful illustration of the value of a TCA approach. Other cases may demonstrate more or less dramatic results.

7.3.1 Company Background

This specialty paper mill is part of a larger corporation of pulp, paper, and coating mills. The mill is not integrated, i.e., does not manufacture pulp. Most of the pulp used by the mill is purchased via pipeline from a neighboring bleached kraft mill. The mill produces approximately 190 tons/year of a variety of uncoated, on-machine and off-machine coated papers and carbonizing, book, and release base paper. The coating used is a latex (i.e., nonsolvent) formulation containing clay, styrene butadiene, starch, and polymers.

7.3.2 Project Background

Paper machine *white water*—a mixture of water and residual fiber and filler (clay and calcium carbonate) that drains out of a sheet of paper as it travels across the paper machine—is typically captured by a white-water collection system dedicated to one paper machine. Some of or all the white water is usually recycled into the papermaking system to recapture water, fiber, and filler. In some cases white water is passed through a save-all screening device to separate fiber and filler from water; fiber, filler, and water are then recycled into the system. The save-all screen produces a clear stream of water that can be used in numerous paper machine operations.

In this mill, two paper machines, sharing a common white-water system, produce a variety of paper grades made with acid, neutral, or alkaline sizing chemistry.[8] Machine 1 has a save-all system that filters fiber and filler prior to discharging into the joint white-water system. This material is recycled into the papermaking system. When the machines are using different sizing chemistry, e.g., when machine 1 is producing acid-sized paper and machine 2 is producing alkaline-sized paper, the mixed white water from both machines is not reusable and must be sewered. Under these conditions, a large flow of potentially reusable water from both machines, and fiber and filler from machine 2, is lost to the sewer.

Prompted primarily by the lack of spare water effluent pumping capacity and a desire to better understand the rather complex, old white-water piping system, the mill commissioned a study entitled "White Water Recycle Feasibility Study." The study had several objectives: "...to review the design and operation of the mill and recommend changes that would help reduce peak effluent flows, reduce BOD in the effluent and reduce total fresh water intake on a mill wide scale." The resulting report contained detailed engineering drawings of the freshwater, white-water, and paper machine systems and a recommendation for process modifications.

7.3.3 Project Description

The feasibility study recommended installing a second save-all system to handle the white water from machine 2, and splitting the white-water systems so that each machine would have a dedicated system. This would permit fiber, filler and water reuse on both machines at all times, thereby conserving raw materials and reducing water consumption, wastewater generation, and energy use for freshwater and wastewater pumping and freshwater heating. The project would require installation of a new save-all system, a new pump, piping, and controls. Available pulping and stock storage capacity could be used to pulp separately for each machine.

7.3.4 Project Financial Analysis

The feasibility study's capital estimate for the project was $1.4 million, including purchased equipment (including save-all system, stock chest, clear white-water chest, and associated equipment), process control instrumentation, electrical controls and lighting, a new building for the save-all system, piping, installation (in-house and contracted labor), engineering, and contingency.

7.3.5 Company and TCA Analyses

The company analysis consists of the capital estimate and only those operating costs and savings that the company typically includes in project financial analyses for projects of this type. These are:

1. Raw material—fiber and filler
2. Energy and chemical use for new equipment

3. Wastewater treatment fees

4. Changes in labor costs

The TCA contains these and other relevant operating costs and savings. On the benefit side, the TCA includes the following:

1. An average reduction in fiber and filler loss of 1200 tons/year, for a savings of $421,530 per year

2. A reduction in freshwater use of 1 million gal/day and a commensurate reduction in cost for freshwater treatment and pumping, for a savings of approximately $112,420 per year

3. A reduction in energy use for freshwater heating amounting to a savings of approximately $393,400

4. A reduction in wastewater generation of approximately 1 million gal/day, for a savings of approximately $54,750 per year in wastewater pumping and $68,240 per year in wastewater treatment fees

Annual operating costs are expected to increase in the following areas:

- Chemical flocculating agents used in the save-all system to promote solids and water separation will cost approximately $28,700 per year.
- Electric costs for new equipment operation will increase operating costs by approximately $107,280 per year.
- An increase in labor cost of approximately $3120 per year is expected for operation of new equipment.

The project does not affect waste streams that require on-site management or disposal, nor does it affect any regulatory compliance activities at the site; therefore, the financial analysis does not include costs for these activities. In addition, no impacts on revenue are expected since neither product quality nor production rates will be improved, nor does the mill expect to visibly enhance its product or company image. Finally, no tangible impact on avoided future liability is expected for this project.

Table 7.2 summarizes the cost categories addressed in the company analysis and the TCA for this project, and Table 7.3 reports the results of the financial analysis. Including savings associated with freshwater pumping, treatment, heating, and wastewater pumping in the TCA analysis dramatically increases the annual savings and financial indicators compared to the company analysis; all three financial indicators improve for all time horizons in the TCA. These savings, which would typically not be included in the mill's calculation of profitability, meet the mill's 2-year-payback rule of thumb. By excluding these savings from the company analysis, the project looks reasonably "profitable" only over the longer time horizon of 15 years.

Pollution prevention projects are especially susceptible to costing errors because costs and savings from these projects are often long-term, indirect, and less tangible. The extent to which TCA improves a pollution prevention investment's profitability depends on the firm's current cost structure, project evaluation practices, the specific project, and the degree to which less tangibles are significant and quantifiable. However, TCA clearly helps produce unbiased information for the support of rational management decision making.

TABLE 7.2 Comparison of Cost Items in Company and TCA Cost Analyses

	Company	TCA
Capital costs		
Purchased equipment	X	X
Materials (e.g., piping, electrical)	X	X
Utility systems	X	X
Site preparation	X	X
Installation (labor)	X	X
Engineering and contractor	X	X
Contingency	X	X
Operating costs		
Direct costs*		
Raw materials, supplies	P	X
Labor	X	X
Indirect costs*		
Utilities		
Energy	P	X
Water		X
Sewerage (POTW)	X	X

The column labeled "Company" shows the results of the original project financial analysis performed by the company. The column labeled "TCA" shows the results of the more comprehensive financial analysis using the total cost assessment (TCA) approach. The TCA was performed by Tellus in collaboration with company staff.

X = cost(s) included; P = cost(s) partially included.

*We use the term *direct costs* to mean costs that are typically allocated to a product or process line (i.e., not charged to an overhead account) and are typically included in project financial analysis. *Indirect costs* here mean costs that are typically charged to an overhead account and typically not included in project financial analysis.

TABLE 7.3 Summary of Financial Data for the White-Water and Fiber Reuse Project

	Company analysis	TCA
Total capital costs	$1,469,404	$1,469,404
Annual savings (BIT)*	$ 350,670	$ 911,240
Financial indicators		
Net present value—years 1–5	($ 476,453)	$ 783,187
Net present value—years 1–10	$ 47,168	$2,072,234
Net present value—years 1–15	$ 359,455	$2,849,636
Internal rate of return—years 1–5	1%	37%
Internal rate of return—years 1–10	17%	46%
Internal rate of return—years 1–15	21%	48%
Simple payback (years)	4.2	1.6

*Annual operating cash flow before *i*nterest and *t*axes.

7.4 LIFE-CYCLE COSTING

Life-cycle costs include all internal costs plus external costs incurred throughout the entire life cycle of a product, process, or activity. External costs are beyond the realm of even TCA because these costs are not borne directly by the company (or the ultimate

- Natural resource depletion
- Human health impacts
- Ecological impacts
- Building/infrastructure impacts
- Crop impacts
- Wetlands impacts
- Habitat loss
- Biodiversity loss
- Climate change

FIGURE 7.3 Examples of external cost.

consumer of the company's goods and services) and do not enter the company's decision-making calculus. In economics vernacular, these costs are called *externalities*. Figure 7.3 lists examples of external costs.

Differences between internal and external costs can be illustrated through the example of electricity generation. Developing and using energy resources impose a variety of impacts on society. Some of these costs are incurred by electricity generators (e.g., utilities) such as the direct costs of facility construction, operation and maintenance costs, fuel consumption, or the cost of pollution control equipment—and are recouped by the utility through its electricity prices. Other impacts, however, are not directly borne by the utility and therefore are not embodied in electricity prices and, by extension, are not included in the price of goods or services that use energy (virtually everything in modern society). Depending upon the extent of regulation, these may include damages to the environment and human health that may result from construction of power plants; extracting, processing, transporting, and combustion of fuels; and disposal of wastes from these activities. For example, fossil fuel plants emit sulfur dioxide (SO_2) and nitrogen oxides (NO_x), precursors to acid rain, which may cause acidification of lakes and streams and contribute to fish kills and loss of biodiversity. Constructing dams for hydroelectric facilities floods land, potentially destroying a wide range of wildlife habitats and flora.

A life-cycle inventory of the energy fuel cycle would quantify emissions and resource use while the impact assessment would address the environmental and human health effects from emissions and resource use. Life-cycle costing extends the impact assessment by taking an additional step—placing a dollar value on those impacts. Methods of assigning costs are described below.

7.4.1 Methods of Developing Monetary Values

The life-cycle impact assessment chain differentiates between three stages or levels of environmental "impacts" leading to damages: (1) initial loadings [i.e., emissions quantified in the life-cycle inventory (LCI)], (2) intermediate effects, and (3) ultimate impacts. In the case of glass packaging manufacture, these correspond to (1) the pounds of SO_2 per glass container produced, (2) the increased acidity in water bodies due to those SO_2 emissions, and (3) the fish kills and loss of biodiversity resulting from increased acidity, respectively. Life-cycle costing distinguishes between these levels as well, using different costing approaches and techniques that vary by where in the impact chain the impacts are assessed.

Monetary values for ultimate impacts can be determined for certain types of impacts. The market value, for example, of crop loss or damages caused by air pollutants can be valued directly by assessing the market value of the lost output. However, quantifying the impact chain leading to revenue loss may be difficult. Translating nitrogen oxide emissions from the life-cycle inventory of a glass bottle to an incremental change in ambient ozone concentration and quantifying crop loss from that increment are, at best, highly uncertain. Additionally, placing monetary values on many impacts (e.g., adverse health effects) is difficult from both an economic and an ethical perspective.

Several methods are available for indirectly valuing impacts. The methods involve (1) assuming or creating a fictitious market in order to elicit the value that individuals might assign to an externality (contingent valuation); (2) examining behavioral responses that are, or might be, influenced by an externality (e.g., hedonic pricing); or (3) analyzing the implicit value placed on pollution abatement by society through the actions of its regulatory agencies (e.g., regulators' revealed preferences).

Contingent valuation relies on surveys to estimate how much people would be willing to pay to prevent environmental degradation or other adverse impacts. By asking people (through interviews or surveys) what they would be willing to pay to preserve the environment or to reduce adverse impacts from pollution, a value for preventing that impact can be inferred. As in the crop loss example, a life-cycle inventory item (e.g., water releases) must be linked to the adverse impact (e.g., fish kills) through the life-cycle impact assessment to render the monetary value meaningful.

Contingent valuation has been used in a wide range of studies valuing air quality improvement in the Los Angeles area and valuing nuclear plant injury reductions, and many others.[9] The main drawback of this approach is that survey responders may give biased answers. For example, to ensure that a favorite fishing resource is preserved, anglers may bias their answers toward a high value if they know that a decision will be based upon the survey's outcome. Additionally, because anglers will not ultimately pay for preserving the site, the values elicited from a survey may be higher than what people may actually be willing to pay.

The U.S. National Wildlife Service has used contingent valuation to value a day of recreational fishing.[10] In its 1975 survey, the agency polled anglers to determine how much money is spent in pursuing their activity and how much more they would be willing to spend before considering the sport too expensive.

Hedonic pricing is an alternative approach that examines market behaviors for the environmental impact in question. Hedonic pricing rests on the assumption that non-market characteristics such as clean air have values that are reflected in what people are willing to pay for tangible goods. For example, property values may reflect the environmental condition of the land and its location. Given two properties with similar characteristics except environmental surroundings, (e.g., one property is situated near a municipal solid waste landfill and the other is not), hedonic pricing assumes that differences in the market value of the properties are attributable to the willingness to pay for the differences in local environmental quality.

Hedonic pricing requires considerable data and accurate use of statistical techniques, but even then it may be difficult to extract a value for a specific externality, given the myriad variables involved in market decisions. An important limitation is the likelihood, in many instances, that the requisite information on existing or potential environmental risk that such a method presumes is not available or apparent, for example, to the home buyer purchasing the home near the landfill. This method also requires establishing links between inventory emissions and resource use to ultimate damages.

The *regulators' revealed-preferences* approach is an empirical means of establishing willingness to pay, without directly engaging in the complex task of identifying and estimating all the various physical environmental damages and "polling" all the affected parties. The approach identifies specific instances where control measures have been required, in order to determine the cost that society, represented by its regulators, is willing to pay to reduce emissions, thereby avoiding environmental damages. By requiring specific control equipment, regulators imply a willingness to pay up to the associated cost per unit of pollution (or damage) avoided, even though there may exist opportunities for pollution reduction at lower costs. For example, some state regulations require fossil fuel power plants to be equipped with *selective catalytic reduction* (SCR) to reduce nitrogen oxide emissions. Under the revealed-preferences approach, dividing the cost for SCR by the tons of nitrogen oxides controlled provides a dollar-per-ton estimate of the cost that society is willing to pay to avoid damages from an additional ton of NO_x. For energy planning, state utility regulators in several states have required that externality values developed by this method be applied.

The main drawback of this approach is it assumes that regulators are fully informed about a pollutant's adverse effects and can accurately assess the costs and benefits of more stringent regulation. Additionally, because society's preferences may change with time as information and policy change, past or current regulations may bear little resemblance to actual impacts and their value to society. Finally, many pollutants remain unregulated; this method cannot be applied to these pollutants.

Generally, the contingent valuation and hedonic pricing techniques for costing have been grouped along with direct market costs (such as crop loss) under the heading of damage costing methods, while the regulators' revealed-preference technique has been referred to as the *marginal cost of control* method. This nomenclature is somewhat misleading. Both types of approach provide imperfect means of estimating willingness to pay to avoid a variety of adverse impacts. Nonetheless, two major differences are noteworthy.

First, the contingent valuation, hedonic pricing, and market price techniques attempt to determine *consumers'* willingness to pay when acting in actual or hypothetical markets, while the regulators' revealed-preference technique attempts to determine *society's* willingness to pay through its environmental regulators acting on behalf of citizens. Second, in the damage costing techniques, the impacts are represented to consumers, and willingness to pay is estimated at the "endpoints" of the many impact pathways—visibility, crop damage, lost habitat, additional mortality, additional adverse health effects, etc.—and aggregated to account for all the effects of the additional pollution. In contrast, with the "marginal cost of control" technique, the impacts are represented to the environmental regulators, and willingness to pay is estimated at the point of release of the pollutant. Thus, the regulators' revealed-preferences approach can be applied directly to the environmental loadings resulting from a life-cycle inventory.

7.4.2 Example of Life-Cycle Costing

One area where life-cycle costing techniques have increasingly been applied is the electricity utility industry. Energy regulators (i.e., state public service commissions or public utility commissions) in several states including California, Massachusetts, Nevada, New York, Wisconsin, and Oregon have proposed or adopted pollutant-specific monetary values to be used in energy planning. While most states only require monetizing impacts from the end of the fuel cycle (i.e., emissions from power plants), some states and/or utilities have included the entire fuel cycle beginning at the coal mine or oil and gas well.

To date, monetized environmental costs have been added to the direct costs of producing energy for purposes of resource evaluation and selection only; these values are not reflected in the rates charged to electricity customers. Utility regulators oversee a utility's resource planning process (how the utility plans to meet its customers' energy needs) to protect ratepayers by ensuring prudent decision making by the utility. By placing monetary values on environmental impacts and including those costs with direct economic costs of energy production, the state ensures that utilities select fuels with the lowest total cost (internal plus external, according to our earlier terminology). Thus, monetizing environmental costs ensures that these impacts are considered in utility resource planning.

Monetizing environmental impacts also levels the playing field for pollution prevention. Energy conservation programs, such as replacing older equipment with more up-to-date and energy-efficient equipment or installing weather stripping and insulation, require outlays of capital. This cost can be balanced against not only the savings achieved by using less energy but also the benefit of reducing pollution from the power plant. Thus, monetized avoided environmental loadings can be added to energy cost savings to evaluate the total savings from an energy conservation program.

California's approach to life-cycle costing is particularly revealing as the state has used both the regulators' revealed-preferences and damage costing approaches in valuing environmental impacts from electricity. Two state agencies have taken the lead in these efforts—the California Public Utilities Commission (PUC), which controls utility rates and the California Energy Commission (CEC), which oversees utility resource planning. In 1991 the PUC required utilities to adopt values based on control costs reflecting air quality in each electric utility's air basin. The values developed for utilities located in the South Coast Air Quality Management District (SCAQMD), an area known for its poor air quality, are the highest in the state. Based upon costs of applying *best-available control technology* (BACT), the environmental costs in Table 7.4 were developed for SCAQMD.[11]

TABLE 7.4   Pollution Costs Used in Los Angeles Basin Control Cost Approach

Pollutant	Cost, $/ton
Nitrogen oxides (NO$_x$)	$24,500
Reactive organic gases (ROGs)	$17,500
Sulfur oxides (SO$_x$)	$18,300
Particulate matter	$ 5,300

In 1993, the CEC developed environmental cost values for each of the state's 13 air quality management districts, reflecting differences in air quality, population density, health costs, and agricultural production among these regions.[12] CEC developed an air quality valuation model (AQVM) that modeled air pollution sources and emissions, translated emissions to air quality, and modeled exposure and susceptibility to pollutants to quantify a physical response to air quality (e.g., crop damage and adverse health effects). In the final step, these responses were converted to monetary values. For SCAQMD, the values in Table 7.5 were determined. CEC values for NO$_x$, ROGs, and

TABLE 7.5   Pollution Costs Used in Los Angeles Basin Damage Cost Approach

Pollutant	Cost, $/ton
Nitrogen oxides (NO$_x$)	$14,734
Reactive organic gases (ROGs)	$ 6,911
Sulfur oxides (SO$_x$)	$ 8,469
Particulate matter	$46,479

SO_x are much lower than the PUC regulators' revealed-preferences values, while the PUC value for particulate matter is much lower than the CEC value. CEC acknowledges possible sources of underestimation and overestimation of these damage costs. While damages from acute health effects were considered, chronic health effects were not, potentially underestimating damages. In calculating damages, it was assumed that the peak daily ambient pollution concentrations occur for the entire day (rather than, say, a 1-hour peak), which may overestimate damages.

Electric utilities are the first sector incorporating environmental costs in their resource plans because, as a state-regulated industry sector, states can mandate—and have mandated—this step. However, other industry sectors may be encouraged to consider environmental costs in the near future. The widely discussed carbon tax, placing a dollar value on carbon emissions contributing to global warming, is one such initiative. Various states have proposed levying disposal fees on municipal solid waste (MSW) to reflect the environmental cost of incinerating, landfilling, and recycling MSW. These efforts reflect regulators' attempts at quantifying the costs and benefits of policies affecting environmental quality.

7.5 CONCLUSIONS

No single definition or protocol exists for process and product life-cycle costing. To look beneath the range of commonly used terms (e.g., total cost accounting, full cost accounting, total cost assessment, true costs) is to find much inconsistency and confusion as to which costs are included and which are excluded from the analysis. Thus, well before any data development or analysis begins, it is incumbent upon the analyst to define in unambiguous fashion an assessment's three key boundary conditions: (1) the stages of the life cycle, (2) the elements of the inventory within each stage, and (3) the types of human health and environmental effects associated with various impacts. Timely determination of these conditions is the foundation for subsequent life-cycle costing, regardless of which costing method is ultimately applied.

To date, firms have adopted a pragmatic approach to defining these boundaries. Boundaries typically are drawn to encompass costs for which the firm is currently held responsible, i.e., those contained within the two inner boxes in Fig. 7.1. While costing methods vary, the goals of firms are commonly twofold: (1) to modify existing costing practices to more effectively link environmental costs with specific processes and products and (2) to facilitate identification of promising pollution prevention and waste reduction opportunities. For firms like Dow, du Pont, Ciba-Geigy, Amoco, and 3M—all with a professed interest in full, true, total, or some other descriptor of improved cost accounting—the choice of boundaries is driven first and foremost by the realities of the marketplace and regulations which create the labor, equipment, liability, waste management, and other costs for the firm. Although the discussion of TCA demonstrates substantial opportunities for improving costing methods, there is little doubt that the point of departure for the vast majority of firms is *internal* costs, *not* full life-cycle costs, as defined in Fig. 7.1.

The major exception to this generalization is the regulated utility industry. Spurred by state regulators with a mandate to promote least-cost planning, where least cost includes both internal and external costs, various approaches and absolute values have been assigned to major pollutants associated with electric energy generation. Under the banner of integrated resource planning, various costing methods have been applied to develop estimates of per-ton pollutant costs. While criteria pollutants have been the target to date, the future may well see additional pollutants (e.g., CO_2 and air toxics) subject to similar cost analysis.

How should industry managers in other sectors respond to such trends? Should they move proactively toward broadening cost boundaries in the direction of area C in Fig. 7.1? If the experience of the last two decades is indicative, then the future will witness a slow but consistent expansion of area B into area C. If this premise is correct, the appropriate response of management logically follows. To get off the "regulatory treadmill," to remain at the forefront of international competitiveness, and to achieve and retain the image and reality of leadership—all these objectives are served by life-cycle costing methods which reveal in clear, unbiased, and comprehensive fashion both the internal and external costs of doing business. A firm need not commit to immediate incorporation of such costs into all aspects of its decision making. To do so is neither feasible nor desirable. But in the long term, life-cycle costing offers managers a valuable tool to operationalize the continuous environmental improvement to which all leadership firms should be committed.

REFERENCES

1. To keep this example simple, use and postuse (disposal) impacts are not considered, although they rightfully form part of an LCA.

2. TCA refers to costing in the context of capital budgeting and investment analysis. However, its principles are applicable to all types of costing activities of the firm.

3. R. Cooper and R. Kaplan, "How Cost Accounting Distorts Product Costs," *Management Accounting*, pp. 20–27, April 1988.

4. R. Cooper, "The Rise of Activity-Based Costing—Part One: What Is an Activity-Based Cost System?" *Journal of Cost Management*, 2(2): 45–54 (Summer 1988).

5. J. Kreuze and G. Newell, "ABC and Life-Cycle Costing for Environmental Expenditures," *Management Accounting*, pp. 38–42, February 1994.

6. A. White, M. Becker, and J. Goldstein, *Total Cost Assessment: Accelerating Industrial Pollution Prevention through Innovative Project Financial Analysis, with Applications to the Pulp and Paper Industry,* Report prepared by Tellus Institute for EPA, Office of Pollution Prevention, December 1991, Revised Executive Summary, June 1993.

7. A. White, M. Becker, and D. Savage, "Environmentally Smart Accounting: Using Total Cost Assessment to Advance Pollution Prevention," *Pollution Prevention Review*, pp. 247–259, Summer 1993.

8. Sizing is added to pulp to reduce water absorbency in the final paper. The pH (i.e., acidity or alkalinity) of the pulp must be adjusted according to the type of paper desired and sizing used.

9. Tom Tietenberg, *Environmental and Natural Resource Economics*, 2d ed., Scott, Foresman, Glenview, IL, 1988.

10. W. Vaughn and C. Russel, *Freshwater Recreational Fishing: The National Benefits of Water Pollution Control,* Resources for the Future, Washington, 1982.

11. California Public Utilities Commission Decision 91-06-022, June 5, 1991.

12. California Energy Commission Docket no. 90-ER-92S, Appendix F: Air Quality, January 1993.

FURTHER READING

Acton, J., and L. Dixon, "Superfund and Transaction Costs—The Experiences of Insurers and Very Large Industrial Firms," RAND, The Institute for Civil Justice, Santa Monica, CA, 1992.

American Institute for Pollution Prevention (AIPP), *A Primer for Financial Analysis of Pollution*

Prevention Projects, Document prepared for EPA, Pollution Prevention Research Branch, Risk Reduction Engineering Laboratory, Cincinnati, OH, April 1993.

Bernow, S. S., and D. B. Marron, *Valuation of Environmental Externalities for Energy Planning and Operations—May 1990 Update,* Tellus Institute, Boston, MA, May 18, 1990.

Curran, M. A., "Broad-Based Environmental Life-Cycle Assessment," *Environmental Science & Technology,* **27**(3): 430 (1993).

General Electric Corporate Environmental Programs, *Financial Analysis of Waste Management Alternatives,* Fairfield, CT, 1987.

Jacobs Engineering Group, *Source Reduction and Recycling of Halogenated Solvents—Lifecycle Inventory and Tradeoff Analysis,* prepared for Source Reduction Research Partnership for the Metropolitan Water District of Southern California and Environmental Defense Fund, Pasadena, CA, 1991.

Kreuze, J. G., and G. E. Hewell, "ABC and Life-Cycle-Costing for Environmental Expenditures," *Management Accounting,* pp. 38–42, February 1994.

Northeast Waste Management Officials' Association (NEWMOA) and Massachusetts Office of Technical Assistance (MA OTA), *Costing and Financial Analysis of Pollution Prevention Projects: A Training Packet,* Boston, MA, 1992.

Shapiro, K., R. Little, and A. White, "To Switch or Not to Switch: A Decision Framework for Chemical Substitution," *Pollution Prevention Review,* Winter 1993–1994.

Shapiro, K., A. White, and R. Little, *Incorporation of Life-Cycle Assessment Concepts in Rule-Making Procedures—A Discussion Paper,* submitted to the Environmental Protection Agency, Office of Pollution Prevention and Toxics, Tellus Study no. 91-083A, 1993.

Shapiro, K., R. Little, and A. White, *Chemical Substitution: A Conceptual Approach and Application to Printing Inks, Paint, and Glycol Ethers,* prepared for The Massachusetts Toxics Use Reduction Institute, University of Massachusetts, Lowell, MA, November 1992.

Shapiro, K., "Life-Cycle Assessment and Evaluation of Packaging Materials," presented at the Association of State and Territorial Solid Waste Management Officials 1992 National Solid Waste Forum, Portland, OR, July 20–22, 1992.

Society of Environmental Toxicology and Chemistry, *A Conceptual Framework for Life-Cycle Impact Assessment,* SETAC, Pensacola, FL, March 1993.

Tellus Institute, *Energy Implications of Integrated Solid Waste Management Systems,* prepared for New York State Energy Research and Development Authority, Tellus Study no. 92-255, Boston, MA, 1993.

Tellus Institute, *CSG/Tellus Packaging Study. Assessing the Impacts of Production and Disposal of Packaging and Public Policy Measures to Alter Its Mix,* prepared for The Council of State Governments, Lexington, KY, and Environmental Protection Agency, New Jersey Department of Environmental Protection and Energy, Tellus Study no. 89-024, Boston, MA, 1992.

Tellus Institute, *Valuation of Environmental Externalities for Electric Utility Resource Planning in Wisconsin,* prepared for Citizens for a Better Environment, Boston, MA, November 1991.

Tellus Institute, *Environmental Impacts of Long Island's Energy Choices: The Environmental Benefits of Demand-Side Management,* Boston, MA, September 1990.

U.S. Environmental Protection Agency, Office of Research and Development, *Life-Cycle Assessment: Inventory Guidelines and Principles,* EPA/600/R-92/245, prepared by Battelle and Franklin Associates, February 1993a.

U.S. Environmental Protection Agency, Office of Air Quality Planning and Standards, *A Framework and Methods for Conducting a Life-Cycle Impact Assessment,* prepared by K. A. Weitz and J. L. Warren, Draft, August 1993b.

U.S. Environmental Protection Agency, Office of Solid Waste (OSW) and Office of Policy, Planning and Evaluation (OPPE), *Pollution Prevention Benefits Manual,* vol. 1: *The Manual,* July 1989.

White, A., M. Becker, and J. Goldstein, *Alternative Approaches for the Financial Evaluation of Industrial Pollution Prevention Investments,* Report prepared by Tellus Institute for the New Jersey Department of Environmental Protection, Division of Science and Research, November 1991, Revised Executive Summary, June 1993.

White, A., "Accounting for Pollution Prevention," *EPA Journal,* **19**(3): 23–25 (July–September 1993).

White, A., N. Talbot, and D. Savage, *Internal Cost Accounting: Concepts, Cases, and Recommendations for the New Ontario Hydro,* Report prepared by Tellus Institute for Ontario Hydro, Task Force on Sustainable Energy Development, Full Cost Accounting Team, August 1993, revised November 1993.

White, A., and K. Shapiro, "Life Cycle Assessment: A Second Opinion," *Environmental Science & Technology,* **27**(6) (1993).

CHAPTER 8
PUBLIC POLICY APPLICATIONS OF LIFE-CYCLE ASSESSMENT

Eun-Sook Goidel
ENVIRONMENTAL PROTECTION SPECIALIST

Mary McKiel
EPA STANDARDS NETWORK COORDINATOR
ENVIRONMENTAL PROTECTION AGENCY
OFFICE OF POLLUTION PREVENTION AND TOXIC
SUBSTANCES
WASHINGTON, DC

8.1 INTRODUCTION

Public policy ranges over everything from soup to taxes in the United States. Ideally, public policy should reflect, preserve, and help shape the social, cultural, ethical, economic, and political well-being and diversity of the represented public. Policy can be codified through formal, legislative processes resulting in federal, state, or local regulation. Policy can also be formulated in nonregulatory public statements of intent, such as intent to act according to certain principles. For example, presidential executive orders state specific policy intentions. The Executive Order on Federal Acquisition, Recycling, and Waste Prevention[1] establishes a policy to encourage the use of environmentally preferable products, which federal agencies must then implement through organizational and operational policies. Certain states and municipalities have made localized smoking bans a matter of public policy.

For the purpose of taking a look at the implications and potential impact of the life-cycle assessment (LCA) tool, this chapter touches upon a few examples where attempts either have been made or are in the process of being made to apply LCA principles to developing a specific public policy. It is not meant to be a comprehensive listing or an in-depth analysis. This chapter also discusses a number of factors that will impact the development of LCA methodology as it relates to its use in public policy.

Setting aside debates on the efficacy of existing policies, is there a role for life-cycle applications in shaping public policies? And how might such thinking be incorporated? Do life-cycle considerations enhance policy applications and outcomes? The intent here is to begin asking questions rather than to provide answers. As LCA is evolving and maturing, it is reasonable to expect that both questions and answers relating to public policy will likewise change.

8.2 OVERVIEW OF CURRENT USES AND POTENTIAL APPLICATIONS

8.2.1 Life-Cycle Assessment in Europe and the United States

There are numerous instances where life-cycle concepts are potentially beneficial in both the making of and the resulting public policy.[2] Generally speaking, European countries have been much more willing to use some form of life-cycle assessment as a basis for their public policy, with full acknowledgment that the methodology for LCA has not been fully developed. Thus, European examples are more plentiful. The willingness of Europeans to use an evolving tool more practically is most apparent in ecolabeling programs that have cropped up in many European countries. Ecolabeling, in fact, is perhaps the most widely publicized area where life-cycle assessment has been used as an underpinning for public policy. This is particularly true for countries in the European Union (EU) and for the Scandinavian countries. In the EU, apart from a communitywide program, a number of individual member countries have established national labeling programs, with Germany's Blue Angel probably being the most notable.

All these programs are either government-run or -sanctioned and incorporate the concept of life-cycle assessment, at least in principle. The European Union formally articulated in a directive that the EU ecolabeling program shall be based on LCA, and the EU has farmed out to member countries specific product categories for which the countries are responsible for conducting LCA. The use of life-cycle assessment and its concepts in ecolabeling programs has already been well documented and will not be discussed in detail in this chapter.[3]

The use of LCA in public policy is not just limited to ecolabeling. In Sweden, research is being undertaken by the Swedish Waste Research Council for a Low-Waste Society [*Avfallforskningsrådet (AFR)*], to examine solid waste management from a life-cycle perspective, and findings from this research will support public policy making.

In another policy initiative, the United Nation's Economic Commission for Europe has examined and pilot-tested the concept of an *environmental product profile* that would facilitate the exchange of information on environmental issues among suppliers, producers, and professional users of the product.[4] Under this system, environmental information would be "built up" along the various life-cycle stages; i.e., during each stage of the life cycle, a supplier or manufacturer that is adding value to the process or product would also document environmental information relevant at that stage and pass that information along to the next stage, thereby building an overall product profile.

The assumption behind this is that with an increased flow of information, "companies, rather than focusing solely on the environmental implications of their own activities without considering subsequent production phases" would "make an additional contribution to the reduction of the use of energy and natural resources, and the reduction of emissions and wastes in the product chain as a whole...."[5] Although this system has not been adopted throughout all Europe, the Netherlands is implementing a similar system for certain consumer products.

In the United States, the concept of life cycle, in a more limited sense, has been used by the Department of Energy since the late 1960s for analyses of energy use in certain processes and products. In fact, the current LCA methodology has origins in DOE's *fuel cycles.* More recently, the use of life-cycle assessment and its concepts has been much more widespread in the private sector but has not gained a strong following in the public sector. The Department of Energy has revitalized its interest in LCA, but its use still remains largely research-oriented rather than for specific public policy making.

8.2.2 Framework for Life-Cycle Assessment Potential

The use of life-cycle assessment concepts in public policy making is still in its infancy, and a discussion of it fits better in the realm of potential applications than current or past uses. A number of forces are at work that will facilitate adoption of tools such as life-cycle assessment in public policy making.

First, there has been a fundamental change in the philosophical paradigm and in the mix of tools available and used by policy makers for solving environmental problems. Rather than relying solely on end-of-pipe control technology, which has been successful at addressing certain problems but not others, policy makers are more willing to look to market-based incentives, pollution prevention approaches, and other innovative ways to get at environmental problems. A change in philosophical paradigm, however, has not necessarily resulted in actual practices that reflect this change.

Second, passage of the Uruguay Round of the General Agreement on Tariffs and Trade (GATT) confirms that global trade is upon us. Inclusion of the Standards Code[6] into the body of the agreement significantly changes how the United States and all the GATT signatories view policies relating to the use of international standards affecting the environment, health, and safety as well as aspects of trade. Government requirements impacting goods in trade may be evaluated and even disputed on the basis of recognized international life-cycle standards.

International trade, the regulatory process, and the public acquisition process provide a variety of venues from which the potential of LCA may be viewed.

8.3 POTENTIAL PUBLIC POLICY APPLICATIONS OF LIFE-CYCLE CONCEPTS

8.3.1 Legislation

Legislation can create as well as solve problems. Unprecedented improvements in the environment and human health over the last two decades have occurred because of tough legislation. Ironically the very laws responsible for improvement may be barriers to continued improvement. Once a crisis situation requiring legislation has abated, often multimedia problems ensue. *Medium* is the term given to an individual environmental arena, e.g., water or air or land. *Multimedia,* as the term suggests, refers to a combination of all or at least some of the individual arenas. Many federal environmental laws are focused on a single medium. The Clean Air Act and the Clean Water Act are two examples. Other laws, such as the Toxic Substances Control Act (TSCA), cover specific substances which may be released in multiple media. Problems may occur when one law fails to take into account cross-media impacts.

Enforcement of Clean Air Act (CAA) provisions relating to pipe stack emissions has led on more than one occasion to the regulated company or industry adjusting processes in order to achieve compliance with the CAA. The process adjustment may change the manner in which wastes are released, diverting the releases from it to another medium. The diversion may be perfectly legal—at least for a time—or may simply result in a less expensive fine. The same scenario is repeated for the Clean Water Act and for the Resource Conservation and Recovery Act. The situation is hardly simple, and the scenario above does not do the entire issue a great deal of justice. Multimedia environmental issues provide an excellent forum for considering the potential for LCA incorporation into legislation and regulatory enforcement. Since regulators can only enforce in accordance with legislation and implementing rules and regulations, the first place to look for use of life-cycle principles and concepts may be in the legislative language itself.

Lawmakers cannot be expected to be seers. LCA is not a completely developed tool and at best is still *only* a tool. However, lawmakers might serve their own and everyone's best interests by learning how and when to use the tool, in order to create more effective and enforceable environmental laws. Ultimately environmental improvement, not just incorporation of LCA, is the yardstick by which environmentally related legislative, regulatory, and policy actions should be judged. And U.S. business and industry, in partnership with federal and state regulators, are beginning to seek ways to reduce pollution at its source and to address multimedia waste release problems in a holistic way. LCA has the potential to become an essential tool or means in that process.

8.3.2 Regulatory Development: A Case Study

LCA use in the development of U.S. environmental regulations can be illustrated by looking at the halogenated solvent[7] cleaning industry, commonly referred to as the *degreasing* industry,[8] which is subject to regulation under Title III of the Clean Air Act Amendments of 1990. In an effort to meet both existing and upcoming regulations aimed at reducing emissions of air toxics, as well as for other reasons,[9] many companies are looking for alternatives to halogenated organic solvents.

In effect, all these factors have contributed to the decreased acceptability and will impact the availability of these solvents. Thus, many companies are looking to substitutes that can largely replace certain halogenated solvents.

What are the substitutes? Although there are a number of alternatives, e.g., other solvents (aqueous, semiaqueous, and organic), supercritical fluids (supercritical CO_2, uv and ozone), and other emerging technologies, often there are no "drop in" alternatives. In other words, it is very difficult to replace one solvent with a substitute without creating a change in cleaning performance or without having to make some type of retrofit of the cleaning equipment.

More importantly, the primary concern with the switchover from halogenated solvents to alternatives is that the environmental preferability of substitutes (e.g., halogenated solvent degreasing versus aqueous-based cleaning) is not clear-cut. By switching, there may be cross-media transfers that precipitate future environmental problems. Some substitutes may require increased raw material use, energy use, etc., which, when taken as a whole, may not necessarily lead to environmental improvement. Thus, in this example, given the multiple effects to different media associated with the substitutes, it would be difficult to provide the regulated industry with a clear, consistent message about safer alternatives to halogenated solvents.

Although these types of issues arise in many rule-making scenarios, there is no agreed-upon method to determine the cross-media impacts and tradeoffs of alternatives. Life-cycle assessment, with its multimedia basis as well as a holistic framework, seemed to offer a good approach to solve this type of problem.

In cooperation with the Environmental Protection Agency, the Tellus Institute undertook a study to help identify various tradeoffs and relative impacts associated with alternatives to halogenated solvent cleaning. More generally, Tellus proposed to take the halogenated solvents cleaning NESHAP (National Emissions Standards for Hazardous Air Pollutant) as a case study to examine how LCA concepts could be incorporated into EPA's rule-making procedures to broaden consideration of the environmental impacts routinely evaluated.

Introducing LCA concepts into the rule-making process extends the regulatory analysis upstream and downstream within and across all affected media to account for both direct and indirect effects of a proposed standard which may otherwise escape a traditional regulatory impact analysis.

As an approach, it was envisioned that a set of protocols would be developed for assessing alternatives under the degreasing NESHAP which would capture the indirect impacts in both physical units (e.g., pounds of pollutants or Btu's of energy per unit of parts cleaned) and possibly monetary terms. The goal was to develop a procedure capable of flagging major life-cycle advantages and disadvantages of a proposed standard that could facilitate decision making without unduly burdening the rule-making process with additional analytical requirements. In its simplest form, the procedure could be a set of questions to expand in a qualitative fashion the traditional economic, environmental, and health impact assessments of proposed rules. In a more complicated version, the procedure could require a quantitative assessment of these life-cycle impacts to accompany the traditional assessment practices.[10]

The results of the degreasing case study were meant to help in developing a generic protocol which could be used in other rule-making processes as a tool to facilitate identification of major tradeoffs and decision making among alternative standards.[11]

For a number of reasons,[12] including resource constraints, the case study was not completed. The proposal of the regulation was governed by a court-ordered deadline that could not accommodate the additional time needed to complete the case study. Although methodological issues arose (e.g., lack of data that would allow tradeoff analysis), these were not the main barriers to applying life-cycle concepts to the specific rule making.

The exercise points to the need for active support from the regulatory and legislative communities to incorporate life-cycle analysis into rule making. A challenge that lies before life-cycle advocates is to demonstrate benefits from LCA incorporation to the legislator, regulator, and regulated communities alike. Nevertheless, experience from the Tellus study illustrates how life-cycle assessment concepts and principles could serve as a decision-making support tool for development of a more holistic and multimedia-based regulation.

Note that other attempts are being made to incorporate life-cycle considerations into the rule development process. EPA's Office of Water intends to apply LCA concepts in its development of effluent guidelines for industrial laundries and will look at disposable versus reusable cloths. Given that this effort was initiated internally and in the early stages of the regulation development process, the prospect for life-cycle concepts facilitating this particular rule-making process is greater.

8.3.3 Executive Order on Federal Acquisition, Recycling, and Waste Prevention: Another Case Study

In October 1993, President Clinton signed the Executive Order on Federal Acquisition, Recycling, and Waste Prevention.[13] The order provides another context within which to apply life-cycle concepts to public policy making.

Under the executive order, the Environmental Protection Agency is required to "issue guidance that recommends principles that Executive agencies should use in making determinations for the preference and purchase of environmentally preferable products" and services. *Environmentally preferable* is defined in the executive order to mean those "products or services that have a lesser or reduced effect on human health and the environment when compared with competing products or services that serve the same purpose."

Ideally, environmental preferability of a product or service should be determined by comparing the severity of environmental damage that it causes to human health and ecological health across its life cycle with competing products—from the point of raw materials acquisition through product manufacturing, packaging and transportation, use, and ultimate disposal. However, translating this to a workable policy will be a challenge.

Even the term *life cycle* itself is often interpreted by different people to mean very different things. To some, it connotes an analysis that is exhaustive, extremely time-consuming, and very expensive. To others a life-cycle approach can refer to an abbreviated process whereby a long list of potential environmental attributes and/or impacts is narrowed down to just a few which provide the basis for comparison across a particular product category.

In either case, however, neither the full methodology nor the abbreviated process is well defined. Thus, a number of practical questions arise in trying to apply LCA concepts to actual purchasing decisions. First, information on environmental releases or impacts across a product's life cycle may be very difficult to get, particularly for upstream stages such as raw materials acquisition. The degree to which this type of information is available may also depend on whether the vendor is vertically or horizontally integrated. Yet, it may be in the upstream stages of the product life cycle that environmental impacts are most severe.

Furthermore, it may be difficult to measure and verify certain life-cycle information. Another issue related to a life-cycle approach is that practical, user-friendly tools that can facilitate application of the concepts are still in development. Of particular relevance in incorporating environmental considerations into purchasing decisions may be life-cycle costing. To date, life-cycle costing is done mostly for internal costs, such as capital costs, operating and maintenance costs, and disposal costs. Apart from some energy-related costs, environmental issues are not part of the costing structure. Efforts are being made to broaden life-cycle costing tools to more fully integrate external and environmental costs associated with products, services, and systems.

Within the context of public policy making, other considerations quite apart from methodological and technical aspects must be taken into account. For example, in trying to encourage reporting of life-cycle information, one must think about the potential impacts on small businesses.

Yet, despite these challenges faced by applying the life-cycle concepts, the life-cycle framework offers the holistic and comprehensive perspective needed to address adequately the issue of environmentally preferable products and services. In addition, no other feasible alternative exists to replace the life-cycle approach. As efforts are made to apply the concepts more broadly, in both the private and the public sector, and as the work of those developing the methodology or establishing standards for life-cycle assessment continues, tools will evolve that can facilitate application of the life-cycle perspective to environmentally preferable purchasing.

8.3.4 Federal Trend toward Commercialization

In 1982 the Office of Management and Budget (OMB) issued Circular A-119, *Federal Participation in the Development and Use of Voluntary Standards.* The circular, which was revised and reissued in 1994, directs federal agencies to use product and testing standards developed through private-sector standards bodies. Federal agencies are directed to use these private-sector standards in preference to federal or military specifications and standards wherever possible and not otherwise prohibited.

In addition to using voluntary standards and incorporating them into acquisition practices, the circular specifically encourages federal personnel to participate in standards-developing bodies. The idea, at least in part, is to save tax dollars by using commercially available products and standards instead of developing government-unique ones. In addition, participation by federal personnel can help ensure that agencies' product requirements are adequately addressed as products and technologies are in the developmental stages.

The combined effect of presidential executive orders on the acquisition of environmentally preferable products and the OMB circular is to enhance the potential for use of life-cycle concepts in product standardization and commercialization. The partnership of federal interests and private-sector processes can foster national environmental, health, and safety goals.

8.4 ISSUES

8.4.1 Methodological

The above examples of current and potential uses of LCA concepts and principles in public policy raise a number of methodological as well as other issues. For example, within public policy making, how well defined must the methodology be, before it can be reasonably and effectively applied? What level of analysis is needed, before decisions can be made in an application? An attempt should be made to make connections between LCA and other assessment tools that currently exist. This is needed not only to avoid reinventing the wheel, but also because existing tools could help advance life-cycle methodology and application.

8.4.2 Trade Implications

Until internationally recognized and accepted standards for life-cycle methodologies are available, differences in life-cycle applications are likely to be challenged in the trade arena, whether under GATT, the North American Free Trade Agreement (NAFTA), or any number of bilateral agreements.

Ecolabel programs, for example, are a means of distinguishing products in trade and often are marketed as being based on life-cycle considerations. Ecolabels communicate product information to the consumer and may be used to foster competition and sway markets. Properly administered, many labeling programs serve as a legitimate means of identifying environmentally preferable products to the consumer.

Trade issues arise when a label program in one country acts as a barrier to the import of similar products from another country or when access to a label (and corresponding market advantage) is denied or overly burdensome. Developing countries, for example, have been concerned that ecolabels would be used in protectionist ways to keep foreign competition under control.[14] Labels based on life-cycle parameters heavily weighted in favor of the import country's economic, environmental, and technological infrastructure may inadvertently balance "apples and pogo sticks" when one is determining the environmental impact of a product and therefore its accessibility to the importer's ecolabel.

Is LCA a barrier? The problem arises when assessment values change because of varying local situations. In Germany, disposal problems strongly favor recyclable materials for product packaging. In fact, German regulations applying to national and imported products require specified levels of recyclability and may even require that an importer take back packaging materials once the consumer unwraps the product in question. Packaging materials are a much smaller consideration in the life cycle of Malaysian products imported to Germany. But transportation and energy expenditures associated with collecting, transporting, and recycling of packaging materials are prohibitive to effective export of some products under the German regulations.

International representatives discussed this and similar situations at the 1994 UNCTAD (United Nations Committee on Trade and Development) conference on ecolabeling.[15] One conclusion of the conference was that many countries such as Malaysia might be able to adjust packaging to meet Germany's requirements, but importers need timely information on national requirements in order to adjust manufacturing and distribution systems. Importers also need to have access to the bases, including the LCA methodology, of national and regional standards. Better yet, life-cycle considerations applied in the development of international standards for products could reveal common elements of both agreement and concern and could spawn new, nonborder mechanisms to address the issues.

8.4.3 Need for International Standards

The lack of standardized life-cycle methodologies for both inventory and impact assessment[16] contributes to the potential for misleading consumers about the environmental preferability of one product over another. Participants in the UNCTAD conference agreed that countries working together to create international standards is one way to help alleviate problems like those encountered by Germany and Malaysia.

GATT underlines the importance of international standards and conformity assessment. Conformity assessment can be likened to an agreement that, in specified situations, the following holds true: If $A = C$ and $B = C$, then $A = B$. In other words, if a product (A) from one country meets the requirements or standards (C) and a similar product (B) from a second country also conforms to the standards (C), then the two countries have a basis for treating the products (A and B) as equivalent. The concept is not difficult, but the application turns out to be extremely complex, especially when one is trying to evaluate regulatory requirements based on life-cycle methodologies. Is it possible, for example, to put competing interests on the table while determining the boundaries for a life-cycle inventory assessment when the natural resources of countries can vary so widely?

Wherever possible, use of international standards as a basis for conformity assessment can help reduce the costs of doing trade by eliminating duplicative testing. A great deal of work has yet to be accomplished[17] before GATT trading partners are comfortable with many of the conformity assessment issues related to environmental, health, and safety concerns across the borders.

8.5 WHERE DO WE GO FROM HERE?

8.5.1 Life-Cycle Concepts and Environmental Management Systems

In 1993, the International Organization for Standardization (ISO)[18] formed the Technical Committee on Environmental Management Systems Standards, known as TC-207.[19] This committee has the task of developing international[20] environmental management systems (EMS) standards for management to use in addressing an organization's environmental goals, needs, and requirements at every level. The standards are intended to help a manager answer the question, How do I get my hands around every existing and potential environmental consideration, including regulatory compliance, that's associated with my doing business?

In the last decade, the use of another set of ISO management standards, namely, the ISO 9000 quality management standards, has pervaded the international trade arena like a spreading tree root. The "9000," as the quality standards are commonly called, have become almost de facto requirements for doing international business. Even U.S. companies that do not engage in overseas trade are getting certified to ISO 9000 because certification is becoming a market advantage at home as well.

Many believe that the ISO 14,000 EMS being developed in TC-207 will carry as much weight as or more weight than the ISO 9000. In other words, as certification to ISO 14,000 becomes available and is spurred on by international market use, environmental management systems may be the basis on which many U.S. organizations identify acceptable suppliers and are, in turn, identified through marketing strategies to the U.S. consumer. It is conceivable that certification to ISO 14,000 may "sell" to the public as green manufacturing or environmentally preferred manufactures in much the same way as ecolabels identify environmentally preferable products.

In developing the EMS specification standard which will be the basis for auditing and certification, TC-207 through its subcommittee structure is also undertaking the development of guidance standards. These include standards for life-cycle assessment, environmental performance[21] evaluation, and ecolabeling.

In the area of life-cycle assessment, ISO is attempting to standardize both the life-cycle inventory (LCI) and life-cycle impact assessment procedures. ISO has the dubious distinction of being the only international and treaty-recognized standards-setting body that is undertaking this enormous task. The potential for LCA advancement is great, however, for two reasons. First, through ISO there is a large international constituency currently gathered under one roof, as it were, committed to producing consensus standards. Second, EMS could provide a standardized structure or LCA laboratory—a consistency of approach that can yield the kind of application data LCA practitioners sorely need to improve the tool.

While use of specific LCA models or standards is not required in the current draft of the EMS standard, for organizations producing products, LCA use is inherent in setting organizations' environmental goals, and setting relevant environmental goals is required by the EMS. In effect, as the EMS standards are adopted, there is the potential for greater generation of LCA data, within similarly structured certification programs, throughout the international trading arena. Sharing and evaluating data may be a hurdle to cross in and of itself, but from the current vantage point, it seems that widespread EMS use could be a tremendous boost for refining the LCA tool.

8.5.2 Taking on the Life-Cycle Challenge

Given that public policy application of LCA concepts and principles is still in its infancy, and given the potential benefit of such application, it is important to reflect on ways to encourage incorporation of LCA concepts into policy making. In part, there needs to be more concerted effort by LCA practitioners to draw a clearer connection between the methodology and the potential for use within the public policy domain as well as to increase the acceptability of a new tool for the mix of tools on which policy makers rely.

But the demonstrated benefits of taking a life-cycle perspective will not be apparent unless LCA is actually used even in its imperfect stage. Looking to the Europeans for their more pragmatic approach to dealing with the methodological inadequacies at this time, the United States needs to learn by doing. The methodology should evolve based on real-life applications. It will be an incremental process, with the methodology undergoing continuous improvement. Science will evolve to fill in the gaps, and the tool will be fleshed out and make applications more sound.

An added benefit of having increased public policy application of LCA concepts is that involvement of the public sector helps establish a baseline of information and more publicly available results. Public access to data can lead to increased access to the tool, and this can help overcome some of the intellectual property rights issues associated with the private sector.

Overall, the use of LCA concepts and principles in public policy making needs to be put in perspective. It is not anticipated, nor should anyone expect, that LCA can serve as a "golden parachute" capable of saving every situation and solving every problem. LCA does not obviate the need to make difficult decisions on tradeoffs and does not replace value judgments. Properly understood and applied, LCA can help identify tradeoffs and help make decisions more transparent and explicit.

LCA should be seen as one of several tools available to policy makers. Because it can bring a more holistic and comprehensive framework to policy making, LCA is sure to be one of the policy makers' most important tools.

REFERENCES

1. Executive Order no. 12873, October 1993.
2. In August 1994, the Society of Environmental Toxicology and Chemistry (SETAC) sponsored a week-long conference on "Application of Life Cycle Assessment to Public Policy." An upcoming publication from this workshop will document a wide array of examples from the United States, Canada, and European and other countries.
3. Readers are referred to *The Use of Life Cycle Assessment in Eco-Labeling Programs,* Environmental Protection Agency, September 1993.
4. From the "Final Report of the Task Force on Environmental Product Profiles," presented at the seventh session of the Senior Advisors to the United Nations Economic Commission for Europe (ECE) on Environmental and Water Problems, May 30–31, 1994.
5. Ibid.
6. The Standards Code provides rules on the treatment of regulatory and voluntary standards in the context of the trade agreement. The Uruguay Round of GATT negotiations resulted in the Standards Code being incorporated into the body of the agreement. Both GATT and NAFTA place specific emphasis on the use of international standards as a primary consideration for tools that governments use in achieving environmental, health, and safety measures.
7. Halogenated solvents commonly used in degreasing operations include chlorofluorocarbons (CFC 113), methylene chloride, perchloroethylene (PERC), trichloroethylene (TCE), and 1,1,1-trichloroethane (TCA).
8. Degreasing is not an industry per se. Instead, it cuts across many industries (e.g., automotive, electronic, aerospace, metal fabrication) and is an essential step in the production process of these industries.
9. These factors include increased concerns about environmental and health effects of solvents; federal and state regulations limiting emissions of hazardous air pollutants and volatile organic compounds; international agreements, such as the Montreal Protocol, to which the United States is a signatory, with scheduled phaseout of ozone-depleting solvents; and other regulations.
10. Excerpted from "Incorporation of Life Cycle Assessment Concepts in Rule-Making Procedures—A Discussion Paper," submitted by Tellus Institute to EPA, Office of Pollution Prevention and Toxic Substances, June 1993.
11. Ibid.
12. A more expanded discussion of lessons learned from this case study can be found in "Using LCA in Public Policy Analysis—A Five Year Retrospective," submitted by Tellus Institute to EPA, Office of Pollution Prevention and Toxic Substances (to be published).

13. Executive Order 12873 is one in a series of executive orders that President Clinton has signed since 1993 that emphasize federal government purchasing practices to promote environmental goals. Other executive orders include Executive Order 12843, Procurement Requirements and Policies for Federal Agencies for Ozone Depleting Substances; Executive Order 12844, Federal Use of Alternative Fueled Vehicles; Executive Order 12845, Federal Procurement of Energy Efficient Computer; Executive Order 12856, Pollution Prevention and Right-to-Know in the Government; Executive Order 12902, Energy Efficiency and Water Conservation at Federal Facilities; Presidential Memorandum on Environmentally and Economically Beneficial Practices on Federal Landscaped Grounds.

14. The following paper gives a good discussion of this issue: "Ecolabelling Initiatives as Potential Barriers to Trade—A Viewpoint from Developing Countries," prepared by Veena Jha and Simonetta Zarilli for the Informal Experts Workshop, Organization for Economic Co-operation and Development, Environment Directorate on Life-Cycle Management and Trade, July 20–21, 1993.

15. See "Ecolabelling and International Trade," UNCTAD Discussion Paper 70, United Nations, October 1994.

16. *Life Cycle Assessment Methodology Development,* EPA Project Update (issued periodically).

17. See *Summary Report: Workshop on Life-Cycle Management and Trade,* Organization for Economic Co-operation and Development, ENV/EPOC(93), Paris, France, 1993.

18. The International Organization for Standardization (ISO) is a voluntary standards-setting body headquartered in Geneva, Switzerland. More than 90 countries have "member body" participation in ISO. In the United States, the ISO membership is held by the American National Standards Institute (ANSI), located at 11 West 42d Street, New York, NY; (212) 642-4900.

19. Readers are referred to ASTM, 1916 Race Street, Philadelphia, PA, for complete information on U.S. participation, by means of a TAG (Technical Advisory Group), in this particular ISO Technical Committee. ASTM has been delegated by ANSI as the TAG administrator. The EPA participates formally in the U.S. TAG by means of the EPA Standards Network. An article on the formation of TC-207 is by M. McKiel, "EPA: Is Sage Enough for the World?" *Pollution Engineering,* Feb. 15, 1993.

20. A number of countries, including Great Britain, France, and Ireland, already had environmental management systems (EMS) standards, arguably the most famous being the BS-7750 standard for the British Standards Institute. Other examples include the Responsible Care Program from the Chemical Manufacturers Association and the GEMI Principles from the Global Environmental Management Institute (GEMI).

21. ISO does not set environmental performance standards typically associated with regulatory activities. The performance evaluation guideline standards from TC-207 will focus on methods for measuring and improving the system's ability to identify and manage environmental performance.

CHAPTER 9
EUROPEAN PERSPECTIVE

Dennis Postlethwaite
LIFE CYCLE ANALYSIS MANAGER
UNILEVER RESEARCH PORT SUNLIGHT LABORATORY
BEBINGTON, WIRRAL, ENGLAND

Nico T. de Oude
EXECUTIVE DIRECTOR
SETAC-EUROPE
BRUSSELS, BELGIUM

9.1 INTRODUCTION

The pressure to assess the environmental characteristics of products and processes has been more severe in Europe than elsewhere, especially in Scandinavia. This has led to a more urgent development of the life-cycle assessment (LCA) approach, from which two major needs have become prominent, namely, for data and for a practical and acceptable approach to impact assessment. As a consequence, developments on these fronts in Europe have been relatively rapid. This has generated some notable advances, although the situation is still in a state of flux. The interest and activities of regulatory and official bodies have also been a major factor influencing both the pace and the nature of LCA development in Europe. The current status in Europe on these three issues, namely, regulatory activities, data, and impact assessment, is reviewed briefly below.

9.2 USE IN EUROPEAN LEGISLATION

European regulators started around 1980 to include references to the LCA methodology in draft legislation without using the term itself. Instead terms such as *research, ecobalances,* and *cradle-to-grave* were used. This section discusses two major areas of application, ecolabels and packaging, and gives some examples of more limited scope.

9.2.1 Ecolabel Regulation[1]

The European Union (EU, formerly named the European Community) is implementing a Community Eco Label Award Scheme. The legislative form chosen is that of a regulation, the most stringent form, requiring all member states to implement the new legislation into their national legislation without any modification.

The European Council stated that specific ecological criteria for different product categories will be established to recognize major environmental improvements. The regulation does not quantify the size of such an improvement, but informally it has been mentioned that roughly 20 percent of products on the market in a category will comply with the initial criteria.

Member states were requested to develop criteria for the product categories listed in Table 9.1. The last category in Table 9.1 is for a material, not a product. It would, for

TABLE 9.1 Product Categories in EU Ecolabeling

Product category	Lead country
Textiles, T-shirts	Denmark
Shoes	The Netherlands
Antiperspirants, deodorants	United Kingdom
Shampoos	France
Hairsprays	United Kingdom
Hair-styling aids	United Kingdom
Cleaning agents	Germany
Laundry detergents	Germany
Household cleaning products	Germany
Kitchen towels, toilet paper rolls	Denmark
Ceramic crockery	Portugal
Glassware (table and decorative)	Portugal
Refrigerators	Italy
Washing machines, dishwashers	United Kingdom
Lightbulbs	United Kingdom
Batteries	France
Paints and varnishes	France
Ceramic tiles	Italy
Insulation materials	Denmark
Building materials	Italy
Cat litter	The Netherlands
Soil improvers	United Kingdom
Growing media	United Kingdom
Packaging materials	Italy

example, be difficult to define a functional unit for a packaging material without knowing the nature of the product it is to contain. Hence, the intention appears to be that a packaging ecolabel can only be awarded to a package for a specific product.

Criteria have been established for washing machines, and ecolabels have been awarded. Groups of experts have proposed criteria for laundry detergents, tissue products (paper kitchen towels and toilet paper rolls), paints and varnishes, and soil improvers. The final step is adoption by the commission. Criteria for the other categories are still being defined.

Basically all countries are consistent in not requiring a true LCA. This is largely the result of a dichotomy in statements by the European Council. On one hand, it requires that "the specific ecological criteria for each product shall be established using a 'cradle-to-grave' approach." On the other hand, the council states that "the criteria must be precise, clear and objective so as to ensure uniformity of application by the competent bodies." It is the common conflict between the lack of absolute certainty in science and the need for absolute truths in Napoleonic law. Napoleonic law assumes that certain things are absolutely true. Science states a certain theory to best explain the available facts but recognizes that theory can be changed if new facts emerge that do not fit the theory. Hence, the member states set about defining specific criteria for each of the product categories.

Many of the lead countries already had established national ecolabels or were in the process of doing so. Hence, the selection of criteria was influenced by existing practices in each of the member states, resulting in a lack of consistency. To remedy this problem, in December 1993 the EU appointed a group of experts to

- Support the member states in establishing ecolabeling criteria which are based on a methodology that is both scientifically sound and workable in practice
- Improve the uniformity in the methods applied in different member states

The group made the first part of its report[2] available in May 1994, pointing out the fact that LCA methodology is still in development. It is recommended that criteria be defined for the EU as a whole, assuming that products and their impacts are substantially the same throughout the EU. If this were not accepted by the member states, then the conclusion must be that only national labels are feasible. The second and final report, published in 1995, defines the research required to support and strengthen the ecolabeling scheme.

9.2.2 Packaging and Packaging Waste Directive[3]

The EU decided to use the regulatory format of a *directive* to manage the amount of packaging and packaging waste used and discarded in member states. A directive must be implemented by member states in their national legislation, but it allows—under specific conditions—for the addition of more stringent requirements.

The draft directive dates back to 1992 and was finally accepted in December 1994. The draft sets targets for recycling and recovery of packages and packaging materials, but allows these to be changed as the results of a life-cycle assessment:

> If scientific research, or any other evaluation technique, such as eco-balances, prove that other recovery processes show greater environmental advantages, the targets for recycling can be modified.

However, the European Council also recognized that this might be simpler said than done: "As there is not yet a generalized agreement on life cycle analysis methodology and interpretation, comparison in terms of environmental soundness between types of packaging, systems of packaging and materials used is very difficult." This has proved to be the case: years of debate between regulators, politicians, and industry followed. The draft packaging directive illustrates that social valuation and acceptance of the results of a life-cycle assessment are a difficult, novel process. Different value systems clash, and some of these systems may see their established opinions challenged.

One opinion is that there exists a clear order of preference for dealing with packaging and packaging waste:

Prevention

Reuse and recycling

Incineration with energy recovery

Incineration without energy recovery

Landfill

Agreement exists that the first and last items are ranked properly in the hierarchy, but the case can be made that a balanced combination of the other three processes may be environmentally superior to recycling to the maximum extent possible. The directive acknowledges the current state of the art and establishes a framework and temporary objectives (for an initial 5-year period). It further creates a "technical" committee to follow up on developments in the member states and to make specific recommendations to the European Council and the Parliament.

Another element confirming this inability to reach definite goals today is demonstrated by the existence of a range for the objectives for the first 5 years after entry into force, namely, 50 to 60 percent for recovery and 25 to 45 percent for recycling with a minimum of 15 percent per material (all percentages by weight). It also recognizes the variability of situations throughout Europe, hence the possibility for some countries to reach higher or lower targets.

9.2.3 Other Examples

Life-cycle assessments were specifically included in a covenant between the Dutch government and industry.[4] An article in this covenant requires that

> If research shows that replacement of one-way packaging by re-usable packaging would cause clearly less damage to the environment and that there are no preponderant objections to such a change-over on market economic grounds then the packaging industry undertakes to switch over to using re-usable packaging rather than one-way packages.

It took about 3 years to produce the LCAs for some 10 different product categories. Not surprisingly, reusable packaging will decrease the amount of municipal waste. However, such waste in itself is not an LCA parameter. It only becomes one after the waste has been treated and residues enter the environment. Then its impact can be weighed against that of transporting and cleaning returned cans and bottles made from glass or plastic.

Industry developed, during the 3 years of life-cycle assessment, a number of novel packaging options. These make it probable that the packaging waste reductions required by the covenant will be met. Hence, the LCAs helped industry to recognize improvement opportunities, rather than choose between options existing at the time of signing the covenant.

The final outcome has been mixed: Partly packages already existing (or developed after the covenant was signed) are preferred environmentally; partly returnable packages are to be introduced after a further period of evaluation in pilot programs.

The Belgian government decided in 1993 to levy a tax on packages and products with the level of tax depending on the environmental burden caused. Polyvinyl chloride (PVC) was earmarked to be most heavily taxed. However, the government commissioned an LCA before imposing the tax and found that the environmental disadvantages of PVC were much less than had been assumed when the tax rates were discussed. The scope of this LCA was clearly more restricted than those discussed in Secs. 9.2.1 and 9.2.2, which suggests that such LCAs may generally provide more usable results.

The rigid order of preference for dealing with packaging and packaging waste has, for example, encouraged a German study into the environmental preference of different waste management options.[5] A study by the German Institute for Energy and Environment assessed different routes for disposing of waste newsprint. The study focused on CO_2 emissions. The results showed—under simplifying assumptions—a preference for incinerating waste paper with replacement newsprint produced from Swedish timber.

These, and similar studies, show that European regulations are now routinely using LCAs. However, with increasing understanding of the possibilities and limitations of the LCA methodologies, regulators are moving toward studies of more limited scope and are defining their questions more accurately. The conclusion is that the LCA methodology has been accepted by European regulators as a useful tool, be it not the answer to all human questions.

9.3 DATA

LCA is a data-intensive technique, and the lack of data has hindered, or prevented, many applications. The situation is particularly acute when LCA is advocated as a tool for implementing public policy decisions, such as ecolabeling or product regulation.

Data pertaining to the inventory phase of LCA are becoming increasingly available, in essentially two forms, that which is openly published and freely available and that which is available by subscription to databases and software systems engineered by LCA practitioners and institutes. Data sources currently available in Europe in these categories are reviewed briefly below. Emphasis is mainly on the primary databases, rather than on the software systems developed from them. The latter are now appearing in a number of forms, many with commercial interests. Reference is, however, made to these where possible.

9.3.1 Openly Accessible Databases

Almost invariably, these databases contain industry-averaged data, usually produced by contracted agencies or consulting bodies. The latter generate the data via individual secrecy agreements with each participating company to preserve the confidentiality of the individual data sets. Thus, the source of the data is ostensibly transparent, although their validity can be, and has been, challenged, principally on the grounds that they are, by definition, an average, in some cases for materials produced by very different processes and because they invariably are not fully comprehensive and, at best, represent a "snapshot in time." Nevertheless, such data are arguably of great value because they do represent the overall situation prevailing at that time and, particularly, provide a uniform and unequivocal base from which LCAs can be undertaken. The latter is especially valuable where such LCAs are used publicly for product compositions. Care is needed to distinguish primary databases from software clones based on them; the clones replicate the data and provide proprietary software for their manipulation.

Two openly accessible databases have been published so far. They are specific to European sourcing, processing, and energy utilization conditions and comprise:

BUWAL.   This database was developed for the Swiss Federal Ministry of the Environment, Forestry and Countryside (BUWAL—*Bundesamt für Umwelt, Wald und*

Landschaft) by the ETH of Zurich in 1991. It is an updated and revised version of an earlier BUWAL study undertaken in 1984 by EMPA and essentially comprises ecobalance data for the following packaging materials:

- High-density polyethylene (HDPE)
- Low-density polyethylene (LDPE)
- Polypropylene (PP)
- Polyethylene terephthalate (PET)
- Polystyrene (PS)
- High-density polystyrene (HI-PS)
- Polyvinyl chloride (PVC)
- Paper, cardboard, corrugated cardboard
- Tinplate
- Aluminum
- Glass

The data include production and transport of each packaging material but exclude conversion to final packaging and are representative of *average* Swiss production processes. Electricity generation is based on the European average (UCPTE).

Because of its ready availability and early publication, the BUWAL database has been widely adopted and used throughout Europe. Thus, many companies have incorporated the BUWAL data into their LCA and packaging optimization systems. Additionally, it has formed the basis of LCA data and software packages, some of which have been made freely available by their creators and others of which have been issued as commercial packages. These currently mainly comprise

Oko-base II	Migros, Switzerland	Subscription
Procter & Gamble model	Procter & Gamble, Belgium	Free
Ecopack 2000	Landbank Consultancy, United Kingdom	Subscription

A further update of the BUWAL system is now in progress with a view to rendering the data compatible with those of the APME study described below.

APME. The Association of Plastic Manufacturers in Europe (APME), formerly known as PWMI (Plastics Waste Management Institute), is in the process of issuing comprehensive data sets (ecobalances) for European commodity plastics. The overall exercise is one of the most comprehensive life-cycle inventory (LCI) studies yet undertaken. It involves all major European plastic manufacturers and was carried out by a consortium of four leading European LCA practitioners. The data so far published cover

- Polyethylene (PE)
- Polypropylene (PP)
- Polystyrene (PS)
- Polyvinyl chloride (PVC)

Reports on PET and other plastics are currently in progress. The intention is to eventually cover all major European plastics.

The above activity, together with the growing pressures to undertake LCAs and to ensure that they are done objectively, has stimulated a number of other initiatives to generate industry-averaged LCA data. Currently these include:

- *Aluminum*—being undertaken by the European Aluminium Association
- *Surfactants*—being undertaken by the ECOSOL sector group of the European Chemical Industry Council (CEFIC)
- *Oxygenated organic solvents*—being undertaken by the OSPA sector group of CEFIC
- *Detergent zeolites*—being undertaken by the ZEODET sector group of CEFIC
- *Steel for packaging*—being undertaken by the Association of European Producers of Steel for Packaging
- *Plastic packaging films*—being undertaken by the Packaging and Industrial Films Association

A major, and highly important, feature of the above databases is that they provide data on not only the materials referred to, but also many raw materials and intermediates used in their manufacture. Additionally, all the above databases necessarily include data relating to energy generation, fuel use, and transport.

9.3.2 Subscription Databases

There are a growing number of commercial LCA databases and software systems available now in Europe. The following is not intended to be an exhaustive survey, but outlines briefly the more advanced and widely-used systems.

BOUSTEAD.   This is the foremost and best-known European system. It was initiated by Dr. Ian Boustead in 1972 and is one of the most comprehensive LCA systems available, covering some 2000 industrial operations. It was originally focused on fuels and energy but now covers a wide range of materials and processes.

ECOLOGIC.   Developed by Chalmers Industrieteknik (Sweden). This is an inventory tool system primarily covering packaging and pertains mainly to Swedish industry.

IDEA (International Databases for Ecoprofile Analysis).   Originally developed by the International Institute for Applied Systems Analysis (IIASA) in Austria, but now managed by VTT Technical Research Institute in Finland, this is a comprehensive system based on western European-averaged data covering, in particular, basic material manufacture, energy, and transport.

PEMS (PIRA Environmental Management System).   This is a two-part system developed by the Packaging Industry Research Association International comprising inventory and impact assessment modules. It was originally based on packaging, utilizing BUWAL and PIRA's own data. It is now being extended to cover many other materials. PIRA has since linked with Franklin Associates, Ltd. (a U.S. company), and they offer a joint database and software system (Ecomanager).

VDU.   This packaging database was developed by the Fraunhofer Institute and the German UBA (*Umweltbundesamt*).

PIA (Product Improvement Analysis).   This database was developed by TME/BMI [Dutch Bureau for the Environment and Information in conjunction with Van den Berghs (Holland)]. It covers consumer product ingredients, packaging, and energy.

TEMIS.   This system was developed by the Ökoinstitut (Darmstadt, Germany). The focus is on energy and transport, and it was developed as a tool for research and decision making in energy policy.

SIMAPRO.   This process and materials system was designed as a decision support tool. The system has been updated and now includes an impact assessment facility based on the Swiss critical-volumes approach. The system was developed by the Centre for Environmental Management Studies (CML), University of Leiden (The Netherlands), and the PRE Consultancy. The system incorporates the BUWAL packaging data.

ECOPACK 2000.   This software program developed by the Landbank Agency (United Kingdom) is based essentially on the BUWAL and Boustead systems. It mainly covers packaging and includes an impact assessment component.

TEAM (Tools for Environmental Analysis and Management).   TEAM was developed by Ecobilan (France) and is an English-language software system having advanced features, such as built-in spreadsheet and facilities for computer-aided design. It is intended to be used in conjunction with standard Ecobilan database modules (DEAMS, e.g., energy, transport, raw materials). A unique feature is encapsulation (nesting) to generate standard aggregated modules. The TEAM system can be modified or added to by the user to suit individual requirements.

ÖfE (Ökoinventare für Energiesysteme).   This very comprehensive system covering energy generation was compiled by the ETH (Technical University of Zurich, Switzerland). It covers generation from oil, gas, coal, nuclear, hydro, biomass, geothermal, solar thermal, and photovoltaic sources and comprehensively quantifies emissions, including radioactivity. The system is modular and available in report and diskette formats.

AIM (Ambiente Italia Model).   This database for LCA and ecobalances was produced by the IRAI (Instituto di Recerche Ambiente Italia, Milan, Italy). It contains data for 8 energy production scenarios, 20 transport systems, and 4 waste management systems. It is primarily aimed at deployment in Italy.

LIFEWAY.   This educational system was developed by the Technical University of Denmark. It is limited in scope but includes a valuation component.

Other databases also exist in Europe. These are generally held by LCA practitioners and consulting organizations and are used by them to undertake commissioned LCA studies. As such, they are not directly accessible. Specific examples are Sundström (Sweden), CAU (Germany), Chemsystems (United Kingdom), TNO (The Netherlands), and the EPS system (Sweden—see below).

9.3.3 Centralized Database Systems

There is a real danger of incompatibilities between various databases now in use or being developed. This has been recognized and the feasibility of developing a harmonized Pan-European system has been investigated by the Society for the Promotion of Lifecycle Development (SPOLD). The study of this concluded that a universal LCA database is, in principle, feasible. There are four basic requirements:

- Transparency
- Completeness
- Temporality
- Quality

and some kind of electronic format would be necessary. Data would need to be carefully scrutinized and qualified, and the system made available in the major European languages, not just English. Major problems foreseen were time (to organize), access, and cost. Although considerable, these problems are not seen as insurmountable, and SPOLD has recently embarked on the assembly of the database as one of its major projects.

9.4 IMPACT ASSESSMENT

Information from an LCA inventory is often diffuse and multifarious. As such, it is difficult to interpret, although the necessity to do so is real. The impact assessment phase of LCA attempts to translate the inventory information to comprehensible environmental effects and to provide at least an overview, if not a measure, of their overall and relative significance. Impact assessment is recognizably difficult because judgment issues and criteria are involved. There is also an expectation by some that this can be done simply, even to an extent which results in a single number or "ecoscore," but this is ill-founded and irrational. Others contend that impact assessment, because of its inherent subjectivity and complexity, is too difficult to be undertaken rationally and that LCA should stop at the inventory. However, for many (even most), this view is also unacceptable, especially in light of the progress made so far.

Because the inventory is detailed and contains many nonrelated parameters, and because the pressures, certainly in Europe, to develop methods which are both relatively simple and easily intelligible are severe, it is essential that impact assessment methodology development be coordinated across all interest groups. At present, as described below, a number of schemes have emerged in Europe, many differing in fundamental characteristics. Considerable effort is now being made by the SETAC LCA working groups on impact assessment in both Europe and North America to achieve such coordination and to ensure that a sensible and consensual option, or options, ultimately emerges and can be implemented.

A basic framework for impact assessment was developed by SETAC at the specialist workshop held in Florida in February 1992. This workshop identified four major impact categories—resource depletion, human health, ecological health, and social health and welfare—to which the inventory items, notably emissions, are linked via chains of stressors. Examples of intermediate stressors are acid rain and global warming. Stressor pathways are as yet but only loosely defined and characterized. What is more rigorously characterized are the phases of impact assessment:

- *Classification* is the step in which the data from the inventory table are grouped into a number of environmental impact categories.
- *Characterization* is the step which attempts to aggregate the impacts within each category, with the objective of producing an impact profile.

- *Valuation* is an attempt to apportion weighting to the different impact categories so that the disparate types and amounts of impact can be compared.

Many of the basic concepts have been embodied to a greater or lesser extent in the impact assessment schemes and methodologies which have emerged or are being developed in Europe. The more established or notable European impact assessment schemes are reviewed briefly below, where a distinction has been made between systems which include valuation (i.e., valuative) and those which do not (i.e., nonvaluative). Again, the review does not claim to be exhaustive but rather seeks to describe the more important systems.

9.4.1 Nonvaluative Approaches

Critical Dilution Volume.   This is one of the leading methods and is now widely used in Europe. It was developed by the Swiss Federal Ministry for the Environment (BUWAL) and basically characterizes each emission in terms of the volume of air or water required to dilute it to the legal limit set for that emission. Overall results are expressed as a total volume, i.e., the sum of the individual dilution volumes. The method has advantages in that it is comprehensible, feasible, and relatively simple. However, the approach has a major disadvantage in that it is critically dependent on the legal-limit specifications. The latter are not science-based, are not available for all emissions, are often country-specific, and do not account for mutual interactions between emissions. The method is also limited because it takes no account of fate or exposure. Despite the disadvantages, the critical-volumes approach is now being applied widely by many LCA practitioners in Europe, if only for broad screening purposes ("sighting shots"). The approach has also been incorporated into many database and software systems.

Dutch System.   One of the most formative and comprehensive European impact assessment systems is being developed by the Centre of Environmental Studies (CML) at the University of Leiden, The Netherlands. At present, this covers only the classification and characterization stages; valuation is excluded. There is thus little subjectivity. Assessment is in terms of environmental effect categories, according to this list:

- Scarce, renewable resources
- Nonrenewable resources (raw materials)
- Global warming
- Human toxicity
- Ozone depletion
- Environmental toxicity
- Acidification
- Eutrophication
- COD (chemical oxidation demand) discharge
- Photo-oxidant formation
- Space requirements
- Nuisance (smell, noise)
- Occupational safety
- Final solid waste, hazardous

- Final solid waste, nonhazardous
- Effects of waste heat on water

This list has been expanded from earlier versions to allow a more precise classification in some of the categories and to include additional ones. Characterization is accomplished by using environmental indices (equivalency factors) for the appropriate emissions and categories, many of which are available in the published literature. The system thus has merit in that not only is it comprehensive, but also it is both objective and transparent. There are reservations, namely, that the system, like many others, estimates potential, rather than actual, effects and that some double counting is inevitable (i.e., the same emission can have an effect in different environmental compartments).

9.4.2 Valuative Approaches

Ecopoint Method. This comprises a further development of the critical-volumes approach of the Swiss BUWAL agency and again is based on regulatory limits. The fundamental concept is *ecological shortage,* defined as the resilience of an environmental resource to the current pollution level or, alternatively, as the ratio of critical flow of pollutant to actual flow. Thus, ecological shortage is measured as an ecological factor from the relationship between total pollution and maximum permissible pollution. The results are calculated in terms of *ecopoints,* which comprise the product of the actual pollution (emission) and the ecological factor. Finally, an overall assessment is obtained by summing the ecopoints for the individual emissions to give a single number, or *ecoscore.* The ecopoint system has been developed to cover all impact categories (including resource depletion and waste disposal to landfill). It is again limited by a total dependence on regulatory limits and by the fact that the "critical flows" can only really be defined for relatively small geographic regions. For these reasons, application of the ecopoint system has largely been confined to its country of origin, i.e., Switzerland, where it has been used to assess packaging.

EPS System. The EPS (Environmental Priority Strategies in Product Design) has been developed in Sweden by the Swedish Environmental Research Institute (IVL), and it is another country-specific system. It is a materials-intensive system designed for assessing a wide variety of product types. For each basic material, an *environmental load index* (ELI) is evaluated. This index assigns values to emissions and resource consumptions based on five criteria: biodiversity, human health, ecological health, resources, and aesthetics. These indices are then multiplied by the materials loadings to give what are termed *environmental load units* (ELUs), which are then summed to quantify the total environmental load. The system has disadvantages in that neither the ELIs nor the ELUs calculated from them are transparent; that ecological, social, and economic effects are intermingled in the ELIs; and that the system is specific to Sweden. However, the system does have the advantage that sensitivity and error analyses can be undertaken routinely, a facility which is not predominant in other systems. Overall, the EPS system is an interesting and relevant development because it does demonstrate the extent to which impact assessment, in the LCA sense, can be, and is being, developed.

DTI System. A different impact assessment approach has been adopted by the Danish Technological Institute (DTI). This focuses on human health effects, although ecological health and resource consumption effects are included. Both chronic and acute health effects are considered, and emphasis is placed on occupational health and the working environment (including accidents). The system is an expert-based, semiquantitative one and attempts to account for fate and exposure as well as loadings. Classification of impacts is made on a three-point scoring basis, the scores subsequently being combined by expert judgment panels to give an overall assessment, which is heavily risk-oriented. The system is essentially targeted at the use of new materials, each of which is characterized in the scheme by an *impact profile* or fingerprint. Like the EPS system, the DTI system suffers from being country- or region-specific and lacks transparency.

DKT System.   This is another Danish system developed by DK Teknik, again targeted at new materials coming into Denmark's technology development program. Full details are not yet available, although it has been claimed that the method builds on but is more transparent than the older DTI system.

German Systems.   Development of impact assessment methodology is now being undertaken by the Umweltbundesamt (UBA). The system currently being devised is being based on environmental effect categories, which closely follow those of the Dutch approach (see above), but, unlike the Dutch approach, a valuation component is incorporated. Interestingly, the nonvaluative and valuative components are being developed separately, the former by CAU (Frankfurt) and the latter by IFEU (Heidelberg). Human toxicity is assessed by MIK (maximum emission concentrations). NOEL values are used to measure ecotoxicity. For the valuation phase, it is likely that in many studies not all effect categories need to be considered, in which case an adequate qualification for those omitted is required.

Landbank System.   An expert-based approach to impact assessment has been developed and used by Landbank Consultancy in the United Kingdom. This utilizes a Delphi technique to evaluate the inventory data, in which members of the expert panel individually assess the human toxicological and ecotoxicological effects of the system. The individual views are collated and summarized, following which they are iteratively fed and refed back to the panel members for ratification, leading to either convergence or divergence of opinion. The technique is very different from the earlier ones and is of interest because of this. It is criticizable on the grounds that it is totally subjective, nontransparent (since panelist confidentiality is a requisite), and, unless they are large, dependent on panel size and constitution. Nevertheless, the technique in principle does have merit in that it addresses the difficult issue of valuation and in doing so attempts to involve a spectrum of judges whose views and experiences are intentionally very broad.

As stated earlier, it is acknowledged that this brief review is not exhaustive; nor can it be, given the current depth and breadth of activity on impact assessment. Only the more significant European impact assessment approaches have been described. Others are being developed and, additionally, many of the databases and software systems described earlier incorporate an elementary form of impact assessment, almost invariably at the time of writing based on the critical-volumes approach.

In summary, serious effort and major resources are being put into the development and use of impact assessment techniques in Europe. The developments are all relevant, and practicable systems are emerging. These need now to be proved by practical experience. It is also likely that more systems will continue to evolve in the future, both new and modified. Eventually, there will be some consolidation and merger of the most appropriate of these, engineered by debate and consensus. The SETAC working groups will play a major role in this. This will take time. Some attention will need also to be directed to data needs, availability, and quality, and this will draw on the resources and findings of other initiatives.

REFERENCES

1. Council Regulation on a Community Eco Label Award Scheme, no. 880/92 of 23 March 1992, *O.J. L-99,* April 11, 1992.

2. H. A. Udo de Haes, "Guidelines for the Application of Life-Cycle Assessment in the European Union Ecolabeling Programme," Society for the Promotion of Lifecycle Development (SPOLD), Brussels, Belgium, 1994.

3. Draft Council Directive on Packaging and Packaging Waste, European Union, Brussels, Begium, 1994.

4. Dutch Packaging Covenant, Ministry of the Environment, The Hague, The Netherlands, 6 June 1991.

5. M. Flood, "Life Cycle Assessments: Understanding the Limits," *Warmer Bulletin,* no. 42, p. 5 (1994).

CHAPTER 10
MATERIALS IN LCA

Steven B. Young
DEPARTMENT OF METALLURGY AND MATERIALS SCIENCE
UNIVERSITY OF TORONTO, ONTARIO, CANADA

OVERVIEW

Materials, along with energy, are fundamental to the life-cycle assessment (LCA) of any manufactured product. Moreover, LCA is important to the materials sector, both as a new tool for environmental management and as a new field of study. It is this connection between LCA, materials, and materials industries that is considered here. The intent is to introduce some important and relevant considerations of materials in LCA. Discussion includes, first, the place of materials in the LCA approach. Second, the materials sector's response to LCA, to supply materials information and participate in LCA activities, is reviewed. Third, the use of LCA to achieve environmental improvements is examined. Internally, LCA might be used by materials producers to implement process improvements. Externally, life-cycle environmental design will incorporate materials selection to reduce product life-cycle environmental burdens. The use of LCA as a tool for environmental map making is illustrated to support decision making.

10.1 MATERIALS IN LCA

10.1.1 Materials Are Fundamental to LCA

Industrial materials are a significant and determining factor in the outcome of LCA studies performed on manufactured products, packaging, and buildings. Whether they be steel, aluminum, paper, glass, wood, or plastic, materials are analyzed at each of the life-cycle stages (Fig. 10.1). Moreover, materials production is, itself, one of the generic product's life-cycle stages, and raw materials is one of the main categories of inputs in the LCA framework. At other life-cycle stages, product manufacturing is affected by input materials, their composition, and their processing characteristics; product use is directly related to materials' performance and properties; and at the end-of-life stage, product disposal is usually characterized in terms of waste materials recovery and pro-

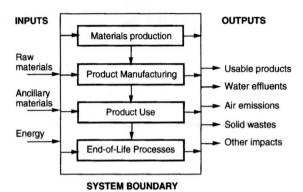

FIGURE 10.1   The generic product life-cycle stages. In LCA, a product system is defined by the system boundary and divided into stages for the life-cycle inventory (LCI) analysis of environmental inputs and outputs. Materials production and raw materials inputs are fundamental.

cessing. At the process level (Fig. 10.2) materials may enter the system either in the main production or as ancillaries. Note also in Fig. 10.2 that energy plays a fundamental role both in the main life-cycle sequence and as an input to materials production processes.

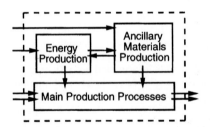

FIGURE 10.2   At each stage of the life cycle, the sequence of main production processes is supported by the production of energy, whether fuel or electricity, and the production of ancillary materials.

10.1.2   LCA's Importance to Materials Producers

Given the importance of materials in LCA, it follows that LCA is important to the materials sector, as both a tool and a field of study. As materials users are starting to apply LCA and life-cycle design, materials producers are responding by providing information and support for studies and applications. Materials industries, along with other sectors, are participating in ISO 14000 and the field of LCA, in general, as they continue to take shape.

10.2   METHODOLOGICAL CONSIDERATIONS

10.2.1   Dimensions of LCA

Instead of the "LCA triangle" that is often used to describe the basic methodology (see Chap. 2), consider Fig. 10.3. This plot illustrates the essential dimensions of the LCA method along three axes. The first dimension is the *life cycle,* which is essentially tem-

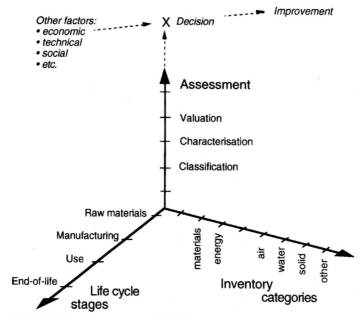

FIGURE 10.3 The dimensions of full LCA.

poral and represents the product's life stages. The second axis is the *inventory cate-gories,* which is the physical dimension that describes the resource and environmental inputs to and outputs from the system. These two dimensions form the quantitative basis of LCA and describe the framework for the life-cycle inventory (LCI). The third axis is the vertical axis, *assessment,* which represents a qualitative dimension. It is in this direc-tion that the life-cycle impact assessment is undertaken based on the LCI. The endpoint of a LCA study is a final assessment (valuation) of the product system.

Above and beyond the LCA, both conceptually and in Fig. 10.3, are other factors— economic, technical, social, etc.—that make up the context of analysis. The LCA tool will result in a life-cycle assessment that, along with consideration of other factors, will help generate a decision that in turn leads to system improvement. Note that ultimately *improvement* is defined with respect to considerations both within and without the LCA. For example, the results of an LCA study may indicate that product *A* is preferable to either product *B* or product *C.* However, when other factors outside the scope of LCA are included, the decision goes to product *B,* which is environmentally preferred to product *C* but is also more cost-effective and socially acceptable than product *A.* The ultimate improvement, in this illustration, is thus characterized in terms of economic, social, and life-cycle environmental factors.

10.2.2 Methodological Issues

From Figs. 10.1 and 10.3, it is clear that materials fit into only a portion of the frame-work of LCA. A *full LCA,* by definition,

- Considers all life-cycle stages from earth to earth
- Inventories multiple resource and environmental issues
- Includes final assessment

It follows, then, that an LCA of a material alone does not make sense; furthermore, LCA cannot, by definition, be used to evaluate the *total* environmental merits of a material or of competing materials. Analysis of the production of a material resulting in a material *ecoprofile* would cover only the stages relevant to its production. Other processes downstream would not be included, nor would impacts that occur beyond material production. The whole product life cycle would have to be factored into a full LCA. A materials ecoprofile may still consider the full list of inventory categories and include a limited degree of impact assessment, but valuations would be limited to the scope of the materials production system boundary.

In decisions arising out of the use of LCA, several material-related alternatives for improvement are possible. The basic goal is to reduce gross environmental impacts over the whole life cycle, including reductions of resource requirements, multimedia pollution, and wastes. The net effect should be fewer and lower negative impacts, or their potential, on human health, ecosystem integrity, and resource sustainability.

Given the above considerations, LCA as a method is a very useful tool for the environmental analysis of materials. This is pertinent both on a stand-alone basis, as is discussed below for the development of materials ecoprofile databases, and as an integral part of assessments that would constitute full LCA studies. A couple of issues that influence results, particularly as the method is applied to materials, will be mentioned.

Alternative Production Routes.   Many materials are produced in essentially identical forms from alternative production routes. Polyvinyl chloride (PVC), for example, is produced by three methods: suspension polymerization, emulsion polymerization, and bulk polymerization.[1] Zinc metal is produced both hydrometallurgically and pyrometallurgically, and within the latter category there are several alternative extraction procedures.[2] The ecoprofiles of zinc produced by these routes would be significantly different. Hydrometallurgical production uses water as a reaction medium and mostly electric power, whereas pyrometallurgical methods use combustion processes based on carbon fuels which result in the common types of air emissions—oxides of carbon, sulfur, and nitrogen. Although there may be slight chemical or physical differences in materials resulting from alternative production routes, the major differences will be *extrinsic* to the material itself. Both economic cost and ecoprofile results reflect the processing history of a product—a fact that engineers and designers will increasingly have to reckon with as they incorporate environmental criteria into their decisions.

Coproduct Allocation.   Many metals come from mixed ores. Zinc, for example, is usually associated with lead and, sometimes, gold, silver, cadmium, copper, and arsenic. Thus in an analysis of zinc, coproduct allocation would be required to share fairly between the coproducts the resource and environmental burdens associated with mining, transportation, ore preparation, and metal extraction. The principle upon which the partitioning is undertaken might logically be economic, mass-based, calorific, or other. In many systems, the method of allocation can greatly affect the resulting profile; however, the rules of allocation, it has been agreed, are largely arbitrary.[3,4]

A second example is illustrative. In an integrated steel works, there is about 3 tons of possible by-products generated for each metric ton of finished steel produced.[5] This includes slags, acids, steam, electricity, chemicals, and iron oxides. Sometimes these by-products are put to good use, e.g., the use of slag for road aggregate; but sometimes they are not, because it is neither economically nor technically feasible. In this case, mass is not an appropriate allocation measure because steel could be allotted only one-fourth of the total inventory quantities, even though it is the "real" product and the basic reason that the whole operation exists in the first place. Perhaps an economic allocation is more appropriate in this case, or perhaps a zero-allocation principle could be applied to some of the by-products.[6]

The allocation issue applies equally to nonmetals. Plastics are derived from crude oil and natural gas. In the refinery, coproducts include numerous fuels and hydrocarbons for lubricants and feedstocks to the plastic industry. Traditionally, in this case, a calorific allocation method has been used. This makes sense for the process: About 95 percent of the output is fuels for combustion, and most data are structured around this fact. Moreover, a mass allocation would not dramatically change results determined by using a calorific allocation.[7]

Generally, in any study using an LCA method, there have to be an explicit and transparent selection and execution of allocation rules. This point is simply emphasized for materials production by the above examples.

10.3   MATERIALS INFORMATION FOR LCA

The implementation of LCA, privately or publicly, will affect the resource industries most significantly: pulp and paper, chemicals, petroleum, and metals. These sectors account for a large portion of air pollution, water pollution, and waste management spending; consequently, they will be greatly affected by new environmental management approaches, like those proposed in ISO 14000. Companies either may respond to activities devised by others or can proactively participate in the development and evolution of the tools and their subsequent application. To a large extent, materials producers have chosen the latter option.

In the life-cycle analysis of product systems, *materials information* is necessary wherever materials are used in manufacturing, used in products, or needed as ancillary inputs; hence materials data are essential to a life-cycle inventory (LCI) and to a full LCA. Even very limited studies will involve industrial materials and thus require profiles describing materials production and materials recycling. Materials industries and other groups are now meeting the need for reliable and accurate data. Materials producers have realized that materials are directly linked to the application of the LCA method and, more broadly, that their products will be affected by decisions arising from LCA studies. One materials company representative suggested the following incentives for undertaking LCA studies of its products:

1. Refute damaging statements and misinformation from other sources.

2. Fulfill requests for inventory information from others.

3. Improve in-house understanding of processes and their implications.

4. Provide data to legislators.[8]

Environmental profile databases for materials, based on the LCA approach, are constructed as generic accounts of environmental inputs and outputs and are usually restricted to the consideration of the cumulative processes required to produce a specific material. A materials profile database may be described as a *cradle-to-gate* inventory generated by using the LCA method. Several European studies, concerned mostly with packaging, set the stage for LCA studies concentrating on materials as a determining factor in the environmental analyses.[9–11]

It is expected that LCI profiles will be utilized internally and by downstream customers in manufacturing, distribution, and retailing (e.g., through environmental labeling). Nongovernment organizations, academics, and government agencies have also voiced interest in using life-cycle materials information. Although many of the activities are not complete at this time, several important new projects are mentioned here.

10.3.1 Multimaterial Projects

Department of Energy Database. The Department of Energy, Battelle Pacific Northwest Laboratory, with industry and other U.S. government departments, has initiated the Life-Cycle Computer-Aided Data Project. The project goals are:

- To develop and successfully deploy to industry and government a computer modeling system that supports management, control, and manipulation of life-cycle data, thus expediting the conduct of consistent LCAs
- To collect and disseminate energy and environmental data for industrial commodities (such as primary metals, bulk chemicals, forest products, plastics, glass, and cement) to support the conduct of LCAs[12]

Data on about 30 materials will be presented in the DOE database.

Canadian Raw Materials Database (CRMD). A Canadian project involving a cross section of materials industries has been initiated to develop a database of life-cycle inventory data characterizing the production of aluminum, steel, commodity thermoplastics, glass, paper, and wood. Industry groups are participating on a volunteer basis along with Environment Canada and the University of Toronto, and with committee support from the Canadian Standards Association. The project's purpose is to provide Canadian LCI data for improvements within industry and for small and medium-size companies to improve their environmental performance. The project is not intended to be a full LCA. Results should be available in 1997.[13]

U.S. Automotive Materials Partnership LCA Project. The USA Consortium for Automobile Research has a project under the Automotive Materials Partnership (AMP) to do an LCA of a generic midsize automobile. Approximately 20,000 different components and dozens of types of materials are present in a modern automobile. Participating are the three major U.S. automobile manufactures (Chrysler, Ford, and General Motors) and the Aluminum Association, the American Plastics Council, and the American Iron and Steel Institute. The results of the study will be used as benchmark data and for new product design.[14]

ASM International. ASM International has a life-cycle analysis committee that is collecting and coordinating materials-related information and has organized an LCA session for its annual conference.

American Institute of Architects' Environmental Resource Guide. The American Institute of Architects and the Environmental Protection Agency have an ongoing project on building materials published as part of the *Environmental Resource Guide.* The LCA framework was modified to consider the unique aspects of buildings and building materials, like the very long use phase of a building. Quantitative and qualitative LCI data have been collected for all life-cycle stages, describing common generic materials like steel, aluminum, concrete, vinyl flooring, and wood. Expert judgment has been applied in the impact assessment step, emphasizing that environmental effects will substantially be a function of design as well as materials selection. Recommendations for architects to reduce environmental impacts and achieve design improvements will soon be added to the published technical reports.[15]

IVAM Database on Building Materials. At the University of Amsterdam, the IVAM Environmental Research group has developed a database of building materials for LCA studies. More than 250 processes and 100 materials are characterized for the Dutch situation. Although the data were collected for the building sector, IVAM supports the use of its data in general LCAs across other product sectors.[16]

10.3.2 Steel

Both the American Iron and Steel Institute (AISI) and the International Iron and Steel Institute (IISI) have established committees on LCA. The AISI is participating in the US-AMP project, discussed above, and has contributed information to the American Institute of Architects' *Environmental Resource Guide.* Several steel companies, particularly in Europe, have undertaken LCA-type studies and have provided LCA-type data to third parties.

10.3.3 Aluminum

The aluminum industry in North America and Europe has similarly undertaken LCA activities. Some LCI studies involving aluminum products have been completed but are unpublished and are being used within aluminum companies for management and improvement activities. The Aluminum Association is participating in the US-AMP project. Aluminum Company of America (Alcoa) has published a series of reports on "Environmental Life Cycle Considerations of Aluminum in Automotive Structures."[17]

10.3.4 Other Metals

Zinc, copper, nickel, and other base-metal producers are involved in LCA and related activities to varying extents. It is expected that ISO 14000 activities, in particular, will facilitate more LCA-type projects within the metals sector.

10.3.5 Plastics

The plastics industry has a recent history of responsiveness and proaction regarding environmental issues. Energy and waste studies are typical of the kind of projects that have been carried out over the last several years.[18] With respect to LCA, in particular, the industry is more advanced than others in its development and publication of studies and data using the LCA method.

Association of Plastics Manufacturers in Europe (APME). One set of LCI studies has been done for the Association of Plastics Manufacturers in Europe (APME) and represents probably the most comprehensive set of published materials ecoprofiles to date. The APME's published technical papers are timely and comprehensive analyses of olefin feedstock sources, polystyrene, polyethylene, polypropylene, and polyvinyl chloride. The full set of reports should cover the production of major commodity thermopolymer resins, including polyurethanes, acrylics, polycarbonates, acrylic/styrene copolymers, nylons, and unsaturated polyesters.[19] Data are specific to western European production and practices and are thus subject to geographical, resource, and technological limitations. The APME ecoprofiles are intended to be used by member companies for improving manufacturing processes and to provide "valuable inventory data for downstream users of plastics, such as packaging manufacturers, who will be able to produce their own eco-balance assessments of individual products."[20]

Another European project, which would be the next step after plastic resin production, has been initiated by the European Plastics Converters Association to obtain data on the manufacturing of plastic products.

American Plastics Council (APC). The American Plastics Council has undertaken a project similar to that of the APME, characterizing North American production of basic thermopolymer resins. Published data should be available in 1996.[21]

10.3.6 Pulp and Paper

Wood and pulp and paper industry groups are participating in LCA developments, like the CRMD. A Canadian project coordinated by the Canadian Standards Association is developing a methodology for life-cycle impact assessment of pulp and paper production.[22]

10.4 DISCUSSION

The objectives behind the development and use of materials databases for LCA are twofold. First, there is the goal of improving environmental performance within producer companies by using ecoprofile data to baseline process improvements. Actions of this sort would be undertaken internal to a company's normal environmental management practices and, presumably, as part of ongoing pollution prevention programs. The life-cycle concept might also be extended to include materials recycling processes and thus "close the loop" between primary and secondary materials production, while reducing overall environmental impacts.

The second goal of databases for LCA is external to the materials producer—to supply reliable information to downstream users. Purchasers, designers, and engineers would use materials ecoprofiles to add environmental content to their activities. Generic information could be particularly useful to small and medium-size companies that conduct their own "streamlined" LCA studies, whereas larger organizations might contact suppliers for more specific and detailed data.

It is expected that, in the long term, there would be a feedback of environmental improvement as materials producers improve the environmental profiles of their products based on selection criteria expressed by their customers. Thus, both basic materials and final products would be on a path of continuous environmental performance improvement.

10.4.1 LCA as Environmental Mapping

To understand how the life-cycle concept might be used in decision-making activities, such as design, consider Fig. 10.4. Products can be grouped into four basic types accord-

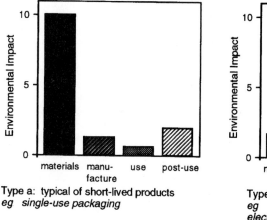

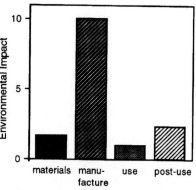

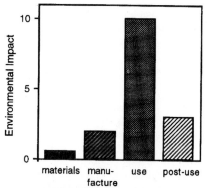

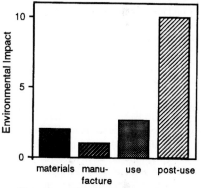

FIGURE 10.4 Products may be categorized into four generic ecoprofile types. LCA results can be used as an "environmental map," thus providing the decision maker with a broad-based picture for assessments and improvement.

ing to their LCA profiles; this hypothetical categorization of different products provides the decision maker with a sort of broad-based "environmental map" for life-cycle decision making. (Note that the environmental impact axis is generic and in a full LCA would be defined by a number of different environmental impact indicators.) Generally, four product types can be distinguished by their length of useful life. Shorter-lived products generally place lower stresses on the environment during use than at other stages and thus probably are categorized as *type a*. Long-lived products, by their very durability, impose greater burdens during their use than at other stages and thus are *type c*. Products of *type b* and *type d* are unique but are categorized depending on specific resource or environmental characteristics.

Note that type a products, like packaging, have a profile that is indicative of high *materials intensity*; i.e., for a given utility, the system exhibits a high throughput of materials. Even if they are used in products for just a short lifetime before discard, materials must still be extracted, processed, and manufactured. A typical beverage can, whose retail and consumer use stages may extend for only weeks, could easily be composed of aluminum that spends most of its lifetime being extracted, processed, filled, or recycled.

The profiles of products that fall into other ecoprofile types may also be determined by their materials composition or materials use. For example, the manufacturing requirements for an automotive component (*type c*) are affected by its materials makeup, and its use characteristics are largely a function of material performance criteria such as stiffness, weight, and repairability.[23]

The role of materials in products perceived to exhibit a *type d* profile has been widely discussed in terms of "the solid waste crisis" and materials recycling. Obviously, material composition is a fundamental variable for issues and actions regarding materials recovery and recycling. But in actuality, it would appear that *type d* life-cycle products are rare, and little evidence has emerged to demonstrate examples of products whose major burdens arise in postuse. Even for life-cycle studies that focus on solid waste, which is just one of many LCA inventory categories, results indicate that significantly more waste and more waste-related stresses occur at other life-cycle stages. This does not undervalue the significance, particularly at the municipal level, of waste generation and disposal, but the solid waste problem should be placed in perspective relative to other resource and environmental issues—and LCA is a good tool for this.

10.4.2 Life-Cycle Design

One of the most far-reaching, complex, and long-term ramifications of the life-cycle concept will be the implementation of life-cycle design (see Chap. 6).[24-27] More generally, *design for environment* (DFE) initiatives are growing and will certainly be a factor in the future selection of materials in design. But note that, as yet, life-cycle design activities are mostly undemonstrated.

Some design programs focus on specific environmental factors such as recycling or air emissions reduction; however, the life-cycle concept is expected to become the dominant model for "green design." In many cases, life-cycle tradeoffs will have to be weighed, perhaps environmental stresses in front-end materials production stages versus back-end stresses involving materials disposal. For example, materials recycling, as a specific strategy for environmental improvement, is perhaps better viewed from a full life-cycle perspective. The indication is that recycling is most beneficial not in terms of end-of-pipe solid waste management but rather for the prevention of upstream burdens associated with primary materials production that are displaced by the use of recycled materials. Those prevented burdens, of course, include not only solid waste generation but also air and water emissions and resource requirements.

Materials Selection.   Bringing environmental considerations into technical design and consequently to materials selection is fundamentally different from designing with conventional technical criteria. Whereas the conventional physical properties of a material, such as density, strength, and electrical and thermal conductivity, are *intrinsic* to the physics and chemistry of a material, environmental characteristics are *extrinsically* characterized by processing history, geographic circumstance, and management practice. In this manner, environmental criteria are similar to economic costs.[28]

This integration of life-cycle information requires energy and material balances across the life-cycle system, given the proportions required at each stage for a specific system. Clearly, the environmental profiles of different materials cannot be compared on a simple mass-to-mass basis, although databases may be constructed in this format. For example, an automotive component, which performs a specific function on a vehicle, might be manufactured with 1.0 kg of steel versus 0.55 kg of aluminum or 0.70 kg of high-density polyethylene, depending on specific properties and processing requirements. In LCA, alternatives are compared on the basis of a *functional unit* which defines product systems of equivalent utility.

10.4.3 Future Needs

For the designer or other decision maker who wishes to consider the whole life cycle, inventory data requirements for manufactured products fall into several categories across the life cycle (Fig. 10.5). Each ecoprofile could be inventoried as a stand-alone

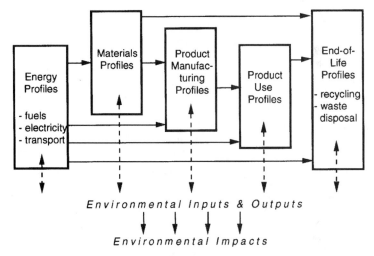

FIGURE 10.5 To do a full LCA, several types of data-intensive environmental profiles are necessary—materials profiles are central.

database, as is being done for materials. Assembled together, they could be employed by a user to construct a complete LCA system profile. At this time, of the five stages shown in Fig. 10.5, materials profiles are most available. Some ecoprofile work has already been considered for energy profiles[29] and waste disposal.[30] It will be especially challenging, if it is undertaken, to develop generic profiles that characterize manufacturing, use, and end of life.

In the future, more databases will be developed. Data that are already available will facilitate more LCA studies which, in turn, will require more high-quality information covering other processes and practices. There will be an interesting conflict between generic data that are available but may be too broad-brush for many users and specific data that will be more difficult to acquire but will be a necessary input to detailed decision making by engineers and designers. Numerous companies and organizations have already developed internal databases that are tailored to their specific needs, finding their own balance between accuracy and breadth.

10.5 CONCLUSIONS

LCA of manufactured products is fundamentally dependent on the analysis of materials. To meet the need, groups are developing materials databases for LCA. Practitioners who wish to consider materials in LCA studies will have to deal with a number of methodological concerns, such as alternative production routes and coproduct allocation.

The LCA method can be used to develop stand-alone materials ecoprofiles, but it is not an appropriate tool to evaluate just materials. Materials cannot be judged directly on a mass-to-mass basis, but some measure of utility must be introduced to facilitate a meaningful basis of comparison.

LCA, used quantitatively and qualitatively, can provide a life-cycle environmental map for decision makers. Consequent improvements may be facilitated both by materials producers, who can reduce the environmental burdens of production processes, and by materials users, who can use materials ecoprofiles and the full LCA tool for their own environmental improvements—in design, engineering, and procurement. Consequently, materials selection and use will be affected by new LCA-related approaches, such as life-cycle design. Materials selection in design that incorporates environmental criteria should consider a full list of resource and environmental issues, across all life-cycle stages.

REFERENCES

1. I. Boustead, *Eco-profiles of the European Plastics Industry. Report 6: Polyvinyl Chloride,* Association of Plastics Manufacturers in Europe (APME), Brussels, Belgium, April 1994.

2. J. D. Gilchrist, *Extraction Metallurgy,* 2nd ed., Pergamon Press, Oxford, 1980.

3. *Proceedings of the European Workshop on Allocation in LCA,* at CML-S&P, Leiden University, The Netherlands, February 24–25, 1994, eds. G. Huppes and F. Schneider, SETAC-Europe, Brussels, Belgium.

4. I. Boustead, *Eco-profiles of the European Plastics Industry. Report 5: Co-Product Allocation in Chlorine Plants,* Association of Plastics Manufacturers in Europe (APME), Brussels, Belgium, April 1994, pp. 19–20.

5. G. L. Montgomery (Stelco Inc.), "Waste Minimization and Recycling in the Steel Industry," paper presented at the *Ontario Air and Waste Management Association (AWMA), Annual Spring Conference,* Toronto, Canada, May 3, 1994.

6. Canadian Standards Association, *Environmental Life Cycle Assessment,* CAN/CSA-Z 760, Toronto, February 1994, p. 59.

7. V. Matthews and P. Fink, "Database Generation for Olefin Feedstocks and Plastics," *J. Cleaner Prod.,* **1**(3–4): 178 (1993).

8. L. Wibberley (BHP Steel) presentation at International Iron and Steel Institute (IISI) ENCO 32 meeting, Hamilton, Canada, September 8–9, 1994.

9. K. Haberstatter and D. F. Widmer, *Ecobalance of Packaging Materials, State of 1990,* Bundesamt für Umwelt, Wald and Landschaft (BUWAL)/Swiss Federal Office of Environment, Forests and Landscape (FOEFL), Environment Series no. 132, Berne, Switzerland, February 1991.

10. A. M. Tillman, H. Baumann, E. Eriksson, and T. Rydberg, *Packaging and the Environment: Life-Cycle Analyses of Selected Packaging Materials—Quantification of Environmental Loadings,* Chalmers Industriteknik, Goteberg, Sweden, September 1991.

11. I. Boustead and G. F. Hancock, *Resource Use and Liquid Food Packaging,* EC Directive 85/339: UK data 1986–1990, Report for Industry Council for Packaging and Environment (INCPEN), London, United Kingdom, May 1993.

12. Pacific Northwest Laboratory, "Life-Cycle Assessment," project information sheet, Battelle, Richland, WA, February 1995.

13. *Ecocycle* (Environment Canada, Solid Waste Management Division, Ottawa), no. 1, Winter 1995.

14. John Sullivan (Ford Motor Company), presentation at "Environmental Challenges: The Automobile Industry in Germany and the United States," organized by the University of Michigan National Pollution Prevention Center, Detroit, April 20–21, 1995.

15. American Institute of Architects, *1996 Environmental Resource Guide,* John Wiley and Sons, New York, NY, 1996.

16. Marcel Brinkkemper, personal communication, IVAM Environmental Research, University of Amsterdam, The Netherlands, August 1, 1995.

17. Alcoa Automotive Structures, "Environmental Life Cycle Considerations of Aluminum in Automotive Structures," Reports 1–4, Aluminum Company of America, Southfield, MI, December 1994.

18. Franklin Associates, Ltd., for the Society of Plastics Industries, Inc., "Comparative Energy Evaluation of Plastic Products and Their Alternatives for the Building and Construction and Transport Industries," Prairie Village, KS, March 1991.

19. V. Matthews and P. Fink, "Database Generation for Olefin Feedstocks and Plastics," *J. Cleaner Prod.,* **1**(3–4): 178 (1993).

20. I. Boustead, *Eco-profiles of the European Plastics Industry, Reports 1–6,* Association of Plastics Manufacturers in Europe (APME), Brussels, Belgium, 1993–1994.

21. American Plastics Council and Society of the Plastics Industry, "Life-Cycle Inventory in Progress," reported in *Chem. Eng.,* p. 33, July 1993.

22. Canadian Standards Association, *Guideline for Life Cycle Impact Assessment—Pulp and Paper Production Phase*, Z 810, Toronto, Canada, 1996.

23. S. B. Young and W. H. Vanderburg, "Applying Environmental Life-Cycle Analysis to Materials," *JOM,* **46**(4): 22–27 (1994).

24. U.S. Congress, Office of Technology Assessment, *Green Products by Design: Choices for a Cleaner Environment,* OTA-E-541, Government Printing Office, Washington, October 1992.

25. U.S. Environmental Protection Agency, *Life Cycle Design Guidance Manual, Environmental Requirements and the Product System,* EPA 600/R-92/226, EPA, Cincinnati, OH, January 1993.

26. G. Keoleian and D. Menerey, "Sustainable Development by Design: Review of Life Cycle Design and Related Approaches," *Air and Waste,* **44:** 645–668 (May 1994).

27. Canadian Standards Association, *Design for the Environment,* CAN/CSA-Z 762, Toronto, April 1995.

28. S. B. Young and W. H. Vanderburg, "Applying Environmental Life-Cycle Analysis to Materials," *JOM,* **46**(4): 22–27 (1994).

29. "Ökoinventare für Energiesysteme," Institute for Energy Technology, Laboratory for Energy Systems, ESU-Unit, ETHZ/ML, Zurich, Switzerland, 1994.

30. "Using LCA to Evaluate Municipal Solid Waste Management Options," in *EPA Life-Cycle Assessment Project Update,* EPA Office of Research and Development, Cincinnati, OH, March 1995.

CHAPTER 11
APPLICATION OF LIFE-CYCLE ASSESSMENT TO BUSINESS PERFORMANCE

James A. Fava
DIRECTOR, PRODUCT STEWARDSHIP AND
MANAGEMENT SYSTEM
ROY F. WESTON, INC.
WEST CHESTER, PA

Frank J. Consoli
PRESIDENT
CONSOLI CONSULTING
MEDIA, PA

11.1 INTRODUCTION

The early 1990s have proved to be a period of dramatic change for environmental professionals. Today industry and broader multisector organizations place greater emphasis on pollution prevention in developing solutions to environmental problems. Additionally, broader concerns about products' environmental impacts, such as solid waste and materials acquisition, as well as the influence of international regulations on environmental problem solving have created new opportunities for environmental performance.

A number of voluntary pollution prevention programs have surfaced in the last several years. Among these are the Environmental Protection Agency's 33/50 Program and Common Sense Initiative, the Executive Order on Environmentally Preferable Products, and the international Organization for Standardization (ISO) environmental management tools and systems, which includes life-cycle assessment (LCA). Collectively, these programs demand a radical change in corporate culture to identify and manage the environmental vulnerabilities associated with an organization's entire operations.

In examining an organization's operations, it is product sales which drives the success of any business. One implication of the shift toward an awareness of pollution prevention concepts is the incorporation of environmental considerations into product design, development, and evaluation processes. This is the best way to manage the areas where products affect or interface with the environment. A product interfaces with the environment throughout all stages of its development from extraction of natural resources to obtain materials, to fuels used in manufacture, to the product's ultimate disposition. Graphically this is portrayed in Fig. 11.1 as a cycle from raw materials acquisition to final disposition, including recovery, reuse, and recycling. Pollution prevention strategies are being developed to maximize the continued use of products and materials while minimizing environmental releases related to production as well as energy and material consumed over the entire product life cycle.

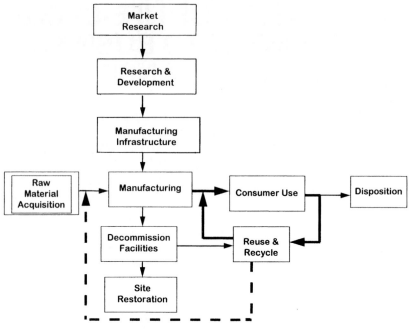

FIGURE 11.1 Life-cycle concept.

The purpose of this chapter is to describe how one pollution prevention tool—life-cycle assessment—can be used to identify and manage the environmental impacts associated with product systems. Specifically, this chapter will describe what life-cycle assessment is, determine the key players in its development and application, and present ideas on how LCA can be used today.

11.2 DEFINITION OF LIFE-CYCLE ASSESSMENT

Life-cycle assessment is a systematic approach used to manage the environmental impacts of product and service systems, and it is applied at two levels. It is applied

- *Conceptually as a thought process* to guide the selection of options for design and improvement
- *Methodologically* to build a qualitative/quantitative inventory of environmental burdens or releases, evaluate the impacts of those burdens or releases, and consider alternatives to improve environmental performance

In any application, LCA considers the environmental impacts along the continuum of a product's life (i.e., from cradle to grave) from raw materials acquisition to production, use, and disposal or recovery. The environmental impacts to consider include resource depletion, human health, and ecological health.

An important feature in this definition of life-cycle assessment is that it involves both a conceptual element and data-intensive methodology elements. The concept of

Life cycle thinking is a unique way of addressing environmental problems from a systems or holistic perspective. In this way of thinking, a product or service system is evaluated or designed with a goal of reducing environmental impacts over its entire life cycle. The essential difference is that life-cycle thinking does not attempt to do so in a quantitative fashion but rather in a conceptual or qualitative fashion.

11.3 SETAC'S ROLE IN LCA DEVELOPMENT

The Society of Environmental Toxicology and Chemistry (SETAC) was the first international organization to recognize LCA's potential value. In the early 1990s, SETAC established an LCA Advisory Group whose mission was to advance the science, practice, and application of LCAs to reduce resource consumption and environmental burdens associated with products, packaging, processes, and activities. To achieve this mission, the SETAC Advisory Group

1. Serves as a focal point to provide a broad-based forum for the identification, resolution, and communication of issues regarding LCAs
2. Facilitates, coordinates, and provides guidance for LCA development and implementation

SETAC's role is not to develop standard methods but to develop initiatives that will improve the science behind the LCA methods. Organizations such as ISO have the responsibility for harmonizing LCA methods. The following two sections outline the results of two SETAC LCA initiatives. Additional results of SETAC efforts can be found in *Guidelines for Life-Cycle Assessment: A "Code of Practice"* (Consoli et al., 1993) and in *Life-Cycle Assessment Data Quality: A Conceptual Framework* (Fava et al., 1994).

11.3.1 Technical Framework for LCA

SETAC's first LCA workshop, conducted in August 1990, resulted in the workshop proceedings entitled *A Technical Framework for [Product] Life-Cycle Assessment* (Fava et al., 1991) in which the following three-component model for LCAs was developed:

1. An *inventory* of materials and energy used and environmental releases arising from all stages in the life of a product or process, from raw material acquisition to ultimate disposal
2. An *impact assessment* examining potential environmental and human health effects related to resource consumption (energy and materials) and environmental releases
3. An *improvement assessment* of the changes needed to effect environmental improvements in the product or process

The majority of *A Technical Framework for Life-Cycle Assessment* focuses on defining concepts and developing a framework for the inventory component of an LCA; however, it also identifies the need to conduct other workshops to evaluate other LCA components.

11.3.2 Impact Assessment

SETAC also sponsored an Impact Assessment Workshop in February 1992 to provide a forum for continuing discussion of the second LCA component. The resulting work, *A*

Conceptual Framework for Life-Cycle Impact Assessment (Fava et al., 1993a), further defined impact assessment in the following three-step conceptual framework for impact assessment:

1. *Classification*—the process of assignment and initial aggregation of data from inventory studies to relatively homogeneous stressor categories (e.g., greenhouse gases or ozone depletion compounds) within the larger impact categories (i.e., human and ecological health, and resource depletion).

2. *Characterization*—the analysis and estimation of the magnitude of impacts on the ecological health, human health, or resource depletion for each of the stressor categories, derived through application of specific impact assessment tools.

3. *Valuation*—the assignment of relative values or weights to different impacts and their integration across impact categories to allow decision makers to assimilate and consider the full range of relevant impacts across impact categories. Use of formal valuation methods makes this process structured, rather than based on implicit, individual value judgments.

During the workshop on impact assessment, participants investigated general impact assessment tools, such as environmental assessments (EAs) and environmental impact statements (EISs) under the National Environmental Policy Act (NEPA). Some of these tools may have practical application to LCAs. Additional research is needed to determine whether methods developed for human health and environmental risk assessments, particularly at the generic or program level, can be adapted to the practice of LCAs. Similarly, conventional resource analysis methods may be adapted for interpreting resource use data in an LCA, but this will require practical demonstrations to assess their feasibility.

In the context of LCA, impact assessment is usually comparative. This places a different requirement on life-cycle impact assessment from what would be required for an absolute stand-alone impact assessment of a single product or process. Comparative analysis can more readily use stressors as surrogates for impacts. For the purposes of life-cycle impact assessment, there is less need for detailed assessments, such as site-specific risk assessments.

The valuation phase, which assigns value or relative weights to the various impact categories, was judged to be inherently subjective and value-laden. An individual's or a group's view of the relative importance of one impact category compared to others was recognized as fundamentally subjective. A variety of tools (often referred to as *decision theory techniques*) that offer the potential to make valuation a rational, structured process were described in *A Conceptual Framework for Life-Cycle Impact Assessment* (Fava et al., 1993a). These techniques use both expert judgment and input from interested or affected parties or publics. Although it was recognized that not all applications of LCAs require the use of decision theory techniques, the tools described hold promise for application to LCAs.

One of the challenges of enhancing the LCA methodology is to incorporate practical and realistic impact assessment components into the conduct of an LCA. Although approaches have been developed for impact assessment for internal application within a company, these have been applied primarily to assist in product or process designs. Applications outside this internal screening-level application of life-cycle assessment have been limited to presenting the results of the inventory analysis. Approaches to interpreting the results of an inventory analysis will likely surface in the near future. This will provide a preliminary model as organizations like SETAC further develop impact assessment methods. One of the concerns of which we must be aware is to avoid burdening the LCA methodology with conditions that cannot be achieved in a realistic time frame, thereby reducing the LCA methodology's value and application.

11.4 *ISO TC-207 LCA STANDARDS*

The International Organization for Standardization (ISO) is developing standards worldwide in an effort to standardize and thus streamline the international marketplace for industry. One of the greatest and fastest-moving trends is the development of ISO's 14000 series, Environmental Management Standards. In 1993, because of a serious concern shared by industry, government, and the public about the proliferation of local and national environmental standards, ISO established TC-207 to develop environmental management tools and systems that would be applicable worldwide. Among the tools under development are environmental management systems, auditing, environmental performance evaluation, life-cycle assessment, and environmentally friendly or "green" labeling (Fig. 11.2). Excluded from the scope of these standards are test methods, setting limit values or performance levels, and specific product standards.

The development of the ISO 14000 series has been a global effort, with more than 30 countries participating. Currently there are more than 15 specific standards in various stages of development. The environmental management system and environmental auditing standards will be finalized in 1996, with the remaining standards finalized over the next 2 to 4 years.

Soon ISO 14000 certification will be a requirement for doing business in the international marketplace. The ratification of the ISO 14000 series standards is fast approaching, and their impact on companies doing business internationally should not be underestimated. Philips Components of Austria, for example, has achieved the first certification to ISO 14001 (Environmental Management System specification—Committee Draft). Their effort helped them achieve worldwide visibility that accompanies certification.

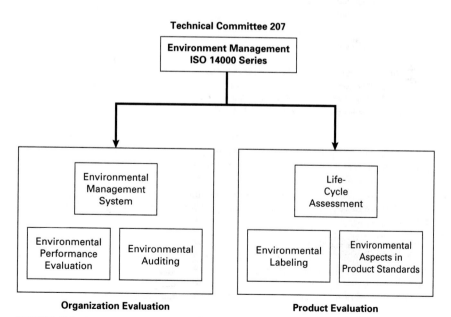

FIGURE 11.2 International Organization for Standardization.

11.4.1 Summary of Standards

The life-cycle assessment subcommittee is comprised of the following five working groups:

- WG 1   Principles and Framework
- WG 2,3   Goal and Scope Definitions/Inventory Analysis
- WG 4   Impact Assessment
- WG 5   Interpretation

11.4.2 Status of Activities

Overall, the ISO LCA standards are directed at product and process evaluation and use of life-cycle concepts as tools for improving environmental performance and reducing environmental impacts. All standards in this group fall under the category of guidance rather than specifications.

Table 11.1 summarizes the status of each ISO LCA working group.

TABLE 11.1   Status of ISO LCA Activities

Document name and number	Comment
ISO 14040 (WG 1) *Principles and Framework*	Expected to be final in 1997
ISO 14041 (WG 2,3) *Inventory Analysis*	Expected to be final in 1997
ISO 14042 (WG 4) *Impact Assessment*	Expected to be final in 1998 or later
ISO 14043 (WG 5) *Interpretation*	Expected to be final in 1998 or later

In addition to the ISO efforts, the American Society for Testing and Materials (ASTM) and the Canadian Standards Association (CSA) are developing LCA standards. The Canadian Standards Association standard on LCA has been published, while the ASTM LCA standards are currently under ballot.

11.5 DESIGN FOR ENVIRONMENT—A PATH FORWARD

When one considers the implications of current environmental, health, and safety trends, the following goal comes to light: *Make health, safety, and environmental protection an integral part of designing, manufacturing, distributing, using, recycling, and disposing of products.**

This goal suggests a shift in corporate culture and requires us to "think outside the box." Environmental, health, and safety considerations should be integrated into an organization's day-to-day decision-making processes. Additionally, thinking about a business's operations quickly makes clear that the manufacture and sale of individual

---

*Products refer to products, processes, and service systems.

TABLE 11.2   DFE Core Principles*

- Maximize efficiency in the use of depletable material resources.
- Minimize the use of energy, where practical; maximize the use of renewable forms of energy, and maximize efficiency in the use of depletable forms of energy.
- Minimize the use of materials or processes which are known to contribute to global warming, ozone depletion, or acidification
- Minimize the risks associated with the use of hazardous materials and/or processes which result in human or ecological exposures
- Eliminate or minimize the use of materials or processes which are known to compromise the local land, air, and/or water

*Modified from Canadian Standards Association.

businesses' products and services drive the global economy. To effectively and efficiently integrate environmental, health, and safety considerations into business operations, the processes used to design and evaluate products and services are the points where the application of these considerations can be most beneficial.

Efforts are under way to develop guidelines for designing products based upon life-cycle environmental principles. The Canadian Standards Association, the secretariat for the ISO 14000 series, has developed a *design for environment* (DFE) standard. Included in that standard are five core DFE principles (see Table 11.2). Applied over the entire life cycle of products, processes, or services, DFE core principles lead to life-cycle reductions in product waste, risks, and harmful effects.

DFE is not new. BMW developed a design for disassembly. Detergent manufacturers design their products and packaging for biodegradability and recycling. However, DFE often continues to be a single-issue focus. We need to expand our thinking beyond these single issues to a broader array of environmental issues over the entire life cycle of the product, process, or service system.

Product designers have long understood and practiced the complex science of integrating functional, technical, financial, and legal requirements into the design process. However, few designers have mastered the ability to include environmental considerations. LCA can quantify the environmental impacts along the entire life cycle of the product system.

What is needed is a tool (or a series of tools) that is simple to use, that follows the design process, and that embeds life-cycle information within business, financial, and technological measures. These tools will integrate the product life cycle (from market research to decommissioning) and the environmental life cycle (Fig. 11.1). For example, market research uses techniques such as quality function deployment. Research and development defines the technical parameters, and manufacturing is responsible for operational characteristics. During the design of a product, all these elements including decommissioning issues are considered.

11.6   EXAMPLES OF APPLICATION OF LIFE-CYCLE PRINCIPLES TO PRODUCT EVALUATION

The following three examples illustrate the application of life-cycle assessment and principles to assist companies in developing a better understanding of the environmental vulnerabilities associated with their products.

Rohm & Haas.   Rohm & Haas has been using life-cycle concepts for several years in implementing its Product Stewardship Program. This example is based upon work published in Fava et al. (1993b).

The Chemical Manufacturers Association developed its Responsible Care Program, which included the practice of *product stewardship.* The purpose of product stewardship is to make safety, health, and environmental protection an integral part of design, manufacture, distribution, product use, recycling, and disposal. The underlying premise is to identify and manage products' environmental quality.

Rohm & Haas, a specialty chemical manufacturer, is a member of the Chemical Manufacturers Association (CMA). Their initial efforts were aimed at understanding what the product stewardship practice entailed, what implications it held for their operations, and who should be responsible for its implementation. As part of its membership in the CMA, Rohm & Haas was required to implement the product stewardship practice.

Once Rohm & Haas was committed to implementing the product stewardship practice, it found that one of the barriers to successful implementation was the lack of a readily available method of product evaluation. Traditionally, the company managed its products based upon financial or market indicators. Often the potential human health and environmental vulnerabilities did not enter into the decision-making process. As part of an effort to develop a product stewardship tool, a preliminary exercise was conducted to incorporate health and environmental concerns into decisions concerning product growth and product development.

This process included the integration of life-cycle assessment and risk assessment concepts into a *health and environmental ranking* (HER) index (Fava et al., 1993b). This index was developed by a multifunctional team and included three life-cycle stages: manufacturing processes, distribution, and primary customers. The results of the pilot study were presented in a product strategy matrix (Fig. 11.3). The matrix provided

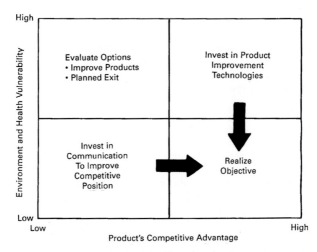

FIGURE 11.3   Product strategy matrix.

strategic guidance as to the relationship of the HER index to the product's competitive advantage. Thus additional information was available for decision making.

Overall, the pilot study was successful, and additional application to other business units is occurring. Implementation of the HER index as one of the tools for product stewardship is still being evaluated. What was learned from this effort was that one should ensure that the evaluation could be performed in a short time (say, 2 hours), education of the participants was needed to ensure an efficient operation, and each business area needed a slightly modified index to reflect its product system characteristics.

Scott Paper Company. This example is based on a number of European publications and material available from Scott Paper Company describing its approach to pulp procurement. It represents an attempt to incorporate life-cycle considerations as one of the decision criteria for material and supplier selection.

Scott Paper company was one of the largest tissue producers worldwide. With significant operations in most major worldwide markets, Scott has long been aware of the importance of environmental stewardship to its business. Scott has been one of the leading manufacturers in applying volunteer techniques to improve its environmental position. Examples include its active involvement in the development and implementation of the Coalition of Northeastern Governors (CONEG) Voluntary Packaging Guidelines and its involvement in the European ecolabel work.

Historically, Scott, like many large producers, addressed environmental issues at a local or site level. In the late 1980s, based on the evolving needs of the marketplace, Scott investigated several environmental issues and provided a dedicated corporate focus. This effort yielded a clear set of corporate worldwide positions on environmental matters and committed the company to pursue an LCA cradle-to-grave approach rather than continuing to track and act on single issues. This position was developed following the execution of several internal studies which provided vastly different insights when viewed from a cradle-to-grave perspective versus a single-issue perspective.

The corporate focus initially was positioned on developing corporate strategy and external communications. In late 1991, Scott formalized its LCA-based environmental policy. In this statement, the company committed to understanding the life cycle of its products, to minimize the impact of its own operations, to conduct supplier assessments, and to conduct employee training and communication.

Within the supplier portion of this program, Scott Europe committed to develop and implement (as a first step) a supplier assessment program to build environmental criteria into pulp purchasing decisions. All European pulp suppliers were required to complete a detailed questionnaire covering

- Emissions (air, water, land)
- Energy use and type
- Manufacturing processes
- Forestry practices

Initially suppliers were reluctant to participate; however, Scott provided unidentified information back to suppliers as a benchmark, and as a result supplier cooperation was high. The questionnaire produced a mass of data, both qualitative and quantitative. Manufacturing emissions were easily quantified. Forestry practices tended to be more qualitative by nature, and the ability to rank suppliers and ultimately recommend decisions required significant work and judgment.

To help in the internal decision process, Scott developed a ranking system to reflect regional environmental priorities. Relevant issues, such as contribution to global warming; pollution to air, water, and land; and forestry practices were ranked in the United Kingdom through research among opinion leaders.

Figure 11.4 demonstrates some of the results of the assessment for SO_x and NO_x emissions. Somewhat surprisingly, considerable variations occurred between suppliers, reflecting the variation in environmental standards from country to country or, as in this

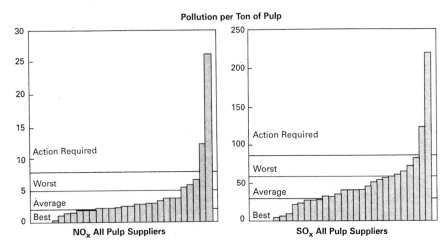

FIGURE 11.4   Scott supplier assessment results. (*Source: Scott Limited U.K.*)

case, the difference in electric utility source. Suppliers that were the worst on individual scales tended to have the worst overall emissions against every category measured representing overall poor practice. This assessment demonstrated to Scott that significant environmental improvement opportunities existed. As a result, Scott went back to each supplier to share the results and encourage improvement. Some suppliers chose not to proceed, and as a result, Scott dropped them as suppliers. Overall, approximately 10 percent of Scott's pulp supply base was changed through this program.

The results of this effort were broadly communicated to Scott's customers. Follow-up surveys confirmed that while Scott was previously considered "one of the pack" in environmental issues and was constantly playing catch-up, after engaging in this supplier assessment activity and communicating the results, Scott broke away from competition as being preferred from an environmental perspective among consumer and pressure groups. As a result, Scott currently is engaged in furthering this work in other life-cycle areas.

Hewlett-Packard.   This example is based upon an article appearing in the July 1994 issue of *Business and the Environment.* It represents an approach by a computer and electronics company to evaluate and implement a product stewardship program.

Hewlett-Packard views product stewardship as the philosophy and practice of designing products and processes to prevent and/or minimize adverse health, safety, and ecological impacts throughout their life cycle. In this example Hewlett-Packard applies the concept of life-cycle thinking to its operations as part of a product stewardship initiative.

One of the first steps was to revise its environmental management objective to read, "To provide products and services that are environmentally responsible throughout their life cycles and to conduct business operations worldwide in an environmentally responsible manner." Additionally, Hewlett-Packard embraced the life-cycle management philosophy.

Hewlett-Packard selected a business area which represented the most significant opportunity to reduce environmental impacts through product and life-cycle design. It selected the Computer Products Organization because it represents high-volume production of printers and personal computers.

Within the Computer Products Organization, Hewlett-Packard appointed a full-time product stewardship manager who was responsible for communication and strategy development and deployment. Because product stewardship is a cross-functional issue, no single function had the clear mission and broad array of capabilities needed to handle product stewardship. As such, product stewards were recruited from various division functions.

During the early stage, the following steps were taken to advance the product stewardship program:

- Established mechanisms to track, evaluate, and communicate the business implications of global legislative and market developments
- Deployed DFE guidelines for products and packaging
- Developed and made a pilot study of product environmental profile sheets (primarily for external use) to describe a product's environmental attributes, including material content and energy use
- Made a pilot study of a set of product stewardship metrics
- Developed a brochure that describes Hewlett-Packard's environmental management policy, programs, and performance progress for customers, employees, and other stakeholders

Collectively, these steps provided the basis for the decision to broaden its product stewardship efforts worldwide.

In 1993, Hewlett-Packard established a corporate-level Product Process Organization, whose mission was as follows: "In partnership with Hewlett-Packard's geographic organizations and other corporate functions, provide a strong facilitation platform to the Hewlett-Packard businesses and be proactive in elevating awareness and leveraging product stewardship solutions for improved business results." This global product stewardship network helped Hewlett-Packard's other businesses launch their own programs.

Hewlett-Packard is continuing with the implementation of its product stewardship program. It believes that the product stewardship program will help its businesses achieve improved results by helping them meet their customers' expectations about product environmental performance. The Computer Products Organization has already released PCs and printers with improved environmental features.

11.7 APPLICATIONS OF LCA

Life-cycle assessment as *both a concept and a methodology* has a valuable role to play in improving our understanding and reducing the environmental burdens associated with products, technologies, processes, and activities from design and development through ultimate disposition. It provides a systematic means to broaden the perspective of a company's decision-making process to incorporate the consideration of energy and material use, transportation, postcustomer use, disposal, and the environmental releases associated with the product system.

LCA provides a framework to achieve a better understanding of the benefits and risks associated with specific change in a product, package, or process. Benefits realized from the application of life-cycle concepts include cost containment, liability management, stakeholder value, and competitiveness (Table 11.3). Companies' use of LCA is encouraged to help plan and begin to design and improve the environmental quality of product systems. However, it should not be viewed as the only tool to solve all environmental problems.

TABLE 11.3 Benefits of Implementing Life-Cycle Concepts

Cost containment	Liability management
• Lower management cost	• Reduce legal fines and penalties
• Lower disposal costs	• Improve relationship with regulators
• Reduce energy consumption	• Limit criminal liability exposure
• Increase productivity	• Increase likelihood of compliance
Stakeholder value	Competitiveness
• Increase revenue	• Better meet supplier and customer needs
• Increase market share	• Revenue potential through recycling
• Enhance company image	• Increase market share
	• New product opportunities

Although the LCA methodology is still evolving, the concept of life-cycle thinking is here today and has applications to business and organizations as an alternative way of addressing environmental problems. It offers us new models for future efforts toward pollution prevention and sustaining our resources for the future.

REFERENCES

Consoli, F., D. Allen, I. Boustead, J. Fava, W. Franklin, A. Jensen, N. de Oude, R. Parrish, R. Perriman, D. Postlethwaite, B. Quay, J. Seguin, and B. Vigon (eds.). 1993. *Guidelines for Life-Cycle Assessment: A "Code of Practice."* SETAC, Pensacola, FL.

Fava, J., R. Denison, B. Jones, M. Curran, B. Vigon, S. Selke, and J. Barnum (eds.). 1991. *A Technical Framework for Life-Cycle Assessment.* SETAC, Pensacola, FL.

Fava, J., F. Consoli, R. Denison, K. Dickson, T. Mohin, and B. Vigon (eds.). 1993a. *A Conceptual Framework for Life-Cycle Impact Assessment.* SETAC, Pensacola, FL.

Fava, J., E. Weiler, and K. Reinert. 1993b. *Product Life-Cycle Assessment: A Tool to Implement Product Stewardship.* Weston Way, Roy F. Weston, Inc., West Chester, PA.

Fava, J., A. Jensen, L. Lindfors, S. Pomper, B. De Smet, J. Warren, and B. Vigon (eds.). 1994. *Life-Cycle Assessment Data Quality: A Conceptual Framework.* SETAC, Pensacola, FL.

CHAPTER 12
LIFE-CYCLE ASSESSMENT: A SYSTEM ANALYSIS

Jacques Besnainou, *President*
Remi Coulon, *Technical Manager*
ECOBALANCE, INC.
ROCKVILLE, MD

12.1 INTRODUCTION

Life-cycle assessment (LCA) is a young tool. It was first used in the 1960s to measure the energy efficiency of companies' products and manufacturing processes. It really began to be widely used in the late 1980s to effectively measure the environmental burdens of a given process or product. Since then, it has been heavily criticized, mostly in the United States, as being an immature science where the assumptions are very important and can be chosen to "stack the deck."[1]

Nevertheless, LCA is evolving and is more and more recognized as a sensible and complimentary way to environmentally analyze products and processes. In Europe, where most progress has been made in this field in the past several years, LCA serves as a basis for the European Ecolabel and the European Directive for Packaging and Packaging Waste. LCA is more and more used internally by U.S. and European companies that want to find savvy ways to reduce their products' environmental burdens while improving their financial bottom lines.

What is life-cycle assessment? It is not, as some believe, only an exhaustive environmental analysis of a product or a process. It is a *complete analysis of a system,* whatever this system may do—manufacture a product, recycle packaging waste, incinerate plastics, etc.

This system can encompass different manufacturing sites or only a small part of them. This system is delimited by system boundaries and can be described graphically by a process tree, as presented in Fig. 12.1.

The ultimate goal of a life-cycle assessment, then, is to report as carefully as possible the environmental emissions (air, water, and solid waste), raw material, and energy requirements at the boundaries of the system, referred to as *flows.*

Therefore, LCA highlights all the tradeoffs within the system. For example, it is helpful to know that while fluorescent lightbulbs require less power than incandescent ones and so contribute to less pollution, they nevertheless contain toxic mercury. It is also interesting that when electric vehicles reduce air pollution on the road, they

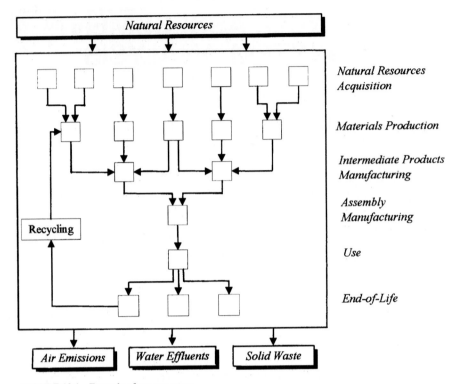

FIGURE 12.1 Example of a process tree.

increase the air pollution generated by power plants and generate a toxic waste problem regarding battery disposal.

Life-cycle assessment, because it provides a system point of view, helps challenge conventional wisdom concerning the environment. It projects a new light on possible cross-media contamination and more generally gives a broader view of all the environmental consequences of a decision. Two applications that illustrate the power and limitations of this system analysis are described in this chapter. The first is the application of LCA in product design, and the second is the application of LCA in waste management. The presentation of these case studies is followed by a discussion of possible improvements of LCA in the near future that will help this new science to attain its maturity.

12.2   LCA'S APPLICATION IN PRODUCT DESIGN: A CASE STUDY

One of the first applications of this system analysis technique was used to compare products. From a historical point of view, this started in both the United States and Europe with packaging and packaging materials, for which comparing two products was often a "simple" choice of comparing two materials. In spite of the various mistakes made in the use of such analyses, the assessment of products' alternatives became widespread and led to the study of more complex multimaterial products.

The following case study is based on an actual project carried out on an electric switch* which shows the profit that can be made from undertaking such a comprehensive assessment, even for products whose complexity would seem to prevent one from doing so.

12.2.1 Background

A large, international company in the electrical industry and headquartered in western Europe started this LCA. It provides products for industrial power distribution control and automation (switches, circuit breakers, relays, controllers, etc.). Several of its markets were close to commodity markets; i.e., competitive products had roughly the same price and level of performance.

In one of these markets ($350 million in Europe alone), that of electric switches, an environmental claim was made by a competitor regarding one of the firm's products, provoking an instant, strong reaction from the market. The claim was that cadmium had been removed from the alloy used in the contact point, therefore yielding a cadmium-free switch. Since all similar products were in the same price and performance range, this claim was highly successful in promoting the product.

The advertisement caught the company unprepared. The cadmium-free technology (use of a cadmium-free alloy in the contact point) was not new, but had not been implemented since there was no *product-related* incentive for it. From a manufacturing perspective, the use and release of cadmium were regulated, but this was the first time in this industry that such pressure was felt at the product level. This type of product-oriented environmental claim generally results from marketing pressure, and therefore it goes beyond regulatory compliance. Actually, all sites involved in the industrial systems of both alternatives (cadmium alloy and cadmium-free alloy) may comply locally, but from a *system* perspective, one may gain an advantage by using a different technology, material, or distribution network.

The company was already manufacturing such a cadmium-free switch for other applications and could have easily prepared a similar claim, but it wanted to put this cadmium issue in perspective and identify where the main contributors were within the life cycle of the product.

12.2.2 Description of Project

Scoping. The project started with the selection of the product for which the LCA was actually carried out. The product range, which was under attack, comprised several hundred different products. A representative one was chosen, in terms of processes and materials. In addition to the selection of the baseline, several scenarios were studied, among which was the replacement of the cadmium-based alloy by a silver-nickel alloy for the contact point.

For such a complex product, the function is defined by many technical parameters (contactor supply voltage, dc or ac nature of the control supply, load, i.e., current taken by the load and frequency of operations, safety features, etc.) and cannot be completely

---

*In such a device, also known as a *contactor,* a low-voltage current is used to control the on and off switching of a high-voltage current. The on and off switching of the high-voltage current is done at a contact point within the contactor. It is widely used in all industrial operations (assembly lines, etc.).

reduced to one parameter. Therefore, the functional unit was chosen as the product itself over its life span, and was a reminder that only functionally equivalent product alternatives should be compared.

System Boundaries.   The first step in performing an LCA is to define the system boundaries. The LCA theoretical principle requires that each material and constituent be studied and traced back to natural resources. The strict application of this principle would lead to the study of almost every industrial process as all industrial operations work within a complex network. This has led to rather extreme examples; e.g., an LCA practitioner studied the "energy needed to make the tire used on the combine that is, in turn, used to harvest the grain, which then is used to feed the cattle that are slaughtered to yield the tallow used to make soap"!

Fortunately, there are some quantitative methodologies available to assess whether a defined process should be included in the system boundaries. These quantitative methods are particularly important for complex multimaterial projects.

However, it should be emphasized that these methods can only reduce the uncertainty associated with the system boundary issue, not eliminate it (using a foolproof methodology would imply an assessment of the environmental impacts of all associated processes and materials, which is precisely one of the final results of the LCA). So far, weight has been used as the sole cutoff criterion since this information is always available and is needed in the subsequent steps of the calculation. This is not satisfactory, however, and a set of cutoff criteria should be used instead of a single criterion. Some of the cutoff criteria that are available for complex products include

- *Weight*
- *Energy requirement.*   The use of energy might seem contradictory since the energy requirement related to a process or a material is a result of the life-cycle inventory (LCI). However, due to the early start of the energy analysis in the 1960s, massive amounts of energy data have been published on almost all products, and the use of approximate, and sometimes dated, values is reasonable at this stage.
- *Toxicity,* either of the component itself or due to its manufacturing process.
- *Price.*   A high price does not directly reflect a high environmental impact; but unless there is a monopoly on a certain product's component, high price does reflect (1) a high raw material cost and therefore scarce natural resources, (2) numerous manufacturing processes, or both.

Although there is no direct relationship between one of these criteria and an environmental impact, when used in conjunction, they provide a correct screening process, as detailed in the example below. This example, presented in Table 12.1, illustrates how six components are selected from a list of nine components. The weight criterion selects components A, B, and C; the energy criterion, components A, B, and E; toxicity, component H; and price, components A, B, and I. As a result, components A, B, C, E, H, and I are included in the system boundaries.

This multicriteria approach is especially needed if weight is considered as a crucial design parameter for the product considered. For instance, in the automotive industry, if weight were the only cutoff criterion in a study of automotive components, that would imply that the lighter the better (a lighter component would not be studied, i.e., included in system boundaries), and thus plastic would be implicitly favored over aluminum, itself implicitly favored over steel.

In this particular project, such a multicriteria approach was used, and the production of the following materials was included in the system boundaries:

TABLE 12.1 Determination of Negligible Components

Component	Weight	Energy	Toxicity	Price	Included in system boundaries
A					Yes
B					Yes
C					Yes
D					No
E					Yes
F					No
G					No
H					Yes
I					Yes

☐ Negligible contribution

▨ Small contribution

■ Large contribution

- Packaging materials (cardboard, shrink wrap, etc.)
- Metals: steel magnetic circuits, enameled copper coil windings, contact points, screws, clamps, blanks, contact support in plated steel or copper, AgNi alloy, AgCdO alloy, etc.
- Plastics: polyamide 6, reinforced polyamide 6,6, thermoset polyesters, etc.

In addition, transportation steps and the production of energy were included in the system boundaries.

Data Collection. As in every LCA, data had to be collected not only from the company's sites but also from suppliers' sites. In-house data collection is often a straightforward exercise, although time-consuming if not carefully prepared (ensuring a strong corporate commitment and delivering properly formatted questionnaires are two critical steps for successful LCA projects). However, data collection from suppliers is often a much more delicate exercise. LCI data are by nature very sensitive, not only because they might contain proprietary technical information (type of additive used, type of energy used, etc.), but also because they could be used by the client to pressure suppliers to reduce prices (material and energy balance can be closely related to costs). In this case, an external practitioner acts as a screen, allowing the delivery of high-quality information to the company undertaking the LCA while preserving the confidentiality of suppliers' processes and products.

Figure 12.2 shows how LCA information can flow between the different partners involved. In this scheme, the external LCA practitioner executes confidential disclosure agreements with the various suppliers involved, works with each one of them on a detailed basis (i.e., having access to information deemed proprietary), and provides the

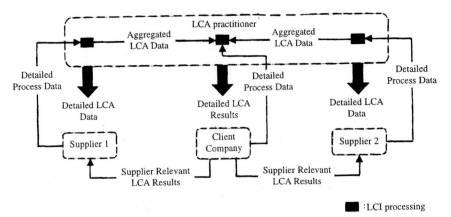

1) The client and suppliers provide the LCA practitioner with detailed process data.
2) After processing those data, the LCA practitioner gives back Ito the suppliers detailed LCA results relevant to their processes.
3) The LCA practitioner gives back to the client detailed LCA results based on the client process data and the aggregated suppliers LCA data.
4) The client may give supplier relevant LCA results to the suppliers.

FIGURE 12.2   Data collection. Relationships with suppliers.

client company with suppliers' aggregated data only. This ensures that the client company has correct LCA data, i.e., checked (no "optimized" data provided by the supplier) and compiled according to the inventory methodology. For the supplier, there is no disclosure of proprietary information that the client could trace to process data.

It is important to highlight the positive returns for suppliers. They receive LCI data on their processes which can be communicated to other clients having the same request and partial results of the overall LCA. It is up to the client company to decide what level of detail of the final LCA can be shared with each supplier. For instance, each supplier could know its contribution within the life cycle of the product. This is of considerable importance and has proved to be a strong incentive for the supplier to participate in the LCA: If the supplier's share is high, the supplier can expect, sooner or later, pressure from the client (and other clients in the same industry) to reduce its environmental impacts (especially if the client company is contemplating an ecolabel based on LCA criteria).

12.2.3   Results and Conclusions

Three types of analysis were conducted: (1) analysis of the life-cycle inventory—analysis of the origin of the flows, (2) life-cycle impact assessment (LCIA), and (3) sensitivity or scenario analysis. The third type of analysis is crucial to ensure the representativeness of both the LCI and the LCIA. However, it was not always properly conducted in the past, and its use is not currently widespread due to poor calculation tools and the lack of accepted methodologies.

The following sections discuss the most salient conclusions that were reached.

Cadmium Controversy.   To put the cadmium issue in perspective (which was a main incentive to initiate the project), two scenarios were studied, silver-cadmium oxide

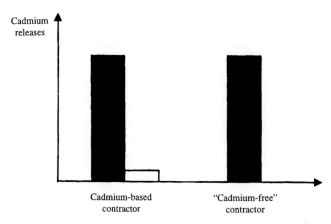

FIGURE 12.3   Origin of cadmium releases.

(AgCdO) versus silver-nickel alloy (AgNi) contact. Figure 11.3 shows the cadmium water releases for both scenarios. Actually most of the cadmium emissions are associated not with the contact point, but with the surface treatment of metal sheets used in other subcomponents. Therefore, getting rid of the cadmium in the contact point was far from producing a cadmium-free contactor.

New Product Design.   For most air emissions as well as the raw material and energy requirements, a surprising life-cycle profile was obtained. Figure 12.4 shows the breakdown of these flows in terms of production (from raw materials to the final product and its packaging) and postproduction (distribution, use, and end of life).

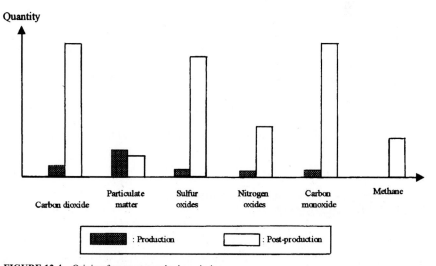

FIGURE 12.4   Origin of some atmospheric emissions.

These results were thought to be disappointing at first, since the company's engineers had little if any control of downstream processes. But actually, analysis of this postproduction step revealed that the use phase (electrical consumption and thus production by power plants) was responsible for more than 97 percent of the impacts of the postproduction phase. Impact assessment results on air indices (global warming potential, acidification potential, etc.) led to the same conclusion.

This result was rather counterintuitive for the company's engineers since the contactor is not an active device (as a computer is) and does not have a high rate of electricity consumption. However, it remains under constant power during its service life (at least 10 years), therefore using an appreciable amount of electric power.

This surprising result was an incentive for the design and promotion of a new low-voltage product that cut by half the electricity consumption and thus the flows associated with the electricity production.

Conclusions. For this company, the benefit of carrying out this LCA was the protection and increase of market share with

- The ability to assess competitive environmental claims
- The identification of environmentally sound products combining an objective environmental edge and characteristics wanted by the market (quality and reduced power costs)
- Rational external communication (a document was prepared for external communication and shown in technical and trade fairs)

From a general point of view, this type of project highlights

- The increasing applicability of LCA on complex products based on database and proper software tools.
- The need for rational methodologies for determining cutoff criteria when system boundaries are defined. In other similar projects on complex products that we have carried out in the electronics industry, silicon-based components (integrated circuits) were included, although they represented only 0.3 percent of the total weight of the product, but 35 percent of the cost of the final product. Subsequently, the 0.3 percent (by weight) of the product proved to contribute up to 40 percent of the total life-cycle impact of the product (in some impact categories).
- The idea that there is not always a need to carry out a valuation (i.e., trading off the various impact categories). The identification of environmental problems itself provides one with a wealth of information, and there is not always a need to trade these environmental issues against each other in order to determine which alternative is "greener."
- The need to go beyond regulations and address product-related issues, which is driven by marketing pressures rather than regulatory pressures. Companies sell products and not manufacturing plants, and therefore they will find (and have already found) that LCA is a strong tool for promoting their products and turning environmental costs (compliance) into a competitive weapon.

12.3 PROCESS DESIGN: THE EXAMPLE OF WASTE MANAGEMENT

Since life-cycle assessment is a system analysis process, it can be easily used to compare environmental impacts of any industrial system (processes, services, etc.), and not only of product life-cycle systems. One particular application of LCA to industrial process design is in waste management. It encompasses several different steps: collection, demanufacturing, sorting, transportation, incineration, landfilling, and remanufacturing. It has also been one of the focal points of both environmental organizations and government agencies which consider waste disposal to be a major environmental issue.

As a result, LCA has been used both by private industry and regulatory agencies to determine which waste disposal option (incineration, recycling, composting, landfilling, reusing) leads to lower environmental impact. This analysis has proved critical for defining integrated waste management schemes, which, if allowed to go unchallenged, could lead to unsubstantiated pollution control decisions with severe economic consequences.

To illustrate the usefulness of LCA in handling waste management issues, two examples are presented:

- A case study with IBM where different waste management options were studied for a monitor housing
- A case study with the European Commission where different waste management options were considered for packaging waste

12.3.1 Private Company Case Study: IBM

Background.   IBM[2] is currently evaluating the environmental burdens associated with the use of various materials, among which is polyvinyl chloride (PVC), in major structural parts for information technology equipment. In applying LCA to materials and subcomponents, IBM can limit its scope of study while including all life-cycle phases of the component or material investigated. A key materials issue for analysis with LCA was identification of environmentally preferable disposal options for plastic components of business equipment. As part of its commitment to developing environmentally conscious products, IBM wanted to understand the environmental soundness of setting product goals for increased recycled content and closed-loop recycling programs. The company identified an experimental closed-loop recycling scheme for PVC covers from personal computer monitors. Then three end-of-life options were studied for disposition of a "clean" (free of paints, labels, coatings and inserts, etc.) PVC monitor housing:

1. A closed-loop recycling option for PVC monitor housings was based on IBM's current cathode-ray tube (CRT) recycling process in the United States. Used or surplus monitor equipment was collected at an IBM site and shipped to a qualified CRT recycling vendor. Reclamation of PVC covers from the CRTs provided the feedstock for the second-use applications in IBM machines.
2. The monitor housings, if not recovered by the CRT recycler, would be disposed of in a landfill as scrap from the CRT disassembly operations.
3. Incineration with heat recovery of PVC monitor housings collected at the CRT recycler was modeled for the third disposal alternative.

Two main technical problems have to be carefully addressed when modeling such an analysis: how to draw consistent system boundaries and how to correctly account for recycling and energy recovery.

How to Draw Consistent System Boundaries.   Determining consistent system boundaries is a crucial point. For waste management systems, this is a two-stage process:

- Determine *general system boundaries* for the compared options, by correctly identifying the function(s) of each alternative.

- Once these general system boundaries are agreed to, *precise system boundaries* can be developed (how far to trace intermediate and ancillary materials, etc.).

The second aspect is well known, although not all the related problems are solved. Its principles have been summarized in U.S. inventory guidelines,[3] and the previous section details how this approach should be refined. But the first aspect has barely been addressed. Actually, as long as LCA was assessing products, the functional unit was often clearly outlined: packaging 1 gal of milk, covering 10 ft^2 of wall for 10 years, etc.

In all waste management options, the same primary function is performed: disposing of wastes. But they often involve several secondary functions—producing energy for waste-to-energy plants and producing recycled materials for recycling schemes.

Figure 12.5 shows that the systems start after the use of the computer, since all the industrial upstream steps (manufacturing, distribution, use) are the same for the three options and therefore do not need to be studied for the purpose of the comparison.

The system then encompasses the transportation of the used monitor housing to the dismantler, the disassembly lines, the transportation of the used monitor housing again to the landfill or the incineration plant, or the grinder. In case of recycling, two additional industrial steps are taken into account: the transportation of the PVC flake to the molder and the molding operation that creates a new PVC monitor housing.

But as explained above, the recycling and waste-to-energy schemes are performing more than the primary function of disposing of a used PVC monitor housing. They also produce energy (through the energy recovery of the incineration process) and produce a new PVC monitor housing (through the material recovery of the recycling process). As a consequence, to draw a meaningful comparison of the three options on the same functional basis (which is disposing of a used PVC monitor), the two additional functions, performed by the industrial system within the system boundaries, have to be eliminated.

In the case of recycling, the manufacturing of a new monitor housing from virgin PVC should be subtracted from the system consisting of disposing of a PVC housing by grinding it and manufacturing a new one. In doing so, the additional function which is producing a new monitor housing (through the material recovery of the recycling process) has been eliminated. Figure 12.6 describes this modeling. This figure shows clearly that all the industrial steps related to the production of a PVC monitor housing have been subtracted from the industrial system describing the recycling options. This operation is called incorporating the *credit for recycling*. It is the right mathematical modeling of the commonsense belief that using recycled materials helps save virgin materials. Consequently, to this modeling, some environmental emissions can have a negative value for the recycling options. A negative value means that the industrial system has lower emissions when manufacturing goods from recycled materials than from virgin materials. This also highlights that the more complex the recycled or recovered materials are, the more data-intensive the project is likely to be. For instance, the reuse of a complex subcomponent of a computer in a specific disposal scheme implies that the production of this subcomponent must be taken into account.

The same type of modeling is applicable to incineration with heat recovery. In that case, the energy production from a conventional source (e.g., power plant) should be subtracted from the disposal of the PVC monitor housing by incineration with energy recovery, as described in Fig. 12.7. The subtraction of energy production from conventional sources can bring to light very counterintuitive results. For example, when air emissions generated by coal-fired power plants are subtracted from air emissions generated from high-density polyethylene (HDPE) wrap films incineration, the overall result of the calculation is often negative, proving that producing electricity from HDPE incineration generates lower air emissions than producing electricity from burning coal.

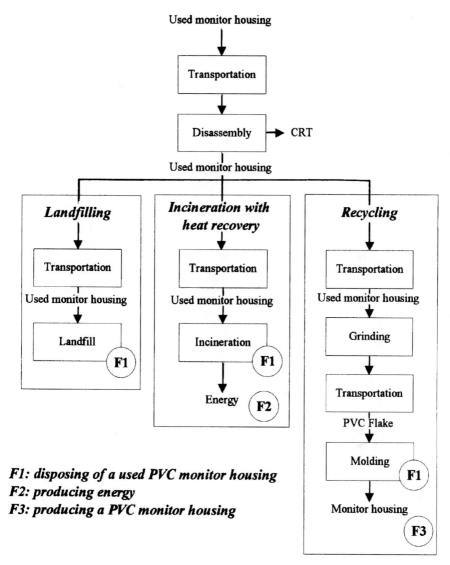

F1: disposing of a used PVC monitor housing
F2: producing energy
F3: producing a PVC monitor housing

FIGURE 12.5   Functional analysis of the three disposal options.

How to Account Correctly for Recycling: The Recycling Efficiency   As shown previously for the recycling system, the subtracted subsystem corresponds to the production of a defined quantity of PVC monitor housing. This quantity of PVC molded from used PVC will be actually the quantity of PVC molded from virgin PVC, which will be subtracted from the recycling system, as shown in Fig. 12.8.

However, it is critical to recognize that the true link between the two subsystems (recycling subsystem and subtracted subsystem) is not a quantity of recycled material, but a function, i.e., a number of monitor housings. This point, often ignored in life-cycle

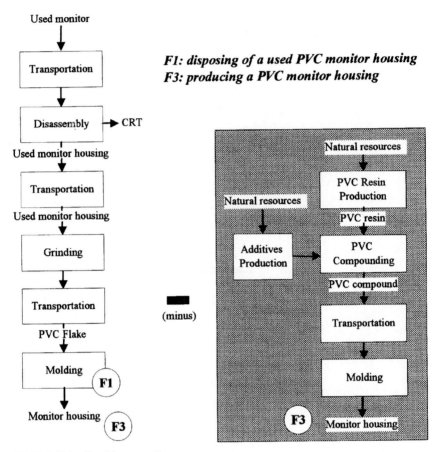

FIGURE 12.6   Closed-loop recycling system.

inventories, is the analysis of the efficiency of recycling (in terms of LCI methodology). Recycling efficiency depends on two independent factors:*

- *Losses of matter* (the higher the losses of matter, the less recycled material is produced, the smaller the subtracted part).

- *Functional efficiency,* i.e., how efficient the recycled material is in replacing the virgin material. In the case of the closed-loop system for the PVC monitor housing, the functional efficiency is 100 percent, meaning that the use of virgin or recycled PVC in the design of monitor housing has no influence on the quantity of PVC in the final product. Figure 12.9 shows how a smaller functional efficiency of recycled material (e.g., due to a bulkier design) would translate to a smaller subtracted part (and thus to higher overall inventory flows for the recycling option).

---

*When necessary, a third factor should be added: the differences in the processes due to the use of recycled materials (in this case study, the energy consumption and other environmental parameters due to the molding of recycled or virgin PVC were the same).

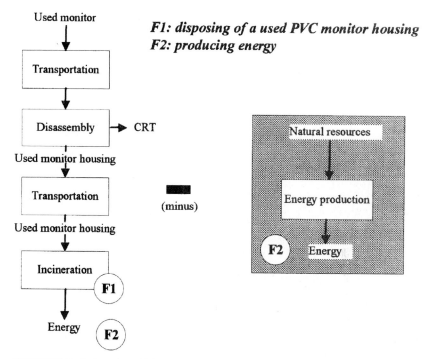

F1: disposing of a used PVC monitor housing
F2: producing energy

FIGURE 12.7   Incineration with heat recovery system.

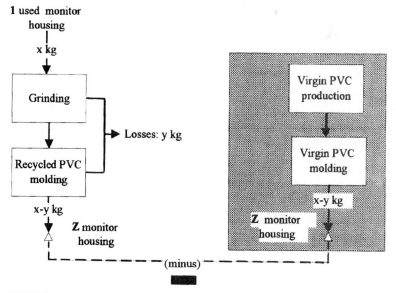

FIGURE 12.8   Recycling efficiency.

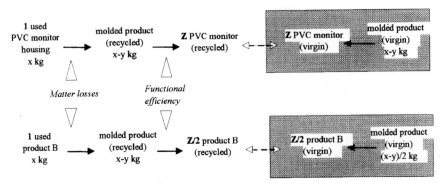

FIGURE 12.9 Influence of functional efficiency.

Results. Table 12.2 presents an abstract of life-cycle inventory results of physical flows for raw materials, energy requirements, air emissions, water effluents, and solid waste generated by each end-of-life option. With few exceptions, the recycling option presents the best inventory profile for

- Raw material requirements, with the exception of coal
- Energy requirements
- Air emissions, with the exception of ammonia
- Water effluents, with the exception of sulfates
- Solid waste, with the exception of hazardous waste or other waste

Several sensitivity analyses were performed to look at the effect of changing the upstream starting point for the study and varying transport efficiency (filling efficiency of vehicles involved in the various transport legs of the three options). None of them altered the comparative outcome of the options; i.e., the previous results were found to be consistent. Scenario analyses were also performed to examine the effects of (1) improved incineration parameters (increased removal efficiencies for particulate matter, acid emissions, and NO_x) and (2) different transportation distances for each disposal option. In each scenario the recycling option proved to be the best environmental performer.

Clearly the economy of PVC savings (replacing production of a new monitor housing from virgin PVC with the recycled material) accounts for the unsurpassed benefits of the recycling option in this study. However, this conclusion is application-specific and is attributable to some unique characteristics of the PVC monitor housing recycling project, such as

- The use of "clean" PVC, minimizing the recycling processes and associated material losses
- The perfect functional equivalency of the recycled PVC monitor housing
- The fact that compounding of the recycled PVC flake (another resource consumption) was not required for this application
- The low heating value of PVC (approximately one-half the value of other classic polyolefins), implying less savings from the energy recovery

For other resins and recycling programs, functional equivalency and resin-specific incineration models would have to be established. Nevertheless, this study demonstrates

TABLE 12.2   Inventory Results for Three End-of-Life Options

		Units	Landfilling	Incineration	Recycling
Raw materials	Crude oil	kg	0.036	0.025	−1.07
	Coal	kg	0.0002	−0.67	−0.44
	Natural gas	kg	0.0001	0.004	−1.28
	LImestone	kg		1.50	−0.004
	NaCl	kg			−1.5
	Water	l	0.007	−0.008	−4.2
Air emissions	Particulate matter	g	0.15	33	−8.3
	CO_2	g	115	2400	−4000
	CO	g	0.41	1.07	−5.3
	SO_x	g	0.16	−13.0	−27
	NO_x	g	1.17	−4.17	−33
	NH_3	g	0.0007	0.0143	0.0011
	Cl_2	g			−0.004
	HCl	g		300	−0.48
	Hydrocarbons	g	0.31	−13.70	−42.6
	Other organics	g	0.00	−0.02	−1.60
Water effluents	BOD_5	g	0.0002	0.0002	−0.18
	COD	g	0.0006	0.0007	−2.46
	Chlorides	g			−89.4
	Dissolved solids	g	0.42	0.48	−2.6
	Suspended solids	g	0.0002	−0.004	−5.3
	Oil	g	0.005	0.007	−0.10
	Sulfates	g			−9.6
	Nitrates	g		−0.0004	0.00004
	Nitrogen — TKN	g			−0.01
	Sodium ions	g			−5.1
	Metals	g			−0.45
Solid waste	Waste (hazardous chemicals)	kg			−0.003
	Waste (landfilled PVC)	kg	2.2	0	0.02
	Waste (slags and ash)	kg		1.7	−0.10
	Waste (others)	kg	0.00005	−0.44	−0.14
Energy	Total primary energy	MJ	42		−103
	Electricity	kWh	0.0012	−2.1	−2.3

the utility of LCA for improving decision making on waste management alternatives and defines criteria that constitute an environmentally positive profile for a closed-loop recycling process for business machine applications.

Also note that meaningful conclusions were drawn from this project just after a life-cycle inventory. That means that the impact assessment stage of an LCA is not always required in order to draw conclusions from a study.

12.3.2   Policy-Making Case Study: The European Directive on Packaging and Packaging Waste

A second example of application of life-cycle assessment to waste management is given below on the European Directive on Packaging and Packaging Waste.[4]

Background.   The project was carried out for the Executive Office of the French Ministry of the Environment, on the basis of actual packaging end-of-life case studies (during the summer of 1993). At that time, a European Directive on Packaging and Packaging Waste was under discussion in the European Commission and Parliament (the process actually started in mid-1992). This directive had been drafted in order to harmonize the differing national measures concerning the management of packaging and packaging waste in the European Community. Its aims were twofold:

- Reduce the impacts on the environment due to the increasing volume of packaging waste in the European Union (50 million metric tons per year).

- Avoid obstacles to trade and restriction of competition within the EC since national recycling programs tend to favor a closed-loop economy that can put imported products at a disadvantage.

In the first draft of the directive, the goals were the following: Within 10 years, 90 percent of the packaging waste should be sorted out, of which 60 percent should be recycled, implying a 54 percent recycling rate for packaging waste. The reduce/reuse/recycle/incinerate/landfill environmental hierarchy was clearly promoted. The French Ministry of the Environment decided to use LCA to study these goals. Based on real case studies of packaging end of life, the aim of this LCA project was to analyze the environmental soundness of the directive's goals. Three cases were studied according to their representativeness over the following criteria: packaging categories (primary, secondary, and tertiary packaging),* material categories (glass, paper products, plastic), and available waste management technologies (reuse, recycling, waste to energy, and landfilling). As a result of selecting these criteria, the three cases studied were glass bottles, corrugated board boxes, and polyethylene wrap. For these packaging groups, actual data were collected representative of the different process technologies currently available in Europe, and several recycling schemes were modeled.

Because a life-cycle assessment is a system analysis that takes all the industrial steps into account, the results of these studies brought interesting, surprising results that challenged the conventional wisdom that reusing and recycling are the most environmentally sound solutions for disposing of packaging.

Results.   The main outcome of this project was to highlight that advocating for a strict environmental hierarchy for packaging disposal options could actually lead to a large-scale pollution transfer phenomenon:

- The promotion of the reuse of glass bottles leads to a major elevation in water pollution (and air pollution when transportation distances increase).

- The recycling of cardboard leads to a massive transfer of pollution from water to air at a high recycling rate.

- Waste to energy is often a sounder environmental solution for disposing of plastics than recycling (lower atmospheric emissions, water effluents, and solid waste).

Figure 12.10 presents the water emission results for glass bottles. The washing of reused bottles implies more water emissions than those corresponding to one-way bot-

---

Primary packaging or sales packaging is the packaging conceived so as to constitute a sales unit to the final consumer at the point of purchase. *Secondary* packaging or grouped packaging is the packaging conceived so as to constitute at the point of purchase a grouping of a certain number of sales. *Tertiary* packaging or transport packaging is the packaging conceived so as to facilitate handling and transport.

LCA of Glass Bottles
Main Water Emissions for Reuse versus Recycling

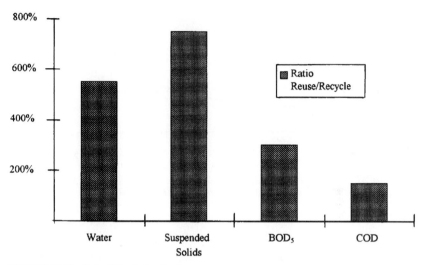

FIGURE 12.10   End of life of glass bottles.

tle production. Moreover, the improvement of glass bottle production technologies in the years to come will likely double that gap. The comparison of air emissions between the two systems leads to less significant results, since it depends on the distance of transportation of the reused bottles.

Figure 12.11 presents the results for cardboard packaging. The LCA shows that a high recycling rate of cardboard is not more environmentally friendly than virgin cardboard, but just leads to a transfer of pollution from water to air. The main reason for this transfer of pollution is that a higher recycling rate requires more and more transportation in order to take back discarded paper and cardboard materials used for the manufacturing of recycled fibers.

Similar results have been found for the end of life of polyethylene wrap. The savings of emissions due to heat recovery in incinerating polyethylene wrap leads to lower air emissions of the incineration alternative compared to the air emissions generated by the recycling alternative.

These totally counterintuitive findings assisted the French Ministry of the Environment in establishing the French position during the European negotiations on the directive and its amendments. The directive was eventually adopted on December 14, 1994, by the qualified majority.* The final directive[5] took into account the findings of the LCA studies:

- The traditional reuse/recycle/incinerate/landfill hierarchy is now explicitly phased out from the European Directive. A case-by-case analysis dependent on local conditions (products, packaging, markets) is favored.

---

*With Belgium, France, Greece, Ireland, Italy, Luxembourg, Portugal, Spain, and the United Kingdom voting for and Denmark, Germany, and the Netherlands voting against.[5]

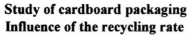

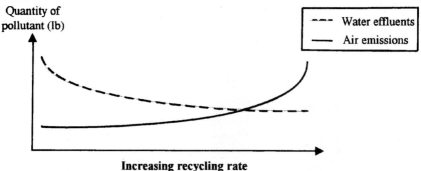

Note: since several curves can be traced for several air and water pollutants (CO_2, NO_x, SO_x, heavy metals, nitrates, suspended solids, etc.), several intersection points could be plotted on such a chart.

FIGURE 12.11   End of life of cardboard packaging.

- The directive now enforces a maximum recycling rate, in addition to a minimum recycling rate. Within 5 years, 50 percent minimum (in mass) and 65 percent maximum of the packaging waste should be diverted from landfills, of which 25 to 45 percent should be recycled, with a minimum of 15 percent per material.

12.3.3 Conclusions

The two previous examples showed how powerful life-cycle assessment can be when it is applied to waste management issues. Generally, LCA studies highlight that

- Recycling is a manufacturing process like any other, requiring energy, water, and often chemical resources.
- Transportation networks associated with waste disposal alternatives may play a significant role and sometimes generate more pollution than the disposal technique itself.
- In terms of emissions, modern waste-to-energy plants operate generally more cleanly than most fossil-fuel-fired power plants.

Here in the United States, it is reasonable to think that LCA studies will play an increasing role in the hot internal debate on municipal waste management (MSW). The latter has become a major issue in terms of environmental impacts. It has become the focus of local, state, and federal regulations, which generally promote the reduce/reuse/recycle/incinerate/landfill environmental hierarchy. As a result, waste incineration has been under increasing scrutiny.

However, recycling is not an easy task technically or economically. For example, when Germany enforced plastic recycling through DSD (Duales System Deutschland), it collected tons of plastic with no possibility of processing it. As a result, DSD lost several hundreds millions of dollars and exported plastic waste to third world countries.

Nevertheless, it is possible through subsidies and tax incentives to develop a broader recycling industry that will help find a market for collected plastic waste. This means that citizens must be ready to pay more taxes to implement recycling. This would sound like a good idea if recycling made the environment cleaner and safer. Unfortunately, the recycling idea is not environmentally friendly in every case, as LCA has demonstrated on many occasions.

12.4 ENHANCING LIFE-CYCLE ASSESSMENT

This section identifies and succinctly describes the main issues that need to be addressed in order to enhance the value of the LCA tool: assessing and using variability and uncertainty in LCA, improving the life-cycle impact assessment (LCIA) stage, and streamlining the LCA process.

12.4.1 Addressing and Exploiting Variability and Uncertainty in LCA

The data inputs, computational methods, results, and conclusions of current LCA methods and tools neglect the multiple sources of uncertainty in the data, the variability in the emissions per unit of output within an industry, and the effects that these both have on analysis results and conclusions.

Users of LCAs obtain numerical results which are reported as if they were certain, while in fact they are based on a host of data sources and are the result of a complex chain of computations. Both considerable uncertainty and variability of the input data are ignored by today's LCA methods and tools, at the expense of the power of the methods and the relevance of the results. For instance (see Fig. 12.12), two different LCA

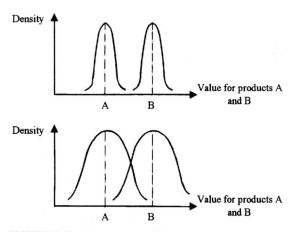

FIGURE 12.12   Point estimates with uncertainty.

values (from either inventory or impact assessment results) might in fact correspond to two opposite conclusions depending on the data distribution curve, and a sharp difference in value between the two alternatives A and B might in fact correspond to no difference at all. Moreover, neglect of variability represents a severe missed opportunity.

Incorporating and processing data on emissions variability (among supplying firms, for example, within a given SIC* category) would provide critical product or process design and supplier evaluation information (see example below).

Second, in communicating to audiences aware of the complexity and uncertainty underlying the final results—fast becoming the bulk of the decision-making and policy-making audience—LCA currently can provide no information about ranges or levels of confidence in the results. Finally, analysts themselves have no systematic way of identifying the most influential uncertainties, so they have little basis on which to prioritize data refinement efforts and resources.

An example of the use of uncertainty and variability is given in Fig. 12.13, in which two product alternatives A and B are compared. When a single numerical value per impact is used, alternative A appears worse than B for impact 1, better for impact 2, and equivalent to B for the third impact. But by using and propagating uncertainty in the search for dominance, impact 2 does not appear as a differentiating factor, and alternative B therefore becomes better than or equal to A (without trying to weight the different impacts themselves).

The solution to this issue relies on the development of both a mathematical framework adapted to LCA and properly formatted databases characterizing uncertainty and variability (use of ranges or, preferably, of standard-deviation-based indicators).

Due to the nature of LCA, several problems might appear when one is propagating uncertainty. For instance, one could compute an industry average LCA for the production of a commodity and indicate ranges associated with each inventory value. However, because LCA values are interrelated, the notion of best and worst sites should be interpreted carefully. Let us suppose that among the sites included in the average are sites A and B, having the same yield and gross waste scrap generation. But because site

*Standard Industry Classification.

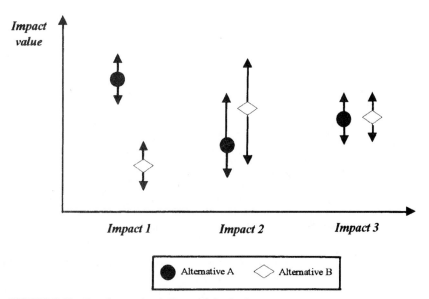

FIGURE 12.13   Use of uncertainty in the search for dominance.

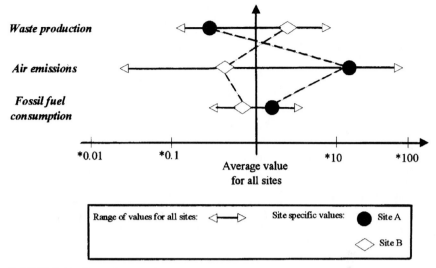

FIGURE 12.14   Uncertainty correlation.

A implements an aggressive solid waste reduction plan, most of its waste is treated (either on-site or off-site), leading to a higher fossil fuel consumption and therefore higher air emissions than site B (see Fig. 12.14). Because LCA results between different media are often interrelated, and not always in the same way (i.e., if A generates less waste than B, this does not imply that A generates lower air emissions than B), one has to take care when speaking about "worst" or "best" sites in such averages.

In summary, the current failure to account for either variability or uncertainty diminishes the power of LCA, and this must be corrected to prevent life-cycle environmental analysis from being dismissed as a pseudoscience. To date, in the absence of a mathematical framework and adequate industry data, the best answer is the extensive use of sensitivity analyses (see section on software tools).

12.4.2   From Analyzing a System to Assessing Its Impact on the Environment

Only recently has the LCA tool actually been concerned with the impacts on the environment of a system. By definition, the inventory component of an LCA, still the single focus of many LCA studies, is only concerned with the flows generated by the system (either consumed or emitted), and by definition, does not address the reception issue, i.e., the impact on the environment. The subsequent stage, life-cycle impact assessment, addresses the issue of how to translate the flows previously compiled to environmental impacts.

Impact assessment methodologies are presented elsewhere in this book and will not be detailed in this chapter. Some issues viewed as crucial for the life-cycle impact assessment are as follows:

- The amount of additional exposure data that would be needed to model actual impacts (as in human health risk assessment) is technically incompatible with the nature of LCA (several hundreds or thousands of processes connected together, each one generating dozens or hundreds of emissions) and does not correspond to its objectives. It should be recognized that LCA is one environmental management tool among several and that LCA cannot replace a specific environmental impact analysis for a specific site (see Fig. 12.15).

- Since LCIA aims at assessing potential impacts, LCA should not be considered as a predictive tool for assessing the actual impacts associated with a system, but rather as a tool providing comparative results for the functional unit considered. Moreover, the functional unit has often no reference to time or space considerations (which would be needed for predictive models), but is solely related to the function and performance of a system. As the modeling of environmental impacts improves, these potential LCIA models should become more and more precise and integrate crucial notions such as thresholds (current approaches are all based on a "less is better" approach). Consequently, as shown in Fig. 12.15, inventory data collection requirements could gradually increase with new parameters characterizing emissions (location, flow rate, etc.).

- Existing approaches that result in a limited number of indices are highly controversial. They have been criticized because they do not separate the objective evaluation

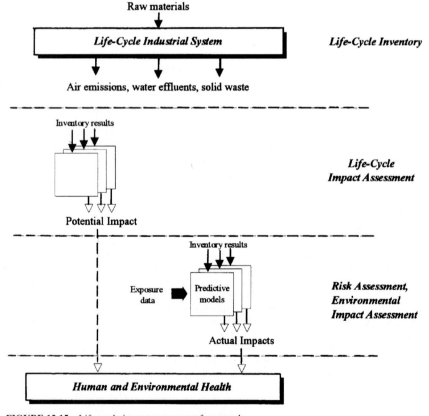

FIGURE 12.15   Life-cycle impact assessment framework.

stage of the environmental impact on scientific grounds from the subjective *valuation* stage in which these impacts are traded off. Using such approaches is very dangerous from an industrial perspective, for the following reasons:

- It tends to favor short-term arbitrary choices while masking their arbitrary nature behind quantitative data which give a false scientific "flavor" to the whole process. Valuation has to rely on these short-term judgments, often based on pollutant-of-the-month conventions. This is incompatible with industrial long-term investment and product design.
- The choices made might hide pollution displacement from one medium to another or from one step to another.

In numerous cases, results of inventory or impact assessment have been conclusive enough that no valuation was actually needed (as shown in the product design case study presented in Sec. 12.2). Moreover, often the existence of tradeoffs is by itself crucial information.

- For most impact categories, variability and uncertainties about impact potentials make any single numerical "equivalency factor" immediately contradictable and discreditable. Instead, LCIA methods need to be developed in which process data and results are considered in probabilistic terms. As for inventory results, uncertainties should be communicated to the decision-making audience.

12.4.3 Streamlining the LCA Resource Requirements

Providing comprehensive databases and powerful calculation engines is the basis for streamlining LCA in order to improve the time spent on data collection and the usability of the results. This streamlining of the LCA *resource requirements* should be promoted instead of the streamlining of the LCA *methodology,* which should remain as rigorous in all cases.

Improving Database Availability and Quality.   Easing the access to reliable LCA data is a crucial step for the widespread use of LCA, along with the development of software tools that can handle large databases and their complexity. Such databases should contain information on transportation (trucks, trains, pipelines, planes, ships), electricity production (several grids available), other utilities (steam production, air conditioning, etc.), plastics and petrochemicals, metals (ferrous and nonferrous), and inorganic chemicals.

Several databases are already available, and numerous industry associations are currently in the process of releasing such information. An important point, however, is that parameter-driven models should be provided rather than plain data, i.e., models accounting for some key parameters editable by the user. Building such models implies much more than collecting data—it involves analyzing them in order to identify these driving parameters.

For instance, an aggregated cradle-to-gate LCI on aluminum production has little meaning, since the electricity production (varying locally) carries a significant share of the burdens. Therefore, in this case, the electricity production should be separated from the aluminum production. The user would therefore have to plug in the correct electricity production module. These key parameters would differ from one product to the other. For instance, in a polyethylene (PE) production model, the electricity production would not need to be separated, whereas this should be the case in PVC production (a large amount of electricity is consumed for the electrolysis of NaCl).

Theses driving parameters should encompass

- Key technical parameters (e.g., type of electricity, type of process, type of feedstock).

- Key methodological parameters. The influence of key LCI methodological choices (e.g., allocation rule) should be identified, and the user should be able to modify the default value and test alternate choices.

These parameters should be understandable to an LCA practitioner and not too specialized (such as the temperature of a PE polymerization reactor).

Toward Powerful and User-Friendly Software Tools

Current Practice and Existing LCA Software Tools. Most LCA practitioners use commercial spreadsheets (or databases) for calculating life-cycle inventories. On top of the spreadsheet program, a specific software or *macro* layer is often added. The main advantages are that very low development costs are involved and, because of the standard functions available in commercial spreadsheets (e.g., formulas, graph construction), one can properly represent process data (e.g., relationships between process inflows and outflows) and achieve a flexible presentation of the results, suited to a particular industry and a specific purpose. Drawbacks are numerous: (1) This practice is incompatible with the elaboration of properly formatted and easily reusable databases; (2) risks of errors are significant; (3) complex projects are difficult to handle; and (4) data entry and calculation are time-consuming, as are simulations and sensitivity analysis.

The same pattern applies to LCA software programs developed on top of an existing commercial database. Balancing the low development costs are the lack of the complex calculation features needed for LCA projects (allocation rules, loops, formulas, etc.) and the near impossibility of handling real-size LCA (i.e., linking several hundreds or thousands of processes and propagating values through such a system).

This is why new software tools are needed, designed with the sole objective of speeding up the process of conducting LCA, without compromising on the methodology used.

In the next section some key features necessary for achieving a useful general-purpose LCA tool are examined. The discussion is focused on inventory analysis only.

Some Important Requirements for an LCA Software Tool

System representation. The LCA practitioner deals with operations or *modules* (industrial processes, transport, commercial activities, etc.) and systems (set of operations linked together). Modules and systems have inputs and outputs (*flows*), corresponding to natural resources, intermediate or finished products, energy sources, wastes, and environmental releases. Modules are connected through their inputs and outputs (a module should accept any number of connections). In addition to the basic numerical values found in every inventory, one should be able to store information on the geographic and technical representativeness, source of information, uncertainty, variability, measurement techniques, etc.

Reusability. One should be able to store modules and systems created for a given LCI project and then reuse them for other purposes, with all original details available as necessary.

Flexible use of LCI methodology. Software tools do not resolve some crucial issues involved in LCI, including the defining of consistent system boundaries, the choosing of allocation rules, and the taking into account of open-loop recycling. It is broadly recognized that these methodological choices can be project- or industry-specific and therefore can differ markedly from one project to another. As a consequence, the software tool should be designed (1) to be able to handle this variety of methodological rules and (2) to let the user handle these choices, change them during the course of a project, and assess their influence on the end results (sensitivity analysis).

Separation of process information from LCI methodological treatment. The software should contain both process information (e.g., without allocation rule) and the methodological assumptions themselves, allowing one to clearly separate the LCI methodological treatment from basic process data and easily link the software with existing process databases.

Flexible presentation of results. The user should be able to group contributions of modules within the system in all possible ways. In other words, it should be possible to identify the contribution of any module (or set of modules) to the LCI results. Similarly, one should be able to present the list of inventory items (inputs and outputs) in several different ways.

Confidentiality. In some instances, confidential information should be protected, depending on the user of the database and the confidentiality level of the data. For instance, only averages (with associated information on variability) might be available to some users.

Search operations. These should be available within the software (e.g., search for all modules or systems which produce electricity, or use soda).

Calculation procedure. When the inventory is computed, the software should deal with loops—recycling or reuse loops as well as other types of loops (take the classical example of electricity production using steel and steel production using electricity). This should be an option, so that pseudolinear approximations can be calculated when necessary.

Functional unit. Changing the functional unit (the reference flow and/or quantity for the calculation) and obtaining new results should be an easy operation.

Simulation formulas. When necessary, the user should be able to introduce parameters, and then vary these parameters, for the purpose of carrying out simulations. For instance, one might want to vary the composition of a multilayer packaging (in terms of materials), the thickness of a steel sheet, etc. Simulation may involve formulas, which describe relationships between some inputs and outputs, for instance.

Sensitivity analysis. Tools for sensitivity analysis should be provided. Automatic sensitivity analysis (i.e., an automatic search for the modules to which the results are most sensitive) would be a very useful feature.

Technical considerations. Object-oriented design and programming seem very appropriate for developing LCA software, as well as object-oriented databases for storing the data. Given the current demand, the software should run on a standard PC (486 or higher, Windows 3.1 or higher) and workstations. The software should also be able to reuse process information from other databases and software programs.

The complex issue is finding the right balance between flexibility and potential, on one hand, and ease of use, on the other. Several versions might exist, depending on the expertise of the user. For instance, some users may only be interested in simulations performed on a single system; in that case, access to the control parameters for the simulation is useful, while access to the details of the system would probably be confusing. But the development of a tool that would be accessible to nonexpert users can only be achieved after a fully functional and satisfactory complex tool has been developed. Aiming at a simple tool first risks letting nonexpert users draw erroneous conclusions, based on an inadequate and oversimplified representation of industrial processes and systems.

The Team Software. A software tool integrating the features listed in the previous section is an important development and calls for many domains of expertise in the field of computer science. These features were included in the development of an LCA modeling tool, the Team software. It allows the user to build a large database and to calculate life-cycle inventories and life-cycle costs for complex systems, in full adherence with the methodological guidelines developed for this technique. This model has been licensed to approximately 40 companies and government agencies worldwide; it includes

- A life-cycle inventory (LCI) and life-cycle cost (LCC) calculation tool: Team (Tools for Environmental Analysis and Management). Team has been developed for Ecobalance by Net-ID, Inc., a California-based company specializing in advanced computer science and computations in hierarchical networks.
- A comprehensive database on processes and materials, Deam (Data for Environmental Analysis and Management). The information provided in the database usually refers to the 1988–1995 period. In all cases, the origin and the geographic and technical representativeness of the data are mentioned, as well as the main underlying assumptions.

Two levels are used in Team (see Fig. 12.16):

- *Database level.*   Information is stored in independent modules representing unit operations (processes, transportation, etc.).
- *Calculation level.*   Calculations are performed for systems, which are sets of connected nodes. The nodes can be
  - Derived from modules. In this case, no change is possible directly in the nodes. The changes can be made only in the original module. If changes are made in a module, all nodes that are derived from this module will be automatically updated.
  - Free, i.e., directly created in the system in which they are used. Free nodes cannot be used by other systems.

This dual structure (database and calculation levels) explains many of Team's improvements over LCA models that are developed from

- Standard commercial spreadsheets (e.g., Excel, Lotus), which lack the database management capabilities needed for large LCA projects
- Standard commercial databases (e.g., Access, dBase), which do not have the complex calculation features needed for LCA projects (allocation rules, loops, formulas, sensitivity analyses, etc.)

Such a tool allows one to perform a wide variety of projects, ranging from simple LCA (built in a few days) to complex projects (the largest system built to date gathers approximately 2200 nodes in several layers of nested subsystems).

Moreover, different levels of use of Team are available for different applications and/or users. If necessary, sensitivity analyses and scenario analyses can be carried out from outside Team, allowing Team to be used as a *design-for-environment* (DFE) tool. End users not specialized in LCA (designers, R&D, etc.) can produce complex environmental and cost simulations by editing simple variables (e.g., transportation distances, recycling rate, coil thickness, fuel economy) in a centralized graphical control panel. This DFE interface accesses the fully elaborated Team model, but hides the LCA complexity so that designers and decision makers can identify influential parameters, test the influence of design changes, and conduct what-if analyses.

The development and use of such tools (database and powerful calculation engine) will be crucial in the coming years in order to ensure the diffusion of LCA techniques.

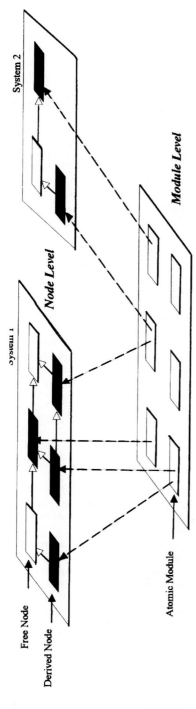

Organization Principle

- **Module level:** Data base

- **Node level:** Connections and calculations

—▷ : Connection

FIGURE 12.16 Team general architecture.

12.5 CONCLUSIONS

Most of the criticisms of the LCA technique are derived not so much from analyses that were not correctly carried out, but from LCAs that were—intentionally or not—misused. Apart from obvious abuses driven by aggressive marketing approaches, most of these misuses are due to the fact that too many people put too much faith in LCA results and do not place these results in perspective. One cannot use LCA in a consistent and sound manner unless one recognizes its limitations in terms of both issues that can be addressed (which implies knowing when the use of LCA is more appropriate than the use of another tool) and intrinsic characteristics, both practical and theoretical. Today's practical limitations (duration and cost of LCA) will disappear with the increasing use of adequate software and properly formatted databases. Some theoretical limitations, such as accounting for and using uncertainty and improving the impact assessment, will require more research and could lead to additional guidelines in a few years.

Moreover, one should keep in mind that LCA, as a technique, helps decision making, but does not replace it. The fact that LCA has often come up with mixed or complex results (i.e., depending on a set of key parameters) should not cast a shadow over the usefulness of these results. They simply reflect complex situations. If deemed necessary, the condensing of such complex results into one single answer should be done with great care. Particularly one should not try to hide decisions in a mathematical model, but rather clearly separate the outputs of the LCA model from the value judgments made in the trading off of different environmental impacts.

When it is properly conducted and used cautiously, LCA can bring extremely valuable information to issues where other environmental and management tools have been helpless.

The very nature of LCA brings *a global picture* of the environmental impacts associated with a product (or any industrial system), based on well-researched facts, and LCA helps in defining *long-term guidelines* for improving product and process design, allowing companies to direct their attention to the sustained health of the business rather than short-term issues. Product-oriented public policy making should gain the same benefit from using LCA.

REFERENCES

1. "How 'Tactical Research' Muddied Diaper Debate," *The Wall Street Journal,* May 17, 1994.

2. Brinkley et al., "Life Cycle Inventory of PVC: Disposal Options for a PVC Monitor Housing," *Proceedings of the 1995 IEEE International Symposium on Electronics and the Environment,* Orlando, Florida, May 1–3, 1995, p. 145.

3. U.S. Environmental Protection Agency, *Life-Cycle Assessment: Inventory Guidelines and Principles,* EPA/600/R-92/245, February 1993.

4. Besnainou, Jacques, and Goybet, Stephanie, "Life Cycle Assessment and End-of-life Management," *Proceedings of the 1995 IEEE International Symposium on Electronics and the Environment,* Orlando, Florida, May 1–3, 1995, p. 310.

5. Common Position (EC) No. 13/94, *Official Journal of the European Communities,* No. C 137/65, May 19, 1994.

CHAPTER 13

VALUATION AS A STEP IN IMPACT ASSESSMENT: METHODS AND CASE STUDY

Jürgen Giegrich
RESEARCHER
IFEU—INSTITUTE FOR ENERGY AND
ENVIRONMENTAL RESEARCH
HEIDELBERG, GERMANY

Stefan Schmitz
FEDERAL ENVIRONMENTAL AGENCY
BERLIN, GERMANY

13.1 VALUATION AS PART OF LIFE-CYCLE ASSESSMENT

The purpose of conducting a life-cycle assessment (LCA) is to answer the questions posed in the process of goal definition and scoping. Some questions can be directly answered by using the results of the inventory analysis:

- What is the contribution of different elements or subsystems of a life cycle compared to the entire system or to other elements or subsystems within the same life cycle of a product?

- How do improvements or alternative systems compare with the status option for all input and output parameters?

Normally, the input and output balances of two options exhibit inhomogeneous results. The substitution of primary material with secondary material for a specific product may reduce the resource demand for the first option while increasing the level of emissions for the second. The use of renewable energies may save fossil fuels but could lead to land degradation and losses of biodiversity.

The implementation of emission control as an improvement for a production unit may result in lower emissions for the production step while increasing the demand for energy which in turn is associated with emissions from energy generation. The reduction of toxic emissions (e.g., dioxins and furans) may conflict with the reduction of greenhouse gases. Similarly, a conflict between environmental impacts such as waste generation versus energy demand has no easy solution. In this example, it somehow must be decided whether waste minimization or energy conservation is more or less "important" in protecting the environment. Figure 13.1 shows schematically the conflict of competing aspects within instruments of environmental assessments like LCA.

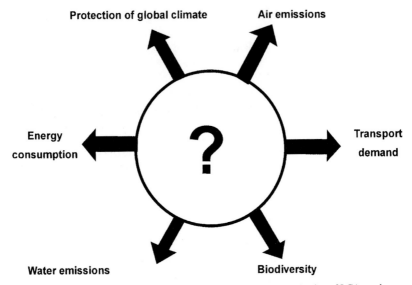

FIGURE 13.1   The judgment of competing environmental goals in valuation of LCA results.

It is obvious that no straightforward answers are possible in such cases. An "objective," scientific way to reach satisfying results does not exist because the presence of personal judgments and preferences for which a broad consensus cannot be expected plays an important role.

Decision making is a normal activity for everyone and is based on rational as well as emotional valuations. Only a few things in life may be so clear that they do not require the setting of preferences. On the contrary, nearly all actions are accompanied by conflicting goals. Valuating and deciding are thus commonly needed from the choice of every day's meal to the decision for a personal career.

It may be easy to derive decisions on an individual basis. Society, however, is forced to make decisions in group situations, ranging from two persons to (theoretically) the whole world population. Decisions are becoming increasingly complex as more people with diverging interests are involved. The participation of people in all kinds of decisions is, in fact, a big achievement of democratic societies. It is a privilege of democracy to have an individual opinion, and we should exercise this right in societal assessments such as environmental assessment methods and LCA.

All who deal with valuation as a methodology should view this complexity, and avoid seeing the valuation step of a life-cycle impact assessment as a mechanistic approach which can be reduced to some computer model. The fact that value judgments are connected with uncertainties may lead to the desire for development of a uniform and mechanistic approach. Rigid, formalistic methods, however, reduce the freedom of people to have their own preferences and apply them in assessment tasks.

With the above concepts as a basis, the *valuation* step in life-cycle impact assessment can be described as follows:

Valuation can be understood as the act of using "objective" information and connecting it with "subjective" value-based environmental goals with some kind of methodology in order to derive a judgment.

Valuation

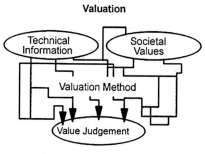

FIGURE 13.2 Graphical illustration of the valuation step in impact assessment.

Figure 13.2 illustrates the principle of how a value judgment in general will be made, not only in any LCA, but also in other assessment situations.

A judgment of an issue depends on facts and issues connected with one's values, emotions, previous judgments, and experience. Connecting information and values can be very different from person to person, and this represents the part of the valuation problem which is open to methodological development. The valuation methodology uses different forms of logic, some of which are described below. Three conclusions can be drawn from the perception of valuation presented in Fig. 13.2:

1. Valuation by definition is strongly influenced by subjective values. Hence, an objective valuation is not possible by definition.
2. Valuation is strongly influenced by facts and information. A value judgment is therefore not totally arbitrary.
3. Valuation as a process becomes more complicated if the number of persons or groups increases, if a complex issue is under judgment, if more than one criterion is used, and if valuation is carried out within a limited time.

A complex value judgment is not an instantaneous act, but a process which has its rules, conditions, and methods. To come to a reliable judgment of options in LCA is to make things as clear as possible. Only if the result of a valuation is transparent can it be communicated to decision makers and to the general public.

One may opt to derive an environmental judgment on the basis of inventory data. In such cases it has to be decided which of the environmental goals will serve as a basis for the valuation. Is waste minimization an environmental goal per se, or should the goal be, for example, the reduction of toxic emissions in waste management (with minimization as the first effective way to do so)? How can waste minimization be compared to the impact-related goal of reduction of health risks?

To be as clear as possible, the problem must be solved as to how to condense the complex information of the LCA inventory analysis in a way which allows a subsequent transparent environmental judgment for a product improvement or comparison.

The LCA step of *impact assessment* deals with the reduction of complex inventory data to impact-related figures and a final judgment of environmental aspects. It is called *impact assessment* because all suggested methods must somehow reflect the environmental impacts related to the inventory input and output parameters. Since the goal of LCA is to reduce overall environmental impacts, an impact-oriented judgment seems to be the appropriate way to deal with complex LCA data.

Impact assessment is defined by SETAC (Society of Environmental Toxicology and Chemistry) as follows:

Impact assessment in LCA is a quantitative and/or qualitative process to identify, characterize, and value the impacts of the environmental interventions identified in the inventory analysis.

Below, some methodological proposals are presented, and basic elements of valuation are formulated. Subsequently, the UBA approach is presented for the case study of milk beverage containers (flexible plastic bag versus refillable glass bottles).

13.2 VALUATION METHODS

Various methods have been suggested to overcome the complex impact assessment and valuation problem for LCAs. Assessment of environmental issues, valuation using ecological scarcity factors, and application of *willingness to pay* or *investments to reduce effects* are some of the approaches (see Table 13.1).

13.2.1 Ecoscarcity Methodology

This approach was developed in Switzerland in 1984 and later revised (BUWAL 1991). The use of environmental scarcity factors served as a starting point for the related Swiss *ecopoint methodology* (BUWAL 1990).

The basic concept is to define a critical load for each parameter under consideration. While BUWAL (1991) focused on toxic emissions, the critical loads for each substance were defined as the environmental quality standards of Switzerland, if available. By dividing the emission of a substance over the life cycle of a product, a critical volume is calculated. For example, 2.7 kg of SO_2, divided by the air quality standard of 0.03 mg/m^3, results in 90 million m^3 of air and can be interpreted as the volume of air which can be polluted by SO_2 while still meeting the air quality standard. Once this is done for every toxic substance, the potentially polluted air and water volumes can be combined in one figure and represent a valuation scheme for the option under study.

TABLE 13.1 Overview of Impact Assessment and Valuation Methods

Impact assessment and valuation method	Characteristics	Source
Ecoscarcity	For every substance a scarcity of toxicity is defined as *critical load*; the particular values are added	BUWAL 1991
Environmental theme	Treats all impacts separately and combines them at the valuation step	CML 1992
Environmental priority strategies	Inventory data are multiplied by weighting factors that are derived by "willingness to pay"	Steen 1992
Impact assessment and valuation of ecobalance	Treats all impacts separately and conducts a discursive valuation	UBA 1994

While BUWAL (1991) works separately with four impact categories (air emission, water emission, energy demand, waste production), the approach by Ahbe et al. (BUWAL 1990) tries to integrate these figures into a single dimensionless number, the *ecopoint*. For that purpose, the environmental goals (e.g., critical flow of air pollutants) are defined in the same unit as the parameters from the life-cycle inventory. Thus the *ecopoint* equals the inventory number divided by the environmental goal. All ecopoints are added to an over-all valuation number of an option under study. The valuation is given by choosing the parameters and the related *critical loads*.

13.2.2 Environmental Theme Methodology

This approach was formulated by CML and has been further developed for the Dutch chemical industry (CML 1992; VNCI 1991). Its basis consists of selecting categories of environmental impacts (environmental themes) and keeping them separate as long as possible. An indicator must be found for each of these categories in order to represent and aggregate all related inventory figures in one number. The environmental impact of ozone depletion in the stratosphere can serve as an example. The ozone depletion potential relative to CFC-11 is the indicator, and all depleting substances can be expressed in and aggregated within this unit.

Various lists of impact categories have been suggested and are currently the topic of general discussion. Since this is the preferred valuation approach within the standardization discussion, the International Organization for Standardization (ISO) and national standardization bodies are developing lists of impact categories. Methodologies must still be found or agreed upon for measuring the related impact for each category. Especially, the impact categories of human health and ecosystem health deserve further methodological development and discussion. The method of dealing with the aggregation here may have valuative elements.

The German Umweltbundesamt (UBA) applied an *argumentative valuation* (UBA 1995) to derive a final conclusion while the approach of the Dutch VNCI used a number-based weighting procedure (multiple-attribute utility analysis) to derive a single decisive *valuation number*. The application and discussion of environmental goals of the society are crucial to these types of valuation.

13.2.3 Method of Environmental Priority Strategies

From the work of two Swedish researchers (Steen and Ryding 1992), the system of *environmental priority strategies* (EPS) is based on the deduction of an index for each emission or resource demand which has been deduced from willingness-to-pay studies. The result, the *environmental load unit* (ELU), can be added for the valuation of the option. ELUs of different options can be compared in order to determine the best option. The valuation step of this methodology is clearly the deduction of the index. Since a valuation step is implied in each ELU calculation, it is not easy to trace the roots of a certain result.

13.2.4 Conclusions Based on Existing Methods

No agreement has been reached yet as to which method should be commonly used. LCA experts still discuss the advantages and disadvantages of the different methods, with the above serving as a limited selection. It is therefore not likely that international standardization activities will render a clear and final statement for the impact assessment step of LCA in the near future, but national standardization bodies may be closer to agreeing to certain conventions.

TABLE 13.2 Comparison of Substance-Related Valuation Figures of Three Different Valuation Methodologies (Baumann and Rydberg 1992)

Substance	Ecoscarcity	Weighted environmental theme	EPS
CO_2	1	1	1
SO_2	197	218	151
NO_x	254	348	6,130
VOC	393	280	258
Hg (gaseous)	68,600,000	4,250,000	250
Hg (aquatic)	68,600,000	28,000,000	250
Pb (gaseous)	349,500	5,138	0.25
Pb (aquatic)	349,500	33,660	0.25
Zn (aquatic)	56,000	86,850	0.00025

Note: Environmental indices for the three methods are normalized to $CO_2 = 1$.

A detailed discussion of the various methods would require in-depth explanations in order to arrive at definite conclusions. An illustrative comparison was provided by Baumann and Rydberg (1992) in order to determine the valuative part of three valuation methods yielding a single number as the result. By setting the CO_2 emission equal to 1 and normalizing all other emissions to CO_2, a comparison of the methods is facilitated (see Table 13.2).

Since these numbers vary over several orders of magnitude for the valuation of a single pollutant (e.g., zinc, aquatic), they can serve as an example of how careful impact assessment and valuation must be handled. The reduction to a single number can hide important information and appears to provide little clarity to communicate the results.

The main difference in the various valuation methods is that some include inherently subjective valuation in early methodological steps, while others try to keep the science-based impact discussion and valuative steps separate.

13.3 ELEMENTS OF VALUATION

The impact assessment approach widely adopted by LCA experts intends to select categories of environmental impacts and keep the results separate as long as possible. The goal is to derive an aggregated number for each impact category which best represents the potential impacts of the category. The following standard list of impact categories has been agreed upon by the German standardization bodies:

- Resource demand
- Demand of land (including biodiversity)
- Greenhouse effect
- Ozone depletion
- Acidification
- Eutrophication
- Toxicological damage to ecosystems
- Toxicological damage to human health
- Formation of photosmog
- Noise

At least one indicator is needed for each impact category. Valuation defines the combination of results of each impact category regarding the question posed in the goal definition. Three basic elements are necessary for the valuation within impact assessment (Giegrich 1995):

13.3.1   Element 1: Results of Inventory Analysis, Classification, and Characterization

All important facts and information of the inventory as well as the information of the classification and characterization step should be available.

The data for the impact indicators could be presented in absolute numbers for the options under study. Thus, unweighted differences between the options can be detected. Further experience with valuation procedures will prove which information is necessary and which information can be omitted at this point. Aside from the aggregated impact indicators, some information about spatial distribution of the emissions could be helpful for valuation.

13.3.2   Element 2: Specific Contribution to the Impact Category

A scaling for a specific contribution of the impacts related to the options under study has to be done regarding either the existing situation or environmental quality standards.

To judge whether a difference in an impact indicator for two options under study can be regarded as big or small, a quantitative procedure is necessary. A 10 percent difference in land use between options may be more important than a 100 percent difference in greenhouse emissions. By calculating the relative contribution of the impact (e.g., greenhouse gas emissions of the system) to the overall impact in the region of concern (e.g., total greenhouse gas emissions in Germany), impacts can be ranked by relative contribution.

13.3.3   Element 3: Ecological Significance of the Impact Category

The significance of the different impact categories in comparison to each other is determined by using qualitative aspects of an impact and the relation distance of the existing level to the environmental quality target.

The most subjective element of valuation is to rank different impact categories, such as the importance of the greenhouse effect in relation to the noise problem or to toxicological health effects. Aspects to be considered in assessing the ecological significance are, for example, the reversibility of the impact, the spatial and temporal distribution, and the degree of uncertainty in the numerical results.

If an environmental goal exists for a certain impact category, the relation of the existing level to the target influences the assessment of the significance of an impact category.

13.3.4   Integrating the Elements

The three elements discussed above must be integrated to derive an answer to the questions posed in the goal definition and scope. Here, a multiple-attribute utility analysis or an argumentative valuation based on hierarchies and stepwise tradeoffs is considered a suitable valuation method. Due to the shortcomings of single-index valuation models, a discursive procedure including the most important groups of stakeholders appears to be the appropriate choice. Their presence is the guarantee of inclusion of all relevant information and personal values. It is the responsibility of the decision maker to take contradictory judgments into account, leaving decisions to people, not machines.

13.4   VALUATION APPROACH OF THE GERMAN FEDERAL ENVIRONMENTAL AGENCY

The German Federal Environmental Agency (UBA) has developed its LCA method in the context of the present international and national debate. It was developed and applied within the framework of the LCA study on beverage containers (UBA 1995) (see Fig. 13.3).

13.4.1   Impact Assessment Results

The evaluation step starts with the results of the impact assessment and the results of the inventory analysis for those criteria and parameters for which impact equivalents could not be determined. The results are presented graphically, separated by impact categories and in a direct comparison of two alternative products (see Figs. 13.4 and 13.5).

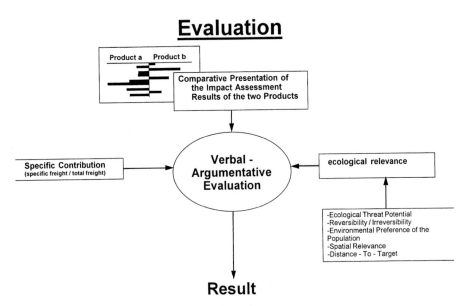

FIGURE 13.3   UBA approach to valuation in life-cycle assessment.

13.4.2 Weighting of the Results

The importance of particular results of the inventory and impact assessment for the over-all impact on the environment varies considerably. To meet general environmental protection objectives, the relative importance must be determined by using a suitable weighting system. Different parameters cannot just be given the same importance a priori; rather we have to establish a special weighting system which takes into account the different relevance of the impact observed categories from an environmental point of view.

13.4.3 Weighting by Specific Contribution

The term *specific contribution* is defined as the results of the impact assessment and/or inventory (related to the functional unit of a certain product, e.g., a type of milk package for 1000 L of fresh milk) divided by the total potential effect and/or total emissions in the area of reference (e.g., Germany).

The specific contribution thus shows the relevance of the product under study for the particular impact category. For example, milk packaging has a greater contribution to the municipal waste problem than to the formation of photo-oxidants. Thus the impact category of landfill must be given a higher weight than the impact category of photo-oxidants by the specific-contribution weighting criterion. All calculated specific contributions of the observed product to the different impact categories are mutually ranked and expressed verbally in a five-stage scale (very great, great, medium, moderate, and small contributions).

13.4.4 Weighting by Ecological Importance

The term *ecological importance* expresses the relative importance of the particular impact category for the generally recognized environmental protection objectives.

While the contribution factor is based on measured facts, the importance factor is especially influenced by subjective judgment. It will have an impact on setting priorities and therefore may influence environmental policy considerably. Although there is no doubt that the determination of the importance factor at the same time means setting priorities with regard to environmental policy, the Federal Environmental Agency of Germany is presenting a proposal on this aspect.

The following criteria influence the determination of ecological importance. It should be kept in mind that this determination is always a subjective one.

- *Ecological threat potential.* It is commonly assumed that the ecological threat potential of the greenhouse effect or of ozone depletion is incomparably greater than, say, the running out of fossil energies or the environmental problems caused by improperly managed waste dumps. Although the ecological threat often cannot be quantified for sure, only estimated, it should be given priority in determining the ecological importance. There is no doubt a major ecological threat to be found in all cases where the consequences of effects cannot be sufficiently assessed yet.

- *Reversibility.* From an ethical point of view and in accordance with the goal of *sustainable development* which was agreed upon internationally, it should not be permitted to pass the burden of the consequences of irreversible effects on the environment to subsequent generations or to nature itself. The question of handling reversible burdens can be answered more easily. In accordance with the trial-and-error principle, impacts can be more easily accepted when they are reversible in the environment and can be "repaired." Subsequent damage repair and damage regulation measures are to be financed exclusively by the generation responsible for them.

- *Spatial relevance.* From the point of view of an institution such as the German Federal Environment Agency which is involved in many international activities, global environment problems such as the greenhouse effect have priority over regional problems, such as acidification, or even more over local problems, such as noise pollution. However, this does not mean that problems on a regional or local level are less important. They are, in fact, indisputably important on their respective levels, and local environmental protection agencies will set priorities in a different way than UBA does.

- *Environmental priorities of the population.* As the supreme scientific federal authority, the German Federal Environmental Agency has to take into account recognizable preferences and views of the population for its determination of the ecological importance. Among the many social science studies available on the subject, there is one outstanding study published annually by the Institute for Practice-Oriented Social Research (IPOSR) entitled *Views on Questions of Environmental Protection.* According to this study, for years the preferences have been ozone layer depletion, atmospheric pollution, waste problems, and death of the forest. A comparatively low importance is placed on noise and the protection of biodiversity.

- *Relationship of actual and/or previous pollution to quality goals (distance to target).* This item takes into account only those impacts and/or effects which have actually been balanced in the ecobalance considered. We also have to differentiate our evaluation, depending on whether the reductions achieved in emissions are sustainable (e.g., as for sulfur dioxide) or whether their level still has to be regarded as too high (as in the case of nitrogen oxide or hydrocarbons—including current emission trends). Actual ecobalances available often do not sufficiently consider the site where pollutants are released.

Estimation is a subjective process. Moreover, it is not possible to relate the decisive arguments systematically and specifically to all the above-mentioned criteria. We therefore have to do without a generally valid weighting of the five criteria to each other. There is, however, agreement that the ecological threat potential and the relationship between actual pollution levels and quality goals (because of the large number of aspects to be considered) should both be given the greatest weight.

As in the case of the specific contribution, a five-stage scale describes the ecological importance: very great, great, medium, moderate, and small importance. In the interest of emphasizing the subjectivity of this evaluation process, UBA has chosen not to do representations of figures in tables and diagrams.

13.4.5 Verbal-Argumentative Overall Evaluation

The final phase of the evaluation process contains the combination of comparative representation of impact assessment and/or inventory results and the weighting via specific contribution and ecological importance to give a verbal-argumentative overall evaluation. It is limited to a consideration of the impact categories compared to each other and consequently refrains from any kind of calculation of the results of the impact assessment.

The basis is the impact profile comparing two alternative products. It determines for the various impact categories (greenhouse effect, input of nutrients, etc.) which of the two products compared is in a worse position and by which factor. The "branches" of this "fir tree" diagram have a defined length. However, this does not tell us anything about their overall importance if we wish to evaluate the branches in comparison to each other or as a whole, or if we wish to set them off against each other.

In accordance with the evaluation method, a certain standardization of the various scales of the fir tree branches can be achieved by observing every impact category (i.e., every branch level) on the background of its ecological importance and at the same time taking into account its specific contribution to the (national) overall problem. Within the scope of scientific studies, there is a certain tendency to perform such standardizations by means of mathematical calculations, e.g., by allocating weighting factors to the five ecological impact categories (very large, large, medium, moderate, small). This may enhance the respective sizes of the relative effect under study by a factor between 1 and 5. One could also do the same, classifying the specific contribution in five weighting classes (within the scope of how far the specific contributions spread), and then combining both weightings to form a matrix, with the weighting factors being between 2 (low ecological importance is combined with low specific contribution) and 10 (very great ecological importance is combined with a very high specific contribution).

Such a procedure, however, is questionable in many respects. It presupposes that mathematical connections do not exist in reality. In addition, it is completely arbitrary to assume that specific contribution and ecological importance scale linearly since an exponential function may also be appropriate. The most severe drawback is that using a scale gives the impression of exactitude and accuracy which do not really exist. In the end, any ecological comparison will always have to be dealt with on a verbal level.

Table 13.3 illustrates one way to summarize statements on specific contribution and ecological importance into a single statement to provide a basis for the final step of a verbal-argumentative evaluation.

13.4.5 Summary of Ecological Importance of Impact Categories

In the verbal-argumentative evaluation of the ecobalance for packaging systems, the importance of the impact categories is determined, as summarized in Table 13.4.

13.5 CASE STUDY ON BEVERAGE CONTAINERS

Within the framework of the UBA project LCA for packaging materials, in which the approach presented in Section 13.4 was developed, different packaging systems for fresh milk and beer were investigated. This section shows a valuation example by comparing two milk containers: a certain refillable glass bottle (white glass, twist-off cap) versus a polyethylene bag, filling volumes of 1 L each.

The results were derived for particular scenarios such as distance of distribution (100 km), return rate of the refillable bottle (25 times), and recycling rates according to the German situation in 1993.

TABLE 13.3 Combining Specific Contribution and Ecological Importance to Show Overall Importance

Ecological importance	Specific contribution				
	Very great	Great	Medium	Moderate	Small
Very great	Very great	Very great	Great	Great	Medium
Great	Very great	Great	Great	Medium	Medium
Medium	Great	Great	Medium	Medium	Moderate
Moderate	Great	Medium	Medium	Moderate	Moderate
Small	Medium	Medium	Moderate	Moderate	Small

TABLE 13.4   UBA Proposal for Ecological Importance of Impact Categories Examined

Impact category	Ecological importance
Scarcity of fossil energy sources	Great
Greenhouse effect	Very great
Damage to human health	Evaluation of particular substances or substance groups
Formation of photo-oxidants	Great
Acidification of soils and waters	Medium
Input of nutrients to soils and waters	Medium
Surface use by waste dumps	Lesser to medium
Noise pollution near residential areas	Medium
Noise pollution at distance	Lesser to medium
Nuclear energy	(Not determinable)
Wood consumption	Less
Water consumption	Less

The ecological comparison of the two packagings is based on the results of the impact assessment, which are listed in Figs. 13.4 and 13.5. The evaluation also includes the specific contributions and the ecotoxicological importance of the impact categories.

At first glance, Fig. 13.4 does not permit any clear judgment. In each system we find impact categories exceeding the overall pollution of the other system. Thus, the plastic bag system leads to a higher consumption of fossil energy sources (great overall importance), a higher contribution to the formation of photo-oxidants (medium overall importance), a higher mileage for waste disposal, and a higher consumption of landfill space (moderate overall importance). The refillable glass bottle system has ecological disadvantages with regard to noise resulting from long-distance truck transport (great overall importance), the greenhouse effect (medium overall importance), and the categories of acidification of soils and waters, input of nutrients in soils and waters, and wood consumption (all moderate importance). In addition, we have to take into account the higher contribution of the refillable glass bottle in the impact category of nuclear energy. However, the ecological importance of this category could not be determined. First, all impact categories with the same overall importance were listed on both sides of the comparison.

In the impact categories with medium overall importance, the refillable glass bottle system lists the contribution to the greenhouse effect with a 100 percent higher load. In comparison, the plastic bag system has a water consumption of a 98 percent higher load. As for impact categories with a moderate overall importance, there are also comparable loads for landfill space and wood consumption.

Among the impact categories with a high overall importance, the category of extraction of fossil energy sources (56 percent higher load via the plastic bag system) matches the subcategory of noise from long-distance truck transport (78 percent higher load via the glass bottle system). This category also includes traffic noise caused by local waste disposal transports (moderate overall importance), with the share of the plastic bag being 22 percent higher. All in all, the result is a higher load via the glass bottle system, equaling the category of extraction of fossil energy sources on the plastic bag side.

Consequently, the following higher pollutant levels remain: contributions of moderate overall importance, refillable glass bottle: acidification (81 percent more), nutrient input (83 percent more), consumption of nuclear energy (not evaluated, 189 percent more);

Packaging systems for fresh milk
Comparison between bag packaging and returnable glass bottle
1. impact categories

Main scenario:
Distribution: 100 km
number of trips (bottle): 25
number of trips (crate): 75
Recycling scenario : 1993

higher loads by returnable bottle   **higher loads by bag packaging**

fossil fuels		46 %
global warming	100%	
photooxidants		460 %
acidification	81 %	
eutrophication	83 %	
land-use for landfill		200 %
noise (overland traffic) 78 %		
noise (urban traffic)		22 %
wood consumption	240 %	
water consumption		98 %
nuclear energy	190 %	

Total relevance of the impact categories:
(ecological relevance & specific contribution)

- ▮ great
- ▤ medium
- ▥ moderate
- ☐ not valued

FIGURE 13.4 Results of UBA case study of two container systems for milk: relative comparison of impact categories.

Packaging systems for fresh milk
Comparison between bag packaging and returnable glass bottle
2.toxicological parameters

Main scenario:
Distribution: 100 km
number of trips (bottle): 25
number of trips (crate): 75
Recycling scenario : 1993

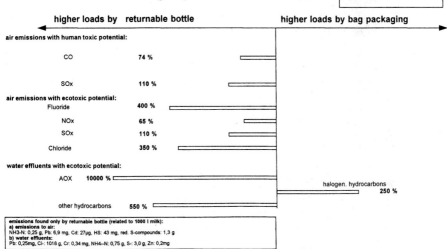

higher loads by returnable bottle   **higher loads by bag packaging**

air emissions with human toxic potential:		
CO	74 %	
SOx	110 %	
air emissions with ecotoxic potential:		
Fluoride	400 %	
NOx	65 %	
SOx	110 %	
Chloride	350 %	
water effluents with ecotoxic potential:		
AOX	10000 %	
		halogen. hydrocarbons 250 %
other hydrocarbons	550 %	

emissions found only by returnable bottle (related to 1000 l milk):
a) emissions to air:
NH3-N: 0,25 g, Pb: 6,9 mg, Cd: 27µg, HS: 43 mg, red. S-compounds: 1,3 g
b) water effluents:
Pb: 0,25mg, Cl-: 1018 g, Cr: 0,34 mg, NH4--N: 0,75 g, S-: 3,0 g, Zn: 0,2mg

FIGURE 13.5 Results of UBA case study of two container systems for milk: relative comparison of toxicological parameters.

medium overall importance, plastic bag: 5 times higher load of photo-oxidants. A comparison of these higher loads is not possible because of their different forms and the unequal overall importance of the impact categories, let alone the non-evaluated category of nuclear energy. However, the refillable glass bottle seems to be slightly advantageous.

The toxicological parameters listed in Fig. 13.5 show that the plastic bag is clearly superior in impact categories such as human health and damage to organisms and ecosystems. There is only a higher load in halogenated hydrocarbons, which is opposed by a higher load of AOX on the glass bottle side.

In summary, neither of the two systems seems to exceed the other clearly. The advantages of the refillable bottle resulting from the overall impact categories are small and have to be balanced against greater toxicological parameters which cannot be easily quantified. Consequently, we cannot conclude that one of the two systems is ecologically superior. The results of this balance evaluation are only valid within the scope of system boundaries mentioned at the beginning of this chapter.

BIBLIOGRAPHY

Bauman, H., and T. Rydberg (1992). *Life-Cycle Assessment: A Comparison of Three Methods for Impact Analysis and Valuation,* Chalmers Industrieteknik, Göteborg, Sweden.

BUWAL (1990). S. Ahbe et al., Methodik für Ökobilanzen auf der Basis Ökologischer Optimierung, Schriftenreihe Umwelt Nr. 133 des Bundesamtes für Umwelt, Wald und Landschaft (BUWAL), Swiss Federal Agency for Environment, Forest and Landscape, Bern, Switzerland.

BUWAL (1991). K. Habersatter, Ökobilanz von Packstoffen Stand 1990, Schriftenreihe Umwelt Nr. 132 des Bundesamtes für Umwelt, Wald und Landschaft (BUWAL), Swiss Federal Agency for Environment, Forest and Landscape, Bern, Switzerland.

CML (1992). *Environmental Life Cycle Assessment of Products, Guide and Backgrounds,* Center of Environmental Science Leiden (CML), Netherlands Organisation for Applied Scientific Research (TNO), Fuels and Raw Materials Bureau (B&G), Leiden, The Netherlands.

DIN (1994). Grundsätze produktbezogener Ökobilanzen, German Institute for Standardisation (DIN), DIN-Mitteilungen 73, Nr. 3.

EPA (1993). *Life-Cycle Assessment: Inventory Guidelines and Principles,* Environmental Protection Agency, EPA/1600/R-92/245, Cincinnati, OH.

Giegrich, J. (1994). *Spatial Information in Life Cycle Assessment, Contribution for Impact Assessment,* Society of Environmental Toxicology and Chemistry (SETAC), Workshop held at Zurich, Switzerland.

Giegrich, J. (1995). Bilanzbewertung in Produktbezogenen Ökobilanzen, Evaluation von Bewertungsmethoden, Perspektiven, UBA-Texte 23/95.

ISO (1995). *Life-Cycle Assessment—General Principles and Practices,* Working Draft 14040 for International Standardisation Organisation (ISO), Technical Committee 207, Subcommittee 5, Berlin, Germany.

Nord (1992). *Product Life Cycle Assessment—Principles and Methodology,* Nordic Environmental Cooperation, Nordic Council of Ministers, Copenhagen, Denmark.

SETAC (1993). *Guidelines for Life-Cycle Assessment: A 'Code of Practice,'* Society of Environmental Toxicology and Chemistry, Sesimbra, Portugal.

Steen, B., and S.-O. Ryding (1992). *The EPS Enviro-Accounting Method,* Report of the IVL— Swedish Environmental Research Institute, Göteborg, Sweden.

UBA (1992). J. Biet et al., Ökobilanzen für Produkte: Bedeutung, Sachstand, Perspektiven, Umweltbundesamt Texte, Berlin, Germany.

UBA (1995). Ökobilanz für Getränkeverpackungen, German Federal Environmental Agency (Umweltbundesamt), Berlin, Germany.

VNCI (1991). *Integrated Substance Chain Management,* Dutch Chemical Industry (VNCI), The Hague, The Netherlands.

CHAPTER 14

INTEGRATING LIFE-CYCLE ASSESSMENTS IN PRODUCT DEVELOPMENT AND MANAGEMENT

Ole Jørgen Hanssen
DIRECTOR
ØSTFOLD RESEARCH FOUNDATION
FREDRIKSTAD, NORWAY

Tomas Rydberg
PRODUCT ECOLOGIST
CHALMERS INDUSTRITEKNIK
GÖTEBORG, SWEDEN

Anne Rønning
RESEARCH MANAGER
ØSTFOLD FOUNDATION
FREDRIKSTAD, NORWAY

14.1 INTRODUCTION

Due to the need for sustainable development in a global society, great efforts are being made to increase environmental performance and resource efficiency in industrial companies all over the world. Until recently, these efforts were first directed toward improvement of industrial processes, with focus on more preventive approaches to minimize waste and emissions to air and water from production plants. However, in the last few years, greater attention has been given to the environmental performance and resource efficiency of industrial products (Hanssen 1994). In this product-oriented approach, the whole product system should be considered from "cradle to grave," i.e., from raw material acquisition to final waste treatment of end products. Government authorities in several countries are developing policies and regulative measures to give incentives to companies to take responsibility for their products throughout the life cycle (Ministry of Environment 1994).

In many companies, tools like life-cycle assessment (LCA) have been used to evaluate specific products. However, up to now, LCA has mainly been used to compare one product with another (often competing) product, to be used in "green marketing" or in discussions with authorities (Hanssen 1994). When applied to the improvement of product systems, LCA has mainly been used to document environmental performance and resource efficiency of a new or modified product, compared to a reference product. Environmental assessment has often been restricted to those areas which are the focus of authorities or the public, and not to get a better understanding of total environmental performance of a product system.

To achieve more sustainable industrial products and processes in the future, it is necessary to integrate environmental and resource parameters more directly in the product development process in companies. Environmental targets must be considered from the very early phase of the product development process, when it is decided which projects should be given priority in the product development work of a company (sustainable product management; see below).

For these reasons, the Nordic Project on Environmentally Sound Product Development (NEP project) was initiated in 1993, in cooperation with the Federation of Swedish Industries and Østfold Research Foundation (STØ). Two other research institutes have participated in the project—the Swedish Environmental Research Institute (IVL) and Chalmers Industriteknik (CIT). The project work has been carried out in cooperation with 22 large Nordic companies.

A simple survey of participants in the project meeting in the NEP project in Stockholm in December 1994 indicated clearly that the main problem or bottleneck in environmentally oriented product development in general is the lack of participation of environmental experts in the product development process, lack of methods for environmentally oriented design, and lack of data and information (Table 14.1). It is thus an

TABLE 14.1   Main Bottleneck to Environmentally Oriented Product Development in Companies*

Type of bottleneck toward environmentally oriented product development (PD) in companies	Number of participants responding on given type of bottleneck (out of total of 26)	Weighted rank of priority among those who prioritized bottlenecks (1.0 highest)
Lack of methods for integrating environmental criteria in PD	16	1.3
Environmental experts do not participate in PD	16	2.3
Companies lack experience in integrating LCA in PD	13	2.4
Lack of environmental data for alternative solutions	12	3.6
Sustainable product development not within strategy	9	3.1
Sustainable product development not given priority	9	4.5
Sustainable products too expensive for customers	7	4.5
There are no regulatory demands for sustainable products	6	6.0
There are no market demands for sustainable products	4	6.5
Environmental regulations work against sustainable products	4	4.5

*As registered in a survey among 26 participants in a seminar for the companies within the NEP project, Stockholm 1994.

important strategy to get the environmental experts in the companies more experienced with and more directly involved with the product development process. Environmental information has to be given to the right person at the right time, and in a format that is understood by members of the product development team (Hanssen 1994).

The main goals for the NEP project have been to:

- Develop data tools for use of LCA in product development.
- Develop methods for environmentally oriented product development based on LCA.
- Create products with better environmental performance.
- Develop educational documents for introducing and implementing environmentally oriented product design in companies.
- Document experiences from the project internationally, as an input to further development and standardization of the LCA methods.

The project has been divided into three subprojects:

1. Development of a relation database structure with interfaces to existing LCA data tools
2. Development of methods for *sustainable product development* (SPD) and testing of the method in case projects
3. Development of educational materials and organization of an international expert workshop

In subproject 2, seven case projects have been carried out to test the method for sustainable product development. The case projects have covered the following products and companies: industrial paints for offshore platforms (Jotun/Statoil), mud gas separator (AMAT), carbon lining paste for ferroalloy plants (Elkem Carbon), light fittings (Glamox), sport underwear (Helly-Hansen), electric low-voltage cables (ABB Bjurhagen), and Tetra Brik milk packaging (Tetra Pak, Stora, Borealis).

This chapter gives a summary of the experiences and results from subproject 2, with examples from the case projects from Elkem Carbon, Glamox, and ABB Bjurhagen. The report is based on the final documentation from NEP subproject 2 (Hanssen et al. 1995).

14.2   AN INTEGRATED APPROACH TO SUSTAINABLE PRODUCT DEVELOPMENT

14.2.1   The Main Concept

One important aspect in the development of methods for SPD has been to integrate life-cycle assessment of products with available methods applied in product development and improvement in general. Three factors are important to consider in product development projects:

- Customer quality
- Economy for the user and the producer
- Environmental performance of products

To get more sustainable solutions, it is necessary to meet requirements, without overemphasizing any one factor. A product with improved intrinsic environmental performance will be a more sustainable solution only if it is implemented in the market as a substitute for products with lower performance.

In the models which have been developed and tested in the NEP project, three tools used to analyze these factors are

- Quality function deployment
- Life-cycle cost (LCC) analysis
- Life-cycle assessment

The correspondences between the three methods are shown in Fig. 14.1. The *product system structure* is the basis for all three methods, as shown in Fig. 14.2. The product

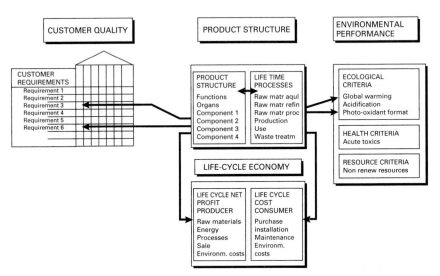

FIGURE 14.1 Correspondences between product system structure, environmental performance, customer quality, and life-cycle economy.

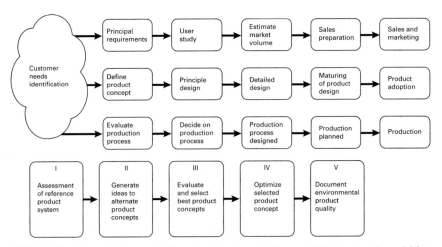

FIGURE 14.2 The model for sustainable product development (Hanssen 1995), based on the model for integrated product development (Andreasen and Hein 1986).

system structure is a way to describe the product in functions, organs, components, and processes. Each product might be divided into subsystems with specific functions (product organs). In the next stage these organs are divided into components, such as materials processed into specific parts. Each component has its own lifetime processes, from raw material acquisition and processing to manufacturing, assembly, distribution, use and maintenance, and finally degradation, incineration, or recovery and reuse.

The basis for the accounting is a *functional unit,* which is similar to the basis for all material and energy balance and conservation calculations in process engineering. In product analysis, a functional unit is a measure of the amount of product needed to satisfy the unit. A mathematical model for the LCA model has been described by Hanssen and Asbjørnsen (1996), and is described in greater detail in Sec. 14.2.4.

In Secs. 14.2.2 to 14.2.4, we describe the relationships between this product structure and the user quality, life-cycle economy, and environmental performance of the product systems.

14.2.2 Customer Requirements and Quality Function Deployment

The ultimate reason for buying a product is that the product fulfills the needs defined by the customer. The challenge for a manufacturer is to identify the main requirements of products, from a heterogeneous group of customers, and transform these into product properties in such a way that the manufacturer's product is preferred to a competitor's product. *Quality function deployment* (QFD) is a method for systematic analysis of the voice of the customers and relationships between these quality requirements and the product structure (Andersson 1991, Mørup 1993, Andreasen and Støren 1994). In a *quality house,* all customer requirements are identified and weighted, and the relationship between these requirements and the technical parameters of the total product is analyzed.

In the next stages of the QFD process, relationships between the important technical parameters and the product system are analyzed stage by stage, from functions and organs (subsystems), components and processes. and finally manufacturing and assembly processes. As shown by Norell (1992), the QFD method is especially important in the early phase of product development, before too much money has been allocated to a specific-product concept. If the results from a QFD analysis are used in specification of basic requirements for the product, it is not necessary to modify the product specification that much later in the process.

One important reason for integrating QFD and LCA analyses is to address systematically the connections between environmental performance and customer quality of a product system. By getting a better understanding of this relationship, which is analyzed through three environmental quality matrices, the product development team can see the consequences of modifications in the product structure.

14.2.3 Life-Cycle Economy and Life-Cycle Cost Analysis

Whereas investments in equipment always are analyzed over a period of, say, 10 years due to depreciation and tax rules, this is seldom the case with products, especially for private consumers. The most important economic factor is thus the purchase price, whereas life-cycle costs seldom are documented. As a result, products normally are compared without consideration of operational costs, maintenance costs, service costs, costs related to failure, and costs related to purchase of new products during a given period, due to different expected product life spans. Such short-term economic considerations will often lead to selection of a low-quality and low purchasing price product.

Within systems engineering, there are well-established methods for calculating life-cycle costs of products (e.g., Blanchard and Fabrycky 1990, Asbjørnsen 1992). Based on the structure and the lifetime processes of a product system, it is possible to calculate life-cycle costs per functional unit of a product for the user (e.g., total costs for maintenance of 100 m^2 offshore platform over 25 years) for different products and to compare life-cycle costs (activity-based costing) on a fair basis. With the same basis, the life-cycle net profit for the manufacturing company can be calculated. The analysis can be a pure cash flow analysis for all costs and incomes related to the product structure and the functional unit. Alternatively, calculation rent and inflation rate can be used as a basis for calculation of the net present value of the cash flow over the lifetime period. This has not been done in the NEP case projects, as we have assumed that calculation rent and inflation rate will balance in the long run.

In life-cycle cost evaluations, both internal and potential external costs can be included. Most industrial products will cause environmental problems in their production, use, or final degradation. Today, the only environmental costs normally included in the economic analysis are internal costs such as waste treatment costs and abatement costs. In the near future, external environmental costs will more and more often be internalized in the budgets and accounts of a company, through environmental taxes, producer responsibility for waste management of products, etc. (the take-back principle). The following cost factors could be evaluated in the initial LCC analyses, but only the major cost factors should be included in the final analyses, based on a sensitivity analysis:

The *net life-cycle cost analyses* should at least consider

- Product purchasing costs
- Energy costs with different energy carriers
- Transport costs
- Environmental control costs (e.g., hazardous waste treatment)
- Maintenance costs
- Operation costs
- Service and repair costs
- Costs related to final waste treatment of product

The *net life-cycle profit analysis* for the producer should at least consider

- Raw material costs
- Energy costs related to different energy carriers
- Production costs
- Transport costs
- Environmental control costs
- Sales income
- Service and repair income
- Other types of income or cost savings

14.2.4 Environmental Performance and Life-Cycle Assessment

The LCA method applied in this project is based on the general SETAC concept (Consoli et al. 1993) and the methods described in the Nordic LCA Guidelines (Nordic Council of Ministers 1995). The following steps have been included in all case projects:

1. Goal and scoping
2. Inventory analyses
3. Impact assessment, with classification, characterization, and valuation

The LCA model has been formulated mathematically by Hanssen and Asbjørnsen (1996), and is briefly described here.

The amount of material and energy flows to produce the amount of product is a vector M of material compounds and energy. Let the mass of product needed to fulfill the functional unit be M_p. Then the material and energy flows may be written as

$$M = f(M_p) \tag{14.1}$$

Each of the components in M may be associated with emissions to air and water, as well as solid waste and hazardous waste. The emissions will be proportional to the flows, assuming constant efficiency of the production process. The emission factors may be grouped into a matrix N similar to the stoichiometric matrix in chemistry. The total vector of emissions from flows M is then

$$\mathbf{e} = NM \tag{14.2}$$

Each emission will contribute to an environmental impact by a similar matrix of impact C. Here the elements $c_{i,j}$ in C are defined as the contribution to an environmental impact i per unit of emission number j. The environmental impact vector i is then simply

$$i = C\mathbf{e} = CNM = CNf(M_p) \tag{14.3}$$

The environmental performance indicator (EPI) is a scalar quantity where the total effect of the environmental impacts is calculated from a weighted average of the impacts:

$$\text{EPI} = \mathbf{w}^T i = w^T cNf(M_p) \tag{14.4}$$

The basis for the EPI model in Hanssen and Asbjørnsen (1996) is the list of environmental impacts given by Lindfors et al. (1995b). A requirement for the practical application of the EPI equation is that conversion factors c and w^T must be available. The EPI is thus a weighted index based on 13 impact categories, within three main groups:

- Resource depletion parameters—resource efficiency (four parameters)
- Health impact parameters—health quality (two parameters)
- Ecological parameters—ecological quality (seven parameters)

14.2.5 Main Project Activities in Sustainable Product Development

Our tools for sustainable product development have to be applied in a procedural framework for product development. We have chosen the method for *integrated product development* (IPD) as a basis for this procedural integration (see Andreasen and Hein 1986). The reason for this choice is that the IPD method is based on a holistic approach to product development, where representatives from marketing, production, and product development are working together in teams throughout the process. Since one of the main obstacles to sustainable product development is the lack of environmental expertise in product development, IPD might be a good framework for further work.

The main activities in the project are shown in Fig. 14.2 where activities related to marketing, production, environment, and product development are shown as four parallel chains of activities during the project.

A modification of the basic framework is the addition of assessment of a reference product. One problem is the lack of precise information about product concepts in general in the early phase of product development. As shown in Fig. 14.3, very little detailed information is hardly available in the idea phase, whereas most of the total life-cycle costs and environmental impacts are disposed of at this stage. It is thus important to improve both the quality and the quantity of information available in this phase. One possibility is to use a reference product as a basis for early analyses, to identify main problems with existing products, as a basis for idea generation for improvements, and for development of criteria for evaluation of solutions. As shown in Fig. 14.2, such a detailed study of a reference product might give a much better basis for the early product development decisions. The initial costs of the project are expected to increase, whereas the total project costs are expected to be lower than they would be without a reference product analysis. Initial information relevant for a new product solution will also increase significantly, whereas the final level of information in general will be only slightly higher.

Another reason for integrating LCA, LCC, and QFD with IPD methods is to set up a well-defined activity plan with milestones in the project.

The intention of the NEP project was to develop comprehensive methods for sustainable product development and management, covering all main activities in the management loop (Andreasen and Hein 1986). The NEP project focused on

- Strategic activities and decisions (business idea development, strategic programs, etc.)
- Tactical activities and decisions (product planning, project selection, resource allocation, etc.)
- Operational activities and decisions (product development projects, sales, marketing, distribution, production, etc.)

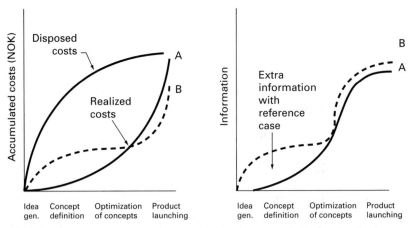

FIGURE 14.3 Development in cost factors and information support during a product development project. A: Project without reference case study (solid line). B: Project with reference case study (dotted line).

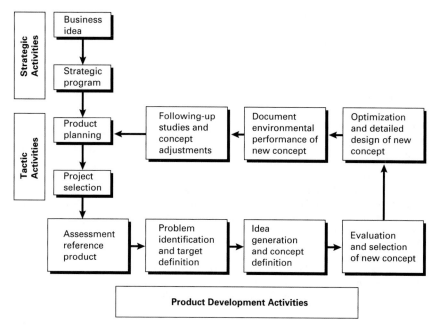

FIGURE 14.4   Correspondence between strategic, tactical, and operational activities in an SPD project.

The relationships among these activities and decisions are presented in Fig. 14.4, in a *management loop*. It is the responsibility of the top management in a company to close the connections between the different parts of this management loop, to ensure that all product development projects fit with the strategic direction of the company (Andreasen and Hein 1986).

14.3   EXPERIENCES FROM CASE PROJECTS

14.3.1   Development of New Light Fittings

Short Description of the Reference Product System.   The case project on light fittings was carried out together with Glamox A/S, the largest producer of light fittings in the Nordic region. The project was initiated as part of an already established product development project at Glamox, with R&D manager Svein Erik Kårvåg as the project manager. The existing product used as a reference product in the analysis is a standard 2×18 W, universal fitting product. The fitting is 0.7 m long and 0.24 m wide, with a traditional reactor system. The fitting weight is about 2.5 kg, mainly consisting of aluzink, plastic materials (acryl and ABS), and an aluminum reflector. The general market situation for the reference product was divided among Norway (68 percent), Sweden (17 percent), and Finland (15 percent). The functional unit for the study was to *light a room area of 25 m^2 over 20 years.*

According to general analysis tools for light fitting planning, it was necessary to use 11 light fittings in an average room. However, from general experience, it was decided to use 12 fittings as the basis for the analysis, as this would be recommended in light planning in general. It was assumed that all fitting products would function in 20 years, with an average lighting time of 3000 h/yr (Førde et al. 1995).

Environmental Performance, Customer Quality, and Life-Cycle Economy of the Reference Product. The results from the LCA studies, with two different valuation methods and a normalization to national emission levels in Norway, are shown in Fig. 14.5. With the given market situation, the main environmental problems related to the fitting system are global warming, acidification, toxic effects from polyaromatic hydrocarbons (PAHs), and consumption of fossil energy. Global warming, acidification, and consumption of fossil energy are most related to the use of the product. This is mainly due to the low share of the products used in Finland, with a relatively high proportion of fossil energy in the national electric grid. The PAH problem is mainly due to emissions from the production of the aluminum reflector and the aluzink components in the fitting.

If the fitting were used only under present Norwegian energy conditions, the evaluation of environmental impacts would be quite different. Since 99.5 percent of Norwegian electricity is produced by hydropower stations, there are no emissions related to the use of the product. Global warming and PAH emissions would be the most important environmental problems under these conditions, with production of light tubes, aluzink, and aluminum for the reflector as the main contributors (Førde et al. 1995).

The most important customer requirements are assumed to be low purchase price; resistance to humidity; simple, functional design; and stable luminance. The most important elements in the product structure to meet these requirements are the plastic shield, the aluzink back and end parts, the reflector, the light tube, and the plastic plugs. However, most of these elements also contribute negatively to the purchase price (Førde et al. 1995)

A life-cycle cost analysis of the reference product with the basis in cost factors for the user over the 20-year period is shown in Fig. 14.6. In the first year, nearly all costs are related to purchase of the 12 fittings. However, over the whole period, energy costs and light tube costs are the same, whereas purchase price is about 50 percent lower than the two other cost factors.

Options for Product Improvements. Based on experiences with the reference product, the following ideas for improvement of the product system were developed by the project team at Glamox:

1. A new design with 30 percent reduction in material consumption, which is easier to disassemble for recovery of materials
2. Substitution of all aluzink parts with black tin
3. Use of recovered aluminum and steel as a substitute for 70 percent of the virgin materials
4. Recovery of the most important weight fractions from the fittings after use

Also considered was a change to other types of fittings, from 2×18 W

5. a. To 23×6 W fittings (six units necessary to fulfill functional unit)
   b. To 2×58 W fittings (four units necessary to fulfill functional unit)   or
6. Integration of energy-conserving equipment (infrared switch, day-light switch, modern electronic reactors, etc.)

Would a change influence customer requirements, life-cycle costs, or environmental performance of the products?

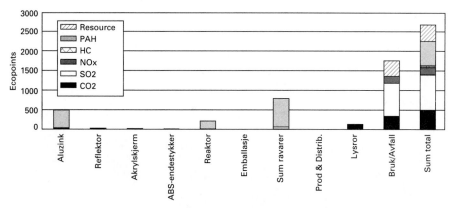

(a) Normalization to total Norwegian emission figures

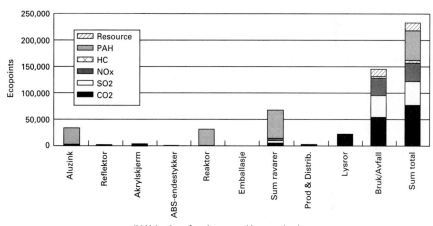

(b) Valuation of environmental impacts by the
Ecoscarcity method (BUWAL-method)

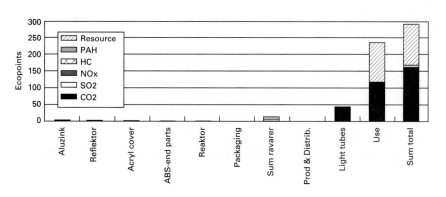

(c) Valuation of environmental impacts by the EPS system

FIGURE 14.5 Evaluation of environmental impacts throughout the life cycle of 12 light fittings by three different methods (based on Førde et al. 1995).

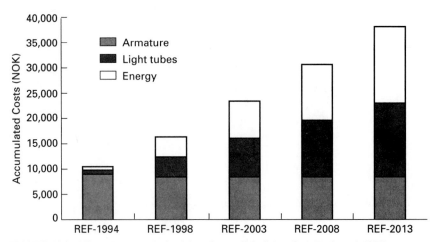

FIGURE 14.6   Life-cycle cost analysis of the reference light fitting (from Førde et al. 1995).

Simulation of Modifications of Product Systems.   The main results from the simulations of effects of the different modifications mentioned in the last section are shown in Figs. 14.7, 14.9, and 14.10. Since energy consumption in the user phase is the dominating contribution to environmental impacts and user costs in countries with a relatively large proportion of fossil energy in electricity production, options which reduce energy consumption will be the most important. Both the LCA and the LCC simulations indicate that integration of energy conservation equipment is the most important option for improvement. The second most important, from the environmental perspective, is reduced material consumption (simulation 1) and recovery of materials after use of the product (simula-

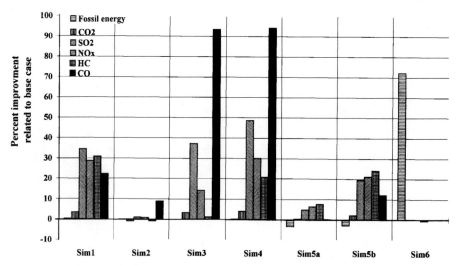

FIGURE 14.7   Effects of different improvement options for environmental profiles of modified products, compared to the reference case.

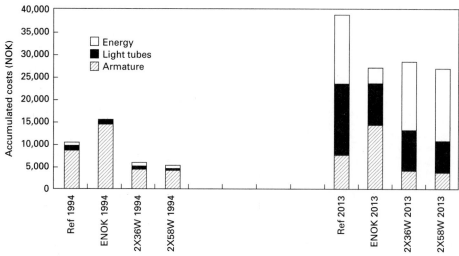

FIGURE 14.8 Life-cycle cost analyses of four different light fitting products.

tion 4). The relationships between the different improvement options and customer requirements, economy, and environmental performance are shown in Fig. 14.9.

The priority given above is also influenced by the market situation of the light fitting. If the fitting is produced only for the Norwegian market, use of recovered aluminum and aluzink (simulation 3), introduction of recovery systems for used fittings (simulation 4), and reduced material consumption (simulation 1) will be the most important options for improvement of the product (Fig. 14.10). Energy conservation will, however, be of minor importance under these assumptions.

Concluding Remarks.   The case project on light fittings shows that the method of sustainable product development might give the company valuable information about a product group, as a basis for further development of a product. Environmental criteria were integrated in the project from the very early stage, and they have been an important element in the development of new products. For several years Glamox has worked hard to integrate energy-conserving equipment in its light fittings. Based on this project, several new ideas will be further evaluated by the company:

- A new product with 30 percent less material has been introduced as a prototype.
- Substitutions of aluzink with black tin are considered.
- Recovery of materials from fitting systems after use is considered.
- A simpler packaging system, with significantly reduced packaging volume, is under development.

Most of these options have been documented to be of significant importance for the total environmental profile of a light fitting from Glamox.

14.3.2   Development of New Lining Paste for Ferroalloy Plants

Short Description of the Reference Product System.   The reference system is a lining paste produced by Elkem Carbon in Kristiansand, Norway. The lining paste is used as lin-

Proposed options for improvements in product system

Criteria for improvement	New product solution with lower material consumption	Substitute aluzink with black iron	Change to use of recovered materials in the product	Recovery of materials from product after use	Change to 2 × 36 W or 2 × 58 W armature systems	Use of energy-conserving equipment connected to the armature
Customer needs						
Simple surface structure (easy to wash)	o	o	o	o	o	o
Simple and functional design	o	o	o	o	—	o
Simple to install in the office	+	o	o	o	—	—
Easy to remove plastic cover (easy to change light tubes)	o	o	o	o	o	o
Stable luminance, without irritating, sharp light	o	o	o	o	o	o
Resistance toward humidity	o	?	?	o	o	o
High level of anticorrosiveness in exposed environments	o	?	?	o	o	o
Low purchasing price	+	+	+	—	++	—
Low life-cycle costs	+	+	+	—	+	++
Environmental targets						
Reduced global warming potential	+	+	+	+	+	++
Reduced acidification potential	+	+	+	+	+	++
Reduced conversion of fossil energy	+	+	+	+	+	++
Reduced emissions of toxic substances (PAH)	o	o	+	+	o	o
Reduced POCP potential	o	o	o	o	o	o

FIGURE 14.9 Relationships between modifications in the product structure and effects in fulfillment of customer requirements, economy for the customer or user, and environmental performance of the products.

ing within the tapping spout for furnaces in ferroalloy plants (Salten Verk is used as an example in this study). Lining paste is carbon mass mixed with a binder. The purpose of the binder is to fill the pores in the carbon mass and act as a binding agent between carbon particles to ensure sufficient strength and conductivity. The lining paste produced by Elkem Carbon consists of calcinated anthracite mixed with a binder made of coal tar.

The anthracite comes from China, Germany, England, and the United States and is transported to Elkem in Kristiansand, where the calcination process takes place. The binder is produced in the Netherlands. Elkem produces the lining paste by mixing the calcinated anthracite with the binder.

The functional unit for the study has been *the amount of lining paste needed in one*

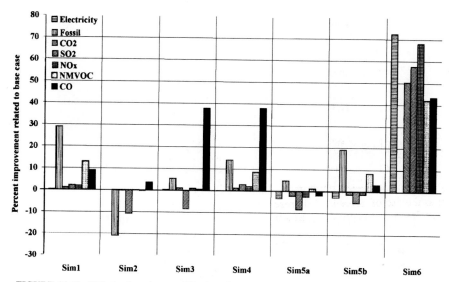

FIGURE 14.10   Effects of product modifications for environmental impacts under Norwegian conditions.

tapping spout for 5 years. Over a period of 5 years, the operation of one tapping spout will require 11,900 kg of lining paste with a coal tar binder (the reference product).
All information from this study is taken from a report by Øksdal et al. (1995).

Environmental Performance, Customer Quality, and Life-Cycle Economy of the Reference Product.   Three different models for valuation and normalization are used to calculate the environmental impacts of the life cycle for the two alternative products. Figure 14.11 illustrates the highest environmental impacts according to the three valuation and normalization models. The figure illustrates that when valuated by the environmental priority strategies (EPS) and Bundesamt für Umwelt, Wald, and Landschaft (BUWAL) methods and normalized to Norwegian emissions, PAH has much greater environmental impact than other emissions and resources in the system. The other impacts from the system are of another and lower magnitude.

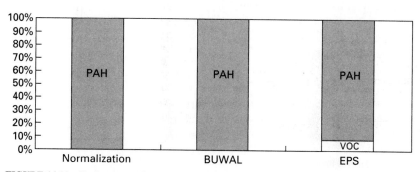

FIGURE 14.11   Environmental impacts according to the three models for valuation and normalization for the reference product (from Øksdal et al. 1995).

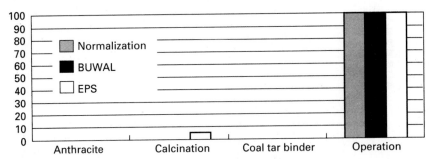

FIGURE 14.12   Environmental impacts over the life span of the reference product according to the three models for valuation and normalization (from Øksdal et al. 1995).

Figure 14.12 illustrates where in the life cycle the PAH is emitted. The figure shows that emission of PAH is a result of the operation of the electrolysis cell, where PAH is emitted during baking of the cathode and operation of the cell.

To demonstrate the other environmental impacts from the system, the emission of PAH is taken out of the calculations. Figure 14.13 shows the contributions from the system after valuation and normalization when emission of PAH is left out of the calculations. The figure illustrates that emission of volatile organic carbons (VOCs) has the greatest environmental impact when one is valuing by the EPS and BUWAL methods (when PAH is left out of the system). By applying the method of normalization, the generation of waste contributes approximately 55 percent of the total, and VOCs contribute approximately 22 percent.

Figure 14.14 illustrates where in the life cycle these impacts occur. In Fig. 14.14 the impacts from the calcination process are set to 100 percent for all three models, and the other stages in the life cycle are seen relative to the calcination step. In the calcination

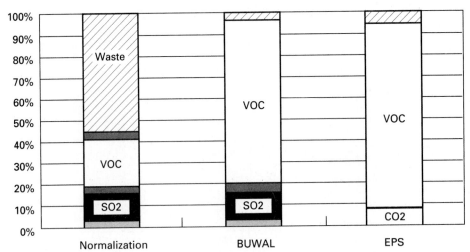

FIGURE 14.13   Contributions to environmental impacts after valuation and normalization when emission of PAH is left out (from Øksdal et al. 1995).

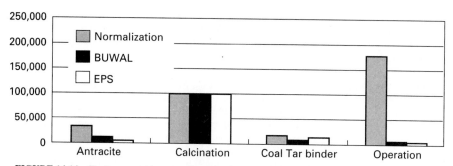

FIGURE 14.14   Environmental impacts after valuation and normalization over the life cycle of the lining paste (PAH emissions are left out of calculations) (From Øksdal et al. 1995).

step, emission of VOCs contributes to almost all the total impacts for the three models. According to the valuation methods, the mining and transport of anthracite and the mining and processing of coal tar binder do not contribute to the total impact as much as the calcination process does. Use of the products (the operation step) gives a higher value than the calcination step when the normalization model is used. The normalization model includes waste, which has a major impact in the operation step according to this model.

A life-cycle cost analysis for the use of the lining paste with coal tar binder has been carried out, and the results are shown in Fig. 14.15. The life-cycle cost analysis of the reference product shows that the most important cost factors of the life cycle of the product are purchasing costs for the lining paste and costs related to installation of the lining in the ferroalloy plant. Since the lining is changed several times a year, the material costs and installation work costs are developing proportionately through the life cycle of the carbon lining. Other types of cost factors which have been considered, such as environmental costs and energy costs, are not important to the total accumulated cost in this study.

Consistent with the method for sustainable product development, there has been carried out a survey of customer requirements related to the traditional lining paste product. This survey is based on communication with one of the customers and should not be regarded as a QFD analysis of the product (Øksdal et al. 1995).

The most important customer requirements seem to be purchasing price and life span of the product. The most important factors contributing to these requirements are the baking and operation of the lining. Other factors which are important to the customer

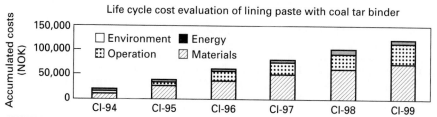

FIGURE 14.15   The accumulated life-cycle costs for the lining paste with the coal tar binder (from Øksdal et al. 1995).

are indoor environment and outer environment. The traditional tar binder contributes negatively to both these factors, whereas baking and operation of the liner are the most important processes contributing negatively to these factors (due to emissions from the binder).

Options for Product Improvements.   Elkem Carbon is developing a new type of lining paste made to remove the emissions of polyaromatic hydrocarbons in the installation and baking process of the existing lining paste. The new synthetic binder does not emit PAH, but will emit small amounts of formaldehyde, phenols, and ammonium. With a synthetic binder, electricity may be used as energy in the baking process, thus reducing the emissions to air from oilburners and open fires.

The lining paste with the synthetic binder will have a longer life span than the lining paste with the coal tar binder. Over 5 years, the operation of one tapping spout will require 6250 kg of lining paste with a synthetic binder. This is 5650 kg (or 47 percent) less than is needed for the lining paste with the coal tar binder.

Simulation of Modifications of Product Systems.   For the methods of valuation and normalization, the environmental impacts of the two lining pastes are compared in Fig. 14.16. The figure shows that the high valuation values of PAH for the three valuation

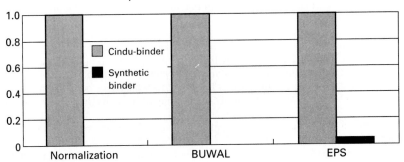

FIGURE 14.16   Comparison of the magnitude of the environmental impacts after valuation and normalization for the two systems (from Øksdal et al. 1995).

and normalization models are dominating the results from the lining paste with the coal tar binder. The impacts of the lining paste with the synthetic binder are of another (and smaller) magnitude and thus are not visible in the figure. Leaving out the PAH, the other impacts from the two lining pastes may be compared. Figure 14.17 illustrates the impacts after applying the methods of valuation and normalization for the two systems when PAH is left out.

When PAH is left out of the calculations of the reference product, the results from the normalization and valuation of the two systems may be compared. Figure 14.17 illustrates that the impacts for the lining paste with the coal tar binder (without the PAH emissions) are 20 to 40 percent higher than the impacts from the lining paste with the synthetic binder.

When the normalization model is used, the higher amounts of waste and VOCs for the lining paste with the coal tar binder give a higher impact than the lining paste with

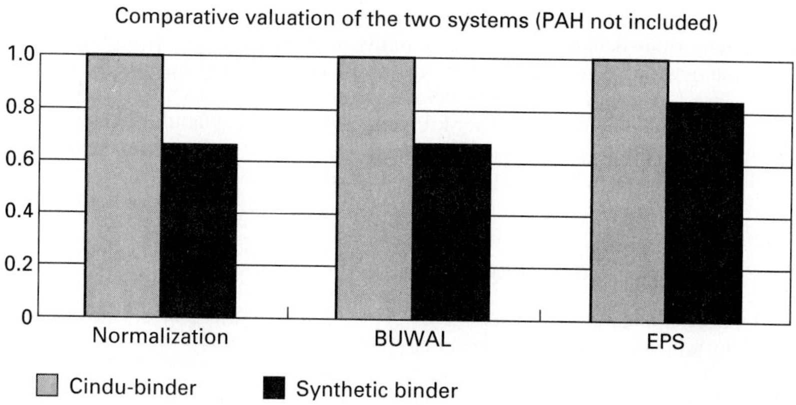

Comparative valuation of the two systems (PAH not included)

FIGURE 14.17 Comparison of the magnitude of the environmental impacts after valuation and normalization for the two systems when PAH is left out (from Øksdal et al. 1995).

the synthetic binder. The reduction of waste for the alternative product (synthetic binder) is a result of the longer life span of the lining paste, and thus the reduced amount of lining paste for deposition. The reduction of the emission of VOCs is also a result of the longer life span of the alternative lining paste, because this will reduce the need for calcinated anthracite.

When the BUWAL and EPS valuation methods are used, the impacts from the lining paste with the synthetic binder are smaller than the impacts from the lining paste with the coal tar binder. The impacts from the use of fossil fuel and emission of CO_2 are higher for the lining paste with the synthetic binder, but the impacts from the emissions of VOCs, NO_x and SO_2 are higher for the lining paste with the coal tar binder.

Figure 14.18 illustrates the life-cycle costs for the two alternative lining pastes. The results from the life-cycle cost analysis of the two product alternatives show that the alternative lining paste with the synthetic binder has significantly lower life-cycle costs than the traditional lining paste with a coal tar binder. The difference is about 50 percent when the accumulated costs for the two alternatives are compared. This shows that the new product gives an added value to the customer by reducing the life-cycle costs.

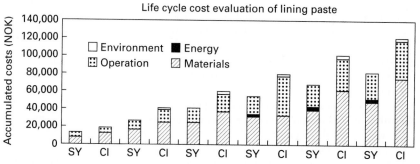

FIGURE 14.18 Comparison of the accumulated life-cycle costs of the lining paste with the coal tar binder (CI) and with the synthetic binder (SY) over 5 years (from Øksdal et al. 1995).

Today, environmental costs are very low for both products. However, if environmental authorities decide to set stricter limits to PAH emissions from the ferroalloy plants, the new binder will give additional value in preventing such costs for the customers. In a U.S. study by Tellus University, the abatement costs for PAH emissions were calculated to about $21,800 per kilogram of PAH. This would increase the annual costs for the traditional binder with about 6 million NOK (based on an exchange rate for U.S. dollars of 6.5, and an annual emission of PAH of 42.8 kg).

14.3.3 Development of New Electric Cable Systems

This section summarizes the results from the work in the NEP project concerning low-voltage installation cables (Rydberg et al. 1995, Sjöström 1994).

Short Description of Reference Product. The producing company, Bjurhagens Fabrikers AB, is a member of the ABB group. ABB has been involved in LCA since 1990 and is an active company in Sweden in the development of methods for environmentally sound product development. As the reference cable, an EKK 3G 1.5 was chosen as one of the cables presently in production at Bjurhagens Fabrikers AB. The reference cable is one of the most important installation cables in Sweden, with close equivalents in most European countries.

The cable in this case has three cords, each with a solid conductor of 1.5 mm². The cords are in different colors for identification while the outer sheathing is white. For security reasons only, the ground cord is allowed to have two colors, green and yellow. Insulation and sheathing material are flexible polyvinyl chloride (PVC) while the material in the filler is an option by the manufacturer. The most commonly used material is a highly filled PVC-based compound.

Environmental Performance, Customer Quality, and Life-Cycle Economy of the Reference Product

Environmental Performance. Figure 14.19 shows the impact of the reference cable as evaluated with three valuation methods, divided among the different steps of the life cycle. From the figure it is obvious that the most important parts of the life cycle are the material production and the discarding of the cable. The following assumptions should be noted:

- The user phase is not included in the analysis. After long discussions, it was decided that this is likely to be a negligible part of the life-cycle impact. Today it is also impossible to change any factor that affects the user phase due to Swedish standards.

- Material production means material in the form that the cable manufacturer purchases.

- Material transport does not include copper transport. This is included in the material production step. It is, however, a short transport and should have no significant effect.

- In the reference case, all waste generated in the system is assumed to be deposited at landfills. In general, no breakdown processes on landfills are considered, while no data about breakdown process from cable disposal could be found.

- A conventional allocation of impacts from production waste deposition has been used in this study. However, the losses in the cable factory are extremely small and any different allocation (see Sec. 14.4.2) would not alter the priorities.

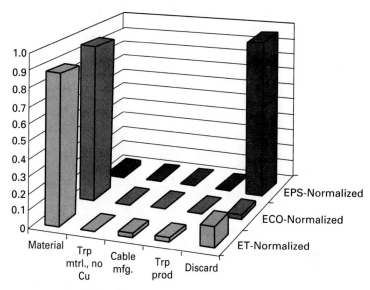

FIGURE 14.19   Normalized (impact for life cycle within each valuation method = 1) impact for the reference product system, divided into five phases of the life cycle, as evaluated with different valuation methods.

Figure 14.19 shows that it is raw material production that has the highest relative environmental impact according to ET and ECO-normalized, while EPS-normalized indicates that discarding of the cable has the highest relative environmental impact. The EPS method result is due to the use of natural resources which are placed as losses in the discard phase.

There are four functional components or product organs in the cable: conductor(s), insulation(s), filler, and sheathing. The environmental impact of the different organs, material production only, and the mass distribution within the cable are shown in Fig. 14.20.

A main component of all three nonconductor organs (i.e., insulation, filler, and sheathing) is PVC-S. It is therefore not very surprising that the relative importance of these organs closely resembles the weight fraction of the organs. Another conclusion that can be drawn at this point is that additives which are unique for one or another of these organs (TiO_2 for the sheathing, PVC-E for the filler) do not change this situation.

Customer Requirements.   Relationships between customer quality and product structure have been evaluated both from the installing company's view and the end user's view, since the installer normally decides which cable system to buy. Priority in customer requirements and relationships with product structure are shown in Figs. 14.21 and 14.23. The most important requirements from the installer's side were purchasing price and properties related to installation friendliness (low weight, simple-to-remove insulation materials, and stiffness). The most important relationships are with PVC content, chalk, lead sulfate, copper, and the production process (Fig. 14.21). End-user requirements are separated into open installation and installation in closed-system cable systems, as shown in Fig. 14.22. For both types of system, reliability and safety of the cables are the most important requirements. Open systems also get high scores for dis-

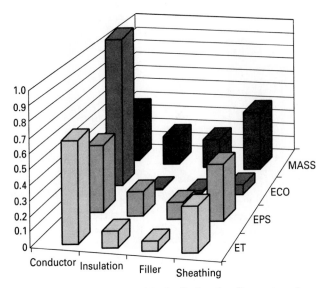

FIGURE 14.20 Assessment of the distribution of cradle-to-gate environmental impacts, i.e., only material production included, according to the three evaluation methods and the mass distribution of the reference cable with respect to the functional components, or organs.

Product structure Customer requirements	PVC-E	PVC-S	DOP	Chalk	PbS	TiO2	Copper	Pigment	Production process	Weighting factor
Low weight	0	−	+	−	0	0	−	0	0	4
Light transport med	0	0	0	0	0	0	0	0	0	1
Soft (easy to install)	−	−	+	0	0	0	−	0	+	3
Stiff (easy to install)	+	+	−	0	0	0	+	0	+	4
Low purchase price	0	−	−	+	−	0	−	0	0	5
Easy to remove insul.	0	0	0	+	0	0	0	0	+	4
Unsensible to dirt	0	0	0	0	0	−	0	0	+	1
Good env. perform.	−	−	−	0	−	−	−	0	0	1

FIGURE 14.21 Relationships between customer requirements (related to the installer) and product structure.

Product structure Customer requirements	PVC-E	PVC-S	DOP	Chalk	PbS	TiO$_2$	Copper	Pigment	Production process	Weighting factor (open)
Discrete design	0	0	0	0	0	+	0	+	+	4
Long life span	0	+	0	−	+	+	0	0	+	4
High reliability	0	0	0	0	0	0	+	0	+	5
Good fire safety	0	+	−	0	0	0	0	0	0	5
High mechan. res.	0	+	−	−	0	0	0	0	+	1
Low purch. price	0	−	−	+	−	0	−	0	0	2
Good color pers.	0	0	0	0	+	+	0	+	0	4
Easy to overpaint	0	0	0	0	0	0	0	0	+	1
Resistant to dirt	0	0	0	0	0	0	0	0	+	4
Good env. perf.	−	−	−	0	−	−	−	0	0	1

FIGURE 14.22 Relationships between end-user requirements and product structure open system.

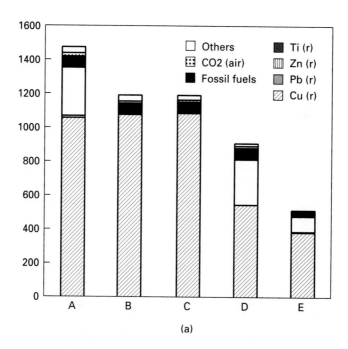

(a)

FIGURE 14.23a Environmental impact for the reference product A and improvement options B to E with respect to contributions from selected dominating parameters, according to valuation in the EPS system (from Rydberg et al. 1995).

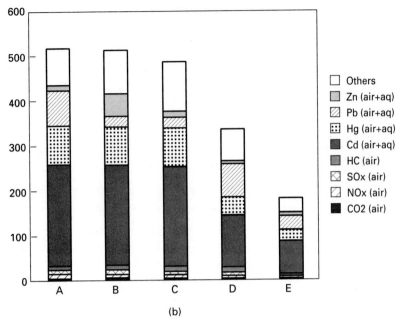

(b)

FIGURE 14.23b Same as Fig. 14.23a but with evaluation by the environmental theme method with Swedish political targets (from Rydberg et al. 1995).

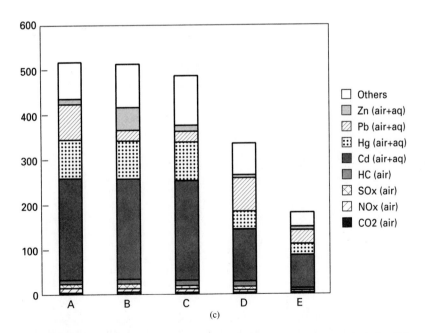

(c)

FIGURE 14.23c Same as Fig. 14.23a, but evaluated by the ecoscarcity method, Swedish indices (from Rydberg et al. 1995).

creet design, long life span, durable colors (white), and washability. Again the most important relations to product structure concern PVC, lead sulfate, titanium dioxide, copper, and the production process (Fig. 14.22).

Options for Product Improvement.   Several potential options for improvement of the product system were proposed during the project. Some of these have been evaluated with respect to environmental performance, as shown in Fig. 14.23*a* to *c*. The reference product is A. The amount of reference product, a functional unit, is 1000 m of cable in the reference case:

A. Reference case.

B. Substitute lead sulfate stabilizer. A stabilizer based on a calcium-zinc complex is used instead.

C. Substitute PVC, in which case a formulation based on polyethylene plastic is used.

D. Recycle copper from cables after use. Use recycled copper in the cable. In the simulations, it has been assumed that 50 percent of the copper in the used cable is recycled, to the smelter process. Process emissions from the smelter are allocated to the virgin production; i.e., no process emissions are assumed from the recycling processes.

E. Installation in closed system, i.e., use of three conducting cables in a hard PVC tube which is placed in the wall. For installation in closed systems, the functional unit was reformulated. The new functional unit is a standard house of 125 m^2, in which electricity is delivered throughout the lifetime of 75 years. In an open installation, the house is completely rewired every 25 years. Assuming 333 m of installed cable means that about 1000 m of cable is consumed over the lifetime of the house. For installation in closed systems, no rewiring is necessary, and the amount of installed cable is therefore 333 m.

Simulation of Modifications of Product Systems

Customer Quality.   For the closed-system installation, the customer requirements will be different than for the open-system installation. Figure 14.24 shows the quality matrix for the closed system. This may be compared with Fig. 14.22, the matrix for the open system.

Life-Cycle Economy.   The analysis shows that life-cycle cost differences will not be very important for the customer in choosing between different cable systems (Fig. 14.25). Although there are relatively large differences with respect to a functional period of 75 years, these will not be sensible costs for the normal private-residence application. For the cable producer, a reduced demand for cables in closed systems will also reduce net profit over the life cycle of the system. Differences between closed and open cable systems in life-cycle costs might, however, be more important in other applications, such as office buildings and industrial plants, where the time between reconstructions often is considerably shorter than in private residences.

Concluding Remarks.   Several options for improvement were not covered in the above simulations of environmental performance. These include replacement of titanium dioxide by another pigment or not used all; reuse of cables (disassembly and reassembly); change of conductor to, say, aluminum, which is already used in certain types of cables (such as high-voltage cables); and change to another voltage in the distribution systems of houses (e.g., either up to 400 V or down to 24 V).

Product structure Customer requirements	PVC-E	PVC-S	DOP	Chalk	PbS	TiO$_2$	Copper	Pigment	Production process	Weighting factor (closed)
Long life span	0	+	0	−	+	+	0	0	+	2
High reliability	0	0	0	0	0	0	+	0	+	5
Good fire safety	0	+	−	0	0	0	0	0	0	4
High mechan. res.	0	+	−	−	0	0	0	0	+	1
Low purch. price	0	−	−	+	−	0	−	0	0	2
Good color pers.	0	0	0	0	+	+	0	+	0	1
Good env. perf.	−	−	−	0	−	−	−	0	0	1

FIGURE 14.24 Relationships between end-user requirements and product structure for closed system.

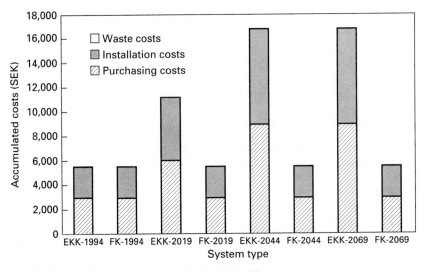

FIGURE 14.25 Life-cycle cost analysis of two electric cable systems.

It was clear from the reference product assessment that titanium dioxide was not a large problem in this case. It was, however, a preconceived option, and this indicates that issues which were regarded as important in advance may not be so important. Similarly, the replacement of PVC with another plastic, or the replacement of the stabilizer, was proved to be less environmentally important than options addressing the consumption of virgin copper or the amount of cable. These issues could be addressed by reformulating the functional unit from 1000 m of cable to the use of electricity in a standard house over the lifetime of the house. Thus, the importance of properly defining the actual requirements and utility of the end user was clearly shown.

14.4 EXPERIENCES WITH THE LCA METHOD APPLIED IN PRODUCT DEVELOPMENT

The discussion of experiences with the LCA method in this project has been structured according to the main elements in the methodological framework presented by Consoli et al. (1993), in the Nordic LCA manual (Nordic Council of Ministers 1995), and by ISO TC 207:

- Goal and scoping
- Inventory
- Impact assessment
- Improvement assessment

In general, the methodology presented in the Nordic LCA manual has been used in most of the case projects.

14.4.1 Goal and Scoping

Three important aspects of the goal and scoping activities which have been a source for discussions in the case projects are

- The definition of goals for the LCA studies
- The definition of the functional unit of the product system
- The definition of relevant system boundaries

Concerning *goal definition,* experience from the case projects shows that the specific goals of the LCA activities related to product development will change from stage to stage in the project. In the initial, tactical stage, there should some type of project superior goals, reflecting systematic selection of case projects. An example of such a goal might be as follows:

> Carry out life-cycle assessments of a representative set of products within a product group, be able to generalize about the environmental performance of the product group in different market situations, and be able to distinguish between product and market situations with high and low performance with a certain degree of precision.

One important reason for such a goal is that the company should have the best possible basis for prioritizing projects where sustainable product development is used.

In the next stage, when the project is selected, and the sustainable product development method is applied, our experiences show that there are at least four different goals for the life-cycle assessment studies which will be carried out throughout the project. In stage 1 in the model in Fig. 14.33, a typical goal for the LCA study will be to

> Carry out a screening LCA of a representative reference product, identify the main environmental problems related to the total product systems under market-relevant assumptions, and identify which parts of the life cycle of the product system have the most significant contribution to these problems.

In stage 2 in the model in Fig. 14.33, where different alternative concepts are compared with the reference product, a typical goal for the LCA study will be to

> Carry out a comparative screening LCA of alternative product systems and identify which alternatives have the best total environmental profile, especially with respect to those problems considered most significant in the reference case.

In stage 3 of the model in Fig. 14.33, the LCA model will be used to make scenarios of one or two alternative system concepts, to evaluate the total system effects of changes in the product structure in the detailed design of a product. Such scenarios will function as sensitivity analyses, which can be of a simple qualitative nature, or more comprehensive and quantitative for significant modifications. In this stage of the product development project, the uncertainty concerning the final product structure and the way the product system will function is normally reduced significantly. This will also make it possible to increase the precision of the LCA studies, by getting more exact data about material composition, product processes, choice of suppliers and transport, and in some cases the user efficiency of the product (although this type of information often is not available before the product has been tested in real-user situations). A typical goal for the LCA study will then be to

> Carry out more detailed LCA scenarios of changes in the product structure in the detailed design of a product system, and evaluate changes in the environmental performance of the total system, from modifications in the design parameters of the product system.

In stage 4 of the product development model in Fig. 14.33, the LCA study would normally be made public for the first time in the project. At this stage of the project, the LCA study will be used to document the environmental performance of the new product and normally will be compared to another, competing alternative. This type of application of LCA will typically have as a goal to

> Carry out a more detailed LCA to document the differences in environmental performance between the new product system and the reference product system.

It is important to recognize that throughout a product development or improvement project, there will typically be several applications of LCA data, often based on the same initial model established for the reference product in stage 1 of the project. However, both the goals of the LCA part of the project and the interpretations made from those different studies will change considerably throughout the project. Also the level of detail of the studies will change from the first stage to the last, where the results normally will be made public in some type of marketing.

This dynamic use of LCA data and interpretations in the product development process makes it very difficult to describe *improvement analysis* as a final stage in a sequential model for the LCA methodology (see Consoli et al. 1993). A further developed, more dynamic model for improvement analysis, based on our experiences from testing of our model in the case projects, will be described in Sec. 14.4.4.

The *functional unit* of the product system is a very important element in the LCA model. In all types of applications of LCA methods, the functional unit must be defined unambiguously and quantitatively. Four elements have proved to be important when one is defining the right functional unit for a product system, to ensure that two systems are compared in a way that really takes into account differences in product efficiency:

1. The efficiency of the product in fulfilling some well-defined user requirements (e.g., kilograms of paint necessary to cover 100 m^2 of platform surface)

2. The life span of the product (e.g., how many times and to what degree we need to repaint a surface of 100 m^2 during 25 years with different products)

3. The fulfillment of user requirements to a certain standard (e.g., the anticorroding properties of a paint should reach a given standard)

4. The fulfillment of different types of functions by one and the same product (e.g., a paint product should have both an anticorroding function and a light-reflecting function; a refrigerator both keeps the food cold and produces heat)

The first two elements are quite easily included in most LCA studies, although it might be hard to get really good data on the user efficiency and the life span of specific products, especially products which are under development. One reason for making a study of a relevant reference product, where such data should be possible to obtain, is, however, to get better documentation of the importance of these factors in the total environmental performance of the product (the system efficiency).

The two last points need more thorough discussion. As stated by Lindfors et al. (1995), it is important that two products are compared with bases in the same functionality. However, to improve product systems, as presented by Hanssen (1996), two important strategies are to change the user requirements to a product and to develop products which fulfill several functions (primary, secondary, and tertiary functions). Regarding the fulfillment of user requirements to a given standard, this has shown up as one of the most important obstacles to development and the use of more sustainable product systems. The standards established by national and international authorities and organizations might often be the most important reason why a given solution is not applicable. Tradition and conservatism by the user are other important reasons. Very often, such standard requirements are general, not taking into consideration different demands in specific situations. In general, such standards are also established without considering environmental impacts of the standard, or especially the impact that a more sustainable system solution will be restricted by the standard. In sustainable product development, one important task is to identify by the QFD analysis which requirements are set by the user or by some external bodies and how these standards eventually can be met or adjusted. In some areas of an offshore platform, e.g., there might be a certain requirement concerning the chemical resistance of the paint, demanding a paint with very special properties. One alternative solution would certainly be to look for options to make the environment less corrosive, by reducing the level of chemical impact on the surface by better operational procedures or by use of less corrosive chemicals. In a sustainable product development project, the project team should thus look for ways to make the standard requirements less rigorous for a given system solution.

Regarding fulfillment of several functions by a given product system, there are several aspects to consider. First, it is important that different system solutions be compared on a sound basis, i.e., that all relevant functions really be included in the study. If one product fulfills three different and independent functions and another system fulfills only one function, then this difference must be included in the calculation, e.g., by enlarging the system boundaries. If a plastic bag system is used three times before it is deposited or incinerated, then all these functions should be considered if they are real and independent. The difficulty with such an approach lies in defining when the fulfillment of a function should be reflected in the functional unit of the product. One example is the refrigerator, where the product produces both cold storage of food and heat. However, if heat is regarded as a by-product fulfilling a secondary function, then there are certain conditions which must be met. The heat must be in a form which makes it possible to substitute for another type of heating system. In practice, the heating function can be included in the analysis only if there is a temperature-regulating meter in the room, which reduces consumption of energy by another source. The environmental performance of production, distribution, and use of this "avoided energy use" can then be calculated in the LCA of the refrigerator.

In some periods of the year, the heat produced by the refrigerator will not be able to substitute for traditional room heating. In fact, in ventilated rooms this extra heat will increase the energy consumption by the ventilator system. This extra energy must also be included in the analysis, reducing the benefits of the avoided energy consumption in periods with a heating demand.

These examples illustrate very well the fact that the multiple-function aspect is a complicated problem, which has to be evaluated carefully when the system boundaries between different systems are considered. However, it is also a challenge to the product development team to use this information to find a solution which takes into account the potential for developing products with multiple functions, and to make the total system more efficient. In the case of the refrigerator, the extra energy produced as heat could, for example, be used more efficiently if applied in water heating instead of room heating, because the need for heated water is not that dependent on the season.

The last important element in the goal and scoping phase is the *definition of system boundaries,* in relation to both other technical systems and what should be included without losing too much information. The last point concerns what constitutes the practical level of detail of an LCA study, since it is possible to use a lot of time without really increasing the information level significantly. A comparative study based on four rather detailed LCA studies in the Nordic LCA project showed that it is not possible to exclude any type of activity or any stage in the life cycle on a general basis (Lindfors et al. 1995). Hanssen (1994) has argued that it is more efficient to use time resources to get complete data from system units which are big contributors to the mass flow through the system, and to follow those back to the acquisition phase, than to use much time on system units with low mass flow contributions.

Based on the system description, it is necessary to define cutoff criteria for which system units should be included in the inventory of emissions from system components. One way is to define the exact cutoff criteria based on a mass fraction of total product weight (1, 2, 5, or 10 percent). The lower the figure, the higher the precision of the study. However, project time consumption increases also steeply with lower figures, and it is probably not cost-efficient to use too low a figure. A better approach is to check how large a proportion of the total mass in the system is covered by the chosen cutoff criteria (as a rule of thumb, 80 to 90 percent of the total mass should be covered). In Fig. 14.26, it is shown how big a proportion of the total mass of the system is included in the quantitative model if we choose 20, 10, 5, 3, 2, and 1 percent as cutoff criteria. The results of the model show clearly that it is more important to include all steps in the life cycle for raw materials with a high mass fraction in the system than to include raw materials with a very small mass fraction. Note, however, that the model does not differentiate between the components with respect to emission or energy consumption factors per unit of material produced. Good knowledge about the relevant processes must thus be combined with such simple cutoff criteria. One simple indication of a need for more detailed information about a raw material occurs when the unit price is much higher than an average for the whole set of raw materials. Price-driving forces could be high energy consumption, high toxicity level, or high scarcity factor for the materials.

Another important aspect of the definition of system boundaries is the strategy followed in some projects—to include only those system units which are different, in comparisons between two alternative products. The reason for such an approach is again to reduce the time needed for data gathering and analysis. This was done initially in the project with electric cables at ABB Bjurhagen, where only those system units which were influenced by a substitution of PVC with polyethylene were considered. The project did not start with an open, problem-focusing approach. Instead, it was taken for

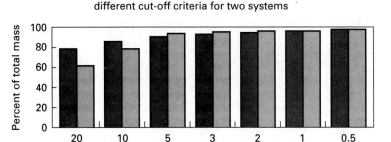

FIGURE 14.26 Proportion of the total mass of a total product system which is included by process-related emissions, if we use different cutoff criteria for defining the system boundaries. In A, raw material acquisition and processing have been included at least three steps behind production of the product. In B, only raw material processing (one step behind production of the product) has been included.

granted that PVC was the main problem, which was the basis for the system boundary definition. However, when a more complete study of the PVC cable as the reference product was done, it was clear that the main problem with the cable system was the copper conductor, not PVC in the insulating shield.

To simplify a system by exclusion of system units, this should be done on the basis of specific knowledge of the system, where only those system units which do not contribute to the total environmental impacts of the system are excluded. Such considerations can only be done on the basis of previous studies of similar systems under similar conditions.

14.4.2 Inventory

Concerning the inventory stage of an LCA project, the main topics include

- Allocation principles for open-loop cascade recovery
- Allocation principles for environmental impacts related to waste generation
- Data quality issues

Allocation principles for cascade recovery have been thoroughly discussed in the report from the Nordic LCA project (Lindfors et al. 1995a) and in other international forums such as the Leiden workshop in 1994. The problem is how to allocate environmental impacts between different products in an open-loop recovery system (see Fig. 14.27). In the Nordic LCA project, a model was introduced which fulfills several requirements of a standard method for such calculations. The model allocates 50 percent of the total impacts from raw material production and final waste disposal or incineration to the first producer and the last producer, respectively. This implies that the producer which uses virgin raw materials and the producer making products without possibility of recovery of materials are both punished for inefficient use of materials (see Fig. 14.28). An incentive for making products with a high degree of material recovery will be when 50 percent of the total impact from raw material production and waste disposal or incineration follows the materials until they are deposited or incinerated.

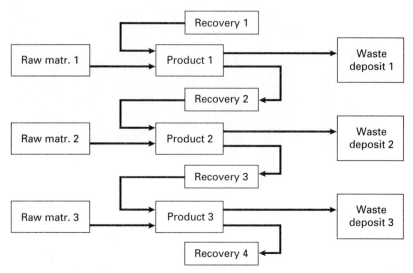

FIGURE 14.27   A typical cascade recovery system for open-loop material recovery.

This 50/50 allocation model will also make it easy to calculate environmental impacts from cascade recovery systems. In most systems, there is a certain ratio between recovered and virgin materials as inputs to a product, and a similar share between products being recovered and waste treated as output from the product system. By establishing a mass balance for one of the product system units within the cascade, it is possible to calculate the environmental impacts for one functional product system in the material chain. The principle behind the mass balance calculation for one system unit in the material chain is shown in Figure 14.28. The Nordic LCA project also used a 50/50 allocation of the environmental burdens related to transport and to processing of the materials between the system which produces recovered materials and the system using recovered materials. From the figures given in Fig. 14.28, the total mass of emissions from producer of product 2 will be

From recovering processes:

$$[(80 \text{ kg} \times 20 \text{ g/kg}) + (80 \text{ kg} \times 20 \text{ g/kg})] \times 0.5 = 1.6 \text{ kg}$$

From raw material processing:

$$[(20 \text{ kg} \times 100 \text{ g/kg}) + (20 \text{ kg} \times 60 \text{ g/kg})] \times 0.5 = 1.6 \text{ kg}$$

From waste treatment:

$$[(20 \text{ kg} \times 60 \text{ g/kg}) + (20 \text{ kg} \times 100 \text{ g/kg})] \times 0.5 = 1.6 \text{ kg}$$

Another important subject concerning allocation of environmental burdens is the problem of waste generation. In all typical LCA handbooks and guidelines, the waste flows are only responsible for environmental impacts related to disposal or other types of treatment activities (see Fig. 14.29). However, a loss of 20 percent of materials in a

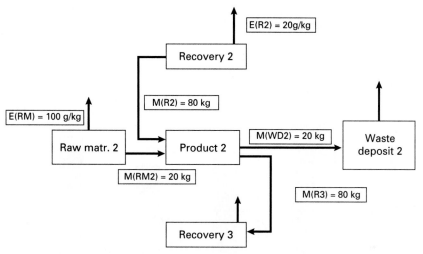

FIGURE 14.28   Allocation of environmental impacts between different parts of an open-loop cascade recovery system. In the model, 50 percent of total environmental impacts from virgin raw material processing and waste treatment is allocated to virgin raw materials and 50 percent as a "latent" punishment for waste to deposits or incineration.

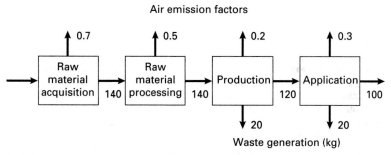

FIGURE 14.29   A life-cycle model of material flows in a product system with waste generation at the production and user phase. Material flows between product system units are in kilograms of material.

production unit as waste means that all upstream units must produce 20 percent more materials than necessary to fulfill the functional unit of the system. In a traditional LCA calculation, the environmental impacts related to these "extra" materials will be allocated to each of the upstream units. When one is looking at options for improvements in the system, the importance of these raw material processing units will be overemphasized. By allocating the responsibility for loss of materials as waste in the production plant, the importance of waste-reducing options will be more in accordance with its role in the system. The difference between traditional LCA calculation of waste flows and the method described in this chapter is shown in Fig. 14.30.

This alternative calculation method has not been used in the case reports presented in the NEP project. The reason is that the method was discovered late in the phase of the

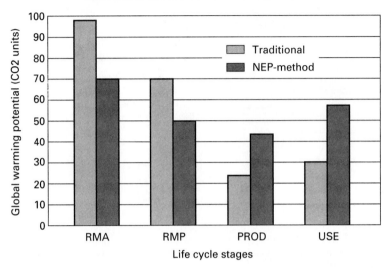

FIGURE 14.30 Traditional LCA accounting method and the NEP project LCA accounting method for allocating environmental impacts from different system units along a product change with waste generation. In calculations done according to the NEP method, 100 percent of the burdens have been allocated to the waste generators.

case project analyses. However, the method will be relevant for several of the case projects, especially the offshore paint project and the super-LIFA underclothes project. In all these systems, there are material losses from the system in the production of the product, which could be treated by the new allocation model. It could be argued that the same 50/50 allocation rule could be used in this type of material loss situation as has been used in open-loop recovery between systems. The situation is principally similar to the open-loop recovery system, although allocation is not between different products, but between different parts of one given product system. A 50/50 allocation between the raw material producer and the waste generator in production and application only shall be used if the material loss is possible to recover and if the raw material producer is not willing or able to substitute for the recovered materials. A 50/50 allocation should thus be used, unless it is clearly stated that the materials are able to be recovered, but no recovering system is available and really functional.

An important element in LCA studies is *data quality,* regarding both emission data and system design variables (e.g., transport distance, material composition, life span). In product development projects, there is much inherent uncertainty, especially in the early phases of development. So far, few LCA studies have used statistical methods to discuss statistical uncertainty (for examples, see Rønning et al. 1993, Førde et al. 1993). In the early phases of a product development project, there is much uncertainty with respect to material composition, design, efficiency, life span, production technology, and market volumes of a new product variety. This is not only a problem with the LCA study, it is also a general problem for the product development team and the company to make decisions under uncertainty. On one hand, it is important to get as reliable data as possible when one is carrying out LCA studies of alternative product concepts in such early stages. On the other hand, one should not set stricter requirements on data quality for environmental information than on other types of information in this stage. The relationship between availability of environmental information and the different stages in product development projects, based on general experiences from product development (e.g., Andreasen and Hein 1986), is shown in Fig. 14.3.

Uncertainty in the LCA model in early stages of development, when the number of degrees of freedom needed to find the optimal concept is high, is the main reason for making an initial study on a relevant reference product. Although this product might be quite different from the new product system, the product development team will learn a lot concerning which environmental problems are related to different parts of the system, which system design variables are important for the total environmental profile of the system, and what the sensitivity is to changes in different parameters. The reference case will make it easier for the product development team to identify those parameters for which good-quality data are important and those which are probably not that important. The reference case will thus increase the information available in the early phases of product development, which will increase the probability of the right concept being chosen. Since the reference case normally will be within the company's own product portfolio, it is possible to get good-quality information for this product.

The quality requirements of LCA data will thus change throughout the project:

- In the initial stage with LCA study on the reference product, there is a requirement for high-quality LCA data.
- In the concept definition and evaluation stage, there will be lower quality requirements for alternative solutions, due to the general high level of uncertainty.
- In the optimization stage, the requirements on LCA data quality will increase, as the precision of the alternatives increases in general.
- In the final stage with product launching, there is a requirement for high-quality LCA data for use in market communications with the customers.

These changes in requirements of data quality are shown in Fig. 14.31. This figure is a general representation for data used in product development.

14.4.3 Impact Assessments

In the case projects, classification, characterization, and valuation have been applied, based on the methods described in the Nordic LCA manual (Lindfors et al. 1995b, Nordic Council of Ministers 1995). In this discussion, we will focus briefly on the incompleteness in covering impact categories, occupational health, and experiences with valuation methods and models in LCA studies.

In the Nordic LCA manual, 13 different impact categories are proposed to be addressed in LCA studies, within three main categories:

- Resource depletion
- Health impacts
- Ecological impacts

In the Nordic manual, models and conversion factors are given for analysis of a number of these impact categories, such as nonrenewable resources, global warming, acidification, ozone depletion, photochemical oxidant formation, nutrification, and ecotoxicity. However, for several other impact categories, there is still a lack of models and impact

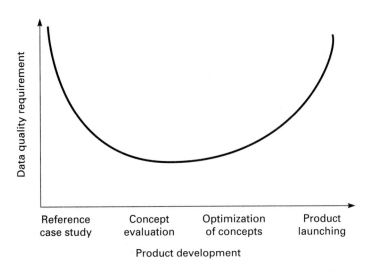

FIGURE 14.31 Changes in requirements of data quality throughout the different stages of product development.

parameters to analyze contributions from product systems to these categories. A question that needs to be addressed is, Should LCA be regarded as a complete method for assessment of environmental impacts from product systems? It is especially important to get better models and conversion factors for habitat changes and biodiversity, for ecotoxicity, and for human health categories. As pointed out by Hanssen et al. (1994), this is not only a problem regarding LCA studies. The systematic structure developed in the LCA method should also be applied in *environmental performance evaluation* (EPE), in *environmental impact assessments* (EIAs), and in other environmental management tools generally. Since all these tools are intended to cover environmental problems in general, it is a weakness that several important impact categories are not covered. In practical studies, this means that these impact categories are not covered in the analyses, which might lead to wrong or suboptimal conclusions. Since the LCA method is the only tool which has the potential to cover all environmental impacts related to products on a superior level, this should be the basis for more research and development in the future.

Occupational health is an impact category which has been analyzed in LCA studies in only a few cases. The reason is partly the lack of models and impact parameters for quantitative analyses of potential health impacts from different materials and emissions and partly the lack of data and information about occupational health factors in a life-cycle perspective. In one case in the NEP project (the Jotun/Statoil project on development of new offshore paints), a semiquantitative method for analyzing occupational health impacts was developed by Rønning et al. (1995). Occupational health impacts were evaluated by considering

- The classification of different raw materials in the paints according to national and international occupational health standards
- The potential exposure to workers through air and skin contact
- The number of working hours the workers were exposed to different materials in production and application of the paints and to substances used in mechanical and chemical pretreatment of the offshore surface

A simple matrix was developed, where the different materials were categorized according to classification and exposure data into four main groups. For each type of activity and for the different paint products, the total exposure to each category was analyzed for production, distribution, and application on the platforms (Møller 1995, Rønning et al. 1995).

The valuation stage is so far the least developed part of the LCA methodology, although there are several methods and models available for valuating different environmental impacts (Baumann et al. 1993, Hanssen et al. 1994, Lindfors et al. 1995). In the NEP project, several methods have been tested in parallel in the different case projects:

1. The EPS system (Ryding and Steen 1992)
2. The ecoscarcity approach (Baumann et al. 1993)
3. The environmental theme approach (Baumann et al. 1993)
4. Normalization of impacts according to national environmental data (see Rønning et al. 1993)

Methods 2 and 3 have their origin in Switzerland and the Netherlands, respectively, originally with country-specific or case-specific weighting parameters. In the case projects, we used weighting parameters with the basis in Norwegian and Swedish conditions, as given by Baumann (1992) and Baumann and Rydberg (1994).

The different valuation methods have been used in parallel in the case projects, to define which are the main product-specific environmental impacts related to a product system. The conclusions are based on the total results from all the valuation models, and not simply those from a single model. Environmental impacts have been divided into three main groups—large, medium, and low potential environmental impacts. For each product system, a given impact category has been allocated to the highest group if it is given priority by *one* of the tested models. In the environmental quality matrices, total weighting of environmental impacts is done with the basis in a total evaluation of all valuation models.

In most case studies, there seems to be a high degree of overlap in conclusions from the different valuation methods. Global warming potential, acidification, photochemical oxidant formation, and conversion of fossil fuels seem to be generally important in many product systems. The priorities of these impact categories will often differ between the different methods. In some cases, there are also other impact categories which are sorted out as important by one or two systems. Toxic releases will often get a relatively high value in the ecoscarcity method and in the normalization method.

There seems to be a general pattern that global and long-term problems such as global warming and resource conversion are chosen as most important by the EPS system. The environmental theme method does often sort out regional problems such as acidification and photochemical oxidation, while the ecoscarcity method gives relatively higher priority to local problems such as toxic releases (e.g., heavy metals).

Most existing valuation systems are based on historical data for the priority of different environmental problems; these are either political goals and target values (ecoscarcity and environmental theme methods) or willingness to pay (EPS system). One problem in using these data as the basis for future strategies is the allocation of priorities among different environmental problems. This is especially the case with long-term problems, which are often given lower priority in society than more acute and local problems (see Hanssen et al. 1994). In the weighting parameters for the ecoscarcity method and the environmental theme method estimated by Baumann (1992), there is a mix of government goals and targets defined in National Environmental Policy documents, and more long-term, voluntary goals set up by industrial-sector programs. When the weighting parameters are applied in situations where LCA data are used for govern-ment purposes, it has been argued that only political goals and targets should be used consistently in the weighting parameters (see Møller and Øksdal 1995). However, when used in long-term product development, the weighting parameters could be based on more long-term *sustainability indices,* in a long-term goal for reduction of environmen-tal problems. These indices could be general parameters for the society or specific para-meters for a given industrial sector. Such sustainability parameters have been discussed by Goedkoop (1995a, b) based on a product development project in the Netherlands.

Although the valuation stage of the LCA method still is in development, it is impor-tant to test the different methods in specific cases, to get more experience with how the different methods are weighting different environmental impacts in various situations.

14.4.4 Improvement Assessment

In the traditional LCA method described by Consoli et al. (1993), *improvement assess-ment* has been defined as the last and final step in the LCA method. By improvement assessment we mean the application of LCA in different types of decision systems, to improve the environmental performance of single product systems, or of a product group in a company, or of a total brand of products in the society (see Hanssen 1994). In the first case, improvement is normally related to product development, product plan-ning, or changes in the different processes and activities or in the infrastructure of a product system. In the second case, improvements can be achieved through environ-mental regulations by authorities, by environmental labeling, etc.

In recent discussions in both the Nordic LCA projects (Lindfors et al. 1995) and the NEP project (Hanssen 1993, Hanssen et al. 1995), the improvement assessment phase of the LCA method has been much debated. Hanssen (1993) has presented a model in which improvement assessment is understood as the interactions between the first three steps of the LCA method and the decision model describing the application situation, e.g., product development (Fig. 14.32). This model has been the basis for development of methods for sustainable product development in the NEP project.

In the final report from the NEP project, it is argued that there are several interac-tions between the LCA model and the product development model during different phases of a product development project (Hanssen et al. 1995). For each of these inter-actions, there are different goals and scopings of the LCA study, although the same model of the product system might be applied. In such a situation, improvement assess-ment is not one final phase in a sequential LCA model. At least four different interpre-tations of LCA results have been identified throughout the product development process, as illustrated in Fig. 14.33.

Although the different LCAs are interrelated, since many of the same data and assumptions are common, there are differences between the studies, depending on what types of interpretation are made from each study. In stage 1 we make a screening LCA to identify main problems and hot spots for improvements; in stage 2 we make a screen-ing LCA to compare concept A with one or several other concepts; in stage 3 we make a more detailed LCA to compare A with A' or with A'' in optimization of a new concept. In the final stage, we make a detailed LCA to compare A_{new} with the original reference product. This iterative nature of the LCA method, as it is applied, say, in product devel-opment and improvement, is illustrated in Fig. 14.33.

In an international expert workshop in Norway in March 1995 (Hankø Workshop), the correspondences between the different types of decision models and the LCA model were documented for improvements of product systems (Christiansen et al. 1995). It is

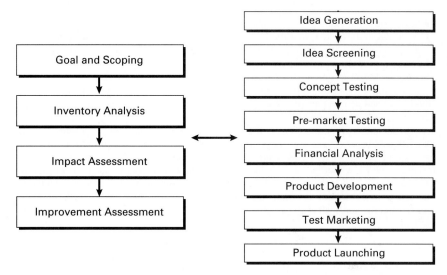

FIGURE 14.32   A conceptual model of interactions between the LCA method and a sequential decision model for product development (from Hanssen 1993).

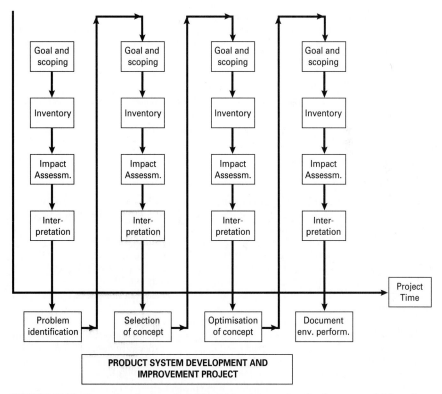

FIGURE 14.33   Interactions between the LCA model and the product development model throughout the different phases of a product development project (from Hanssen et al. 1995).

quite obvious that there will be different requirements for the depth and width of an LCA study and for the quality of LCA data for different types of applications. Documentation of experiences with use of LCA as an integrated part of different types of decision models, and the specific requirements for data quality and organization of the project, has been one of the main goals.

In all these types of applications for improvements, LCA data and information should be used as one part of the decision support documentation. However, the number of applications for improvements mentioned above clearly shows that there is no *one* type of improvement assessment as the last part of the LCA method. Experience shows that different types of applications for improvements will have different requirements in the various stages in the LCA method. The different types of applications will thus influence the LCA method, as it is applied in different decision models. However, the LCA approach will influence the design of the decision model, the types of decisions made, and the content of the decisions. In total, the combined LCA and decision model will be specific for each type of application and will be a modification of the standard methods.

14.5 GENERAL EXPERIENCES FROM THE PROJECT

Most of the people involved in case projects under the NEP project believe that the project has medium to significant importance for the companies in their product development activities. As shown by Table 14.2, the main results from the project have been to help companies to

- Develop strategies for sustainable product development
- Build up knowledge in the companies regarding sustainable product development and life-cycle cost analyses
- Identify the most important materials and processes for improvement of environmental performance of the products
- Identify the most important environmental problems related to a given product or product group

To some degree, the project has also contributed to the development of new product ideas, knowledge of product development in general, and internal cooperation between the environmental department and the marketing department.

The NEP project seems so far to be of minor importance for development of new products with better environmental performance in the companies. One reason is that the project period has been quite short (about 18 months), whereas product development often takes considerably longer. Some of the respondents did also comment that the questionnaire was sent out too early, as most case projects had not been finalized and documented at that time.

The most important obstacle in the case projects has been the access of data for the LCA and LCC analyses. In most of the case projects, the companies had problems with gathering data for all types of materials and processes, especially data concerning special chemical substances. This must be seen in relation to the fact that most companies had little experience with the different methods before the NEP project started (Hanssen et al. 1995). Time limitations for members of the project groups and other experts within

TABLE 14.2 Importance of NEP Case Project for Different Factors Related to Sustainable Product Development in Companies

Type of evaluation factor	No signifi- cance	Minor signi- ficance	Medium signi- cance	Signfi- ficant	Very signi- ficant	Total
Development of new, environmentally sound products	2	5	2	3	0	12
Development of new product ideas	1	3	5	2	0	11
Development of strategies for SPD	1	4	2	5	0	12
Competence building in SPD	1	2	3	6	0	12
Competence building in product development	4	2	6	0	0	12
Competence building in QFD	3	3	3	3	0	12
Competence building in LCC	3	1	4	4	0	12
Increased cooperation with customers in PD	3	3	2	3	1	12
Increased cooperation between environ- ment and marketing departments	3	1	6	1	1	12
Increased cooperation between environ- ment and PD departments	3	1	6	1	1	12
Knowledge about important environ- mental problems with products	0	1	4	5	2	12
Identification of materials, processes, and activities causing problems	0	1	5	4	2	12
Market position of company	4	2	4	2	0	12

the company were also a factor, but less important than data availability (Hanssen et al. 1995).

One of the main ideas behind the method for sustainable product development is to carry out projects in integrated teams within a company. Several departments should thus be involved in the projects, which should have a well-defined priority and commitment from top management.

In the case projects, environmental, marketing, production, and research and development departments have been rather involved in the projects. Most engagement seems to be from the environmental, product development, and R&D departments (Hanssen et al. 1995).

Most of the respondents believe that the knowledge, tools, and methods developed in the case projects should be further disseminated within the companies. Experiences from the projects will be drawn upon in strategic development, in product development, and in marketing of products. Education of employees, communication with authorities, and selection of suppliers are of medium to minor importance for most companies, whereas very few respondents see the potential for using information and experiences from the projects in communication with bank and finance and insurance companies (Hanssen et al. 1995).

In the NEP project, LCA has been used for several different purposes during the product development process, from idea generation to product launching and evaluation of product strategies. The companies seem to be most focused on the use of LCA for idea generation and in developing criteria for new products (Hanssen et al. 1995).

14.5.1 Concluding Remarks

The NEP project has shown that LCA is a well-developed method for analysis and evaluation of environmental performance of products, as an input to product development. However, there is still work to be done, to get a more complete picture of all relevant environmental impact categories. It is also necessary to develop better tools for managing LCA data and presenting them in an easily understood format for the different stakeholders in a company. The SPINE database structure which has been developed in the NEP project is a major step forward in this respect.

In the NEP project, a method has been developed for sustainable product development, where LCA is integrated with other general tools into the integrated product development model. Experience from the case projects shows that this is a good approach, since both economy, customer requirements, and environmental performance are considered in a life-cycle perspective.

The NEP project has shown that it is possible to develop products which give added value to the customer in reduced life-cycle costs, combined with a significant improvement in the environmental performance of the product. The project has shown that the most important environmental problems often are connected with other types of processes and activities in the life cycle of a product. Also, options for improvement of product systems often are quite simple modifications in the system properties, not necessarily influencing the main properties of a product.

BIBLIOGRAPHY

Andersson, R. 1991. *QFD. A System for More Effective Product Development.* Studentlitteratur, Lund (in Swedish).

Andreasen, M. M., and Hein, L. 1986. *Integrated Product Development.* Universitetsforlaget, Oslo, Norway (in Norwegian).

Andreasen, M. M., and Støren, S. 1994. *Product Improvement, with Basis in the "Know Your Product."* Philosophy Institute for Product Development, Note 566-K-94.

Asbjørnsen, O. A. 1992. *Systems Engineering Principles and Practice.* Skarpodd, Maryland.

Baumann, H. 1992. *Utvärdering med index. Beräkning av två uppsättingar norska index.* CIT-ekologic 1992:2, Chalmers Industriteknik, Gøteborg, Sweden.

Baumann, H., Ekvall, T., Kullmann, M., Rydberg, T., Ryding, S.-O., Steen, B., and Svensson, G. 1993. *Miljömömessiga skilnader mellom återvinning/återanvending och förbränning/deponering.* Reforsk FOU Report 79, Malmö, Sweden.

Baumann, H., and Rydberg, T. 1994. "Life Cycle Assessment: A Comparison between Three Methods for Impact Analysis and Valuation," *J. Cleaner Prod., 2:* 13–20.

Blanchard, B. S., and Fabrycky, W. J. 1990. *Systems Engineering and Analyses,* 2d ed., Prentice-Hall, Englewood Cliffs, NJ.

Christiansen, K., Heijungs, R., Rydberg, T., Ryding, S.-O., Sund, L., Wijnen, H., Vold, M., and Hanssen, O.J. (eds.). 1995. *Application of Life Cycle Assessments (LCA). Report from Expert Workshop at Hankø, Norway, on LCA in Strategic Management, Product Development and*

Improvement, Marketing and Ecolabelling and Governmental Policies. Østfold Research Foundation Research Report OR.29.95.

Consoli, F., Allen, D., Boustead, I., Fava, J., Franklin, W., Jensen, A. A., de Oude, N., Parrish, R., Perriman, R., Postlethwaite, D., Quay, B., Séguin, J., and Vigon, B. 1993. *Guidelines for Life-Cycle Assessment: "Code of Practice."* SETAC, Brussels, Belgium.

Førde, J. S., Hanssen, O. J., and Rønning, A. 1993. *Life Cycle Assessment of Fuel Products.* Østfold Research Foundation Report 50.93.

Førde, J. S., Rekdal, E., Kårvåg, S. E., and Hanssen, O. J. 1995. *Environmentally Oriented Product Development for Lighting Armature Products.* Report for a case project under the NEP project at Glamox A/S, Molde. Østfold Research Foundation, Project Report OR.36.95.

Goedkoop, M. 1995a. "Evaluation in the NOH Eco-indicator," in S.-O. Ryding (ed.), *Proceedings from the International Workshop on Environmentally Sound Product Development, Saltsjöbaden,* Stockholm, Sweden, 5 December 1995. Østfold Research Foundation, Working Paper AR06.95.

Goedkoop, M. 1995b. "Impact Assessment for Ecodesign Applications—Beyond Distance to Target," pp. 3–16 (appendices), in K. Christiansen et al. (1995).

Hanssen, O. J. 1993. *Proceedings from International Workshop on Product Systems Development and Improvements in a Life Cycle Context.* Østfold Research Foundation, Working Paper AR02.93.

Hanssen, O. J. 1994. *Sustainable Product Development—A Draft Method Description.* Østfold Research Foundation, Working Paper AR08.94.

Hanssen, O. J. 1996. "Preventive Strategies for Improved Environmental Performance of Product Systems," *J. Cleaner Prod.* (in press).

Hanssen, O. J. and Asbjørnsen, O. A. 1996. "A Life Cycle Optimization Model for Environmental Performance of Product Systems (CYCLOPS)." Paper submitted to the *Journal of Cleaner Production.*

Hanssen, O. J., Førde, J. S., and Thoresen, J. 1994. *Environmental Indicator and Index Systems. An Overview and Test of Different Approaches. A Pilot Study for Statoil.* Østfold Research Foundation, Research Report OR 17.94.

Hanssen, O. J., Rønning, A., and Rydberg, T. 1995. *Sustainable Product Development. Methods and Experiences from Case Projects. Final Results from the NEP project.* Østfold Research Foundation, Research Paper OR 28.95.

Lindfors, L. G., Christiansen, K., Hoffman, L., Virtanen, Y., Juntilla, V., Leskinen, A., Hanssen, O. J., Rønning, A., Ekvall, T., and Finnveden, G. 1995a. *LCA Nordic Technical Reports* no. 1-9, Tema Nord, 1995:503.

Lindfors, L. G., Christiansen, K., Hoffmann, L., Virtanen, Y., Juntilla, V., Leskinen, A., Hanssen, O. J., Rønning, A., Ekvall, T., and Finnveden, G. 1995b. *LCA Nordic Technical Reports,* no. 10, and *Special Reports,* nos. 1, 2. Tema Nord, 1995:503.

Ministry of Environment. 1994. *NOTA Produkt & Milieu.* VROM 93681/h/1-94 (in Dutch).

Møller, H., and Øksdal, E. 1995. *Environmental and Resource Aspects of Packaging Products—Based on Life Cycle Assessments.* Østfold Research Foundation, Research Report OR12.95 (in Norwegian).

Møller, H. 1995. *Methods for Assessing Toxic Properties of Products in Life Cycle Assessments.* Østfold Research Foundation, Unpublished Paper, 1995.

Mørup, M. 1993. *Design for Quality.* Report IK 93.134 A from Institute for Engineering Design, Danish Technological University, Copenhagen, Denmark.

Nordic Council of Ministers. 1995. *Nordic Handbook in Product Life Cycle Assessments.* NORD 1995:(20), Stockholm, Sweden, 1995.

Norell, M. 1992, *DFA, FMEA and QFD in Product Development. Experiences from Six Swedish Companies.* Technical University of Stockholm, TRITA-MAE 1992:5 (in Swedish).

Øksdal, E., Hanssen, O. J., and Larsen, J. A. 1995. *Environmentally Oriented Product Development of Carbon Lining. Report from Case Study under the NEP Project at Elkem Carbon.* Østfold Research Foundation, Project Report OR.30.95.

Rønning, A., Hanssen, O. J., Møller, H., Gade, A. L., and Haug, U. C. 1993. *Life Cycle Assessment of Paint Products.* Østfold Research Foundation, Project Report OR76.93.

Rønning, A., Hanssen, O. J., and Møller, H. 1995. *Environmentally Sound Product Development of Offshore Coatings. Case Study from the NEP Sound Project at Jotun and Statoil.* Østfold Research Foundation, Project Report OR 40.95.

Rydberg, T., Sjöström, K., Karlsson, L., Larson, P., Videsson, A., and Hanssen, O. J. 1995. *Environmentally Oriented Product Development of Installation Cables. Case Study from the NEP Project at ABB Bjurhagen.* CIT report.

Ryding, S.-O., and Steen, B. 1992. *The EPS Environment Method. An Application of Environmental Accounting Principles for Evaluation and Valuation of Environmental Impacts in Product Design.* Swedish Environmental Research Institute report, Gothenburgh, Sweden.

Sjöström, K. 1994. *Life Cycle Assessment on an Installation Cable EKK 3G 1,5.* ABB Technical Report SECRC/KC/TR-94/4104.

CHAPTER 15
APPLICATION OF LIFE-CYCLE ASSESSMENT TO SOLID WASTE MANAGEMENT PRACTICES

Dr. Neil Kirkpatrick
DIRECTOR
ECOBALANCE UK, WEST SUSSEX

15.1 INTRODUCTION

Solid waste management is currently the subject of much topical debate. This has been driven largely by consumer and legislative pressures which seem united in their belief that increasing the levels of recycling of solid waste beyond their present state will provide an environmental solution to what many refer to as the *solid waste crisis.*

Legislators have been active within the European Community and individual Member States, establishing a legislative framework aiming to secure the diversion of solid waste from disposal in landfill to "processing" via alternative routes such as material recycling or incineration with energy recovery.

In the European Union, the Waste Framework Directives of 1975 and 1991 have given rise to daughter directives such as the EC Directive on Packaging and Packaging Waste, which deal with specific elements of the solid waste stream. Other priority waste streams include electronic and electrical equipment and other highly visible components of the waste stream such as automobile tires.

In the United Kingdom, the Secretary of State for the Environment stated, in the first White Paper on the Environment, "This Common Inheritance," that 50 percent of all recyclable content of all household waste (an estimated 25 percent overall) should be recycled by the year 2000. More recently, the Department of the Environment published its proposed Waste Strategy for England and Wales as well as a Consultation Paper entitled, "Sustainable Waste Management—Producer Responsibility for Packaging Waste."

All these documents have one thing in common—the use of the *solid waste management hierarchy* (Fig. 15.1) as a means of justifying the desire to process solid waste by any means other than landfill. The solid waste management hierarchy places alternative waste treatment options in a fixed order of preference, with waste minimization at source as the most environmentally preferred (least environmental impact) option and landfill as the least environmentally preferred (greatest environmental impact) option.

- Waste minimization at source
- Reuse
- Recycle
- Incineration with energy recovery
- Incineration without energy recovery
- Landfill

FIGURE 15.1   Solid waste management hierarchy.

While the solid waste management hierarchy serves a useful purpose, many have come to argue that it should not be viewed as fixed and that one should exercise a degree of caution before coming to any immediate conclusions as to what represents the most environmentally preferred solid waste disposal practice.

One of the main criticisms of the solid waste management hierarchy is that it does not reflect directly environmental concerns such as the use of nonrenewable reserves, global warming, and destruction of the ozone layer. Instead, it is presented as a means to an end, reflecting varying degrees of environmental preference for the processing of solid waste, with landfill assumed to be the least environmentally preferred solid waste disposal practice.

The UK Department of the Environment (DoE) is aware of the desire to integrate other environmental considerations into the decision-making process when it comes to solid waste disposal, and has recently initiated a program of research aimed at adopting a more holistic approach to solid waste disposal. In this work, the DoE is seeking to employ the techniques of life-cycle assessment (LCA) to evaluate waste management practices. Using this approach, each waste management option will be compared on the basis of its ecoprofile, i.e., the consumption of energy and raw materials and associated releases to air, water, and land necessary to facilitate that process. Collectively, in the context of LCA, inputs and outputs are known as *environmental burdens.*

In this chapter, I explain further the methodology of LCA, describing specifically how it is applied to waste management scenarios. I also provide an update on the progress of the DoE initiative in this area as well as indicate how policy options might be defined on the basis of the results generated.

15.2 OVERVIEW OF LIFE-CYCLE ASSESSMENT

Life-cycle assessment is defined as "an objective process to evaluate the environmental burdens associated with a product, process or activity by identifying and quantifying energy and materials used and wastes released to the environment, and to evaluate and implement opportunities to effect environmental improvements" [Society of Toxicology and Chemistry (SETAC), *Code of Practice,* 1991].

LCA, as it is now generally known (other terms used in the past include *ecobalance, ecoprofile analysis,* and *environmental assessment*), has evolved considerably since its inception in the 1970s as an analytical tool to quantify the energy consumption to a holistic methodology to assess the impact on given environmental concerns of a given product or service system.

LCA may be broken down into three stages:

- *Inventory analysis*—quantification of individual environmental burdens
- *Impact assessment*—assessment of the potential effect of the burdens, or environmental impacts

- *Improvement assessment*—an application of the results to facilitate improvement of the system to minimize harmful effects on the environment

In this section, the basic techniques of LCA are described and illustrated with reference to how LCA is applied to waste management practices.

15.2.1 Inventory Analysis

Life-cycle inventory (LCI) analysis quantifies the raw material and energy consumption together with all solid wastes and emissions to air and water (the environmental burdens) for all processes within the system boundary. The results of such a study generate an inventory of the *environmental burdens* (as distinct from *environmental impacts*— see below) associated with the functional unit.

Functional Unit. In order for the results of a comparative study to be valid, comparisons must be made on the basis of equivalent function. In an LCI study, all data will be calculated on the basis of the functional unit.

In waste management operations, there are a variety of ways to define a functional unit, each of which will depend on the goal and scope of the application. Unlike product LCAs, the functional unit for waste management scenarios is based on an input *to* the system rather than an output *from* the system. In all cases, however, the functional unit will be quantified in terms of mass. In the context of waste management, the functional unit will be expressed in terms of mass although the *derivative* itself may be in units of mass, volume, or even energy.

Examples of functional units that might be relevant in the context of waste management include the following:

Mass-derived

- 1000 kg of municipal solid waste
- 1000 household equivalents of solid waste collected
- That quantity of solid waste collected from a given geographic area

*Volume-derived**

- Volume occupied by the waste collected from a given geographic area, transposed to units of mass, allowing for its density when compacted in landfill

Energy-derived†

- Amount of fossil fuels (and associated environmental burdens attributable through precombustion) displaced by recovering energy generated from that waste collected from a geographic area, allowing for efficiencies of conversion

Another factor which should be considered when one seeks to define a functional unit is *time*. The dimension of time in the context of waste management is reflected in two main ways—that time over which data are averaged or normalized and the time period covered by the study, taking into account that proportion of environmental burdens associated with start or shutdown procedures or even (a given portion of those

---

*For example, the focus of the study may be to displace volume that would otherwise be occupied in landfill.

†For example, the focus of the study may be to quantify the environmental benefits of incinerating waste with energy recovery relative to displacing fossil fuels used to contribute energy to the national grid.

environmental burdens associated with) the building and decommissioning of equipment relative to the time specified. For example, if it is assumed that a particular item of capital equipment will function for 5 years at a given rate of throughput, then for a functional unit reflecting the total environmental burdens occurring over a period of 1 year, one-fifth of those environmental burdens associated with the manufacture of that equipment might be assigned to the functional unit.

A further difference between waste management LCAs and LCAs for conventional single-product systems (e.g., packaging) is that waste management LCAs necessarily deal with a much wider range of material types. For every reference to the mass of solid waste, one must further reflect the composition of that waste (on a mass-by-mass basis) to enable the environmental burdens specific to those material types present to be recorded for the given scenario (e.g., environmental burdens associated with corrugated board manufacture if that corrugated board is separated at source for the purposes of recycling).

System and System Boundaries.   A *system* is a collection of connected operations which together perform a defined function.

Conventionally, the main life-cycle stages included in any LCA are the extraction and processing of raw materials, manufacture of the product, distribution, use, reuse, and disposal. Transport operations should be included, where these occur in the primary production sequence. Each of these main life-cycle stages can be further broken down into a series of substages or subprocesses. The level of breakdown will depend on the nature of the available data. In general, the greater the level of breakdown possible, the greater the transparency of the study.

Ideally, all material inputs should be traced to the extraction of raw materials from the earth. In practice, however, this is rarely feasible, and the manufacture of many ancillary materials is often excluded from the system.

The system boundaries separate the system from its surroundings, or the *system environment*. The system environment acts as a source of all inputs to the system and a sink for all outputs from the system. An LCI study therefore produces a quantitative description of all flows of materials and energy across the system boundaries.

System boundaries generally include

- The main production sequence, i.e., extraction of raw materials up to and including final product disposal
- Transport operations
- Production and use of fuels
- Generation of energy, i.e., electricity and heat (including fuel production)
- Disposal of process wastes
- Manufacture of transport packaging

System boundaries generally exclude

- Manufacture and maintenance of capital equipment
- Maintenance of manufacturing establishments, i.e., heating and lighting
- Factors common to each of the products or processes under consideration

In the context of waste management practices, the systems boundary definition can become extremely complex. At the simplest level, one can define the boundaries artificially by defining the *beginning of the life cycle* as, for example, the curbside or curbside collection (the curtilage). While this approach may be simple enough for the flow of materials (waste) into the system boundaries, there are still complications when one considers the outputs from the system.

The *end* of the life cycle may be defined, as is commonly stated, as occurring when all residues from the system are returned to land. However, when one seeks to evaluate material recycling and incineration with energy recovery, one must further extend the system boundaries since the *benefits* of these options can only be evaluated relative to those activities which are *displaced* or *avoided*. In other words, recycling should be viewed as offsetting the environmental burdens associated with the manufacture, transport, and use of virgin materials; and incineration with energy recovery should be evaluated by considering those environmental burdens which are *avoided* by generating heat and power from an alternative means such as burning fossil fuels.

Once again, as stated above for the functional unit, the systems boundaries for waste management processes must take into account every material and energy flow that will occur as a consequence of each individual component in the waste stream being processed.

Waste management LCAs introduce an interesting dimension to the discussion of LCAs in that theoretically one can argue that there is no such thing as *life-cycle* inventory analysis or assessment—only the application of those techniques to the system you define!

This remark also emphasizes that the system boundaries one sets must be consistent with the goal and scope of the study. In essence, then, the system boundaries are tailored to each application, thereby accounting for different results and conclusions for studies conducted independently which appear to be identical in scope.

Note that in using the system boundaries outlined here, the first two options in the solid waste management hierarchy—waste minimization at source and reuse—are excluded. This does not mean that they are not valuable practices. This simply reflects the fact that waste minimization at source and reuse are dealt with more in the context of product-oriented LCAs than waste management LCAs. Specifically, these practices are dealt with by paying careful attention to the manner in which the functional unit and system boundaries are set. In most cases, waste minimization at source will always be the preferred option, although in the case of reuse, the outcome of comparative LCA studies is often less clear. There are, of course, always exceptions to the rule, and depending on the scope of a given study, waste minimization at source may not be preferred if the savings at one point in the system give rise to greater losses elsewhere (e.g., lightweight packaging at the expense of greater loss of those products packaged therein through breakage and/or damage).

Inventory Compilation.   Once the boundaries for a given study have been set, the next step is to gather the data that will form the basis for all calculations. This is invariably the most time-consuming part of conducting an LCI or LCA, and in the majority of cases, data are drawn—at least initially—from databases. Once these data have been "worked through," one can employ the techniques of sensitivity analysis (i.e., examining the difference between alternative data sets) to prioritize one's effort for gathering site-specific, measured data to fine-tune a study to the needs of a particular situation. Data quality in LCA is a major topic of debate and one which is outside the scope of this chapter.

In compiling the inventory, what one actually does is to build up a profile that quantifies the flow of materials through the system, with the *main* output from one life-cycle stage becoming the *main* input to the next life-cycle stage. At the same time, all other material and energy inputs and outputs occurring as releases to air, water, and land are similarly quantified at each life-cycle stage. In this way, the total quantity of inputs at one life-cycle stage should, by definition, equal the total quantity of outputs occurring at that stage; i.e., their masses balance. Given the complexity of the LCI methodology, this illustrates the importance of maintaining the transparency of reporting in LCI and LCA work so that all raw data are evident (and able to be assigned to a given life-cycle stage) and all elements of the calculation procedures, such as coproduct allocation, are transparent.

One of the main reasons for conducting and reporting LCI studies in this manner is to maximize the potential for minimizing burdens or impacts by identifying where they occur at the most significant levels, i.e., to yield the greatest improvements by making the most beneficial use of resources.

The DoE has identified data quality as a key issue for the evaluation of the relative merits of solid waste management practices and accordingly has given this topic a high priority over the next few years. Indeed, at a national conference covering the first stage of the DoE LCI program—the Development of Methodological Guidelines for the Application of Life Cycle Inventory Analysis to Solid Waste Management Practices— it was announced that the DoE intended to spend £850,000 over the next 3 years to support the compilation of a comprehensive, up-to-date database specific to waste management practices. There will inevitably be a lot of competition to access this pool of funding!

15.2.2 Impact Assessment

Impact assessment facilitates the interpretation and aggregation of inventory data into forms that are more manageable and meaningful to the decision maker. In simple terms, impact assessment serves to transpose the environmental burdens quantified at the inventory analysis stage (e.g., energy consumption, emissions to air and water) to *environmental impacts* (i.e., measures of environmental concern such as depletion of nonrenewable fossil fuels, contribution to global warming, or ozone layer depletion).

The desire to undertake an impact assessment will depend on the purpose and results of a given study. In a comparative study, if the results of an inventory analysis demonstrate that one product or system is better than another product or system across all considerations (i.e., consumes less materials and energy and gives rise to reduced emissions to air and water and solid waste), then the outcome is clear and there is no need to perform an impact assessment.

However, more commonly, one alternative will be better on some considerations but worse on others. In such a case, it is desirable to have an indication of what these results mean when one considers their transposition relative to given environmental concerns, such as impacts to global warming, depletion of nonrenewable resources, and ozone layer depletion.

Impact assessment allows the environmental burdens to be translated to potential environmental effects or impacts. Some argue one can take this further by ranking all impacts against each other to generate an *environmental score*. This approach is controversial and is discussed below under "Valuation."

The methodology for performing impact assessment is currently under development. The approach currently favored is a three-stage process: classification and characterization, normalization, and valuation.

Classification and Characterization.   In the problem-oriented approach, data in the inventory are aggregated according to the relative contributions made to a surveyable number of environmental concerns.

The problem-oriented approach generally incorporates a non-site-specific approach which classifies environmental impact on a global level to obtain a general worldwide classification independent of site-specific considerations. Potential impacts are quantified rather than actual impacts. Actual impacts are dependent on the site of production, i.e., actual concentrations and the sensitivity of the receiving environment.

The following environmental impact categories are generally included in an impact assessment:

- Resource depletion
- Greenhouse effect (direct and indirect)
- Ozone layer depletion
- Acidification
- Nutrification and eutrophication
- Photochemical oxidant formation

The following list includes environmental impact categories less well defined or used by only a few practitioners:

- Landfill volume
- Landscape demolition
- Human toxicity
- Ecotoxicity
- Noise
- Odor
- Occupational health
- Biotic resources
- Congestion

For each of the chosen environmental impact categories, potential impact factors (e.g., global warming potentials) are developed. These factors are used to facilitate the aggregation of a number of contributory environmental burdens into a single value.

Normalization. The effect scores defined above which are the result of the classification and characterization step are difficult to interpret because the order of magnitude and units differ. To overcome this problem, a final step in classification and characterization called *normalization* can be used, which makes the effect scores (classification results) more meaningful by relating them to the total emissions or extractions over a given period.

Valuation. *Valuation* is the assessment of the relative importance of the environmental burdens identified in the classification, characterization, and normalization stages by assigning weighting factors to them, allowing them to be compared or aggregated. There is increasing pressure to achieve a single value to enable the ranking of products and aid in the decision-making process.

The development of valuation methods is still in its early stages and fraught with controversy. It is unlikely that an entirely objective standard valuation method can be developed. Clearly there are as yet no objective criteria on which to decide whether one environmental concern is more or less important than another. It is a subjective choice between dissimilar parameters.

Impact Assessment in the Context of Solid Waste Management. The *treatment* of waste management LCA data is no different from that of conventional single-product or service system LCAs. Solid waste management life-cycle inventory data can be classified, characterized, and normalized; then, if one chooses, one can use weighting factors to yield a single value or score on the results.

Once again, all previous comments concerning the complexity of solid waste management LCAs are applicable with waste being considered as a collection of discrete but often intermingled used products which themselves can be composed of a wide variety of material types.

15.2.3 Improvement Assessment

This stage of LCA is invariably cited as being an integral part of LCA methodology, although, in reality, improvement assessment is what one does with the results. According to the BSI Technical Committee on Life Cycle Assessment, improvement assessment is not a part of the methodology which can be standardized since each and every application of LCA will vary. That being the case, there are no absolute rules to describe here; suffice it to say that one needs to have a clear focus at the outset of a study, or else the scope will shift continually which will increase the chance of making an error or employing an incorrect assumption dependent on the final scope of the application as reached.

15.3 PRESENTATION OF RESULTS

The results of an LCA are best presented in the form of spreadsheet(s) in combination with flow diagrams to facilitate the transparency of reporting, i.e., to ensure that third parties examining the data are able to elucidate the raw data values used as well as determine the precise system boundaries set and the calculation methods employed.

The latter considerations become particularly important if one wishes to use the results of an LCI (or LCA) study externally, e.g., in policy setting or marketing, where one might have the results validated by third-party verifiers in the form of a peer review.

Once a series of spreadsheets have been created, one can readily transpose the data to generate a wealth of graphs to assist in the process of interpreting the results.

A checklist of points for consideration in evaluating the usefulness of LCA reports and a checklist of points for consideration if one wishes to undertake or commission an LCA are given in Appendixes A and B, respectively.

15.4 APPLICATIONS OF LCA

Having gained an appreciation of what LCA is (and, by definition, what it is not), one is now ready to apply this newly gained expertise to assist in the process of managing environmental performance.

Types of application may include the following:

Internal uses:

- Set a benchmark of environmental performance.
- Identify opportunities to improve environmental performance.
- Set environmental targets for management systems.
- Evaluate product and process.
- Select environmentally preferable materials.
- Improve handling and distribution systems.

External uses:

- Back up marketing claims, using scientifically defensible techniques.
- Assist in defining the basis for legislation, standards, or policy.

Many issues surface when one seeks to carry out an LCA. In virtually all cases, the first major hurdle is data quality.

As far as possible, data should have sources that are specific to the product under consideration. In many instances, this is not possible, and data from other sources may be used, e.g., government and industrial databases, published literature, laboratory testing, engineering calculations based on process chemistry and technology, and estimates from similar operations. Data gathered for a particular operation should ideally be averaged over a reasonable time frame, commonly 1 year, to take account of atypical behavior or seasonal changes.

15.5 INTERPRETATION OF THE RESULTS

A detailed discussion of the results of LCA studies generated for solid waste management scenarios is beyond the scope of this chapter. However, it is clear that the solid waste management hierarchy is not fixed, and based on experience, in some cases there is a very clear argument for incineration with energy recovery over material recycling. It is dangerous to make generalized conclusions in this respect, and each scenario will yield its own results which may differ—even for studies which appear similar—depending on the assumptions made.

This emphasizes the need to exert caution when one is interpreting the results of LCA studies—a fact which causes much friction politically when people seek to use the results of LCA studies for marketing applications.

Let me make a plea at this stage! All processes and product systems have an impact on the environment. Use the results of LCA studies (and other environmental management tools) to quantify environmental impacts, to enable you to identify where to prioritize your efforts to minimize those impacts, e.g., through the implementation of an environmental management system. We should all remember that sustainability—both economically and environmentally—is where our attentions should be focused, not on trying to use the results of complex LCA studies to justify a market claim that might be easily challenged if aspects of the LCA studies were conducted in a slightly different way or under different assumptions!

15.6 APPLYING LCA TO WASTE MANAGEMENT SCENARIOS AND USING THE RESULTS TO SET POLICY OPTIONS

15.6.1 Software Tools and Databases

As indicated previously (Sec. 15.2.1), when one wishes to determine the relative environmental merits of waste management options by using an LCA approach, it is necessary to extend the system boundaries to include those activities which are avoided or displaced as a result of recycling or incineration with energy recovery. That being the case, applying the methodology of LCA to a mixed waste stream in which a range of scenarios are to be considered, including various rates of sorting, recycling, and/or incineration with energy recovery, is a horrendous task in terms of the calculation procedures to be employed.

To facilitate that task, a variety of software tools are available which contain the necessary formulas and algorithms to handle all the complex calculation procedures as well as provide baseline data to use in the calculations where the user is not able to provide site-specific data.

As with any software tool, each has its own strengths and weaknesses. Of the LCA software tools now on the market (there are approximately 10 at the time of this writing), only two (to the best of my knowledge) are set up specifically to deal with waste as the main material input. These are a software tool generated by Procter & Gamble and another software tool issued by Ecobilan, one of the world's leading firms of LCA practitioners, with its headquarters in Paris and offices in a number of other European countries as well as the United States.

The Procter & Gamble software comes in the form of one diskette issued with a book entitled *Integrated Solid Waste Management—A Life Cycle Inventory*. The book (together with diskette) is available for approximately £75 and is published by Blackie Academic & Professional, an imprint of Chapman & Hall. The software is relatively user-friendly and comes with a full database drawn from information and data in the public domain.

The other software tool differs from the Procter & Gamble software largely in terms of its sources of data and its ability to be adapted to a much greater number of complex scenarios (including the ability to generate bespoke scenarios, taking into account local, regional, or even national variations).

Unlike most other LCA practitioners, Ecobilan has been able to invest considerable sums of money to compile and refine its database. Accordingly, the data in the Ecobilan software are based on an enormous number of measurements taken on site throughout Europe. The Ecobilan data cover municipal solid waste as well as other "generic products" such as cars and electronic equipment. The Ecobilan data have been gathered specifically with their use in LCI and LCA applications in mind and are updated periodically. This contrasts with the Procter & Gamble software which, as stated earlier, has been taken from a wide variety of sources where—most importantly in the context of LCI and LCA—the data quality is largely unknown. Specifically one considers here issues such as the systems boundaries which the data relate to as well as the period of time which the data represent (e.g., average over 1 year versus steady-state conditions).

The different sources of data in the French software tool may in part account for its greater price (a license to use the ECOBILAN waste management software costs on the order of £5000), although experience shows that at the end of the day, it is access to those data deemed to have the greatest quality possible which demands a higher price, since this is where the value is realized in terms of generating results which represent as much as possible the real situation without having to instigate one's own data collection program.

15.6.2 Formulating an Environmental Policy Based on Results of LCA Studies

Formulating a strategy to facilitate improved environmental performance is a little bit like deciding which came first, the chicken or the egg. The reason is that to facilitate improved environmental performance, one needs to have a clear set of priorities against which one can measure performance—and invariably one cannot begin to define these until one has first a knowledge of what environmental impacts are associated with or attributable to a given product.

Presently, one can define two main approaches to set priorities. In both cases one is dependent upon the goals for environmental performance laid down in a policy. The first such policy is that laid down by virtue of environmental legislation, in other words, the government's strategy to achieve sound environmental performance.

While this seems logical and straightforward, there are number of limitations. Most notably, environmental legislation does not address every consideration dealt with typically in an LCA and—significantly—does not set limits relevant to environmental concerns (*environmental impacts* in the terminology explained above). The UK government's policy toward waste management in general is an obvious example of this, although it is encouraging to note that in the draft of Waste Strategy for England and Wales as well as in the EC Directive on Packaging and Packaging Waste, there is reference to the role of LCA in providing more informed data on which to amend and improve existing targets as laid down.

In general terms, environmental legislation seeks to control the release of given parameters which *contribute* to a given environmental concern, without taking into account the relationship of one contributing parameter to another. Also environmental legislation tends to address *releases* into the environment without due regard for setting limits for those *inputs* to a system which ultimately give rise to those releases.

Arguably, the most relevant UK legislation which one can use as a template against which to measure performance is/will be that encaptured in *integrated pollution control* (IPC) authorizations (where appropriate) for those prescribed processes described in the Environmental Protection Act of 1990.

In these instances, the most appropriate reference values against which to measure performance will be those values laid down in the appropriate *best available techniques not entailing excessive costs* (BATNEEC) guidance notes or, where different, the *best practicable environmental option* (BPEO) criteria as specified at an individual site level.

The second policy one can follow to achieve improvements in environmental performance is that in which one can define *bottom-up* based on the results of an initial LCA.

In this way, one uses the results to identify priority areas for improvement (preferably specified relative to given environmental concerns). Adopting this approach, one can still ensure that regulations for all areas governed by environmental legislation are complied with or exceeded beyond that which is necessary; but at the same time, one can build in that extra dimension of having an environmental policy which actually seeks to facilitate improvements relative to a series of environmental concerns. The latter may reflect the needs and wishes of one's customers as well as taking into account what can practicably be achieved with state-of-the-art technology over a defined period.

The latter approach is consistent with BS7750 or the EC Ecomanagement and Audit Scheme, although there are subtle differences which relate more to the scope of application and the definition of system boundaries which are outside the scope of this chapter.

At the end of the day, however, one has to realize that to facilitate improved environmental performance, it may end up costing money through an initial capital expenditure program. While there is no choice in this matter in the context of compliance with legislation, one should always seek to justify capital expenditure which is designed to tackle issues outside of those parameters which are legislated, from the viewpoint of what short- and longer-term savings can be achieved that will enhance overall efficiency and productivity.

If one takes this viewpoint, then in the vast majority of cases, one comes to appreciate that expenditure to facilitate improved environmental performance can be cost-effective if, at the same time, there is an improvement in efficiency as well as an opportunity to increases sales by meeting more of the needs of environmentally conscious customers.

Examples of cost savings may be through making more efficient use of valuable resources (e.g., by getting more into the final product and thereby diverting less ultimately into waste) and by achieving energy savings.

The ideal situation, then, is to improve environmental performance, to increase profitability, and to safeguard the environment for the benefit of those who will inherit it. Life-cycle assessment can play an essential role in this fulfilling these objectives.

15.7   *CONCLUSIONS*

In this chapter, readers have been introduced to the complexities of the environmental debate concerning the issues of solid waste management in the context of life-cycle inventory analysis and assessment.

The main conclusions reached are as follows:

1. Life-cycle inventory (LCI) analysis serves to quantify the consumption of raw materials and energy as well as releases to air, water, and solid waste for a defined system (theoretically from cradle to grave).

2. Life-cycle inventory analysis is the first stage of life-cycle assessment; the latter relates those parameters quantified at the inventory stage to measures of environmental concern, such as global warming or depletion of reserves.

3. Solid waste management practices are themselves processes requiring inputs of energy consumption and resulting in the generation of atmospheric emissions as well as discharges to a receiving water and solid waste for further disposal and processing.

4. Waste minimization at source is recognized most often to be the most common-sense approach to minimizing environmental impact associated with solid waste management practices.

5. To determine the relative advantages (or disadvantages) of waste management options requires an investigation of complete life cycles in which the potential advantages of recycling and incineration are balanced against those environmental burdens offset by the avoidance of the use of so much of the virgin material or energy source.

6. Life-cycle assessment is an effective tool for benchmarking environmental performance and can be used in comparative studies to determine the relative environmental advantages and disadvantages of products able to perform the same function.

7. LCA is being used *now* to assist companies to quantify and assess their impacts on the environment, to identify opportunities to minimize those impacts, and significantly to realize cost savings by making more effective use of available resources.

8. There is—presently—no universally accepted and scientifically defensible way of prioritizing environmental concerns!

APPENDIX A: CHECKLIST TO DETERMINE THE "USEFULNESS" OF LCI AND LCA REPORTS

To help readers determine the usefulness of LCI and LCA reports, the following checklist has been prepared:

- Who conducted the study?
- Who commissioned the study?
- What material types are considered?
- What product or service systems are considered?
- What functional unit(s) has (have) been used?
- How have the system boundaries been defined?
- Do the systems boundaries take into account the following?

- The manufacture and use of secondary packaging
- Precombustion energy
- Transportation
- Waste management
- Environmental burdens and impacts associated with ancillaries
- Heating and lighting
- Manufacture of capital equipment
- Maintenance of equipment

- Does the scope of the study encompass inventory analysis *and* impact assessment or only inventory analysis?
- What is the data quality? This will involve a determination of:
  - Source of data
  - Age of data
  - Representativeness of data
  - Precision of data
  - Measurement methods used
  - Calculation methods used
  - Methods used to fill data gaps
- Has sensitivity analysis been conducted to assess the data quality?
- Do the environmental burdens' masses balance (i.e., does the weight of material and energy sources—the "inputs"—equal the weight of the releases to air, water, and land—the "outputs")?
- Are the full reports available? If so, how transparent is the reporting (e.g., do the reports contain detailed flow diagrams, spreadsheets, and disaggregated data; and make clear how all aspects of the calculations have been undertaken, in particular with regard to the allocation methods used, impact assessment calculations, assumptions made, etc.)?
- Has the work been critically reviewed by one or more experts, a panel of interested parties, stakeholders?

APPENDIX B: CHECKLIST OF POINTS FOR CONSIDERATION IN CONDUCT OF LCI OR LCA STUDY

To assist the readers of this chapter who may wish to commission an LCI/LCA study, the following checklist has been prepared:

- What benefits are anticipated to be gained from conducting an LCA study?
- How will the results be used?
- Who will have access to the results, and how will those results be presented?
- What demands will be placed upon resources (financial/human) to conduct the LCI/LCA study?

Assuming the study is to proceed:

- Who will carry out the study?
- What material types will be considered?

- What product or service will be considered?
- What functional unit(s) will be used?
- How will the systems boundaries be defined?
- Will the systems boundaries take into account the following?
  - The manufacture and use of secondary packaging
  - Precombustion energy
  - Transportation
  - Waste management
  - Environmental burdens and impacts associated with ancillaries
  - Heating and lighting
  - Manufacture of capital equipment
  - Maintenance of equipment
- Will sensitivity analysis be conducted to assess the data quality?
- Will the scope of the study encompass inventory analysis *and* impact assessment or inventory analysis only?
- What demands will be placed upon data quality? This will involve a consideration of the:
  - Source of the data
  - Age of the data
  - Representativity of the data
  - Precision of the data
  - Measurement methods used
  - Calculation methods used
  - Methods used to fill data gaps
- Will the data included achieve a mass balance in relation to the environmental burdens included?
- What demands will be placed upon the writing of the reports?
- If the reports are to be made available to a wider audience outside the commissioning organization, how will the reports be structured and written (e.g., will the reports contain detailed flow diagrams, spreadsheets, and disaggregated data and make clear how all aspects of the calculations have been undertaken, in particular with regard to the allocation methods used and impact assessment calculations, assumptions made, etc.)?
- Will the work be critically reviewed by an expert panel of interested parties or stakeholders?

CHAPTER 16

INTEGRATING LIFE-CYCLE ASSESSMENT WITHIN AN OVERALL FRAMEWORK FOR ENVIRONMENTAL MANAGEMENT

B. De Smet
ENVIRONMENTAL QUALITY MANAGER
PROCTER & GAMBLE EUROPEAN TECHNICAL CENTER,
STROMBECK-BEVER, BELGIUM

P. R. White
SENIOR ENVIRONMENTAL SCIENTIST
PROCTER & GAMBLE LIMITED, NEWCASTLE UPON TYNE,
UNITED KINGDOM

J. W. Owens
SENIOR ENVIRONMENTAL SCIENTIST
ENVIRONMENTAL SCIENCES DEPARTMENT,
THE PROCTER & GAMBLE COMPANY, CINCINNATI, OH

16.1. INTRODUCTION

Life-cycle assessment (LCA) is a powerful and alluring concept, and understandably so. There are many reasons for its attraction and the level of attention that it has received in recent years, especially within Europe. Among environmental management tools, it possesses two unique attributes. First, it considers the whole life cycle of a product or service, from "cradle to grave." This broad approach differs from other environmental management tools which consider specific parts of the life cycle, such as the releases of individual chemicals, the environmental balances of particular manufacturing sites, or the contributions to a single environmental problem. The life-cycle approach can therefore help prevent "problem shifting," whereby a solution to one environmental problem leads to greater deterioration at another place or time in the life cycle. Second, the life-cycle approach allocates all the environmental burdens to the functional unit, i.e., to the *value* of the product or service to society. It is therefore possible to attempt a *value/impact* assessment[1,2] whereby the value (i.e., performance and cost) of the product or "service to society" can be balanced against its environmental burden.

The aim of this chapter is to place LCA in context. LCA is a new and rapidly evolving tool, and as such it still has many development opportunities which will be highlighted in this chapter. There is a fundamental need at this time to clarify what information an LCA tool can provide to help environmental decision making and what information either it cannot provide or is more effectively provided by other tools. The chapter sets out an overall framework for environmental decision making, using LCA results together with information from other tools, experience, and judgment. It looks at the applicability of this framework for internal use by industry as well as for broader societal decision making about the management of the environment.

16.2. USING LCA FOR ENVIRONMENTAL DECISION MAKING

16.2.1 LCA—What Does It Stand For?

So far, mostly industrialists and academics have been involved in the development of LCA as an environmental management tool. Governments and environmental organizations, even though important potential users of LCA results, have been much less involved. There appears to be a knowledge gap between these two groups. To help bridge this gap, the Society for the Promotion of Lifecycle Development (SPOLD) has begun a dialogue in Europe between LCA practitioners and potential users in society.[3] The work has revealed that this very different degree of involvement of environmental stakeholder groups can, in part, be explained by the fact that each is looking to LCA for different reasons and indeed understands different things from the term *LCA* itself (see box).

The broader group of potential LCA users sees LCA as the concept of holistic environmental management—the notion of considering all environmental aspects from cradle to grave. This includes a framework for organizing all data and information about a product's life cycle necessary for effective environmental decision making. It should contain information coming from a variety of environmental management tools, such as LCA, but also risk assessment, environmental auditing, and environmental impact assessment.

Most LCA practitioners will define *LCA* more narrowly as one specific measuring technique, especially useful for improving resource and waste management of industrial systems on a per-service basis. Here, LCA is basically a quantitative accounting tool of all resources used and wastes generated on a per-service basis.

Both interpretations are valid and relevant, but the scope of the first definition is much broader than the second. There *is* a need for an overall holistic approach to environmental management. It *would* be helpful, for both communication and management reasons, if the different elements and tools involved in managing the environment could be synthesized into one overall framework. The specific LCA measuring technique, as described by LCA experts, *does* provide unique information that would not be available otherwise and that is very helpful in effective environmental decision making. It is essential, however, to recognize that these two interpretations of LCA are different, and perhaps deserve their own specific terms. In this chapter we use the term *LCA* to mean the specific measuring technique, and we use the term *environmental management framework* (EMF) for the holistic, structured approach to integrating the tools.

DIFFERING INTERPRETATIONS OF "LCA"

ACCORDING TO LCA NONEXPERTS

LCA is a concept (taking a cradle-to-grave approach) that provides an organizing framework for overall environmental management.

- Includes use of a whole range of measuring techniques such as risk assessment, environmental impact assessment, and environmental monitoring.
- Referred to here as *environmental management framework* (EMF).

ACCORDING TO LCA EXPERTS

LCA is one specific measuring technique especially useful for assessing efficient resource use and waste management on a per-service basis.

- Some try to extend LCA to become an all-encompassing environmental management tool.
- Others consider LCA within an overall environmental management framework which includes the range of environmental management tools that are available (view taken by the authors of this chapter).

16.2.2   Using the Life-Cycle Inventory

The first two stages of a full LCA, *goal definition* and *inventory analysis,* together constitute the process of *life-cycle inventory* (LCI). LCI itself has been used as a tool for predicting the environmental burdens associated with particular products or services (Fig. 16.1). An LCI is an inventory of all the system inputs (in terms of resources,

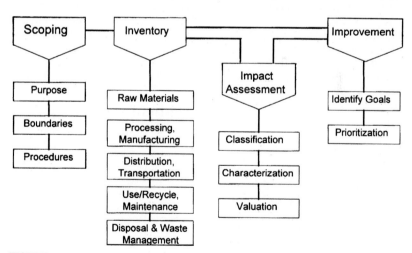

FIGURE 16.1   The structure of a full life-cycle assessment.

including energy) and outputs (in terms of emissions to air, water, and land) associated with providing a given service to society. LCI can therefore identify opportunities to optimize life cycles by the reduction of resource use and the production of fewer emissions (including solid waste). Several LCI tools have been produced for packaging materials[4,5] and are increasingly used. Recently, an LCI tool for solid waste systems has been developed, to help identify sustainable methods to manage society's solid waste in the future.[6]

At present, the greatest challenge to the production of life-cycle inventories is the gathering of sufficient high-quality data.[7] This involves two separate issues, data availability and data accuracy, which are discussed below.

Data Availability. Since it covers all processes in the life cycle, LCI is a data-intensive tool. Unfortunately, such data are generally not readily accessible, in many cases due to their commercial sensitivity. A second problem is data compatibility. To cover all stages of a life cycle, it is likely that many separate sources of data will need to be used. Since different sources often make different assumptions and do not use the same boundaries and definitions, this will commonly lead to data incompatibility. Then there is the further problem that since such data reflect continually changing and dynamic practices, the data will need regular updating.

Several activities are under way to address these data challenges.

To overcome the commercial sensitivity issue, many industrial sector associations are taking the initiative to develop and publish industry-averaged data for the basic materials they are producing. The Association of Plastics Manufacturers in Europe (APME), for example, has published cradle-to-gate data for most of the commonly used plastic resins,[8] and other industries have similar projects in progress. Data thus becoming available may not necessarily be compatible between different industrial sectors, but at least they will be compatible within the industrial sector.

The compatibility issue is also being addressed. Academic institutions and consultants have been actively building comprehensive databases, and several national governments have begun assembling compatible LCI data for their specific geographies.[7]

The Society for the Promotion of Lifecycle Development is currently attempting, in Europe, to coordinate all these diverse activities.[9] There is a need for independent, publicly available, and regularly updated databases for at least those data that are common to all LCIs (see Fig. 16.2). Such basic data modules will include energy generation, commodity materials, transport, and waste management. Several organizations have recognized this need, including SETAC[10] and the Groupe des Sages, a group of experts set up

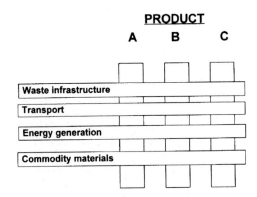

FIGURE 16.2 Some basic infrastructure data are common to most LCI studies. Data on areas such as commodity materials, energy generation, transport, and waste infrastructure could be used for a whole range of individual LCI studies.

to advise the European Commission on LCA.[11] Once such basic data are available, LCI should become a much more practical and easy-to-use tool, especially with the development of relatively simple LCI spreadsheet models running on desktop computers.

Data Accuracy. There is also the problem of data accuracy since much of the LCI information available has an associated level of uncertainty. Because so many individual data points are included in an LCI calculation, these errors will be propagated throughout the calculations and may markedly affect the accuracy of the final result. Sensitivity analysis is needed to give some indication of the reliability of the final calculated LCI result. Many current studies assume that differences in LCI results need to exceed 10 or 20 percent to represent real differences, but these are only rules of thumb. There is a need for research to gauge just how accurate an LCI result can be expected to be. The LCA working groups of the Society of Environmental Toxicology and Chemistry are currently addressing this issue.

16.2.3 Interpreting Life-Cycle Inventory Results

Many decisions about product improvements can be made on the basis of an LCI alone. However, since an inventory is a list of *all* the inputs and outputs of a product system, it is only possible to decide that option A is preferable to option B if option A has lower resource requirements and lower emissions of all materials than B. This is unlikely to occur. One approach to comparing different LCI inventories is to interpret their possible environmental effects by predicting the contribution of consumed and emitted energy and materials to a number of environmental impact categories. This process has been called *life-cycle impact assessment* (LCIA) (Fig. 16.1).

In principle, LCIA takes the aggregated material and energy consumption and emissions over the whole life cycle and converts them to *potential impacts,* using substance- and category-specific conversion factors. For example, all emissions considered as contributing to ozone depletion are aggregated on the basis of their *ozone depletion potential* (ODP) to give an ODP for the functional unit over the whole life cycle. A variety of environmental categories have been included in LCIA schemes, ranging from global issues such as climate change to local issues such as releases of odor and noise.[12] This method has been described as the *less-is-better* approach,[13] since it assumes that all emissions will cause effects, regardless of whether this is actually true. A linear dose/response relationship is assumed, and no account is taken of whether individual emissions surpass *no observable effect concentration* (NOEC) thresholds, i.e., whether any *actual* effects will occur. The basic methodology of converting aggregated mass loadings to potential impacts by means of generic weighting factors means that the spatial and temporal details of emissions (i.e., where, when, and how they are released) are not accounted for. Consequently, this approach cannot evaluate the likelihood of actual, measurable impacts on the environment, but instead provides a worst-case scenario. Thus the term *impact assessment* for this process is a misnomer, and it has caused confusion between practitioners of LCA and those of other tools such as risk assessment and environmental impact assessment, where the term *impact* implies an actual, measurable effect. To clarify this situation, it has been suggested that the term *inventory interpretation* be used for LCIA, since this is actually more descriptive of what is involved[13] (Fig. 16.3).

To assess the actual impacts likely to occur over the life cycle of a product or service, another approach is needed. The LCI can be used as a screening tool, to locate those parts of the life cycle which produce the most significant emissions. Other tools— most notably *risk assessment* (RA), *environmental impact assessment* (EIA), and *envi-*

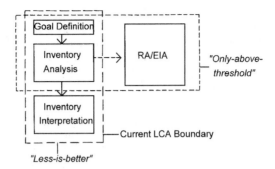

FIGURE 16.3 Two distinct approaches to life-cycle impact assessment. "Less is better" provides a worst-case scenario. "Only above threshold" predicts actual impacts.

ronmental monitoring (EM)—can then be used to predict the likely environmental concentrations and exposures that will result, to predict whether NOEC thresholds are likely to be surpassed, and to monitor the environment for actual effects. This method has been called the *only-above-threshold* approach,[13] since it concentrates on where thresholds are exceeded and actual effects occur, rather than considering every emission equally. Although it uses LCI data, it also relies on other tools, including RA, EIA, and EM, and goes outside the current boundary of LCA (Fig. 16.3).

Both approaches for assessing the likely impacts associated with a product's or service's life cycle can be of use. The less-is-better approach provides a broad macro analysis of the whole system and may provide insight into what is the more efficient way of providing a given service to society. It can be considered a "general tool for general answers" and can be useful in complex strategic comparisons such as between waste management systems or energy generation strategies. It can aid in selection of strategies that *on average* will produce decreased environmental burdens and may also be of use in the design phase of projects, where site-specific data are not likely to be available. However, since it considers a worst-case scenario and does not predict actual impacts, it could mislead future directions. In contrast, the only-above-threshold approach *can* predict actual impacts, and therefore it should be used in the assessment of actual product life cycles. It will identify real environmental improvements in specific product life cycles. The increased accuracy of this approach depends on detailed site-specific information for particular substances or activities, however, and this complexity limits its usefulness on a macro scale.

Both the less-is-better approach and the only-above-threshold approach to LCIA have their applications, advantages, and limitations. These need to be recognized so that the right tool is used for the right job. LCA, with its normal less-is-better approach, provides a macro overview of the system rather than a detailed analytical perspective. As such, it provides unique and useful information that would not otherwise be available, but it cannot predict actual impacts. In contrast, the only-above-threshold approach can predict actual impacts, but relies on the use of a range of other tools such as risk assessment, environmental monitoring, and environmental impact assessment, which lie outside the normal boundaries of LCA (Fig. 16.3). Both approaches are valuable. The next section introduces a framework for environmental management and shows how each most appropriately fits into overall environmental decision making.

16.3   AN OVERALL ENVIRONMENTAL MANAGEMENT FRAMEWORK

Environmental decision making is a complex process for both governments and indus-try, and it comprises many dimensions. However, it is no different from any other deci-sion-making process. It is necessary to define the overall objectives and the essential elements, to assemble and order the available data, and to integrate the information with both experience and judgment to come up with a final decision. A framework can be of considerable use to ensure that all dimensions of environmental management have been addressed and that none have been overlooked[14] (see Table 16.1).

The first requirement is an overall objective for environmental management. Consensus is building that this objective should be *environmentally and economically sustainable development.*[15] Economically sustainable development is essential to improve continuously the standard of living of the world's population. Environmental sustainability ensures that this is achieved without causing environmental deterioration in either this generation or future generations. For industry to contribute to both envi-ronmental and economic sustainability, it needs to embrace a broad approach to envi-ronmental management that goes beyond the traditional boundaries of the factory gates to consider all its interactions with the environment. All manufacturers, handlers, and users involved in the life cycle of a product share the overall responsibility for that prod-uct. The individual share of responsibility for each will vary in the different life-cycle stages, being greatest in the parts of the life cycle under their direct control and least in distant stages of the life cycle.

Such an approach to environmental management can be broken down into separate ele-ments, namely, (1) ensuring human and environmental safety, (2) ensuring regulatory com-pliance, (3) ensuring efficient resource use and management of wastes, and (4) addressing societal concerns (Table 16.1). The first two elements—safety and regulatory compli-ance—are prerequisites for doing business today. The third and fourth elements are emerg-ing business needs which will be important for the long-term success of a company.

Subsequent sections deal with each of the four elements individually and give exam-ples of the tools that can be used to support each one. While this framework has been based on the practice of environmental management within a company, it will be seen that all the elements and most of the tools are equally relevant to governments and other organizations, and to environmental management in general.

16.3.1   Human and Environmental Safety

The safety of products, packages, and operations to humans and the environment is of paramount importance to every manufacturer. Safety must be ensured during all stages of a product's manufacture, use, and disposal.

Safety can be ensured by using the well-established tools of *human health and eco-logical risk assessment* (Table 16.1). Human health risk assessments are performed to protect both workers at manufacturing sites and consumers in the home. Ecological risk assessments evaluate the safety of emissions from manufacturing plants and discharges from the consumer's home. The same basic approach is used in both human health and ecological risk assessments: Each requires an assessment of both exposure and effects (i.e., the level of a substance that comes into contact with a human or the environment and the level that could cause harm).

Products that are used and later disposed of by the consumer often contain many chemicals (natural or artificial), each of which represents a potential environmental risk

TABLE 16.1 Environmental Management—An Overall Framework

Goal	Elements of goal	Available tools
Environmentally and economically sustainable environmental management	1. Human and environmental safety	Human health risk assessment (occupational and domestic exposure) Ecological risk assessment (plant site and consumer releases)
	2. Regulatory compliance	Manufacturing site management system auditing Manufacturing site wastes* reporting (e.g., SARA, Toxics Release Inventory) Material consumption† reporting (e.g., Dutch packaging covenant) New-chemicals testing and registration Product and packaging classification and labeling
	3. Efficient resource use and waste management	Material consumption† monitoring and reduction Manufacturing site management system auditing Manufacturing site environmental auditing Auditing of major and new suppliers Disposal company auditing Product LCI Ecodesign Economic analysis
	4. Addressing societal concerns (i.e., understand, anticipate, and interact)	Understand and anticipate • Opinion surveys • Consumer and market research • Networking (antenna function) Interact: • Information through presentations and publications to key audiences‡ • Academic, policy, and industry work groups (e.g., think tanks, professional bodies, consultants) • Lobbying to influence future policy and regulations • Corporate reporting • Specific problem solving with others

*Wastes are emissions to air, water, and land.

†Material consumption is raw materials and energy consumption for product, packaging, and processing.

‡Key audiences are consumers, employees, retirees, opinion leaders, and legislators.

16.8

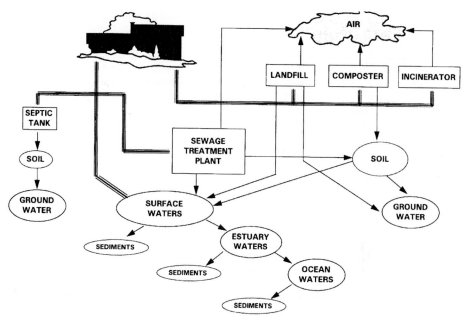

FIGURE 16.4   Products often contain many ingredients. Each needs to be considered separately in risk assessment. As an example, the various pathways that chemicals may take in the disposal of household products and which should be considered in a multimedia risk assessment are outlined.

(Fig. 16.4). Each chemical must be considered separately, because of its unique characteristics when released into the environment. Environmental processes (e.g., biodegradation) may also create new and different substances along the way. To predict exposure accurately, it is important to understand these processes, i.e., to know for how long and with how much of the chemical an organism will be in contact.

The other part of risk assessment concerns the harm that the substance may cause. A wide variety of organisms (e.g., fish, birds, plants) need to be studied to understand the effects that a chemical may have on the environment. Survival, growth, reproduction, and other sensitive ecological effects must be evaluated.

These different inputs then enable an adequate assessment of the associated risk. If the predicted exposure is expected to cause harm, the risk is deemed unacceptable. In that case, the risk must be reduced by limiting or substituting the use of the chemical. The safety margin will be considered adequate only if the predicted exposure is known to be significantly lower than effect levels.[16]

Often risk assessments are done in a tiered fashion.[17] An initial, screening-level assessment may use very conservative assumptions to estimate exposure and effect. Subsequent tiers will then contain more precise information, and assumptions will be replaced by more realistic data. For example, for some chemicals, predicted exposure data can be replaced with actual measurements taken from samples of soil, water, or air. This process is repeated until there is confidence that the assessment of safety is accurate.

By using a similar approach, human health risks are evaluated for workers in the manufacturing plant as well as for inhabitants of surrounding communities and for consumers in their homes. Exposure to the chemical and a wide range of possible effects to humans are carefully studied. Stringent safety margins are used to ensure that no harm will come from either the intended use of the product or reasonably foreseeable misuse. In manufacturing operations, risks can be managed with appropriate training in chemical handling, the use of protective clothing during production, and the provision of safety equipment. However, to ensure safety in the consumer's home, a manufacturer can only rely on carefully formulated products and clear instructions for their use.

This type of assessment relies on a vast amount of very detailed information, far beyond the information typically available in LCAs. Therefore, LCAs (LCI plus less-is-better approach) are not capable of risk assessment. Still, an LCI can provide very useful initial data which can subsequently be used in a risk assessment procedure (i.e., LCI plus only-above-threshold approach). For example, the LCI will identify those parts of the life cycle where the most important environmental loadings occur, hence priority areas for performing risk assessment.

16.3.2 Regulatory Compliance

Additional management systems need to be established as part of the internal environmental management activities, to ensure compliance with specific local and national regulations. These may vary considerably from country to country. Several tools are being used.

One example is *manufacturing-site management system auditing.* At regular intervals, the site's environmental management systems are reviewed and evaluated against criteria of excellence. An essential part of the auditing exercise is the documentation of compliance with relevant requirements and permits. Additionally—and fundamentally more important—there is the assurance that the systems in place do provide the capability for ongoing compliance and continual improvement.

Legislation may also require *manufacturing-site waste reporting* to ensure that emissions meet specific environmental or human health-related requirements or to encourage the reduction of emissions. Under SARA (Superfund Amendments and Reauthorization Act), the U.S. Environmental Protection Agency (EPA) compiled a list of over 300 chemicals. Releases of each of these chemicals need to be quantitatively reported to the EPA on an annual basis as part of the Toxic Release Inventory Program.[18] As these data become public information, a reduction in emissions is encouraged. Governments may also request *material consumption reporting.* For example, under the Dutch packaging covenant, industry reports the annual consumption of different packaging materials as well as progress in achieving reductions.[19]

Chemical substances are also the subject of regulatory compliance. Depending on the tonnage of the chemical sold and the countries involved, *registration of new chemicals* will require that physicochemical, toxicological, and ecotoxicological data be generated to compile a safety dossier. Existing chemicals are also reviewed periodically. Since the U.S. Toxic Substances Control Act (TSCA) was introduced in 1979, 38,000 of the 65,000 existing chemicals have been reviewed.[20]

16.3.3 Efficient Resource Use and Waste Management

This is the element where LCI and LCA (LCI plus the less-is-better approach) are particularly useful. To ensure real improvements, the use of resources and waste management needs to be monitored systematically throughout the whole life cycle of a product or service, to identify ways to increase efficiencies. This includes considering all environmental compartments that may be affected. The use of LCA and LCI hence ensures that any improvement in one part of the life cycle or in one environmental compartment does not cause a greater deterioration elsewhere.

Several other tools also contribute to this element of environmental management. All involve tracking and accounting for material and energy flows, each along a different dimension of the company's operation, and thus together they help optimize systems with different boundaries. For example, *material consumption monitoring and reduction* track and report materials as well as emissions to air, land, and water of individual production sites, of individual business entities, or of individual profit centers. This helps management to follow progress toward internally agreed improvement goals. The individual improvement performance data can also be analyzed to identify how and whether wastes can be "designed out" or otherwise reused. Such *ecodesign* activities provide a useful alternative to the use of end-of-pipe solutions.[21]

Once they are in place, it is necessary to ensure that plant tracking and monitoring systems continue to function effectively. This is achieved through *manufacturing-site management system auditing*. Audits are also used with suppliers, although these are usually less formal. Their objective is to ensure close cooperation between manufacturers and their suppliers to improve the overall environmental profile of products. Bringing the manufacturer, who understands the end product, together with the supplier, who knows the raw materials, often leads to developments with a better overall environmental performance.

Efficient use of resources and waste management will usually minimize costs and so reflect positively on the company's bottom line. The reverse is also true; sound *economic analysis* and management will continuously strive to identify inefficient use of resources, whether in projects, plants, or products. Hence, this is one area where sound environmental and economic management are, virtually always, mutually beneficial.

16.3.4 Addressing Societal Concerns

No company operates in a vacuum. Companies are but one small part of society. They need to understand the society they operate in as well as the people in that society to whom they sell. Because the different parts of any democratic society use political processes to express their views, cooperate, and decide on common rules, it is important for companies to understand and be closely involved in these political processes. Any company needs effective tools to identify and anticipate consumers' needs and society's concerns as they emerge. These concerns may come from government, opinion leaders, or society at large. Some will be data-based, but others may not be. Each of these issues or concerns will need to be dealt with by companies in an appropriate manner, regardless of the origin of these issues and regardless of whether they can be considered data-based. Companies must be prepared to engage in discussion and debate, the nature of which will vary from country to country.

The tools typically used in this area of environmental management are generally less clearly defined, yet fall into two broad areas: anticipation and understanding of emerging societal concerns and interacting with society to appropriately respond to concerns. *Opinion surveys and market surveys* provide an insight into the opinions and perceptions of people and help one to understand societal concerns. The unique value of broad market surveys is that they include the opinions of both the "silent majority" and vocal activists. Effective *networking* with key opinion leaders, scientists, and government officials, who often help frame and develop the public debate, will position the company at the heart of the political process.

Subsequent interaction of the company with the rest of society on specific concerns may take many forms but usually involves—at a minimum—the development and organization of appropriate data to improve understanding of the issue. This data-based information can then be shared in public presentations, in publications, and, to a limited extent, even in advertising. Sometimes, it may also involve active participation and cooperation in public policy, scientific, or industry working groups to find adequate solutions to specific real or perceived problems.

Effective interaction requires trust between the company and other social partners. Given the current suspicion of industry, government, and other organizations held by the general public, transparency and openness are key. Individual companies, and industries as a whole, are (within the limits of legitimate competitive concerns) becoming increasingly more open and informative about what they do in the area of environmental management and why they do it. The growing practice of *corporate environmental reporting* provides one way to start building this necessary trust.[22]

16.3.5 The Decision-Making Process

Any company must be able daily to make short- and long-term decisions on how to run its operations. The decision-making process will involve assimilating data from many different sources, but will also always involve experience and judgment. The framework, described above, has been developed to help guide this process of decision making by (1) indicating a decision hierarchy, (2) ensuring the systematic, appropriate use of the different tools that are available, and (3) making sure nothing is left out.

The framework suggests an existing decision hierarchy: Meeting safety and regulatory requirements are a must. Safety of consumers, workers, and the environment is ensured by the use of risk assessment methods. Once safety and regulatory compliance have been assessed and ensured, improvements in resource use and management of wastes will be stepwise and, in line with Total Quality Management (TQM) principles, continuous. Each opportunity must be considered on its merits, on a life-cycle basis. Every decision made will assess the information produced by the different tools used, taking into account the existing decision hierarchies. The final decision will be an amalgam of environmental and economic influences, since an environmentally improved product will only deliver that environmental benefit if it sells in place of a less environmentally desirable option.[1]

The framework may tend to underplay the important interactions which occur in practice between the different elements of environmental management and the tools that are supporting them. For example, the environmental performance of a manufacturing site will involve compliance auditing; waste reporting; and material consumption, waste, and energy consumption monitoring and reduction. The data for each of these activities will also largely overlap although the focus of the work will differ.

Just as with business and financial data, environmental data will be processed through the sieve of experience and judgment. Decision making is a complex operation. It will be extremely difficult—if not impossible—to reduce it to a single "expert system" that reduces a multitude of complex and often conflicting data to a single number. Effective decision making requires a flexible, well-balanced, and knowledgeable organization to meet the unique demands of each situation. This implies that environmental management involves flexible organizational structures which have overlapping and interwoven responsibilities to cover all facets of environmental management (see box).

A company operates as one part of society, and most environmental issues cannot be solved by one part of society alone. Therefore, environmental management is actually a responsibility that is shared by the company and its many partners (suppliers, customers, consumers, the government). Traditionally, companies have worked—by themselves—to satisfy consumers and shareholders, to comply with the existing laws, and to be compatible with public utilities such as sewage works. Recognizing the need for collaboration to achieve environmental improvements puts more emphasis on other emerging relationships, such as between customers and suppliers, or with waste managers, concerned interest groups, and others.

There are examples of effective shared-responsibility initiatives, especially in the waste management area. More and more systematic shared responsibility, based on increased trust between parties, will be needed for future environmental management. Suggested solutions to particular issues will require a science-based discussion prior to action, to ensure that all aspects are considered. Again, it is essential that proposed solutions to one problem not create or exacerbate other problems elsewhere.

PROCTER & GAMBLE'S ENVIRONMENTAL MANAGEMENT STRUCTURE

Careful management of the environmental safety of products and operations has been a hallmark of P&G for decades. As a large decentralized consumer products company, P&G has business sectors (soap, paper, food, etc.) with day-to-day responsibility for environmental safety. Each sector has a Professional and Regulatory Services (P&RS) group dedicated to ensuring human and environmental safety of products and processes.

In addition, three corporate groups support these sectors. The Environmental Science Department (ESD) is a resource center for basic science which develops procedures, data, and understanding that are used to make business decisions and to develop environmental risk assessments. The Product Supply Environmental (PSE) group within the Product Supply organization has direct responsibility for environmental auditing, measurement, and safety of operations in our manufacturing plants. Bridging these groups is Environmental Quality Coordination (EQC), which has responsibility for establishing overall policy, setting company goals, and measuring progress. Through the coordinated efforts of these three organizations, environmental safety and quality are ensured for each of our products, packages, and processes.

Environmental Science Department (ESD)

The Environmental Science Department is staffed by Ph.D. scientists and professional researchers. As a company resource, its role is to advance science and develop protocols for understanding and evaluating the environmental safety and impact of products and packages. It also conducts basic studies in toxicology, microbiology, and biodegradation.

Research papers from ESD scientists appear regularly in peer-reviewed scientific journals and are presented at regional, national, and international meetings. In 1993, P&G scientists presented technical papers at more than 50 conferences and symposia internationally. Worldwide, there are more than 150 employees in P&RS and ESD with responsibility for issues of environmental safety.

Product Supply Environmental (PSE)

Global, regional, and site Product Supply Environmental (PSE) professionals use Total Quality Environmental Management (TQEM) as their key tool in the effort to prevent pollution at P&G operating facilities. Worldwide, more than 250 employees are dedicated to ensuring compliance and delivering cost-effective results, with an emphasis on environmental safety, energy use, and waste. PSE employs a common set of worldwide standards and measures, which provide the framework for annual site audits. PSE is also engaged in a major pollution prevention effort which emphasizes process modifications, efficient use/recovery of waste materials, and efficient control of residual wastes.

Environmental Quality Coordination (EQC)

EQC works with more than 350 company contacts worldwide to help ensure that environmental practices are consistent in the 56 countries in which P&G operates. EQC also monitors national and international issues as they relate to the company's environmental policy and strategies.

16.4 CONCLUSIONS

The term *LCA* means different things to different people, depending on the specific questions of concern. Typically, LCA nonexperts consider LCA as a holistic concept for overall environmental management. In contrast, most LCA experts will apply a narrower definition of LCA as one specific measuring technique, especially useful for studying resource use and waste management on a per-service basis.

Both interpretations of the term *LCA* are equally valid and relevant. However, if not explicitly recognized, this difference can cause confusion and communication problems between stakeholders with different perspectives. LCA, when narrowly defined as one specific measuring technique, provides unique information that would not be available otherwise and that is very helpful in environmental decision making. However, it cannot form the sole basis for effective environmental decisions. This requires the use of an overall environmental management framework which combines, in the most appropriate way, information gathered from a whole range of measuring techniques, together with experience and judgment.

LCI, by itself, is a very useful tool. It provides a holistic life-cycle overview of all the resources used and wastes generated on a per-service basis. Because of this life-cycle perspective, LCI results can play more than one role in the overall framework. LCI results combined with a less-is-better approach provide useful insights into how to optimize resource use and waste management of industrial systems on a per-service basis. When combined with an only-above-threshold approach, however, LCI data can also be of use in subsequent human and environmental safety assessments for products, packages, and processes.

The environmental management framework discussed in this chapter puts LCA into context and shows how the technique can be most appropriately used as part of overall environmental management. It recognizes that environmental management, like business management, is complex and that the various issues are intricately interwoven. The framework has been developed to provide a means of structuring work processes and organizations to help ensure that the appropriate and necessary data are promptly and properly available for effective decision making.

REFERENCES

1. P. Hindle, P. White, and K. Minion, "Achieving Real Environmental Improvements Using Value: Impact Assessment," *Long Range Planning,* **26**(3): 36–48 (1993).

2. *Who Needs It? Marketing Implications of Sustainable Life Styles—A Sustainability Business Guide,* SustainAbility Ltd., London, 1995.

3. *LCA Social Dialogue Initiative—Summary of Workshop Outcome,* Society for the Promotion of Lifecycle Development (SPOLD), Brussels, Belgium, 1995.

4. P. White, P. Hindle, and K. Dräger, "Lifecycle Assessment of Packaging," in G. Levy (ed.), *Packaging in the Environment,* Blackie Academic and Professional, Glasgow, Scotland, 1993, pp. 118–146.

5. C. R. Hemming, *Directory of Lifecycle Inventory Data Sources,* Society for the Promotion of Lifecycle Development (SPOLD), Brussels, Belgium, 1995.

6. P. White, M. Franke, and P. Hindle, *Integrated Solid Waste Management—A Lifecycle Inventory,* Blackie, London, 1995.

7. B. De Smet and M. Stalmans, "LCI Data and Data Quality—Some Thoughts and Considerations," *International LCA Journal,* accepted for publication, vol. 1, no. 2, 1996.

8. APME/PWMI (Association of Plastics Manufacturers in Europe/Plastic Waste Management Institute), Dr. I. Boustead, *Eco-balance Methodology for Commodity Thermoplastics/Eco-Profiles of the European Plastics Industry,* Reports 1 to 6, APME, Brussels, Belgium, 1992 to 1994.

9. *LCI Database Initiative—Project Outline and Work Program,* Society for the Promotion of Lifecycle Development. A copy of the document can be obtained from SPOLD, Avenue Mounier 83, Box 1, B-1200 Brussels, Belgium.

10. F. Consoli, et al., *Guidelines for Life-Cycle Assessment: A Code of Practice,* SETAC-Europe, Brussels, Belgium, 1993.

11. H. Udo de Haes, et al., *Guidelines for the Application of Life-Cycle Assessment in the European Union Ecolabeling Programme,* SPOLD, Brussels, Belgium, 1994.

12. Society for Environmental Toxicology and Chemistry, *Life-Cycle Assessment—Leiden Workshop Report,* SETAC Europe, 1992.

13. P. White, B. De Smet, H. Udo de Haes, and R. Heijungs, "LCA Back on Track—But Is It One Track or Two?" *SETAC-Europe LCA News,* **5**(3): 2–4 (1995).

14. P. White, B. De Smet, J. Owens, and P. Hindle, "Environmental Management in an International Consumer Goods Company," *Resources, Conservation and Recycling,* **14:** 171–184 (1995).

15. World Commission on Environment and Development, *Our Common Future,* University Press, Oxford, 1987.

16. Commission directive 93/67/EEC, "Laying Down Principles for Assessments of Risks to Man and the Environment of Substances Notified in Accordance with Council Directive 67/458/EEC," O.J. L 227/9, 1993.

17. C. E. Cowan, D. J. Versteeg, R. J. Larson, and P. J. Kloepper-Sams, "Integrated Approach for Environmental Assessment of New and Existing Substances," *Reg. Toxicol. Pharm.,* **21:** 3–31 (1995).

18. Environmental Protection Agency, *US Superfund Amendments and Reauthorization Act,* EPA, 1986.

19. Nederland, Ministerie voor milieu. *Het Convenant Verpakkingen,* 1991.

20. Environmental Protection Agency, *Toxic Substances Control Act—Chemical Substance Inventory,* EPA, 1979.

21. G. A. Keoleian and D. Menerey, "Sustainable Development by Design: Review of Life-Cycle Design and Related Approaches," *Air & Waste,* **44:** 645–668 (1994).

22. United Nations, *Company Environmental Reporting,* United Nations environmental program's technical report, 1994.

CHAPTER 17

BEGINNING LCA: A DUTCH GUIDE TO ENVIRONMENTAL LIFE-CYCLE ASSESSMENT

N. W. van den Berg
G. Huppes
CENTRE OF ENVIRONMENTAL SCIENCE
LEIDEN UNIVERSITY
LEIDEN, THE NETHERLANDS

C. E. Dutilh
UNILEVER (VAN DEN BERGH NEDERLAND)
ROTTERDAM, THE NETHERLANDS

This chapter is a slightly revised version of a booklet published in February 1995 under the title *Beginning LCA: A Guide into Environmental Life Cycle Assessment*. The study was carried out under the auspices of the *National Reuse of Waste Research Program (NOH)*. Copyright of this chapter remains at NOH.

The chapter does not necessarily cover all the opinions on life-cycle assessment (LCA) in the Netherlands. Nevertheless, it probably reflects the main line of thought in that country, including the opinion of the officials. J. Suurland from the Dutch Ministry of the Environment and B. Hanssen of the Dutch Ministry of Economic Affairs wrote the preface to the original book. We quote from that preface:

> The product policy in the Netherlands is based on the principles of environmental life cycle management [...] The LCA method has been developed in the context of the National Reuse of Waste Research Programme of the Netherlands (NOH). The NOH has also commissioned the production of this easy-to-use manual, aiming at a wider use of the LCA method by companies. This manual is the result of a cooperation between the Leiden University, a major contributor to the scientific development of the LCA methodology, and Unilever, a large company which has acquired considerable experience in the implementation of that technique. In our view, this unique combination of expertise provides a good basis to make a manual on how to execute an LCA yourself.

17.1 INTRODUCTION

About This Chapter

In recent years, attention to environmental problems has increased, and as a result, analytical tools have been developed. These include environmental management systems, waste reduction schemes, and environmental analysis methods such as life-cycle assessment (LCA).

This chapter describes LCA for beginners and provides the basic instructions required to conduct an LCA. It shows what can be done with the instrument and when other tools are required.

LCA is a systematic way to evaluate the environmental impact of products or activities by following a "cradle-to-grave" approach. This approach implies the identification and quantification of emissions and material and energy consumptions which affect the environment at all stages of the entire product life cycle.

The possible reasons for executing an LCA include, for example,

- To depict, in as detailed a way as possible, the interaction of a product or activity with the environment
- To ensure thorough insight into the interdependent nature of the environmental impacts of a human activity
- To supply decision makers with information on the environmental impacts of activities and the possibilities for improvement

Until now, LCA has been used only by experts and scientists, mainly due to the complex nature of the analysis, but gradually LCA should become a more generally applicable tool. For instance, an LCA can be conducted for similar reasons and in a similar way to product costing, where everyone knows why and how to do it.

This chapter introduces LCA as a way of thinking, i.e., in a step-by-step approach which allows the reader to start executing an LCA without delay.

In summary, the main goal of this chapter is to provide practical guidance for those who want to start an LCA.

The Structure of This Chapter

This chapter is divided into sections which can be read separately. While working with it, you will soon discover that the LCA process is an iterative one where you move continuously forward and backward between preceding and following sections. The sections themselves have been set up in an instructive way, each consisting of the following items:

- A short description of the section's content
- Starting point
- Approach, stating the instructions to be followed
- Suggestions and precautions where appropriate
- The type of results expected
- How to proceed—a description of the next step
- Example

The structure of this chapter is as follows:

Section 17.2 provides arguments to decide whether LCA is the right tool to use in a particular case. In this section, other ways to study interactions with the environment will be mentioned as well.

Section 17.3 explains the process of formulating the purpose and scope of the study. The results will give a general picture of the characteristics of the LCA. The next step, which is called the *inventory analysis,* represents the largest amount of work and is split up into four parts, i.e., Secs. 17.4 to 17.7.

Section 17.4 gives guidelines and detailed examples of how to construct a flowchart of the study. Section 17.5 describes how to collect the required data, and Sec. 17.6 how to define the system boundaries. Finally, the processing of data is described in Sec. 17.7. The result of the inventory is a list of emissions and extractions for all processes involved in manufacturing and required for the functioning of a product, service, or activity during the entire life cycle.

Sometimes results are so clear that you may decide to stop after the inventory stage. Usually, however, it is useful to carry out the impact assessment, which is split into two parts (Secs. 17.8 and 17.9). Instructions are given on how to translate the list of environmental interventions of the entire life cycle of the product to a table with scores on environmental themes: the classification and characterization. A basic substance list that might be used is added (Sec. 17.8). Also a description showing how to evaluate the results of the classification and characterization is given, so that conclusions may be drawn from the information that has been generated (Sec. 17.9).

Section 17.10, the last section, describes how to complete the LCA. It provides suggestions on how to present the results and indications about the improvement analysis.

How to Proceed and for Further Reading

After finishing this chapter, you may want to do a more comprehensive LCA, in which case more advanced documents are available that may be used as a reference for more skilled practitioners:

- The Centre for Environmental Science of Leiden University, the Netherlands, developed, in cooperation with other institutes, a method to gather and process all the environmental data on a product's life cycle (Heijungs, 1992). This document will be further referred to as the *CML Guide.*

- The Society of Environmental Toxicology and Chemistry (SETAC) has held a workshop on LCA, which produced *A Code of Practice* (Consoli et al., 1993).

   This chapter on beginning LCA follows the rules stated by SETAC in *A Code of Practice.*

17.2 POSSIBLE APPROACHES TO ENVIRONMENTAL QUESTIONS

When a study concerning the environmental aspects of an activity or product is started, you should realize that several, very different methods are available. The choice between these depends on the questions you want to answer. Selecting the right tool can save a lot of time. For that reason this section will explain what can be expected from LCA and what cannot.

Starting Point: A Short Introduction to LCA Principles

Environmental life-cycle assessment deals with the environmental impacts of a product in its entire life cycle. It summarizes all environmental effects to generate a certain function. A *life cycle* consists of all the processes related to the functioning of a product, from the extraction of raw materials through the production and use of the product to the reuse and disposal of all final waste (including the discarded product itself) and the final production waste. The environmental impacts through the entire life cycle are formed by all the extractions from the environment and emissions into the environment.

LCA allows the comparison of different products with the same function by providing a systematic framework to gather the environmental interventions. You may think of using plastic pipes instead of metal ones, glass bottles instead of cans, fibers instead of steel cables, or transport by train instead of by car. When you are redesigning a product, existing products can be compared with the newly designed ones.

In some cases, you may want to identify environmentally dominant stages of the life cycle. For instance, most of the environmental impacts of electric lightbulbs are caused by the electric energy consumption during use. This observation may imply that you have to concentrate on the using phase for the most effective environmental improvements.

When to Use LCA

LCA provides a systematic framework which helps to identify, quantify, interpret, and evaluate the environmental impacts of a product, function, or service in an orderly way. It is a diagnostic tool which can be used to compare existing products or services with each other or with a standard, which may indicate promising areas for improvement in existing products and which may aid in the design of new products.

When Not to Use LCA

LCA cannot make decisions related to the location of a building or an activity. In that case, *environmental impact assessment* (EIA) is more appropriate. Nor can LCA answer questions related to the life cycle of a substance; *substance flow analysis* (SFA) should provide an answer.

LCA is not the tool to evaluate the environmental impacts of a company or a production location. For that purpose the *environmental audit* would be appropriate, although it may use elements similar to LCA. Also environmental improvements related to only one single process would not be evaluated by an LCA but with a process technology study. LCA does not provide answers to risk-related questions; in that case, *hazard* or *risk assessment* should be applied. Neither do LCA studies cure environmental problems, although a process change or technology development can be evaluated with the help of LCA. In redesigning your product, options should be provided by technical experts whereafter these changes can be compared as to their environmental impact by an environmental LCA.

Approach

1. State the relevant questions now that you know some more about the possible applications of LCA.
2. Check whether LCA is the proper tool to answer these questions.

How to Proceed

Move on to the next section if the information in this section has indicated that LCA is the right tool to answer your questions or problems.

Summary: When to Use LCA

- To compare the environmental impacts of different products with the same function
- To compare the environmental impacts of one product with a reference or standard
- To identify the environmentally most dominant stage in a product life cycle and hence to indicate the main routes to environmental improvements of existing products
- To help in the design of new products or services
- To indicate strategically the direction of development

Summary: When Not to Use LCA and What Else to Use

- Not to answer specific environmental questions regarding locations. Instead use environmental impact assessment.
- Not to answer questions related to one substance or resource. Instead use substance flow analysis.
- Not to answer questions related to the environmental impacts of a company. Instead use environmental audit.
- Not to answer questions related to a single production process. Instead use a process technology study.
- Not to answer risk-related questions. Instead use specific hazard or risk assessment.

17.3   GOAL DEFINITION

A very important step in carrying out an LCA is the goal definition. It is rewarding to spend some extra time to define clearly all relevant aspects, as this will help to direct efforts on the main issues.

In the goal definition, both the subject and the scope of a study are defined to determine for what purpose the outcome can be used. In fact, the goal definition provides information on the organization of a study and serves as a reference to the results. Initially a goal may be defined rather quickly. When, in the course of the study, more insight has been gained, it may be worthwhile to consider the goal definition.

Approach

To define adequately the goal of a study, the following issues need to be defined:

1. The purpose of the LCA—what do we want to know?
2. The initiator and the target group—for whom are the results meant?
3. The subject of the study—which product or function is studied?
4. The scope of the study—what is the level of detail and reliability required?

1. Purpose of the LCA.   At this stage, you should identify which types of question you want to answer.

- Do you compare products, or do you want to relate your product to a standard (as in ecolabeling)?
- Are you planning to improve a product environmentally, or are you going to design a completely new product?
- Do you want strategic questions to be answered, related to the place of your company in the market?
- Do you simply want information on your product?

2. The Initiator and the Target Group.   It is important to know who has initiated the study and for whom it is meant. It is, for example, relevant to identify whether a study is meant for internal use only or that results will be made public via government, consumer organizations, or marketing. Studies meant for external target groups usually need more elaboration and more extensive evidence than internal studies.

3. Subject of the Study.   A specification of the subject to be studied is needed. This specification would answer the questions, Which product? What amount of it, during which time span, and which function is relevant? Where appropriate, items like packaging materials and consumer behavior are also described.

Often an LCA will be carried out only on the manufacturing part of a single product. In such cases, any amount can be chosen. However, it will be convenient to choose a large unit, such as 1 metric ton or one pallet, which will make the numbers easy to handle. When you are comparing different products, a description of the function of these products should be added so that equivalent products and amounts are compared. In the SETAC *Code of Practice* and the *CML Guide,* this is a description of the *functional unit.*

Now, define the subject of your study, bearing in mind that a proper description of product and quantity, without any other information, is only sufficient when studying one single product or when improvements only relate to the production phase. When you are comparing products with the same function, a definition of this function is necessary. Subsequently, you need to identify the consequences of such a definition for the product description.

4. Scope of the Study.   You should identify the level of detail required for the application of the results, remembering that the results of this study can never be more accurate than your input allows. Therefore, in this section, you should think of the level of detail required regarding, for instance, spatial and temporal representation.

The questions to be answered include

- Did the product change a lot during the last decades?
- Has the means of production changed substantially?
- Does the means of production vary from country to country?

The outcome of such considerations can largely affect the kind of sources you may want to consult for information: Can you look for generic data, or do you need to find very specific information?

In practice, it is recommended that you spend relatively little time in formulating the scope if you start a new LCA. Experience in gathering information may force you to reconsider and adjust the scope formulation.

Suggestions and Precautions

- Try to clarify the questions, e.g., What exactly do I want to know and why? In which way will the depth of the study influence the outcome? Which function is to be chosen for comparisons?

- Return from time to time to the goal definition when executing other sections and adjust where necessary.

- Do not spend too much time dealing with uncertainties. Just flag these and make a note, or try to cover entire ranges by choosing best and worst cases. The latter approach is also useful for getting a feeling for sensitivities.

- At this stage it would be convenient to consider several functional units, as the same initial data can often answer different questions.

- The goal definition is meant to give an overview of the premises of the study. When there is no overview at the first stage, try to formulate things very briefly and roughly and adjust afterward, where necessary.

- When you are (re)defining the subject of the study, it is important to realize that, on one hand, the functional unit should be large enough to simplify calculations, in order to enable the choice between alternatives and to allow generalizations to be made; on the other hand, the functional unit should be detailed enough to enable the identification of relevant differences.

Example of goal definition I

We produce matches and want to quantify the environmental impact of this product. The subject under study can be defined as *one match* or *1 kg of matches*. We should also indicate how to include packaging materials such as boxes, plastic covers, and one-way pallets. The subject of the study could therefore better be *one pallet of packed matches.*

If it is intended to compare the function of matches with the function of lighters, it is relevant to define the function which is shared by both products, e.g., lighting cigarettes, which may make the functional unit of the study *the lighting of 1000 cigarettes.*

Example of goal definition II

We want to compare two different kinds of paint: water-based paint and organic solvent-based paint. The relevant parameters include the amount of paint needed to cover the object, the expected duration of protection, the way of removing the used paint, and maintenance. Therefore we define the protecting function of the paint, taking into account all aspects, as a *1-m^2 painted surface over 20 years.* In most cases this does not relate to equal amounts of paint.

Results

The result of this section is a text which describes the subject and organization of the study. All choices that have been made should be clearly specified.

Example. Throughout this chapter, an example will be elaborated, regarding the comparison of four different margarines for bread. The goal definition is as follows:

Purpose. For four different margarines an LCA will be carried out to identify differences between alternative products and to point out common areas with major environmental impacts, in order to find the most efficient improvement options.

Initiator and Target Group. This study is an internal exercise, carried out by Van den Bergh Nederland, a manufacturer of spreads. The study has been initiated by the development manager in order to identify improvement options, the results of which are to be discussed with the marketing department.

Subject of the Study. The subject under study is specified in the functional unit *1 kg packed spread.* As a first approximation, all spreads are considered to have the same physical performance. Also, differences in the behavior of consumers of the four various products will be neglected.

The same spreading behavior is assumed; therefore the products can be compared on a weight basis, leaving bread out of the analysis. (Here, these assumptions are flagged, in order to be checked afterward for their possible impact on the final results.)

Scope of the Study. As this is the first time an LCA will be carried out, we do not yet impose restrictions. Any data source seems to be useful at this stage, because we do not know of major changes in the manufacturing of raw materials or products in the last decade. Therefore, even old handbooks can be used. We expect the results to be generally valid. At this stage we decide to consider packaging materials as waste, which appears during the consumption of the spread. We will not consider emissions to water or cleaning operations at the end of the sewage system.

Quality of the Data. At this stage it is not apparent whether a clear distinction can be made between all four spreads. However, because the products have a high similarity, data need to be as detailed as possible.

How to Proceed

When the goal definition has been completed, continue the study by executing the inventory. This means drawing up a process flowchart (Sec. 17.4), collecting data (Sec. 17.5), and constructing system boundaries (Sec. 17.6), sections which should be gone through iteratively. As a result of the inventory, you may wish to go back and modify the goal definition.

For Further Reading

If further information about the goal definition is required, read chapter 1 of the *CML Guide,* especially section 1.3.4 for more information on the functional unit and section 1.2 about the scope of the study.

17.4 INVENTORY PART 1: PROCESS FLOWCHART

The inventory forms the core of LCA and will consume most of the time. It has been split up into four parts: the process flowchart (Sec. 17.4), collection of data (Sec. 17.5), the system boundaries (Sec. 17.6), and finally the processing of data (Sec. 17.7). These steps describe the gathering and processing of the environmental interventions, which appear during the life cycle of a product or service. This section introduces the first part—the process flowchart. It is recommended that you read all sections dealing with the inventory before the execution, as this is an iterative process where you may have to repeat several stages.

The process flowchart forms a qualitative graphical representation of all relevant processes involved in the life cycle of the system studied. It is composed of a sequence of *processes* (represented by boxes), linked by *material flows* (represented by arrows). It is recommended that this definition be used consistently. The main goal of the process flowchart is to create an overview: You should focus on the most relevant processes and environmental interventions rather than strive for 100 percent coverage.

Starting Point

The starting point for a process flowchart is usually the product formulation and the manufacturing condition, on one hand, and information on the consumption (the use) and waste stage, on the other hand. The ingredients and processing steps for the product should be screened: What are they composed of? How are they made? Which services are delivered?

Approach

1. Start the process flowchart with the manufacturing process of the main product.
2. Add the previous and following stages (resources, components, consumption and waste).
3. Combine processes or subdivide where appropriate.
4. Flag unfamiliar processes.

1. Start the Process Flowchart at the Manufacturing Process of the Main Product. Think of the manufacturing process of your own product first. Put this in the center of your process flowchart, and identify relevant processing steps and major material flows.

2. Add the Previous and Following Stages. The complete life cycle, in which the product fulfills its function, has to be followed. Therefore extend the process flowchart with the processes which appear before and after the manufacture of the product under study. On one hand, this will consist of the extraction, manufacturing, and processing of raw materials and components. On the other hand, you will add the use of the product by consumers as well as the recycling and processing of all wastes. Sometimes, especially when you produce a product for different purposes, it is necessary to choose which application of your product will be followed. Also, a process flowchart should indicate where by-products are generated or where recycle loops appear.

3. Combine Processes or Subdivisions Where Appropriate. Usually, various boxes can be combined into one or two boxes in such a way that they can be more easily handled. You can, for example, integrate all transactions of one company into one single block. You will discover that the complexity of a process flowchart largely depends on the way in which data can be obtained. Keep in mind that you should concentrate on those steps that generate the largest environmental impacts. Of course, when you are starting an LCA, this may be difficult, but you will discover that it becomes simpler as the study progresses.

4. Flag Unfamiliar Processes.   Flag those processes that are unfamiliar to you and for which no information can be obtained. Make a note or mark the process in your process flowchart.

Suggestions and Precautions

- Particularly, in this initial stage, try to get a broad view without going into detail. Reduction can take place at a later stage.
- The flowchart is only a model of reality; hence you may draw it up as you wish. For instance, it could help to arrange your flowchart so that it matches your information sources.

Results

The outcome of this section is a graphical representation of the subject under study. In principle, a process flowchart should start at the extraction of materials from the environment, either by a mining step or by agriculture, also including the inputs and their productions. A flowchart ends up with emissions and final dumped waste. In between, all processes involving material upgrading and material use should be shown.

Note: Depending on your goal definition, you will need either a comprehensive flowchart with relatively little detail or a limited flowchart, focusing on a few processes with much more detail.

How to Proceed

After constructing an initial process flowchart, you may start to collect data (see Sec. 17.5). During the collection you may discover that some process steps need to be detailed further because no general information can be obtained. However, remember to concentrate on those steps that are expected to contribute or, at this stage, are suspected of contributing most to the environmental impacts.

For Further Reading

For further reading you are directed to section 2.1 of the *CML Guide,* "Drawing up the process tree."

Example.   In Fig. 17.1 the process flowchart for fat spreads is shown. Spread production consists of a mixing step, followed by a filling step. The main raw materials are oils and fats, milk components, and packaging materials. No detail is shown in any of the process blocks. In the lower part, consumer behavior and waste processing are shown.

Two specific areas are marked—(1) packaging production and (2) spread production. The arrows represent transport processes, either internal (within a factory) or external (between sites).

Now the intention is to gather data for these blocks from suppliers. If they cannot provide any data, it will be necessary to let them specify the underlying steps of the blocks and to find out further data with the help of handbooks or other literature.

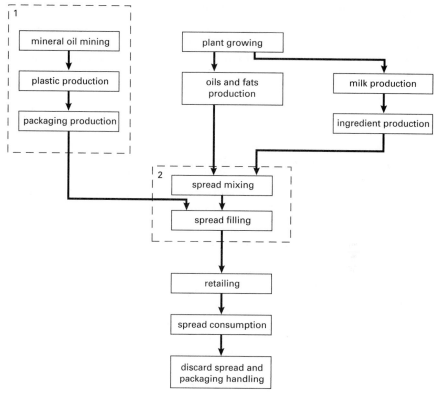

FIGURE 17.1   Process flowchart of fat spread.

17.5   *INVENTORY PART 2: COLLECTION OF DATA*

This section is the second part of the inventory, which is an iterative process: You will go through each of the steps of the inventory several times until the result is suitable for the purpose of the study. This section deals with the collection of data.

In Sec. 17.4 you learned how to describe processes in a process flowchart. In this section you will learn which data need to be collected; also some practical guidance is given on how to collect that information. In Sec. 17.6 you will learn how to define the boundaries of a study.

The collection of data is a time-consuming business, as it deals with many processes and many items per process and because the appropriate data usually are not readily available. Other parties need to be involved, who mostly have only limited interest in the outcome of the LCA or, even worse, who may feel threatened by such studies. Much effort should be spent in informing such parties of the purpose of the study and the way in which results will be handled. Honesty and candor usually score the best.

You should ask for information on physical mass flows or services, regarding the inputs of the processes as well as emissions, defined by their names and expressed in sensible units.

Starting Point: Which Data Do You Need?

In Sec. 17.4, the process flowchart was constructed. Each box in the chart represents a particular process or cluster of processes. For each process, or cluster, you need to collect information on two types of input and output flows: environmental and economic. Figure 17.2 gives examples of these.

	Inflow	Outflow
Economic	Raw materials (e.g. steel), services (e.g transport) energy input (e.g. electricity)	(Semi)final products by-products and waste
Environmental	Mined or grown raw materials (e.g. energy carriers, plant materials, water)	Emissions to air and water (e.g CO_2 or BOD) and solid waste dumped

FIGURE 17.2   Schematic representation of both economic and environmental inflows and outflows.

Approach

1. Choose or design a questionnaire or data information sheet.
2. Collect the data.
3. Check the gathered data for consistency.

1. Questionnaire or Data Information Sheet.   At the data collection stage, a lot of information is gathered. You need to store all the information in a systematic way, so that you can easily retrieve it and trace its origin. A standard information sheet may facilitate this job. An example is shown in Fig. 17.3.

2. Collect the Data.   Relevant data can be found in many places, but it will need some creative thinking to identify the simplest approach. Remember that consultation with others always takes time, especially when they have only limited, or even no, interest in collaborating.

Suggestions.   A substantial part of the data can be found in the literature. Sources of information include

- Standard documents or other literature
- Environmental statistics
- Environmental licenses
- Technical encyclopedia

ENVIRONMENTAL DATA SHEET

PROCESS:		DATE:		

MASS BALANCE

RAW MATERIALS INPUTS	kg/1000 kg	OUTPUTS (Products and solid waste)	
		Main product: By product(s): Solid waste:	1000 kg
AIDING COMPOUNDS INPUTS	kg/1000 kg	REMARKS	

ENERGY INPUTS

ENERGY SOURCES	kg/1000 kg	GJ/1000 kg	REMARKS

TRANSPORT DATA

TRANSPORT ACTIVITY (data per 1000 kg main product)	MEANS (truck. rail. ship)	DISTANCE km	CHARGE SIZE (tonnes)

ENVIRONMENTAL DATA

EMISSIONS TO AIR	kg/1000 kg	REMARKS
EMISSIONS TO WATER	kg/1000 kg	REMARKS
EMISSIONS TO SOIL	kg/1000 kg	REMARKS

DATA SOURCE

FIGURE 17.3 Model for standard information sheet.

- Internal information on processes in your own company
- Manufacturers' associations may have generic information or literature
- Actual or potential suppliers (you are advised to contact these sources through the purchasing department)
- LCA conducted elsewhere or published databases, like the BUWAL Reports (Habersatter, 1991), and ETH data (Frischknecht et al., 1993).

3. Check the Data. As soon as new information is received, it is important to check whether the data are complete and whether they correspond with other sources.

A possible way of checking data is to draw up simple balance sheets for each process, considering the fact that the total input of a process should equal the total output, including emissions and waste:

$$\Sigma \text{ input} = \Sigma \text{ output} + \Sigma \text{ emissions and waste}$$

Such a balance may be based on product mass, but also on a specific element, such as a carbon balance. You will discover that balances never reach 100 percent, but they give some indication as to where and how deviations have their origin.

Suggestions and Precautions

- Save time by planning. Start as soon as possible with the collection of data. This takes most of the time, as it not only contains the largest work volume, but also depends on the cooperation of other parties.
- It is useful to make estimates beforehand, as this could give you a feel for the matter and enable you to find missing data.
- Do not ask for too much information, as it may delay the response or even turn off your respondent. The reduced substance list in Table 17.1 indicates the main substances you could start to ask for.
- When sending out questionnaires, you should keep in mind that most suppliers are unfamiliar with LCA and may easily misinterpret your questions.
- Always remember that the reliability of the final result will depend on the quality of the data. It does not make any sense to get accurate figures for small effects if major contributions can only be estimated.
- In the collection stage, unfamiliar substances may come up. Mark these, just as you flagged unfamiliar processes in Sec. 17.4, step 4.
- Pay attention to the generation of waste because this is to be processed later. If data about the waste treatment processes are not available, quantify the amount of waste and register the way in which it is being processed.
- To avoid mistakes, it is recommended that calculations always be done with the same unit, such as kilograms of emission per 1000 kg of product, and using exponential notation such as 3.5×10^{-6} kg or 3.5E−06 kg.

Remark: Human toxicity should be split into air, water, and soil. In Table 17.1 only one value is mentioned.

Results

The execution of this section results in a growing pile of data sheets, and growing insight regarding the availability of information.

TABLE 17.1   List of Most Common Substances and Their Impact on Various Environmental Themes*

Score: Units: SUBSTANCE NAME	ADP (-/kg)	EDP (MJ/kg) (MJ/m³)	GWP (kg/kg)	POCP (kg/kg)	AP (kg/kg)	HT (kg/kg)	ECA (m³/kg)	ECT (kg/kg)	NP (kg/kg)	ODP (kg/kg)
2-Propanol (isopropanol or $CH_3CHOHCH_3$)						0.022				
Acetylene				0.168						
Acrilonitril (CH_2CHCN)						23				
Ammonia (NH_3)					1.9				0.35	
Ammonium (NH_4^+)						0.02			0.33	
Benzene				0.189		3.9	2.9E+04			
Cadmium (Cd)	1.9E−09					580	2.0E+08	1.3E+07		
Carbon dioxide (CO_2)			1.0							
Carbon monoxide (CO)						0.012				
Chemical oxygen demand (COD)									0.022	
Chlorobenzene (monochloro-benzene; C_6H_5Cl)						5.7		1.0E+06		
Chroom(vi) (Cr^{6+})						4.7E+04				
Dichlorodifluoro-rmethane (CFC12 or CCl_2F_2)			7.1E+03			0.022				1.0
Dinitrogen oxide (N_2O)			270							
Halon 1202 (bromotrifluoro-methane; CF_3Br)										1.3
Hydrogen sulfide (H_2S)						0.78				
Hydrocarbons (C_xH_y)				0.377						
Lead (Pb)	1.3E−11					160	2.0E+06	4.3E+05		
Mercury (Hg)	1.8E−07					120	5.0E+08	2.9E+07		

TABLE 17.1   List of Most Common Substances and Their Impact on Various Environmental Themes*
(*Continued*)

Score: Units:	ADP (-/kg)	EDP (MJ/kg) (MJ/m³)	GWP (kg/kg)	POCP (kg/kg)	AP (kg/kg)	HT (kg/kg)	ECA (m³/kg)	ECT (kg/kg)	NP (kg/kg)	ODP (kg/kg)
Methane (CH_4)			11	0.007						
n-Hexane (hexane or C_6H_{14})				0.421						
Nitrate (NO_3^-)						9.9E−03			0.1	
Nitrite (NO_2^-)						0.26			0.13	
Nitrogen (kjeldahl nitrogen or N)									0.42	
Nitrogen oxide (NO_x)					0.7	0.78			0.13	
PCB (average)							4.0E+08			
Phosphate (PO_4^{3-})						4.8E−04			1.0	
Pyrene						1.7	7.5E+06			
Styrene (vinyl benzene or $C_6H_5CHCH_2$)						0.15				
Sulfur dioxide (SO_2;SO_x)					1.0	1.2				
Trichloromethane (chloroform or $CHCl_3$)			25			3.3	1.7E+05			
Copper (kg)	2.9E−12					0.24	2.0E+06	7.7E+05		
Tin (kg)	2.3E−10					0.017				
Zinc (kg)	6.8E−12					0.033	3.8E+05	2.6E+06		
Crude oil (kg)		42.3								
Natural gas (m³)		35.7								

*A more comprehensive list can be found in the *CML Guide,* annex B.

Abbreviations:

ADP	Abiotic depletion potential, relative to the worldwide stores
EDP	Energy depletion potential, equals energy content
GWP	Global warming potential, relative to 1 kg CO_2
POCP	Photochemical oxidant formation, relative to 1 kg ethylene
AP	Acidification potential, relative to 1 kg SO_2
HT	Human toxicity, relative to 1-kg human body
ECA	Ecotoxicity, aquatic, relative to 1 m³ polluted water
ECT	Ecotoxicity, terrestrial, relative to 1 m³ polluted soil
NP	Nutrification potential, relative to 1 kg PO_4
ODP	Ozone depletion potential, relative to 1 kg CFC-11

How to Proceed

When sufficient data are available, you can continue either by specifying the boundaries in Sec. 17.6 or by processing the data as described in Sec. 17.7.

Example. Various information sources are available for the processes related to the manufacturing of fat spreads. The manufacturing data should be obtained from Van den Bergh itself. Fortunately, for vegetable oil milling and processing, a lot of information is available within Unilever, the mother company. (Otherwise one would have had to search the literature.) Information about the agricultural stage can be obtained from government consultants.

Information on minor ingredients will be requested from suppliers, but this causes great difficulty as they are not familiar with these sorts of questions. On packaging, the BUWAL database (Habersatter, 1991) will be consulted. Finally, for information regarding the behavior of consumers, the internal marketing department will be consulted. In Fig. 17.4 an example is given of data found for soybean growing.

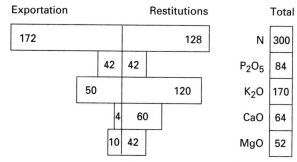

FIGURE 17.4 Detailed information on fertilizer use in growing soybeans. (*Source: Cetiom, La Culture du Soja, Paris, 1991.*)

17.6 INVENTORY PART 3: SYSTEM BOUNDARIES

This section is the third part of the inventory, which is an iterative process: You will go through each of the steps several times until the result is suitable. This section deals with the exact specification of the system boundaries.

In Sec. 17.4 you structured the process flowchart, and in Sec. 17.5 you started to collect relevant data for every process step. Therefore, you now have some insight into the critical processes which must be included in the LCA and the availability of data. That understanding, together with the objectives as stated in the goal definition, will allow you to define the system boundaries, thus defining the limits of your LCA.

Starting Point

To define the system boundaries, you need the (preliminary) results of the three preceding sections—the goal definition, the process flowchart, and the data collected. With these elements you can determine which parts need either less or greater detail.

Approach

1. Define the boundary between the system under study and the environment.
2. Define the boundary between the system under study and other interrelated systems, and subsequently allocate the various effects, if necessary.
3. Define the boundary between relevant and irrelevant processes.

1. Boundary between the System under Study and the Environment.   In Sec. 17.2 you learned that environmental LCA deals with the environmental impacts of a product during its entire life cycle. In principle, this environmental load is formed by all the extractions from the environment, and emissions into the environment, which arise during the entire life cycle. Therefore, ultimately, each LCA inventory should specify these extractions and emissions.

2. Boundary between the System under Study and Other Interrelated Systems. Many processes generate several different products, by-products, or functions in coproduction, recycling, or waste processing. Two cases are distinguished:

1. Sometimes you will have to attribute the environmental impacts of a process to two or more products. For instance, for cattle, milk as well as meat is generated. When dealing with one of these products, you have to define how to allocate the environmental interventions of cattle breeding between the various products. This procedure is known as *allocation,* and it can be conducted along different lines, e.g., mass, commercial value, or energy content. It is carried out by adding all the masses (in the case of mass allocation) of the different products and dividing the relative contribution accordingly.

2. Another situation exists in the production of reusable waste. When metal parts are produced, scrap metal is generated which is reused as a raw material for the production of iron. The commercial value of scrap is slightly positive so that you may cut the flowchart at the point where the reusable waste appears. In this particular case, the one who processes the waste will be held responsible only for the environmental impacts that appear during the processing. In cases where the value represents a substantial share of the total revenue, an allocation should be performed, as described above. In the latter case, the reusable waste is a coproduct.

3. Boundary between Relevant and Irrelevant Processes.   You have to decide how far you want to extend your study: What should be included and what not? This subject is determined, on one hand, by the scope of your study and, on the other, by pragmatic considerations. In other words, you will have to choose whether processes need to be considered. Too much detail costs a lot of time and mostly does not have a substantial effect on the outcome of the study. For instance, the production of capital goods such as machines or buildings (used in the manufacturing of goods) is usually ignored because the environmental impacts of these processes are relatively small when compared to the impacts during the complete life cycle of a product. Also, you may end up going round in circles when delving too far into details. For instance, the production of electricity requires steel; but in the production of steel, electricity is needed. The choice between relevant and irrelevant processes should also be determined by the purpose as defined in the goal definition. Some general rules, based on previous experience, are given under "Suggestions and Precautions."

Suggestions and Precautions

- At this stage, check your flags made in the previous sections. Also register and rejustify all your decisions.

- Transport and packaging should always be included.

- The production of capital goods, used during the manufacturing of goods, usually can be ignored, especially if the contribution from capital goods is similar for the systems compared.

- As a first approximation, concentrate on those processes which represent most of the cash flow or added value and on those processes dealing with notorious chemicals such as chlorine or mercury.

- Allocation is usually carried out according to mass or commercial value. When dealing with a process which produces more than one product or function, you are advised to check both ways of calculation, to see whether there is a major difference in the results. If so, flag this as a point of concern in the evaluation stage (Sec. 17.9).

- Often, it is not possible to obtain a complete set of data as specific information on processes or substances may be missing. Especially in waste processing (incineration, landfill), emission data may be unknown or difficult to allocate to specific wastes being processed. In any case, flag them as a point of concern and make estimates on their relative influences.

Results

As a result of this section, you will have a completed process flowchart in which you have indicated, with arguments, which parts are included and which parts are not:

- A description of how the boundary between environment and the system has been set up—which kind of emissions and extractions will be taken into account

- A description of how the boundary with other interrelated systems has been defined in cases of coproduction, recycling, and waste processing and a motivation in the exclusion of processes

- A description of processes where data are lacking and which are expected to have major influences

How to Proceed

After completion of this section, the collection of data can be continued. When the process boundaries are described and sufficient data have been collected, continue with the next section—the processing of data.

Example. The process flowchart of fat spreads (Fig. 17.1) starts with the agricultural stage in which fertilizer and pesticides are being used. The contribution of the manufacturing of these materials is assumed to be negligible compared to the application stage. Fat spreads contain oils and fats, obtained from oil seeds. It is assumed that, in almost all cases, the environmental impacts of the entire agricultural stage should be allocated to the vegetable oil. Only for soybeans is the market value for seed protein high; so in that case, the environmental impacts will be allocated between the oil and soybean protein fractions. Nonfat ingredients, except milk protein, will be excluded due to a lack of information. It is assumed that this limitation will not seriously affect the outcome of the study, because of the low concentration of these components. In the consumption phase, only packaging waste and nonconsumed material will be included. Human consumption is excluded because it is considered that it causes a low environmental impact. For packaging, all those aspects are included which are dealt with in the BUWAL database (Habersatter, 1991).

All assumptions mentioned here need to be flagged and evaluated in the end.

17.7 INVENTORY PART 4: PROCESSING DATA

This section is the fourth and last part of the inventory, which is an iterative process: You will go through each of the steps several times until the result is suitable. This section deals with the processing of data.

In Secs. 17.5 and 17.6, you learned how to obtain data and how to decide which parts of the process flowchart should be included in the inventory and which left out. In this section you will learn how to process the data in such a way that calculations can be carried out.

The first step is the transformation of all data to a convenient form. Examples of convenient data forms will be given. Subsequently, calculations can be carried out. Initially, such calculations can be done by hand, but at some stage, you may prefer to use a computer program. In this section we assume that you do not have a computer program. For those who are interested, a survey of available programs is given in Chap. 3.

Starting Point

Data processing usually starts when the data gathered give a reasonable coverage of the system under study.

Approach

1. Transform the gathered data to a convenient form.
2. Calculate the specific amounts of the components used in your system.
3. Add the environmental impacts for the system, thus creating an inventory table.

1. Transform Gathered Data to a Convenient Form.   Often, responses will be incomplete or contain irrelevant information. In the ideal case, you should have information for each process step on the nature and quantity of each environmental impact. If this is not the case, at least you should gather, per component, the amount of energy used and qualitative and quantitative information on raw materials used and by-products generated. Try to find information about the waste—its nature, volume, and way of processing. Put all data into a standard form. An example of such a form is given in Fig. 17.3.

2. Calculate the Specific Amounts of All Components Used in Your System.   Now that you have a proper set of data sheets, allocated where necessary, you can do some calculations. First, for every process (every data sheet), find out the relative contribution to the system under study.

3. Add the Environmental Impacts For the System.   After quantification of all the relevant processes, gather the amounts per substance, add these, and put them in a table, the *inventory table*. For instance, all the emissions of CO_2 are identified for the whole system; subsequently add them and put them in the inventory table as x kg CO_2, emitted by the system as a whole. Put all emissions in the same table.

Example.   As an example, we construct an inventory table for the production of bean oil, of which the process flowchart is shown in Fig. 17.5. In Figs. 17.6 to 17.10, the relevant environmental data sheets are shown, whereafter the combined tables are given (Fig. 17.11*a*). See also Fig. 17.1 for the place of the oils and fats production in the complete cycle.

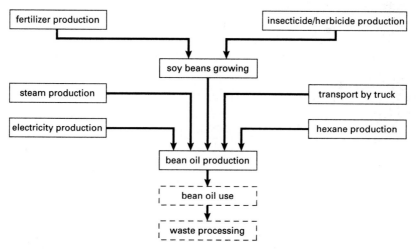

FIGURE 17.5   Process flowchart for the production of soybean oil.

In Figs. 17.6 to 17.10, examples of environmental data sheets for individual processing steps involved in soybean oil production are given.

Contributions from production of fertilizer, insecticides and herbicides, as well as from solvent hexane are neglected for the time being, as they were estimated to be of minor influence. Note that this assumption has to be checked in the evaluation stage.

Environmental impacts of soybean oil use and waste processing have been excluded as well. To simplify further calculation, all impact data are combined in one spreadsheet, which is shown in Fig. 17.11*a* to *c*.

How to Calculate.   The production of 1000 kg of soybean oil needs 175 kWh of electricity. The data we obtained from our electricity supplier relate to 1 kWh of electricity. In calculating the environmental impacts of 1000 kg of soybean oil, for the electricity part these will be based on 175 times the data which were given for 1 kWh of electricity.

ENVIRONMENTAL DATA SHEET

PROCESS:	SOY BEAN GROWING:	DATE: 21-09-'93

MASS BALANCE

RAW MATERIALS INPUTS	kg/1000 kg	OUTPUTS (Products and solid waste)	
Soy bean seeds	30	Main product: Soy beans By product(s): Residue of the plant (used as fertilizer) Solid waste:	1000 kg pm

AIDING COMPOUNDS INPUTS	kg	REMARKS
Fertilizer: N	99	
PO_4^{3-}	28	
K_2O	56	
CaO	21	
MgO	17	
Insecticides	12	Various compounds
Herbicides	1.65	Various compounds

ENERGY INPUTS

ENERGY SOURCES	kg/1000 kg	GJ/1000 kg	REMARKS	
Diesel fuel	13.87	0.58		

TRANSPORT DATA

TRANSPORT ACTIVITY (data per 1000 kg main product)	MEANS (truck, rail, ship)	DISTANCE km	CHARGE SIZE (tonnes)	

ENVIRONMENTAL DATA

EMISSIONS TO AIR	kg/1000 kg	REMARKS
	45.3	
	0.01	
	0.0046	
	0.071	
	0.32	
Particles	0.015	

EMISSIONS TO WATER	kg/1000 kg	REMARKS
Fertilizer: N	99	It is assumed that all fertilizers
PO_4^{3-}	28	insecticides and herbicides go to
K_2O	56	water as emissions. Of course this
CaO	21	is a worst case approach
MgO	17	
Insecticides	12	
Herbicides	1.65	

DATA SOURCE

CETIOM 1991. La Culture du Soja. Centre Technique Interprofessionel des Oléagineux Métropolitains, Paris 1991.

FIGURE 17.6 Environmental data sheet for soybean growing.

ENVIRONMENTAL DATA SHEET				
PROCESS:	STEAM PRODUCTION:		DATE: 22-03-'93	
MASS BALANCE				
RAW MATERIALS INPUTS	kg/1000 kg	OUTPUTS (Products and solid waste)		
Natural gas	68.4	Main product: By product(s):	Steam	1000 kg
		Solid waste:	Industrial waste	0.24 kg
ENERGY INPUTS				
ENERGY SOURCES	kg/1000 kg	GJ/1000 kg	REMARKS	
Natural gas	68.4	3.45		
ENVIRONMENTAL DATA				
EMISSIONS TO AIR	kg/1000 kg		REMARKS	
CO_2 CO C_xH_y NO_x SO_2 Particles	162 0.04 2 0.5 0.14 0.001			
EMISSIONS TO WATER	kg/1000 kg		REMARKS	
Oil	0.0025			
DATA SOURCE				
BUWAL. 1991. Oekobilanz von Packstoffen.BUWAL. Bern. 1991				

FIGURE 17.7

Results

The result of this step is the inventory table for the system studied—a list of environmental interventions, caused by the functional unit.

How to Proceed

If the purpose of the LCA is to compare two or more products or investigate a product improvement process, then evaluations can usually be made on the basis of the inventory table. However, if there are major differences in the various impact parameters, or if you want to relate the environmental interventions to environmental themes, you should continue with Sec. 17.8 (impact assessment, part 1), in which you will learn how to perform a classification and characterization step.

ENVIRONMENTAL DATA SHEET

PROCESS:	TRANSPORT BY TRUCK:	DATE: 15-04-'93

MASS BALANCE

RAW MATERIALS INPUTS	kg/15000 kg.km	OUTPUTS (Products and solid waste)	
Diesel fuel	0.205	Main product: Load performance of a 15 tonnes truck over 1 km a highway. fully loaded	15000 kg.km
		Solid waste:	

ENERGY INPUTS

ENERGY SOURCES	kg/15000 kg.km	GJ/15000 kg.km	REMARKS
Diesel fuel	0.205	0.00857	

ENVIRONMENTAL DATA

EMISSIONS TO AIR	kg/15000 kg.km		REMARKS
CO_2	0.81		
CO	0.002		
C_xH_y	0.0013		
NO_x	0.012		
SO_2	0.00088		
Liquid particles in air	0.0008		

DATA SOURCE

CBS 1990. Various report from the dutch centre for statistics (Centraal Bureau voor de Statistiek)

FIGURE 17.8

The contribution of each process has to be adjusted, by using a contribution factor, to represent the relative contribution of a particular process to the production of 1000 kg of soybean oil. Contribution factors can be obtained by dividing the input figures in the data sheet for soybean oil production by the output figure on the respective environmental data sheet. For instance, for 1000 kg of soybean oil, we need 5000 kg of soybeans; whereas the data sheet for soybean growing amounts to 1000 kg of beans. The contribution factor is calculated as 5000/1000 or 5. When all the environmental impacts have been multiplied by their contribution factors, the totals for all impact parameters can be calculated.

Note that in this case there is a valuable by-product, 4000 kg of soybean meal. Therefore, the totals of the inventory table have to be divided between oil and meal—the allocation step. In this case we choose to base the allocation on commercial value. Assume that the value for soybean oil per kilogram is 3 times higher than the value for soybean meal. The relative contribution for soybean oil can be calculated by dividing the relative value for soybean oil (1000×3) by the relative value of both products (1000×3 + 4000×1), which makes 3/7. The figures shown in Fig. 17.11c represent the inventory table for soybean oil production.

ENVIRONMENTAL DATA SHEET

PROCESS:	ELECTRICITY PRODUCTION:	DATE: 23-04-'93

MASS BALANCE

RAW MATERIALS INPUTS	kg/kWh	OUTPUTS (Products and solid waste)		
Various fuels (Dutch fuel mix for electricity production)		Main product: By product(s):	Electricity	1 kWh
		Solid waste:	High Risk waste Industrial waste	1.7E-06 kg 7.0E-07 kg

ENERGY INPUTS

ENERGY SOURCES	kg/kWh	GJ/kWh	REMARKS
Various fuels		0.00908	

ENVIRONMENTAL DATA

EMISSIONS TO AIR	kg/kWh		REMARKS
CO_2	0.625		
CO	2.9E-05		
C_xH_y	0.000053		
NO_x	0.0012		
SO_2	0.00078		
Liquid particles in air	0.000025		

DATA SOURCE

CBS 1990. Various report from the dutch centre for statistics (Centraal Bureau voor de Statistiek)

FIGURE 17.9

17.8 IMPACT ASSESSMENT PART 1: CLASSIFICATION AND CHARACTERIZATION

Impact assessment is a tool for relating the outcome of an inventory analysis to environmental themes. Usually the inventory process generates a long list of substances, which may be difficult to interpret, especially when you are comparing products. Environmental impacts caused by different products may be of a different nature, which will further complicate the interpretation.

Classification and characterization are a calculation process in which each impact parameter of the inventory table is converted to a contribution to environmental themes. Generally, the following environmental themes are considered: abiotic depletion and energy depletion, global warming, human toxicity, ecotoxicity (aquatic and terrestrial), acidification, nutrification, ozone depletion, and photochemical oxidant formation. A description of these themes is given on page 17.32. Classification and characterization end up with a list of up to 10 figures instead of hundreds of specific emissions. A more

---

ENVIRONMENTAL DATA SHEET

PROCESS:		BEAN OIL PRODUCTION:		DATE: 18-05-'93	

MASS BALANCE

RAW MATERIALS INPUTS	kg/1000 kg	OUTPUTS (Products and solid waste)			
Soy beans	5000	Main product: By product(s):	Bean oil Soy meal	1000 kg 4000 kg	
		Solid waste:			
AIDING COMPOUNDS INPUTS	kg/1000 kg	REMARKS			
C_6H_{14} (Hexane)	3				

ENERGY INPUTS

ENERGY SOURCES	kg/1000 kg	GJ/1000 kg	REMARKS
Steam Electricity	1200 175 kWh/ton		

TRANSPORT DATA

TRANSPORT ACTIVITY (data per 1000 kg main product)	MEANS (truck. rail. ship)	DISTANCE km	CHARGE SIZE (tonnes)
Incoming cargo: Soy beans	truck (diesel. highway)	200	

ENVIRONMENTAL DATA

EMISSIONS TO AIR	kg/1000 kg	REMARKS
C_6H_{14} (Hexane)	3	

DATA SOURCE

Unilever 1991. Internal Unilever reports

FIGURE 17.10

comprehensive survey of environmental themes can be found in the *CML Guide,* chapter 3.

In this section you learn how to perform the conversion by hand, using a reduced list with classification factors. It is obvious that, at some stage, you may prefer to do this process with the help of a computer program.

Remark: According to SETAC nomenclature, the name for this part of the impact assessment is classification, on one hand, which represents the choice of environmental themes considered, and characterization, on the other hand, which represents the transformation from substances to numbers. The *CML Guide* does not distinguish between these two and only talks about classification.

Process	Product outline	Energy Re-sources (GJ)	Emissions to Air (kg)							Emissions to Water (kg)									Solid Waste (kg)	
			CO_2	CO	C_xH_y	NO_x	SO_2	Part-icles	Liq. part. in air	C_6H_{14}	CaO	Herbi-cides	Insecti-cides	MgO	Nitro-gen	Oil	PO_4^{3-}	K_2O	High risk	Indus-trial
Soybeans growing	1000 kg	0.58	45.3	0.01	0.0046	0.071	0.33	0.015			21	1.65	12	17	99		28	56		
Steam production	1000 kg	3.45	162	0.04	2	0.5	0.14	0.0012								0.025				0.24
Electricity production	1 kWh	0.0091	0.625	2.9E-05	5.3E-05	12E-05	7.8E-05		2.5E-05										1.7E-06	7.0E-07
Transport by truck	15.000 kg.km	0.0086	0.81	0.002	0.0013	0.012	8.8E-04		8.0E-04											
Bean oil production	5000 kg									3										

FIGURE 17.11(a) Combined table for all impact data in the production steps of soybean oil.

Process	Contribution factor excluding allocation	Allocation factor on commercial value	Contribution factor including allocation
Soybeans growing	5000 / 1000	3/7	2.14
Steam production	1200 / 1000	3/7	0.51
Electricity production	175 / 1	3/7	75
Transport by truck	5000•200 / 15,000	3/7	28.6
Bean oil production	1000 / 1000	3/7	0.43

FIGURE 17.11(b) Contribution factors, including allocation on commercial value.

Process	Contribution factor	Energy Resources (GJ)	Emissions to Air (kg)										Emissions to Water (kg)						Solid Waste (kg)	
			CO$_2$	CO	C$_x$H$_y$	NO$_x$	SO$_2$	Part-icles	Liq. Part. in air	C$_6$H$_{14}$	CaO	Herbi-cides	Insecti-cides	MgO	Nitro-gen	Oil	PO$_4^{3-}$	K$_2$O	High risk	Indus-trial
Soy beans growing	2.14	1.24	97.2	0.021	0.01	0.15	0.71	0.032			45.0	3.54	25.7	36.4	212		60	120		
Steam production	0.51	1.77	83.3	0.021	1.03	0.26	0.07	0.001								0.0013				0.123
Electricity production	75	0.68	46.9	0.0022	0.004	0.0009	0.0058		0.0019										0.00013	0.000052
Transport by truck	28.6	0.25	23.1	0.057	0.04	0.34	0.03		0.023											
Bean oil production	0.43									1.29										
Total		3.95	250.5	0.101	1.08	0.75	0.81	0.033	0.025	1.29	45.0	3.54	25.7	36.4	212	0.0013	60	120	0.00013	1.0.12

FIGURE 17.11(c) Inventory table for 1000 kg of soybean oil, including allocation on commercial value.

Starting Point

To do the classification and characterization, you need an inventory table, as produced in Sec. 17.7, and a substance classification list. Initially, it is recommended that you use the list of most common substances shown in Table 17.1. A more extensive list can be found in the *CML Guide*.

Approach

First, identify those environmental themes that are relevant for your study. On page 17.32 a short description of common themes is given. You are advised to include all themes in those cases where no specific restrictions have been formulated in the goal definition. Solid waste is often mentioned separately, for instance, when data on waste processing are lacking.

Now take the inventory table and multiply each of the impact parameters by the corresponding weight given in Table 17.1 (characterization step). Note that one substance can score under more than one theme simultaneously!

The simplest way to do the characterization step is to create a new matrix in which you put all environmental interventions from the inventory table on the horizontal axis and the themes on the vertical axis. For each environmental theme, do the following: Multiply the amounts of the interventions by their equivalency factors, thus completing the columns of the matrix. Add the columns, to get the total score for each environmental theme. Repeat this for all the environmental themes. If relevant, add a description of the qualitative environmental aspects of your study.

Example. In Table 17.2 we execute the classification and characterization for 1000 kg of soybean oil, using the inventory table obtained in Sec. 17.7 (Fig. 17.11). First, the totals for each substance from the inventory are repeated. Next, the classification factors for all substances which appear in the example of soybean oil are given. Subsequently, the substance amounts are multiplied by the classification factors and added in the extreme right column of the lower part. All results are shown in Table 17.3. These results are further treated in Table 17.3 for a normalization step.

Explanation of Classification Process on Calculation of Human Toxicity Factor. Five of the substances on the inventory table have a score for human toxicity: SO_2, NO_x, CO, phosphates, and insecticides. Herbicides are used as well, but their classification factors are not known. The classification factors are given for each of these known substances: 1.2 kg human toxicity per kg SO_2, 0.78 kg human toxicity per kg NO_x, and 0.012 kg human toxicity per kg CO. For herbicides the scores are unknown, and for insecticides a range between 1.2 and 12 is assumed. By multiplying the amount of NO_x with its classification factor, the score is (0.75 kg)(0.78 kg/kg), or 0.59 kg human toxicity, which represents the characterized score for human toxicity, concerning the emission of NO_x. In the same way, the score for SO_2 is derived; multiplying 0.81 kg by 1.2 kg/kg gives 0.97 kg human toxicity. For CO, the score is 0.101 kg times 0.012 kg/kg, or 0.0012 kg human toxicity. Finally, the scores for herbicides are shown as a flag, and the score for insecticides is multiplied by a range which gives 30 to 300 kg human toxicity. In the extreme right column of the lower part, the total score for human toxicity is shown, which equals 30 to 300 kg human toxicity.

Explanation of Table for Theme of Acidification. In the same way, the scores for other themes can be derived. This example shows what to do when a certain substance contributes to different environmental themes. In this case both SO_2 and NO_x contribute

TABLE 17.2 Classification and Characterization of 1000 kg of Soybean Oil

		Resources, GJ	Emissions											Total
			CO_2	CO	C_xH_y	NO_x	SO_2	C_6H_{14}	Herbicides	Insecticide	Nitrogen compounds	Oil	PO_4^{3-}	
Inventory amounts, kg		3.95	250	0.101	1.08	0.75	0.81	1.29	3.54	25.7	212	0.00129	60	
CLASSIFICATION FACTORS														
Abiotic depletion	per kg													
Energy depletion	GJ	1												
Global warming potential	kg/kg		1		11									
Photochemical oxidant formation	kg/kg				0.377			0.421						
Acidification potential	kg/kg					0.7								
Human toxicity	kg/kg			0.012		0.78	1.2		??	1.2–12			0.000521	
Ecotoxicity, aquatic	m^3/kg								??	8–80		50,000		
Ecotoxicity, terrestrial	m^3/kg								??					
Nutrification potential	kg/kg					0.13					0.42		1	
Ozone depletion potential	kg/kg													
MULTIPLIED CLASSIFICATION														
RESULTS	per kg													
Abiotic depletion	–/													
Energy depletion	GJ	3.95												3.95
Global warming potential	kg		250											250
Photochemical oxidant formation	kg				0.407			0.541						0.95
Acidification potential	kg					0.53	0.81							1.34
Human toxicity	kg			0.0012		0.59	0.97		??	30–300			0.031	30–300
Ecotoxicity, aquatic	m^3/kg								??	200–2000		64		200–2000
Ecotoxicity, terrestrial	m^3/kg								??					
Nutrification potential	kg					0.98					89		60	149
Ozone depletion potential	kg													

Substances not taken into account, no classification factors available: industrial waste, high-risk waste, particles, liquid particles in air, CaO, K_2O, and MgO.

TABLE 17.3   Example Classification and Characterization Followed by Normalization for Soybean Oil

Description	Score	Unit	Normalized score, $yr \cdot 10^{-12}$
Abiotic depletion	0	—	0
Energy depletion	3.95	GJ	16.8
Global warming	250	kg	6.6
Photochemical oxidant formation	0.95	kg	254
Acidification	1.34	kg	4.7
Human toxicity*	30–300	kg	52–520
Aquatic ecotoxicity*	200–2000	m^3	0.22–2.2
Terrestrial ecotoxicity	0	kg	0
Nutrification	149	kg	1995
Ozone depletion	0	kg	0

*For the themes of human toxicity and aquatic ecotoxicity, the classification scores are unsure.

to human toxicity as well as to acidification. The score for acidification is calculated in the same way: For SO_2 we multiply the amount of 0.81 kg by 1 kg acidification/kg, which gives 0.81 kg acidification. For NO_x we multiply 0.75 kg by 0.7 kg acidification/kg, which gives 0.53 kg acidification. In the extreme right column of the lower part, the total score for acidification is 1.34 kg acidification.

Short Description of Most Common Environmental Themes

- *Abiotic depletion potential* (ADP).   Abiotic depletion concerns the extraction of nonrenewable raw materials such as ores.
- *Energy depletion potential* (EDP).   Energy depletion concerns the extraction of nonrenewable energy carriers. In the *CML Guide,* this is included in ADP.
- *Global warming potential* (GWP).   An increasing amount of CO_2 in the earth's atmosphere leads to an increasing absorption of radiation energy and consequently to an increase in temperature. This is referred to as *global warming.* CO_2, N_2O, CH_4, and aerosol all contribute to global warming.
- *Ozone depletion potential* (ODP).   Depletion of the ozone layer leads to an increase in the amount of uv light reaching the earth's surface. This may lead to human diseases and may influence ecosystems.
- *Ecotoxicity, aquatic/terrestrial* (ECA/ECT).   Exposure of flora and fauna to toxic substances causes them health problems. Ecotoxicity is defined for water (aquatic ecotoxicity) and soil (terrestrial ecotoxicity).
- *Acidification potential* (AP).   Acid deposition onto soil and into water may lead, depending on the local situation, to changes in the degree of acidity. This affects flora and fauna.
- *Human toxicity* (HT).   Exposure of humans to toxic substances causes health problems. Exposure can take place through air, water, or soil, especially via the food chain.
- *Photochemical oxidant creation potential* (POCP).   Reactions of NO_x with volatile organic substances lead, under the influence of uv light, to photochemical oxidant creation, which causes smog.

- *Nutrification potential* (NP).   Addition of nutrients to water or soil will increase the production of biomass. This in turn leads to a reduction in the oxygen concentration, which affects higher organisms like fish, which may lead to undesirable shifts in the number of species in ecosystems and thus to a threat to biodiversity. The main nutrifying elements are nitrogen-containing substances (e.g., ammonia and NO_x), phosphates, and organic material.

Normalization (Optional)

The scores for each environmental theme can be normalized in various ways, in order to relate them to a reference, thus relating the contribution of the functional unit to the sum of all emissions and extractions worldwide. This means, for instance, dividing the effect score for global warming of the functional unit under study by annual worldwide global warming. The same can be done for other effect scores. Global figures for most common environmental themes are given in Table 17.4.

Suggestions.   A convenient way to do the classification and characterization is to use a spreadsheet program.

Results

The result of the classification and characterization is a table in which up to 10 relevant environmental themes may be represented, describing the environmental profile of your functional unit in absolute or normalized figures. Where relevant, a description of the qualitative environmental aspects of your study can be added.

TABLE 17.4   Global Figures for Most Common Environmental Themes. Data Can Be Used for Normalization Purposes

Environmental theme	Unit	World	Netherlands
Abiotic depletion (W)	yr	1.06	0.0106
Energy depletion (W)	$GJ \cdot yr \cdot 10^9$	235	2.35
Global warming (W)	$kg \cdot yr \cdot 10^{12}$	37.7	0.377
Photochemical oxidant creation (N)	$kg \cdot yr \cdot 10^9$	3.74	0.0374
Acidification (N,W)	$kg \cdot yr \cdot 10^9$	286	2.86
Human toxicity (N)	$kg \cdot yr \cdot 10^9$	576	5.76
Aquatic ecotoxicity (N)	$m^3 \cdot yr \cdot 10^{12}$	908	9.08
Terrestrial ecotoxicity (N)	$kg \cdot yr \cdot 10^{12}$	1,160	11.6
Nutrification (N)	$kg \cdot yr \cdot 10^9$	74.8	0.748

Remark: The data in Table 17.4 have not been obtained independently. For each theme, data from either the Netherlands or the world were available. The constant ratio between the Netherlands and the world has been derived from the fact that the national income of the Netherlands is 1 percent of the global income. The numbers marked W are primarily derived from the world situation; the numbers marked with N are primarily derived from the situation in the Netherlands.

For acidification, data are combined. For depletion of resources (abiotic and energy depletion) data are recalculated.

Source: Guinee (1993).

How to Proceed

The result of this section is formed by a number of factors, relating the functional unit to environmental themes. When you are comparing products, it is possible to compare the scores per environmental theme, which together form the environmental profile.

17.9 IMPACT ASSESSMENT PART 2: VALUATION

The classification and characterization step in Sec. 17.8 has provided an environmental profile, consisting of a fixed set of scores on environmental themes in absolute figures. In some cases those scores may have been related to the local or global situation, following a normalization step. In other cases, however, you may prefer to have a single score instead of a set of figures which are difficult to compare. This is particularly true when two or more products have very different environmental profiles, or when it is required to relate a specific product to a standard.

Simplification introduces the risk of losing sight of the underlying assumptions and information. Therefore you will have to explore the soundness of the conclusions. This section provides some tools to help you convert an environmental profile to one score and to evaluate the reliability of such a figure.

Starting Point

The basis for a valuation is the environmental profile for the function under study, as it was produced in Sec. 17.8. Each environmental theme can be weighted in order to allow a direct addition. Weighting factors may differ from country to country, or even within one country, due to differences in local conditions. Also, political views affect the weighting process, due to different opinions on the relative importance of local or regional themes (e.g., nutrification or acidification) versus opinions on global issues, such as global warming or depletion. However, when consensus has been reached in how to use weighting factors, the result of this method is reproducible.

Approach

1. Weight environmental themes.
2. Convert the environmental profile to an environmental index.
3. Check the soundness of the outcome.
4. Seek a peer review.

1. Weight Environmental Themes. In the weighting of environmental profiles, every environmental theme gets a weight, representing the relative seriousness of that theme. Several methods are available. The *CML Guide* provides technical requirements for weighting factors. Until now, a number of sets of weighting factors were available: the EPS factors (Steen and Ryding, 1993, pp. 34–53), ecopoints (Braunschweig and Muller-Wenk, 1993, p. 146), and NSAEL factors (Kortman et al., 1994). Recently a distance-to-target method has been developed on behalf of the Dutch Ministry of Housing, Spatial Planning and the Environment, in which the environmental levels of durability are used as a standard. Note that weighting factors, to a large extent, have a subjective nature. Until now, no consensus has been reached regarding a preferred approach.

Remark: Once individual weighting factors for each environmental theme have been identified, the mathematical procedure for valuation is similar to the characterization step: The score for each environmental theme is multiplied by its weighting factor.

If you decide to design your own set of weighting factors, you may use a multicriteria analysis. The principle behind multicriteria analysis is to develop a set of weighting factors by asking a reference group to have members indicate their preferences. Such groups may consist of experts, but also of politicians or key managers in a company. In choosing the participants, it is important to check the goal definition (Sec. 17.3), as they should reflect the target group of the study.

A simple method used to establish preferences is to ask for a priority ranking of environmental themes, by giving paired choices, e.g., global warming versus human toxicity, global warming versus acidification, human toxicity versus acidification, etc.

Remark: In case only a few themes are dominant in the environmental profile, you can choose to concentrate on these in the weighting process, ignoring other themes.

Example. Four different fats A, B, C, and D will be ranked in order of their environmental score in two different ways. The weighting will be performed by using two sets of weighting factors on the normalized scores. First, in Table 17.5 we show the normalized scores for all four fats. Note that the profile for fat A (soybean oil) has been calculated in Sec. 17.8. The profiles for the other fats have been calculated elsewhere.

Now we calculate the environmental index with two different sets of weighting factors. In Table 17.6 these sets are shown. In method 1 we assume all factors to be equal. Since the total amount has to be 1 and we have 7 environmental themes, all weighting factors equal 1/7 (approximately 0.143). In method 2 we take a set of weighting factors derived within Unilever during the execution of the spread case.

A slightly more quantitative approach would be to score in a semiquantitative scale, e.g., by ranging from $---$ to +++ instead of using a bipolar choice.

2. Convert the Environmental Profile to an Environmental Index. Multiply the scores on the environmental themes by their respective weighting factors. Subsequently add the outcomes, to obtain an environmental index (dimensionless). To get a feel for

TABLE 17.5 The Normalized Figures (in yr•10^{-12}) of Classification and Characterization for Four Different Fats, Used to Perform the Weighting*

Theme	Fat A	Fat B	Fat C	Fat D
Abiotic depletion*	0	0	0	0
Energy depletion	16.8	30.4	17.8	23.5
Global warming potential	6.6	12.1	6.9	9.4
Photochemical oxidant formation	254	406	390	460
Acidification potential	4.7	14.1	3.1	5.1
Human toxicity	520	17.9	16.6	24.8
Ecotoxicity, aquatic	2.2	0	0.2	0.8
Ecotoxicity, terrestrial*	0	0	0	0
Nutrification potential	1995	2086	479	1965
Ozone depletion potential*	0	0	0	0

*Note that the scores for the themes of abiotic depletion, terrestrial ecotoxicity, and ozone depletion equal zero; therefore these need not be taken into account in the weighting procedure.

TABLE 17.6   Two Different Sets of Weighting Factors to Perform Weighting of Fats Studied

Theme	Method 1	Method 2
Energy depletion	1/7	0.361
Global warming potential	1/7	0.240
Photochemical oxidant formation	1/7	0.113
Acidification potential	1/7	0.039
Human toxicity	1/7	0.039
Ecotoxicity, aquatic	1/7	0.106
Nutrification potential	1/7	0.102
Total	1.0	1.000

the value of the index derived, it is essential to execute the next step—checking the soundness.

Suggestions and Precautions.   To get a feel for the sensitivity of the outcome, it may be useful to try different sets of weighting factors. In the example we show how results change depending on two different sets of weighting factors.

3. Check the Soundness of the Outcome.   To get a feel for the level of reliability, some analysis needs to be performed. For instance, a sensitivity analysis can be used to identify the consequences of uncertainties and deviations in the data. It is worthwhile to estimate the range of uncertainty for the main process data. A mathematical method of calculating the effects of these uncertainties has been developed in the *CML Guide,* section 4.2. A practical way to perform this analysis is to gather all your notes and construct best- and worst-case scenarios. Identify whether different scenarios fundamentally affect your final conclusions.

4. Peer Review.   LCA studies, as you have seen, are rather complex. Therefore you should consult experienced people, once you have finished a study. These people should review assumptions and conclusions to see if they are sufficiently clear and whether you have followed the right approach.

SETAC suggests that each LCA study include an official peer review, produced by an independent third party. Such a review should enhance the credibility of the outcome.

Example.   Having identified the weighting factors, we perform the weighting, by multiplying the environmental scores with their weighting factors. As an example we calculate the environmental index for fat A by the two methods:
Method 1:

$$(16.8 + 6.6 + 254 + 4.7 + 521 + 2.2 + 1995) \cdot \frac{1}{7} = 400 \cdot 10^{-12} \text{ yr}$$

Method 2:

$$16.8 \cdot 0.361 + 6.6 \cdot 0.240 + 254 \cdot 0.113 + 4.7 \cdot 0.039 + 521 \cdot 0.039$$
$$+ 2.2 \cdot 0.106 + 1995 \cdot 0.102 = 261 \cdot 10^{-12} \text{ yr}$$

The results are shown in Fig. 17.12.

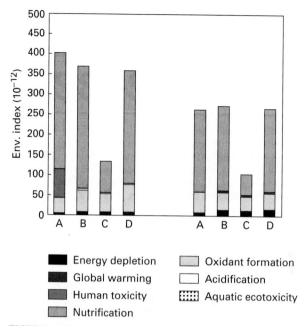

FIGURE 17.12 The results of the weighting with different methods for the four fats. Note that the different methods each give different highest index and also change the order of the alternatives!

Example. The study on spreads indicated that the results for the environmental index largely depend on the data for nutrification elements, such as pesticides, herbicides, and insecticides. Therefore the reliability of the results will depend on the information on these process data. A further study on fertilizer use in various parts of the world should indicate how sensitive the soybean growth is to fertilizer use, in order to get an idea about the reliability and improvement options.

Peer review: Colleagues from the University of Leiden were asked to comment on the approach. One of their main comments was that more information is needed on the environmental impacts of using both pesticides and herbicides in the agricultural stage.

17.10 HOW TO COMPLETE AN LCA STUDY

The preceding sections have provided you with the inventory, the environmental profile, and maybe also the environmental index of your system. This section offers some suggestions on how to report these results and how to structure an improvement process.

Starting Point

At this stage, consult your goal definition, to check both purpose and target group for your study. In some cases, you may want to communicate the outcome of the study. In other cases, you will use the results as a basis for an improvement analysis.

Approach

1. Structure the results.

2. Perform the improvement analysis.

1. Structure the Results.   LCA studies intend to increase insight into the environmental impact of a product or service during its entire life cycle. To maximize this insight, the results should be represented in an effective way. Some people may want to present the absolute numbers in tables, but in general, graphs and pie charts are far more informative.

    Various options exist for representing the data, an example of which is shown in Fig. 17.12 in Sec. 17.9, the subdivision of the total environmental index per theme. You may also want to present the results for all the environmental themes, subdivided per stage of the life cycle, or for the most important processes. Various options to present the results exist. Some have been elaborated on in Figs. 17.13 to 17.15. An example of the subdivision per stage of the life cycle (extraction or growing of raw materials, production, product use, waste stage) is given in Fig. 17.13.

    You may also want to use the results of Sec. 17.8: here it may be useful to subdivide the relevant substances for all the environmental themes considered, as shown in Fig. 17.14.

2. Perform the Improvement Analysis.   To improve the system studied, identify areas of possible improvement. As noted in Sec. 17.2, to perform any improvement, you need knowledge of production processes and of the system studied. LCA does not cure environmental problems, but acts as a decision support in identifying those areas which have the highest improvement potential.

    The simplest way to identify promising areas of improvement is to use the structured results as described in step 1 of this section. Once that picture is available, you can start to select improvement options, for which an environmental profile should also be made. Next, you may compare the various improvement options. The main questions to be answered are, Which processes or stages do have improvement potential and which

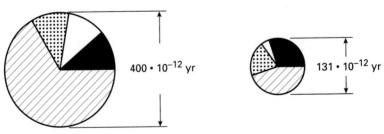

FIGURE 17.13   An example of the presentation: resubdividing the environmental index in stages of the life cycle for fat A and fat C.

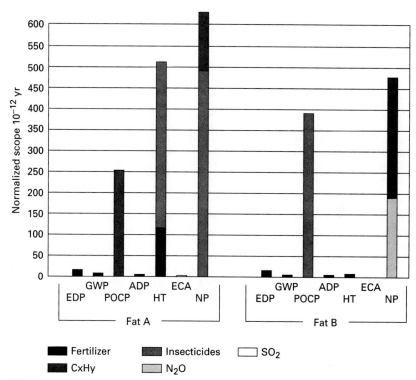

FIGURE 17.14 An example of the presentation: resubdividing the environmental themes for the main causing substances.

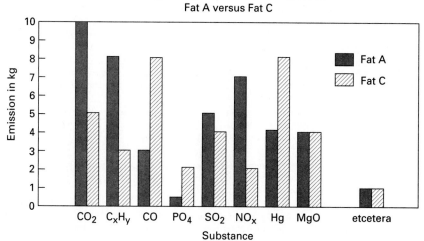

FIGURE 17.15 The comparison of alternatives, based on the emissions in kilograms.

alternatives offer the best scope? Examples of this approach can be found in literature on ecodesign, for instance Brezet et al., 1994; Crul, 1994; Mazijn, 1994; and Ter Riele and Zweers, 1994.

Suggestions and Precautions

- Try to formulate what is important to know in performing improvement analysis. Do you want to find out which process is dominant, or do you want to find the main substances? Note that the way the results are structured may depend on the way in which your process flowchart has been constructed.

- Keep in mind that the reliability of the outcome depends on the reliability of the data used. It is possible to find out the influence of the reliability of the data by performing a marginal analysis or sensitivity analysis. The idea is to find out in which way small changes in the data influence the final results. The main question is, How much do the results depend on the data used? Such a sensitivity analysis may highlight which data need further elaboration.

Example.   The spread case gave a first insight into the environmental impacts of the products. The most significant contribution can be attributed to the agricultural stage. Here, the main polluting factors are the use of fertilizer and insecticides or pesticides. Upon closer observation it appeared that the data used for these components were obtained from one information source only. Before further action is taken, it should be clear whether other data sources give similar figures. Meanwhile, alternative sources on oil data should be checked to see whether they show a substantially improved environmental profile.

BIBLIOGRAPHY

Braunschweig, A., and R. Müller-Wenk, *Ökobilanzen für Unternehmungen; Eine Wegleiting für die Praxis,* Haupt, Bern, 1993.

Brezet, H., et al., *Handleiding voor milieugerichte produktontwikkeling* (in Dutch), Gravenhage, 1994.

Consoli et al., *Guidelines for Life-Cycle Assessment: A "Code of Practice,"* SETAC, Brussels, Belgium, 1993.

Crul, M. R. M., *Milieugerichte produktontwikkeling in de praktijk, ervaringen, belemmeringen en oplossingen,* NOTA, Den Haag, 1994.

Frischknecht, R., Hofstetter, P., Knoepfel, I., Dones, R., and Zollinger, E. *Environmental Life Cycle Inventories for Energy Systems, An Environmental Database for the Inclusion of Energy Systems Comparison for Swiss Conditions,* Laboratorium für Energiesystème, ETH Zürich/PSI Villingen, 1993. Available in German and in English.

Guinée, J. B., *Data for the Normalization Step within Life Cycle Assessment of Products,* Leiden, The Netherlands, CML paper no. 14, 1993.

Habersatter, K., *Ökobilanz von Packstoffen,* BUWAL, Bern, 1991.

Heijungs, R., et al., *Environmental Life Cycle Assessment of Products. 1: Guide. 2. Backgrounds (CML Guide and Backgrounds),* Centre of Environmental Science, Leiden, The Netherlands, 1992. Dutch version: NOH nos. 9253 and 9254; English version: nos. 9266 and 9276. Japanese version available from Science Forum, Tokyo.

Kortman, J. G. M., E. W. Lindeijer, H. Sas (CE), and M. Sprengers, *Towards a Single Indicator for Emissions, An Exercise in Aggregating Environmental Effects,* Interfaculty Department of Environmental Science, University of Amsterdam, Amsterdam/Delft, March 1994.

Mazijn, B., *Van tekentafel tot afvalberg; LCA, een instrument voor ecodesign, eco-label en eco-tax* (in Dutch), Monografieën Stichting Leefmilieu nr. 32, Pelckmans, 1994.

Pederson Weidema, B., *Environmental Assessment of Products, A Textbook on Life Cycle Assessment,* 2d ed., UETP-EEE, Helsinki, Finland, 1993.

Society for the Promotion of Lifecycle Development (SPOLD), *LCA Source Book, A European Business Guide to Life-Cycle Assessment,* Brussels, Belgium, 1993.

Steen, B., and S. O. Ryding, *The EPS Enviro-Accounting Method, An Application of Environmental Accounting Principles for Evaluation and Valuation of Environmental Impact in Product Design,* AFR-Report 11, Swedish Waste Research Council, Stockholm, 1993.

Ter Riele, H., and A. Zweers, *Eco-design: acht voorbeelden* (in Dutch), TNO Produkt-centrum, 1994.

CHAPTER 18
FUTURE PERSPECTIVE

Thomas D. Foust
TEAM LEADER
U.S. DEPARTMENT OF ENERGY
WASHINGTON, DC

Douglas D. Gish
SENIOR CONSULTANT
SRA INTERNATIONAL, INC.
ARLINGTON, VA

18.1 OVERVIEW

The previous chapters of this book explain the history and current status of the life-cycle assessment (LCA) methodology, applications of LCA, cost and design issues, software systems and databases, streamlining issues, public policy applications, and some other pressing current topics. This chapter will provide perspectives on future directions for LCA and will present three possible scenarios for the continued development of LCA tools.

18.2 DRIVERS

In the past, attempts were made to classify LCA studies as being either internally or externally focused; however, in practice, this distinction is difficult to make. Companies routinely perform LCAs for "internal" reasons such as cost reduction, product life-cycle studies, and liability assessment. Similarly, companies perform LCAs in support of activities that are "external" to the organization such as justifying a company policy or action, gaining a marketing advantage, or influencing public policy. Since in many cases an LCA is performed for both internal and external reasons, this distinction will likely disappear in the future.

To grasp where LCA is headed, we must understand how the LCA discipline has evolved to where it is today. A variety of driving factors have helped to shape and focus the LCA discipline and specifically LCA tools. A recent survey[1] showed the motivations for conducting LCAs to be as shown in Fig. 18.1. These drivers will likely remain relatively constant in the near term. LCAs performed for product and/or process improvement and/or cost reduction will remain the primary drivers. LCAs performed for cost reduction reasons will likely increase in the future, as waste disposal costs continue to increase. The second tier of motivators—decision making, proactive environment, and customer requirements—will continue as important drivers. LCAs driven by customer requirements will increase. Many companies have recently began marketing products as "environmentally friendly" or "green." And in order to make this claim,

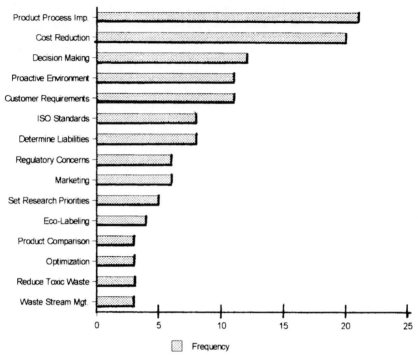

FIGURE 18.1   Motivations for implementing LCA.

they require suppliers to provide environmentally benign materials and components. A common method for justifying the environmentally friendly claim is to perform an LCA to compare alternative products. Although customer requirements and marketing are listed as two separate drivers, in many cases they are indistinguishable. The green product claim is increasingly being used as a marketing tool. This trend will increase in the future as the average consumer's awareness of environmental concerns is heightened. Market research has shown[2] that if two products are equal in every way, the product that can show an environmental advantage will always gain a market advantage. A significantly more complex issue that companies are struggling with is the amount of cost and/or performance penalty that consumers should or will bear for an environmentally preferable product. Most of the debate to date on this issue has been theoretical, but in the future this will become more of a concrete issue. The other lower-tier drivers listed in Fig. 18.1 will vary slightly in significance but will remain as lower-tier drivers.

18.3 REGULATIONS

Although there are currently no regulations or planned regulations mandating the use of LCAs in the United States, there have been a variety of actions within the executive and legislative branches of government recently addressing the use of LCA in the nonregulatory sense. Several of these actions are outlined in the following sections.

18.3.1 Executive Orders

In recent years there have been a number of executive orders and proposed legislation addressing the use of LCA. The two recent executive orders by President Clinton addressing the use of LCA are

- Federal Acquisition, Recycling, and Waste Prevention
- Energy Efficiency and Water Conservation at Federal Facilities

Federal Acquisition, Recycling, and Waste Prevention. On October 20, 1993, President Clinton signed Executive Order 12873,[3] which seeks to achieve these four goals:

1. As the nation's largest consumer, the federal government seeks to safeguard natural resources through the acquisition of recycled products and through waste prevention.
2. The executive order seeks to instill in the federal government the practice of environmental stewardship.
3. The federal government will serve as a role model for others by reducing landfill use through waste reduction and recycling.
4. The federal government will serve as a catalyst to strengthen U.S. economies by supporting "environmentally preferable products and services."

The order calls for the use of LCA in achieving these goals. Section 507 of the order states, "National Institute of Standards and Technology (NIST) shall work with the Environmental Protection Agency (EPA), General Services Administration (GSA), and other public and private sector organizations that conduct life cycle analysis, to gather information that will assist agencies in making selections of products and services that are environmentally preferable."

Part 2 of the executive order defines *environmentally preferable* as products or services that have a lesser or reduced effect on human health and the environment when compared with competing products or services that serve the same purpose. This comparison may consider raw materials acquisition, production, manufacturing, packaging, distribution, reuse, operation, maintenance, or disposal of the product or service. Section 2.11 of the executive order defines *LCA* as "the comprehensive examination of a product's environmental and economic effects throughout its lifetime including raw material extraction, transportation, manufacturing, use and disposal."

Part 4 of the executive order requires the EPA, in consultation with other federal agencies as appropriate, to endeavor to maximize environmental benefits, consistent with price, performance, and availability considerations, and to adjust bid solicitation guidelines as necessary to accomplish this goal. Section 402 (b) states, "agencies shall ensure that 100 percent of their purchases of products meet or exceed the EPA guideline unless…a product…is only available at a unreasonable price."

Energy Efficiency and Water Conservation at Federal Facilities. On March 8, 1994, President Clinton signed Executive Order 12902, which seeks to achieve many goals including the following:

1. Reduce the energy consumption by federal facilities by 30 percent within 9 years, with 1985 as the baseline.
2. Increase energy efficiency by 20 percent in 9 years, with 1990 as the baseline year, and institute cost-effective water conservation within federal facilities whenever possible.

3. Support the construction of new federal facilities, which will be designed and erected as showcase facilities that will "highlight energy or water efficiency and also shall attempt to incorporate co-generation, solar and other renewable energy technologies, and indoor air quality improvements."

In section 309, the Department of Energy (DoE) is charged with reporting "...on the issues involved in instituting LCA for Federal energy and product purchases that address the full fuel cycle costs, including issues concerning energy exploration, development, processing, transportation, storage, distribution, consumption, and disposal, and related impacts on the environment." The report is to examine methods for conducting LCA and implementing such analysis in the public sector and to make appropriate recommendations. The report is to be forwarded to the president for review.

In addition to the above two executive orders promoting the use of LCA, the Clinton administration is also quite active in promoting sustainable development. The "Technology for a Sustainable Future" report calls for life-cycle approaches to be used in evaluating alternatives for new environmental technology development.

18.3.2 Congressional Action

Although, by comparison, the U.S. Congress has been more conservative in promoting the use of LCA, two bills have been proposed in recent years. Several bills and initiatives were recently proposed or are currently pending in both the Senate and the House of Representatives. Senator Max Baucus (D-Montana) and Senator Claiborne Pell (R-Rhode Island) led the Senate effort. Senator Baucus wrote in his sponsorship of the Environmental Technologies Act of 1994, "Our environment and economy are inseparable. In order to prosper, we need a healthy economy; in order to service, we must have a healthy environment."[4] He points out that the application of environmental technology prevents waste and saves money. Environmental technology means the broad application of science to the entire production process. "It means life-cycling planning. It means, in short, a new way of thinking."

In the House, Congressman Brown (D-California) sponsored a companion bill to the Environmental Technologies Act of 1994 (HR 3870). Section 202 is entitled *Life-Cycle Assessment*. HR 3870 directs the Office on Science and Technology Policy or other presidential designee to "...coordinate ongoing Federal activities to develop life-cycle assessment and design-for-environment resources to facilitate the development and utilization of analytic data and methods for greater environmental sustainability and industrial efficiency."[5] An interesting note made by the House (HR 3870) states that while this measure embraces the value of LCA, it advises caution in its use as a regulatory tool by stating, "Any attempts by government to impose the use of LCA must be carefully assessed and should be avoided in this early stage of its development."

These executive and congressional actions are indications of increased government pressure to encourage the use of life-cycle thinking and methodology in public policy as well as the private sector. However, this pressure stops short, as pointed out previously, of mandating the use of LCA in a regulatory framework until the methodology and techniques are more fully developed and standardized. This sentiment is also echoed in the private sector, as evidenced by a number of recent surveys on LCA use and trends[6] as well as public testimony given to EPA. The results of these surveys overwhelmingly indicate that LCA is considered a useful environmental decision-making tool, but its use should not be mandated until techniques and data used in LCA analysis become more standardized. In addition, the majority of respondents oppose the use of LCA to formulate regulations in the near term. The results also indicate that experts in both the public and private sectors feel that eventually LCA will become an integral part

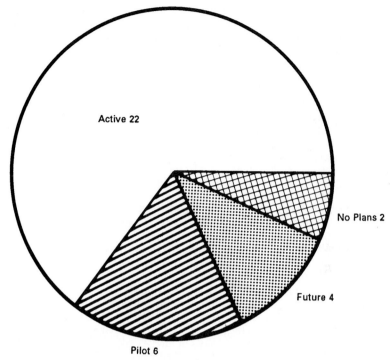

FIGURE 18.2   Level of LCA involvement.

of environmental legislation. In fact, LCA has already been mandated in European countries for use in areas such as ecolabeling. Most organizations surveyed, both public and private, currently have an LCA program in place or plan to implement one in the near future. Figure 18.2 depicts an analysis of 34 organizations surveyed on the current status of LCA programs in their own organization.[7]

18.3.3   Tools

The same situation holds true for LCA tools as it did for drivers. To determine the future direction of LCA tools, one has to look at present-day tools. Chapter 2 covered the present state of LCA inventory, impact, and improvement methodologies. The discussion on software systems and databases covered in Chapter 3 addressed the current tools available for assisting the practitioner in performing an LCA. Additionally, it covered characteristics of an ideal software package, and likely future trends in this area. Additional insight into the future of tool development can be found by comparing Chaps. 2 and 3.

As stated in Chap. 2, *life-cycle inventory* (LCI) analysis has been practiced both in the United States and in Europe for well over 20 years. Based on this experience, LCI methodology is widely accepted and used. In comparison, Chap. 3 stated that there are numerous software packages available to assist the user in performing an LCI analysis. Earlier versions of this type of software were, for the most part, based on commercial spreadsheets and inherently very limiting. Very recently, largely because of the overall trends in software development, tools are becoming more graphically oriented and, as stated in Chap. 3, moving toward *object-oriented programming* (OOP). These types of programs have embedded databases for manipulating the data and performing the analysis, which is inherently more powerful than spreadsheet-based approaches. Future trends in the development and refinement of LCI-type software will likely continue in these two primary areas: enhanced graphical interfaces and more powerful computational engines.

A recent trend in LCA software tools is that programming is being coded in high-level program languages (such as C/C++), allowing them theoretically to be run on a wide variety of platforms. The tool will require some optimization for the particular platform selected. This approach requires greater up-front developmental cost and effort, but makes the tool available to a greater variety of users while also making future improvements and extensions to the tool easier.

Impact assessment methodology is still in the development stage. Although conceptual guidelines for impact assessment have been published by SETAC, the EPA, and the Canadian Standards Association, these guidelines are conceptual and do not represent a consensus standard. Impact assessment methodology is likely to remain under development and refinement for the immediate future, although considerable advances are being made in this area.[8] There are currently no tools available for performing an impact assessment in the classical sense, although a few software packages will do some impact assessment type of analysis. There are several impact assessment tools currently under development. However, without an accepted methodology for performing an impact assessment, it is unlikely these tools will receive wide-scale acceptance.

In the context of improvement assessments, one could logically state that improvement assessments have always been performed as part of an LCI analysis. However, performing an improvement assessment based on an LCI analysis forces the choice of the option with the lowest overall emissions or lowest emissions in a specific category. In many cases there is not a clear "winner." Usually one alternative is lower in certain areas and higher in others, thus making it difficult to decide which alternative is more beneficial. Most experts agree that a superior way to perform an improvement assessment would start with the results of an impact assessment and proceed from there. In this way the user would have a scientifically based method for making decisions. As stated in Chap. 2, an impact assessment combines complex LCI data outputs into a small number of impact categories. The improvement analysis could then be based on whichever impact is deemed the most detrimental and on minimizing this impact. However, as mentioned in Chap. 2, without an agreed upon methodology and standardized data, this analysis is subjective and greatly limited by the quality of data.

18.4 SOFTWARE TOOLS AND FUTURE ENHANCEMENTS

Although LCA methodology has been utilized by industry and government for over two decades, the applications have been limited in number and scope due in part to the constraints on computation power and the manual cataloging of mass quantities of data. As indicated earlier in this text, life-cycle assessments were often conducted as stand-alone efforts focused on specific materials or processes. The preparation of these assessments was expensive and time-consuming, and the practitioners had no standard approach for cataloging the information they developed from their assessment. Consequently, LCAs were conducted on an ad hoc basis, and the knowledge gained from the assessments was often not transferred within the organization, let alone to others external to the organization. However, recent technological advances, increasing risk awareness, total quality management (TQM) principles, and other factors have moved LCA from its cursory role to the mainstream of business planning, design, and operation. Just as design engineers now have the capability to model and simulate complex process designs with simulation tools, the designer in the near future will have interlinked, PC-based LCA tools available to assist in the design process. As top-level tools, these LCA tools will provide initial life-cycle impact, inventory, and improvement analysis to allow various alternatives to be assessed. LCA tools will be linked to more detailed simulation and evaluation tools such as Aspen and Chemcad. Several factors will help bring this about.

Notwithstanding the dramatic increases in both memory and computational capabilities of the microcomputer, the most significant technological advances in the future will be realized in the interchange and linking of information from across the world through the Internet or Intranet. Stand-alone computational and process design tools are limited by the breadth and depth of information available to product and system designers. In the future, these designers will be linked to a vast network of technological and environmental data. Linking the design efforts of individual engineers with these databases will provide the designer with access to not only site-specific analytical information but also the materials, technology, and environmental experiences of literally thousands of other designers. This wealth of "expert knowledge" will facilitate the evaluation of alternatives in terms of environmental performance and risks. The development and deployment of the national information superhighway is but one example of the drive to create an information-sharing infrastructure in both the public and private sectors.

In the context of utilizing LCA tools, the interlinking and sharing of information will enable designers to more thoroughly evaluate design alternatives by providing direct access to information on process reactions, by-product emissions, and environmental impacts generated by hundreds of thousands of organizations with similar design experiences. Clearly, this capability will have dramatic impacts on the selection of environmentally benign materials and processes that can meet product performance requirements. The continual process of data input and revision will enable thousands of organizations (both large and small) to move quickly up the learning curve, as the expert knowledge about the economic and environmental aspects of various technologies becomes available almost instantaneously.

As an example, consider a product designer who is to design a new computer housing. In the traditional design paradigm, the designer would select a short list of materials that best met the design requirements. In many cases, the list of potential materials would be limited to materials with "corporate history"—materials used successfully in other similar products. Often, the environmental impacts of these materials would not be addressed until the product went into production; in which case, the efforts to mitigate pollution and environmental impacts would be focused on the process used to manufacture the product. If the designer were interested in comparing environmental data on the materials, she or he would have to undertake an arduous process of data searches and then attempt to integrate data from multiple sources. Even then, the designer might not be able construct a complete life-cycle profile of the material from raw material to disposition.

In contrast, consider the future design engineer empowered with a desktop LCA model interlinked with a worldwide web of technological and environmental databases. The product designer will be able to search a global database of materials against specified criteria such as material durability, density, and cost. With a short list of potential materials available, the designer can rapidly evaluate the relative environmental impacts of the materials by inputting the various alternative materials into the life-cycle model. The model, interlinked with environmental databases, will systematically evaluate the waste, energy, and hazards associated with the material throughout its life cycle. This analysis will generate a comprehensive environmental impact assessment as an input to the design process. In both cases, the designer is designing an environmental impact into the product. However, the LCA model enables the designer to rapidly make a decision based on a comprehensive knowledge of the environmental performance of alternative materials, processes, and technologies. The designer can then evaluate the environmental considerations in the design process concurrent with performance and economics considerations. Three key developments that will have a significant impact on the future of LCA tools are discussed in the next sections.

18.4.1 Data and Databases

Although an entire book could be devoted to data issues, the purpose of this text is to provide an introduction and overview of LCA. Consequently, this section will briefly discuss some of the likely future trends and advances in this area. As mentioned in Chap. 2, the lack of good-quality, consistent data has been an issue in the field of LCA, since the first LCA was performed in 1969. Although considerable progress has been made in this area, the lack of good-quality, consistent data and the availability of these data still remain major obstacles to performing an LCA. There are many very diverse reasons why this problem has never been solved, including such issues as proprietary concerns, lack of consistent reporting requirements, regulatory concerns, questionable benefit to organizations collecting data, and, most importantly, cost.

It is difficult for any organization, public or private, to justify the cost of developing a comprehensive database. Individual companies often have very good data on in-plant processes and vendor-supplied data, but must rely on outside data of questionable quality for upstream and downstream processes beyond the scope of their direct control. Certain industry trade associations have collected and compiled very comprehensive data on their particular industrial sector (i.e., steel, aluminum, plastics, pulp and paper). However, these data were collected for internal use of the trade association and member companies, and they are often reluctant to release the data to outside interests.

Private consulting firms have the expertise and desire to collect and compile these data. Certain consulting firms have built business over the last 20 years based on their ability to collect and analyze data. Most of these consulting firms are small and simply lack the resources to collect, compile, and maintain a comprehensive industrywide database. The same holds true for environmental trade associations such as SETAC. The cost of initially developing a database of this magnitude would easily run well into the millions, and maintenance costs would be in the hundreds of thousands per year. It would be very difficult for an environmental trade association to justify this cost to its members and to raise the necessary funds.

Finally, government agencies have been reluctant to pursue development of a public database, again due to cost and reluctance to enter into a long-term maintenance commitment. One recent attempt to collect and compile good LCI data on a specific industrial commodity—aluminum—from publicly available sources met with marginal success, high cost, and considerable delays in collecting the data. Due to these problems the effort was terminated.

Unfortunately, the lack of good-quality, consistent data is not a problem that will be solved quickly or easily. In fact, the reality of the situation is that we probably will never have as good data as we would like. As mentioned in Chap. 3, the issues of software systems and databases are closely linked. A software tool is only as good as its input data, and although we are becoming very sophisticated in tool and database development, data quality standards are lagging behind. Only by all parties working together can this issue be addressed in the best possible manner.

Information and data are at the core of all assessment tools, process simulators, and decision models. Consequently, as mentioned previously, the revolutionary advances in communications and information systems will have a profound impact on the adoption and utilization of LCA tools. Many organizations now subscribe to the vision of a virtual office where individuals have access to data, information, and decision support tools which will help them do their jobs regardless of organizational or geographical location.[9] When applied in the context of LCA, the concept of a virtual office implies that the designer has access to systems that will enable data and information to flow in a seamless fashion through the product development chain, all the way from product design through manufacturing and ultimate disposition. The drive toward a seamless communication system has led to significant advances in "open-architecture" systems that enable communication between various computing platforms. Despite these advances, numerous challenges must be overcome in order to achieve a truly seamless information process, two of which are mentioned here.

One of the first major obstacles to overcome is the development of standardized data transfer methods to replace specific data translators that operate between individual applications and databases. Some international data transfer standards exist, and more are being developed. Technical data transfer methods are currently being developed within the International Standards Organization Technical Committee 184, better known as "ISO-STEP." Nontechnical commercial and financial data are being addressed by the United Nations EDIFAC standards, which are international in scope.[10] Many organizations are following the lead of these two standards-setting bodies, and the eventual adoption of their standardized data transfer methods will enable truly seamless communication. This will allow LCA tools to be linked with environmental, process, and materials databases worldwide.

Another significant issue that must be addressed, before the vast quantities of data can be utilized effectively in LCA models, is data integrity. To ensure that the integrity of data is maintained, data quality standards must be established. Since it is not economical to maintain large numbers of individual databases, organizations will begin or continue to migrate data into common databases. As an example, several major chemical companies are pursuing common databases for chemical processes and materials, but the chemical industry as a whole has a long way to go to achieve the goal of consolidated, common databases. In many cases, databases will be built up and supported with both public and private data. The consolidated databases will develop maintenance plans that will allow information to be updated on a regular and periodic basis. This will also establish a formal process for modifying, changing, inputting, and deleting information. To facilitate the use of the databases, information will be input in a common, standardized format.

The adoption of international data transfer standards and data quality standards will dramatically enhance the capabilities of LCA models. Information about materials or technology that was once painstakingly generated will be available on-line to product and process designers. In addition, the adoption of standards will simultaneously enhance the economics of LCAs while providing higher-quality data as an input to the assessment process. The breadth and quality of information available to process designers will expand their decision-making capabilities, particularly in the area of environmental impact.

One of the best examples of how future LCA tools will be linked to the design process through information systems is the Clean Process Advisory System (CPAS) being developed by a coalition of industry, academia, and government. CPAS is a computer-based pollution prevention process and product design system that will provide environmental design data to individual designers. As currently envisioned (see Fig. 18.3), the CPAS will be composed of many separate but integrated software applications containing design information for new and existing clean process or product technology, technology modeling tools, and other design guidance.[11] The objective of CPAS is to tap into the vast body of information on clean technologies, health and safety issues, and economic issues that resides in industry, academia, and government and to make this expert information avail-

CPAS

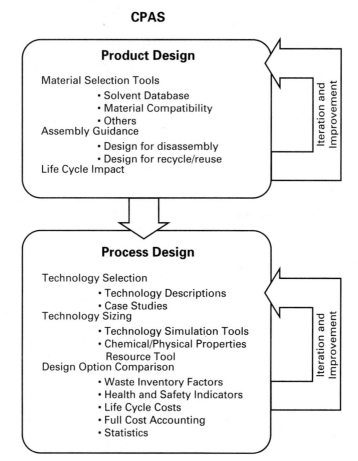

FIGURE 18.3

able to product and process designers during the design process. This information will be provided to designers by linking numerous databases through a user-friendly, menu-driven interface. Several design comparison tools are being developed, including a life-cycle analysis and full-cost accounting tool. The CPAS will allow process designers to rapidly evaluate alternative design concepts by using the LCA tool to assess the true costs of products, including the long-term environmental burden.

18.5 ENVIRONMENTAL RISK ASSESSMENT AND ANALYSIS

Over the last two decades, industry has become increasingly concerned about minimizing the risk (probability) of products and operations causing adverse impacts to human health and the environment. This could include the release of hazardous or toxic materials into the air, land, or water. In addition to industry trends toward greater environmental responsibility, public and private organizations have been driven to seriously address these risks by legislation such as the Comprehensive Environmental Resources Conservation and Liability Act (CERCLA), commonly known as the Superfund Act. This act was originally designed to (1) provide money for the cleanup of abandoned hazardous waste disposal sites and (2) establish liability so dischargers could be made to pay for injuries and damages.[12] More recent environmental regulations such as the Pollution Prevention Act of 1990 require both public and private organizations to seek ways to prevent or minimize adverse environmental impacts by instituting source reduction, material substitution, and recycling where practicable in their operations. It is anticipated that the tolerance for environmental degradation will trend downward while the standards of environmental performance will continue on an upward path. Both trends will accelerate the development and use of more analytical approaches to environmental management, specifically environmental risk analysis and assessment. Because the elements of environmental risk analysis and assessment can be addressed within the framework of life-cycle impact analysis, LCAs will play an increasing role in the environmental management decision process of public and private organizations. As defined in the SETAC publication *Technical Framework for Life-Cycle Assessment,* life-cycle impact analysis is a characterization and assessment of effects associated with a product, process, or activity. The assessment, which may be quantitative and/or qualitative, should address effects such as environmental and health considerations, habitat modification, noise pollution, socioeconomic impacts, and other impacts.[13]

Environmental risk assessments and analyses may be a component of an LCA impact analysis. However, they, like other LCA applications, are currently limited by the lack of detailed data on the chemical, physical, and biological properties of specific materials. "This information translates into an understanding of both the inherent toxicity of the material as well as the environmental exposure. Both parts of this equation are necessary to fully assess the potential of an emission to the environment to cause and environmental effect."[14] The anticipated advances in data standards and data transfer described in the previous section will have a profound impact on the use of LCA impact analysis tools to support risk assessments and analyses. With these advances, the LCA inventory tool will be able to provide both specific process and material information as well as aggregated data for generic processes and facilities, giving the decision maker or designer a credible basis for assessing risks at a macro as well as micro level.

Another important component of LCA impact analysis is the impact model. The impact model provides a means of translating raw inventory data to a format that is meaningful and useful for evaluating alternative decisions. Specifically, decision analysis techniques are used to weight and measure the relative impacts of various materials and emissions. For example, the emissions from a generic facility might include 3 metric tons (t) of carbon dioxide and 1 t of ozone-depleting chlorofluorocarbons. Without a knowledge of the relative impacts on the environment of these two compounds, it would be difficult or impossible to decide which of these emissions should be reduced. However, by weighting the impact of the two emissions based on the knowledge of the negative impacts of each compound on the environment, the decision maker and designer can make sound choices that minimize environmental risk and result in an overall reduction in the impacts on the environment.

A technique called *multicriteria decision analysis* provides decision makers with an analytical and systematic way of evaluating alternatives based on user-defined objectives, characteristics, and weights. Since the evaluation and solution of complex problems nearly always involves competing objectives, multicriteria decision analysis enables the decision maker to assess how well various alternatives satisfy the objectives. This technique has been used extensively to evaluate complex decisions in numerous applications such as facility siting, technology selection, and political issue analysis. By defining the elements of the multicriteria analysis tool, the decision maker is essentially developing a model of his or her own decision-making process. Similarly, an organization can develop a quantitative model of its decision process including specific objectives with varying degrees of importance. In the context of environmental risk analysis and assessment, these decision models are used to convert LCA inventory data on various alternatives to a meaningful decision process. Organizations may have a stronger interest in reducing one type of emission over another based on environmental or health impacts.

Another mathematical decision analysis technique called the *analytic hierarchy process* (AHP) has been adopted for use in LCA impact assessments. AHP is closely related to multicriteria decision making but has a significant difference. AHP allows the decision maker to conduct pairwise comparisons of the objectives and subobjectives. This is significant because, by assessing the objectives through pairwise comparison, a mathematical coefficient of correlation can be determined to provide a measure of how consistent the decision maker is in setting up weights and the importance of objectives. In the context of environmental risk assessment, this technique helps avoid building inconsistencies into the risk or decision model. Comparisons can incorporate both objective (quantitative) and subjective (qualitative) factors in evaluating alternatives.[15]

18.6 ORGANIZATIONAL AND TQM CHANGES

Some of the most significant changes that will affect the future utilization of LCA tools in design are being driven by changing organizational structures and operational philosophies. U.S. corporations have been streamlining their business units since the late 1980s to reduce costs and improve operational efficiency. As part of these efforts, many of these organizations are redesigning how their personnel work. Traditionally, organizations were broken up into major units such as production, research and development, and marketing, and these units often operated as if they were independent entities. This model is now being discarded as more and more companies adopt cross-functional organizational structures that include personnel from multiple business units. This development is significant to the use of LCA tools because these work teams will be engaged in the whole life cycle of new products and services. In the traditional organizational structures, if an environmental analysis of a product were performed, it would likely be conducted with a limited scope, such as from the production point of view. The use of teams will facilitate the use of LCA tools to evaluate new products to determine their true environmental impacts all the way from research through production, utilization, and disposal. This will provide organizations with an opportunity to institutionalize the concept of design for environment.

Another significant organizational change that will have a marked effect on the use of LCA tools in the future is the transition to total quality management principles. TQM places the responsibility for the quality of products or services on the individuals designing, manufacturing, and selling the products. Certainly, environmental performance is one of the important measures of quality for a product. Moreover, the use of LCA tools during the product design phase is consistent with the TQM philosophy of identifying problems before they arise. Designers will use LCA tools to help them select product designs that have the least environmental impact or risk over the entire life of the product.

18.6.1 Possible Scenarios

This section will cover the possible scenarios in the future development and refinement of LCA. Although predicting the future is difficult, if not impossible, and the future development of LCA could potentially follow thousands of different scenarios, for argument's sake, all the possible scenarios will be grouped into three general categories:

1. Business as usual
2. Lead group or organization
3. Multipartnership venture

It is not possible to predict specific accomplishments or milestones that the LCA discipline will achieve in any of the three scenarios, nor is it possible to predict the state of the science at a future date, say 2005, and compare the differences. However, it is possible to make general assumptions about the evolution process for each of the three scenarios and draw general conclusions about the differences.

18.6.2 Business as Usual

As the name implies, this scenario is based on the premise that the science of LCA will continue to evolve and advance in the same manner as it has so far. In this scenario there are many diverse organizations working in the field of LCA, applying LCA techniques for very diverse reasons, and, for the most part, working independently. Central guidance would be provided by organizations such as SETAC or the EPA on issues of interest to everyone, such as methodology, data, policy, or other common issues.

The field of LCA has evolved considerably since the late 1960s by essentially following this scenario. Great strides have been made in standardizing methodology for performing LCIs, and there has been and continues to be a considerable effort made to standardize the methodology for performing an impact assessment and/or an improvement assessment. Software tools have come a long way and promise to continue to improve rapidly. The cost of performing a full LCA has been significantly reduced, and advances will continue to reduce the cost.

An advantage of this approach is that given the lack of rigid requirements for performing an LCA, individual companies and organizations have been free to structure the performance of an LCA to best meet their needs. Front-runner companies and organizations that were the first to realize the benefit of performing LCAs have set up in-house procedures and methodologies for performing LCAs. In most cases, these procedures and methodologies dictate how an LCA will be performed to best meet the performing organization's needs. These procedures and methodologies, while for the most part generally consistent with each other and the SETAC and EPA guidelines,[16] differ significantly in the specifics from organization to organization. Some of the earlier methodologies predate the SETAC and EPA guidelines.

Software and database development will continue to evolve under this scenario. Most of this work will be done by individual organizations or small groups developing a particular tool or database. Under this scenario, a few tools and databases will emerge as superior to the others and receive wide acceptance, forcing the others to gradually disappear.

The disadvantages of this scenario are that the problems of the past will continue, because the framework to adequately address these issues does not exist. The lack of a standardized methodology, although possibly an advantage to those already established in the field, is a major impediment to newcomers. Organizations that are looking to establish an LCA program are confronted with what often appears to be conflicting guidance, questionable benefits, and perceived high costs.

The major disadvantage of this scenario is that the lack of good-quality, consistent, publicly available data will continue to be an issue. Any one organization cannot justify the cost and resources required to develop a comprehensive industrywide database.

Since the lack of good-quality data has been identified as one of the premier problems facing the field of LCA, many have suggested the lead-organization scenario for overcoming the lack of data.

18.6.3 Lead Organization

This scenario differs from the business-as-usual scenario in that one organization assumes the lead role in advancing the field of LCA. The lead organization would serve as the focal point in the following areas:

- Resolve questions in methodology.
- Develop and maintain a public life-cycle database.
- Coordinate the development of a software tool.

As mentioned earlier, the lack of standardized methodology can serve as an impediment to acclimating newcomers to LCA. A lead organization would serve as the focal point in resolving methodological questions and guide the process toward issuance of a standardized methodology for performing an LCA. In many ways, SETAC and the EPA are already functioning in this role. The only change under this scenario is that either SETAC or the EPA would assume a more prominent and/or authoritative role. The lead organization would set a timetable with specific milestones toward the eventual issuance of standard LCA methodology, including the scoping, inventory, impact, and improvement segments.

The lack of publicly available high-quality data has been a difficult issue to address. Under this scenario the lead organization would assume responsibility for developing these data and compiling them in a public database for use by all in the field. This scenario would work quite well for development of a database, assuming the lead organization has the required resources. The major drawback of this type of approach is that it would be quite costly and resource-intensive for one organization to develop a database of this magnitude. Additionally, the time required for one organization to develop a life-cycle database would be excessively long.

In this scenario one organization would assume the lead role in developing a comprehensive software tool. The logistics of this scenario work out quite well in that the lead organization that develops the database also develops the software tool. In this way compatibility is ensured. However, the same drawbacks exist here—the development of a software tool with the capabilities required would be quite expensive. The software tool development cost compounded with the database development cost would be quite expensive and difficult for one organization to absorb. Development of a software tool and database would cost at least $5 million and could easily exceed this value.

The lead organization could theoretically be an industrial trade association, an environmental association, or a government agency. Industry trade associations have collected very high-quality life-cycle data on commodities or resources vital to their particular industry. However, it would be very difficult for an industrial trade association to justify the whole effort and cost to its members. Environmental associations would face similar problems. Even though many of these associations have a wide cross section of members representing many diverse interests, it is still very difficult for these associations to justify a cost of this magnitude.

The most likely organization to assume the lead role would be a government agency. Assuming the organization has support at all levels of the organization for LCA work, it should be able to justify the funds for development of a software tool and embedded database. The problem with this scenario is that this support cannot be counted on for the long term. Management at the upper levels is very volatile in government agencies and very subject to political pressures. Additionally, this support is most often generated throughout the organization at the working level or first-line supervisory level. Individuals at this level research the project, determine the necessary participants, and secure the necessary resources from their management. If these individuals move on in their careers and their replacement does not share the same conviction for LCA work, the support quickly dries up. Therefore, although government agencies assuming the lead organization role is a temporary solution, this scenario cannot be counted on for a long-term solution.

18.6.4 Multipartnership Venture

This scenario has most of the benefits of the lead organization scenario without some of the major drawbacks. In this scenario, organizations having a vested interest in LCA work in collaboration to advance the science. Industry, government, academia, and non-government organizations all play a part in this scenario. This would be the best of all possible scenarios, but the most difficult to implement.

A process would be set up to establish a framework for all stakeholders to collaborate to standardize methodology, develop data, and create a software modeling tool. In this scenario all stakeholders are involved from the beginning and work in collaboration. The advantage of this type of approach is that it is an open process and all are invited to participate. The final product is more likely to receive wide acceptance since all were invited to participate. The other major advantage of this approach is that with a wide involvement of multiple parties the whole effort is not overly dependent on any one party. Therefore, if individual parties can no longer participate in the process, the effort can continue.

With multiple-party participation, the cost to any one participant will be minimized. This is an especially attractive aspect of this scenario, since the financial benefits of having a standardized methodology, high-quality comprehensive data, and a good modeling tool tend to be spread out across all stakeholders. However, it is a slow and arduous task to get such a diverse group to agree and cooperate on all levels. The more players, the greater the compromises. Someone will still have to lead and coordinate the whole effort but will not have to shoulder the entire burden.

REFERENCES

1. B. Breville, T. Gloria, M. O'Connell, and T. Saad, "Life Cycle Assessment, Trends, Methodologies and Current Implementation," Department of Civil and Environmental Engineering, Tufts University, Medford, MA, August 1994, pp. 145–155.

2. "Technology for a Sustainable Future—A Framework for Action," Office of Science and Technology Policy, Washington, DC, 1994, pp. 65–80.

3. President, "Federal Acquisition, Recycling, and Waste Prevention, Executive Order 12873," *U.S. Office of the Press Secretary of the White House,* October 20, 1993, p. 1.

4. *The Environmental Technologies Act of 1994,* 103d Cong., 2d Sess., H.R. 3870, June 8, 1994, p. 46.

5. Breville et al., note 1, p. 14.

6. M. Sullivan and J. Ehrenfeld, "Reducing Life-Cycle Environmental Impacts: An Industry Survey of Emerging Tools and Programs," *Total Quality Environmental Management,* Winter 1992/1993, pp. 147–157. K. Habersatter, "Experts' Survey," in *Proceedings from SETAC LCA Data Quality Workshop in Wintergreen, Virginia, October 4–9, 1992,* Society for Environmental Toxicology and Chemistry, 1992, pp. 3–13. B. Vigon and A. Jansen,

"Practitioner Survey," in *Proceedings from the SETAC Data Quality Workshop in Wintergreen, Virginia, October 4–9, 1992,* SETAC, 1992, pp. 2–13. Breville, et al., note 1, pp. 151–165.

7. Breville et al., note 1, pp. 149–151.

8. B. Barnes, B. Gockel, K. Hsu, C. Ischey, and R. Watkins, "Life Cycle Analysis: Integrated Inventory, Environmental, and Economic Analyses," prepared for U.S. Department of Energy, Idaho National Engineering Laboratory, Idaho Falls, Idaho, April 1994.

9. B. L. Ramaker, issue paper on "Computers in Manufacturing," prepared for the Chemical Manufacturers Association Information Management Work Group, February 1995.

10. Joseph Halford and Risdon Hankinson, "Data Transfer: A Review and Concept," Chemical Manufacturers Association Information Management Work Group, February 1995.

11. P. P. Radecki, D. W. Hertz, and C. Vinton "Build Pollution Prevention Into Process Design," *Hydrocarbon Processing,* August 1994.

12. Vesiland, P. A., Pierce, J. J., and Weiner, R. F., *Environmental Pollution and Control,* Butterworth-Heinemann, Boston, 1990, p. 236.

13. J. A. Fava, R. Denison, B. Jones, M. A. Curran, B. W. Vigon, S. Selke, and J. Barnum (eds.), *A Technical Framework for Life-Cycle Assessments,* Society of Environmental Toxicology and Chemistry (SETAC), Pensacola, FL, 1991, p. 118.

14. Ibid., p. 124.

15. R. Dyer and E. Forman, *An Analytical Approach to Marketing Decisions,* Prentice-Hall, Englewood Cliffs, NJ, 1991, p. 87.

16. See note 13.

APPENDIX
LIFE-CYCLE ASSESSMENT CASE STUDIES AND RELATED STUDIES TABLE

Prepared by
U.S. EPA & Reynolds Research, Inc.
July 18, 1995

Title of LCA case study or related study	Category	Performed for	Performed by	Date
Beverage container life-cycle assessment (not exact title)	Beverage containers	Coca-Cola	Midwest Research Institute	1969
Environmental Impacts of Polystyrene Foam and Molded Pulp Meat Trays	Polystyrene	Mobil Chemical Company	Midwest Research Institute	April 1972
Resource and Environmental Profile Analysis* of Nine Beverage Container Alternatives	Beverage containers	Environmental Protection Agency (EPA)	Midwest Research Institute	1974
Resource and Environmental Profile Analysis of Plastics and Competitive Materials	Plastics	Society of Plastics Industry	Midwest Research Institute	1974
Beer container life-cycle assessment (not exact title)	Beer containers	Unknown	Midwest Research Institute	1974
Resource and Environmental Profile Analysis of Plastics and Non-Plastics Containers	Plastics	The Society of the Plastics Industry Canada	Midwest Research Institute	November 1974
Resource and Environmental Profile Analysis of Selected Disposable and Reusable Consumer Products no. 00875	Disposable versus reusable products		Franklin Associates	1975
Resource and Environmental Profile Analysis of Five Milk Container Systems with Selected Health and Economic Considerations	Milk container systems	EPA	Midwest Research Institute	1976
Comparative Analysis of Selected Characteristics of Disposable and Reusable Napkins	Napkins	American Paper Institute	Arthur D. Little, Inc.	1977
Comparative Analysis of Selected Characteristics of Disposable and Reusable Towels	Towels	American Paper Institute	Arthur D. Little, Inc.	1977

A.2

Title of LCA case study or related study	Category	Performed for	Performed by	Date
Comparative Analysis of Selected Characteristics of Disposable versus Reusable Diapers, Napkins, and Towels	Diapers, napkins, and towels	American Paper Institute	Arthur D. Little, Inc.	1977
Resource and Environmental Profile Analysis of Five Milk Container Systems	Milk containers	EPA	Midwest Research Institute and Chemtech†	1978
Family-Size Soft Drink Containers—A Comparative Energy and Environmental Impact Analysis	Soft drink containers	Goodyear Tire and Rubber Company	Franklin Associates	January 1978
Energy and Materials Flows in the Fabrication of Aluminum Products	Aluminum products	Department of Energy (DoE)	Argonne National Laboratory	1979
Energy and Materials Flow in the Fabrication of Iron and Steel Semifinished Products	Iron and steel semifinished products	DoE	Argonne National Laboratory	1979
Voluntary Recycling Targets for the Paper and Paperboard Industry no. 05278	Paper and paperboard		Franklin Associates	1979
A Case Study Analyzing the Volume of Residential Plastics	Residential plastics		Franklin Associates	1979
Discarded Tires: Energy Conservation through Alternative Uses	Discarded tires		Argonne National Laboratory	December 1979
Energy and Material Flows in the Production of Olefins and Their Derivatives	Olefins	DoE	Argonne National Laboratory	August 1980
Energy and Materials Flows in the Copper Industry	Copper	DoE	Argonne National Laboratory	December 1980
Energy and Materials Flows in Air Products	Air products	DoE	Argonne National Laboratory	1981
Energy and Materials Flows in the Pulp and Paper Industry	Pulp and paper industry	DoE	Argonne National Laboratory	1981

A.3

Title of LCA case study or related study	Category	Performed For	Performed By	Date
Energy and Materials Flows in the Cement Industry	Cement	DoE	Argonne National Laboratory	1981
Energy and Materials Flows in the Primary Aluminum Industry	Primary aluminum	DoE	Argonne National Laboratory	1981
Energy and Materials Use in the Production and Recycling of Consumer Goods Packaging	Packaging (bags, milk containers, disposable cups, meat trays, beverage containers)	DoE	Argonne National Laboratory	1981
Plastics: The Energy Saver‡	Plastics		Franklin Associates	1981
Total Energy Impacts of the Use of Plastics Products in the United States	Plastics	The Society of the Plastics Industry	Franklin Associates	January 15, 1981
Energy and Materials Use for Production and Recycling of Consumer Goods Packaging	Consumer goods packaging		Argonne National Laboratory	February 1981
Energy and Materials Flows in Petroleum Refining	Petroleum refining	DoE	Argonne National Laboratory	February 1981
Industrial Waste Exchange: A Mechanism to Save Energy and Money	Industrial waste		Argonne National Laboratory	July 1982
Energy and Materials Flows in the Iron and Steel Industry	Iron and steel	DoE	Argonne National Laboratory	1983
Estimating Environmental Costs and Benefits for Five Generating Resources	Generating technologies (coal, dual-fired combustion turbines, cogeneration from biomass and municipal solid waste, geothermal, solar central receiving stations, and wind turbines)	Bonneville Power Administration	ECO Northwest	1986 (partially updated in 1991)

Title of LCA case study or related study	Category	Performed For	Performed By	Date
Laundry detergent packaging LCA (not exact title)	Laundry detergent packaging	Procter & Gamble	Franklin Associates	1988
Piping Applications Case Study	Piping	U.S. Bureau of Mines	U.S. Bureau of Mines	Circa 1988
Beverage Container Case Study	Beverage containers	U.S. Bureau of Mines	U.S. Bureau of Mines	Circa 1988
Automobile Bumper Case Study	Automobile bumpers	U.S. Bureau of Mines	U.S. Bureau of Mines	Circa 1988
Environmental Fate, Effects and Recyclability of 135 Film Packaging Components	Film packaging components	Eastman Kodak Company	Battelle	1989
Surfactants LCA (not exact title)	Surfactants	Procter & Gamble	Franklin Associates	1989
Comparative Energy and Environmental Impacts for Soft Drink Delivery Systems	Soft drink delivery systems	National Association for Plastic Container Recovery	Franklin Associates	March 1989
Environmental Costs of Electricity	Energy-related	New York State Energy Research and Development Authority and U.S. DoE	Pace University	1990
Disposable versus Reusable Diapers—Health, Environmental and Economical Comparisons	Diapers	Procter & Gamble	Arthur D. Little, Inc.	1990
Energy and Environmental Profile Analysis of Children's Disposable and Cloth Diapers	Diapers	American Paper Institute, Diaper Manufacturers Group	Franklin Associates	1990
Good Things Come in Smaller Packages, the Technical and Economic Arguments in Support of McDonald's Decision to Phase Out Polystyrene Foam Packaging: Why and How the Environment Benefits	Burger containers	Environmental Defense Fund	R. A. Denison, J. Prince, and J. Rusto	1990
Resource and Environmental Profile Analysis of Foam Polystyrene and Bleached Paperboard Containers	Foam polystyrene and paperboard	Council for Solid Waste Solutions	Franklin Associates	1990

A.5

Title of LCA case study or related study	Category	Performed for	Performed by	Date
Polystyrene Foam (Plates, Clamshells, Cups) versus Paper Equivalents	Polystyrene and paper	Council for Solid Waste Solutions	Franklin Associates	1990
Resource and Environmental Profile Analysis of Polyethylene and Unbleached Paper Grocery Sacks	Paper grocery sacks	Council for Solid Waste Solutions	Franklin Associates	1990
Life-Cycle Cost Assessment (includes a life-cycle inventory)		An unnamed utility industry research organization	Gauntlett Group, Inc.	1990
Cost and Energy Consumption Estimates for the Aluminum-Air Battery Fuel Cycle	Aluminum-air battery fuel cycle		Battelle, Pacific Northwest Laboratories	January 1990
Estimates of the Volume of Municipal Solid Waste and Selected Components in Trash Cans and Landfills	Waste management	The Council for Solid Waste Solutions	Franklin Associates	February 1990
A Comparison of Energy Consumption by the Plastics Industry to Total Energy Consumption in the U.S.	Plastics	The Society of the Plastics Industry	Franklin Associates	November 1990
Comparative Energy and Environmental Analysis of Three Interior Packaging Materials, Final Report	Packaging	Free-Flow Packaging Corporation	Franklin Associates	November 1990
Resource and Environmental Profile Analysis of Sandwich Bags	Sandwich bags		Franklin Associates	January 1991
Diapers: Environmental Impacts and Life Cycle Analysis	Diapers	National Association of Diaper Services	Lehrberger & Jones	January 1991
Resource and Environmental Profile Analysis of High-Density Polyethylene and Bleached Paperboard Gable Milk Containers	Polyethylene and paperboard containers		Franklin Associates	February 1991

Title of LCA case study or related study	Category	Performed for	Performed by	Date
Comparative Energy Evaluation of Plastic Products and Their Alternatives for the Building and Construction and Transportation Industries no. 28190B	Plastics	The Society of the Plastics Industry	Franklin Associates	March 1991
ESRG Energy Systems Research Group Study 1990	Packaging materials and plastics		ESRG (Program Manager, John Schall)	Was to be completed by March 1991
Comparative Energy, Environmental Analysis, and Cost of Various Poultry Boxes	Poultry boxes		Franklin Associates	April 16, 1991 (draft copy)
Vinyl Product Lifecycle Assessment	Vinyl	Vinyl Institute	Chem Systems	September 17, 1991
Resource and Environmental Profile Assessment of Packaging for Laundry and Cleaning Products	Laundry and cleaning products	Procter & Gamble	Franklin Associates	November 1991
Life Cycle Inventory of Virgin versus Recycled Paperboard Folding Cartons	Paperboard folding cartons	Eastman Kodak Company	Battelle	1992
Life Cycle Inventory of Lithographic Inks and Gloss Coatings	Lithographic inks and gloss coatings	Eastman Kodak Company	Battelle	1992
The Energy Requirements and Environmental Emissions for Removing Silver from Photoprocessing Solutions	Removal of silver from photoprocessing solutions	Eastman Kodak Company	Franklin Associates	1992
Resource and Environmental Profile Analysis: A Life Cycle Environmental Assessment for Products and Procedures	General	Procter & Gamble	Franklin Associates	1992 (publishing date)
Case Study: A Product Life-Cycle Assessment of Arm & Hammer Baking Soda	Baking soda	Church & Dwight's Arm & Hammer Division	Arthur D. Little	1992

A.7

Title of LCA case study or related study	Category	Performed for	Performed by	Date
Environmental Resource Guide—Building Materials: [life-cycle analysis on] Aluminum	Aluminum	American Institute of Architects, EPA	Scientific Consulting Group, Inc. (SCG)	1992
Environmental Resource Guide—Building Materials: [life-cycle analysis on] Particleboard	Particleboard	American Institute of Architects, EPA	SCG	1992
Environmental Resource Guide—Building Materials: [life-cycle analysis on] Steel	Steel	American Institute of Architects, EPA	SCG	April 1992
Environmental Resource Guide—Building Materials: [life-cycle analysis on] Linoleum	Linoleum	American Institute of Architects, EPA	SCG	April 1992
Environmental Resource Guide—Building Materials: [life-cycle analysis on] Vinyl Flooring	Vinyl flooring	American Institute of Architects, EPA	SCG	April 1992
Project Synopsis: Resource and Environmental Profile Analysis of Hard Surface Cleaners and Home Remedy Cleaning Systems	Hard surface cleaners and home-remedy cleaning systems	Procter & Gamble	Franklin Associates	April 14, 1992
Tellus Institute Packaging Study (This study included five separate case studies on the following products: soft drinks, juice, fast-food hamburgers, microwave dinners, and hardware.)	Packaging materials	New Jersey Dept. of Environmental Protection, EPA, and Council of State Governments	Tellus Institute	May 1992
Environmental Resource Guide—Building Materials: [life-cycle analysis on] Sealants	Sealants	American Institute of Architects, EPA	SCG	July 1992
Environmental Resource Guide—Building Materials: [life-cycle analysis on] Carpet, Carpet Cushion, and Adhesive	Carpet, carpet cushion, and adhesive	American Institute of Architects, EPA	SCG	July 1992

Title of LCA case study or related study	Category	Performed for	Performed by	Date
Environmental Resource Guide—Building Materials: [life-cycle analysis on] Paint	Paint	American Institute of Architects, EPA	SCG	July 1992
Resource and Environmental Profile Analysis of Polyethylene Milk Bottles and Polyethylene-Coated Paperboard Milk Cartons	Milk cartons and milk bottles	The Society of the Plastics Industry	Franklin Associates	July 21, 1992 (publishing date)
Environmental Life-Cycle Inventory of Detergent-Grade Surfactant Sourcing and Production	Detergent-grade surfactants from oleochemical and petrochemical sources	Procter & Gamble	Franklin Associates	Accepted on September 28, 1992
Environmental Resource Guide—Building Materials: [life-cycle analysis on] Concrete	Concrete	American Institute of Architects, EPA	SCG	October 1992
Environmental Resource Guide—Building Materials: [life-cycle analysis on] Tropical Woods	Tropical woods	American Institute of Architects, EPA	SCG	October 1992
An Energy Study of Plastics and Their Alternatives in Packaging and Disposable Consumer Goods no. 34191	Plastics	The Society of the Plastics Industry	Franklin Associates	November 1992
Life-Cycle Environmental and Cost Assessment: Examining Adhesives from a New Angle	Adhesives		Bruce Vigon (Battelle Columbus Labs)	1993
Resource and Environmental Profile Analysis of Children's Diaper Systems	Diapers		Franklin Associates	1993
Eco-Profile Studies of Fabrication Methods of IBM Computers: Sheet Metal Computer Covers	Computers	IBM	IBM	1993
Single-Use versus Reusable Drapes and Gowns: A Health, Economic, and Environmental Comparison	Surgical drapes and gowns	Johnson & Johnson	Arthur D. Little	1993

A.9

Title of LCA case study or related study	Category	Performed for	Performed by	Date
Life-Cycle Assessment on Recycled Office Paper	Virgin white paper and recycled paper	DoE	DoE	1993
Life Cycle Inventory Demonstrating Residential Nylon Carpeting	Carpeting	EPA	Battelle Columbus Labs	1993 (interim report)
Environmental Resource Guide—Building Materials: [life-cycle analysis on] Plywood	Plywood	American Institute of Architects, EPA	SCG	January 1993
Environmental Resource Guide—Building Materials: [life-cycle analysis on] Thermal Insulation Highlights	Thermal insulation high-lights	American Institute of Architects, EPA	SCG	January 1993
LCA of a Computer Work Station	Computer workstation	MCC		March 1993
Resource and Environmental Profile Analysis of a Manufactured Apparel Product: Woman's Knit Polyester Blouse	Woman's blouse	American Fiber Manufac-turers Association	Franklin Associates	June 1993
Environmental Resource Guide—Building Materials: [life-cycle analysis on] Steel Framing: Technical Report	Steel framing	American Institute of Architects, EPA	SCG	July 1993
Environmental Resource Guide—Building Materials: [life-cycle analysis on] Wood Framing: Technical Report	Wood framing	American Institute of Architects, EPA	SCG	July 1993
Environmental Resource Guide—Building Materials: [life-cycle analysis on] Plaster and Lath: Technical Report	Plaster and lath	American Institute of Architects, EPA	SCG	July 1993
Environmental Resource Guide—Building Materials: [life-cycle analysis on] Glass	Glass	American Institute of Architects, EPA		October 1993
Biomass-Ethanol Total Energy Cycle Assessment (Fuel Cycle Evaluations of Biomass-Ethanol and Reformulated Gasoline)	Biomass-ethanol and reformulated gasoline alternative	DoE	Pacific Northwest Laboratory, National Renewable Energy Laboratory, Oak Ridge National Laboratory, others	December 1993

Title of LCA case study or related study	Category	Performed for	Performed by	Date
Mandated Recycling Rates: Impacts on Energy Consumption and Municipal Solid Waste Volume			Argonne National Laboratory	December 1993
LCA on electricity options (not exact title)		DoE	DoE	End of 1993
Life Cycle Assessment of Reclamation Options for a Photographic Fixer Used in Graphic Arts Image Processing	Photographic fixer	Eastman Kodak Company	Ecobalance, Inc.	1994
Energy Implications of Integrated Solid Waste Management Systems	Waste management	New York State Energy Research and Development Authority	Tellus Institute	1994 (finalized version)
Electrotechnology Case Studies 1. Automobile, electric 2. Canoe, electric 3. Car warmer, electric 4. Clothes drying, heat pump 5. Clothes drying, microwave 6. Cold vaporization 7. Commercial cooling 8. Commercial laundry, ozone 9. Copper melting 10. Dairy processing 11. Dishwashing, ultrasonic 12. Electric airport shuttle 13. Electric mill 14. Electric moped 15. Electroreactivated carbon bed 16. Farm chore tractor 17. Farm pump 18. Fax 19. Flash bake cooking 20. Forging, direct resistance	See first column	The Edison Electric Institute	Mills, McCarthy & Associates/Chem Systems	Published 1994

A.11

Title of LCA case study or related study	Category	Performed for	Performed by	Date
Electrotechnology Case Studies	See first column	The Edison Electric Institute	Mills, McCarthy & Associates/Chem Systems	Published 1994
21. Forging, induction				
22. Freeze concentration, dairy				
23. Freeze concentration, sugar				
24. Freeze concentration, water				
25. Garbage disposer				
26. Gas-line compressor				
27. Glass bottles				
28. Grill, electric				
29. Heat pump, geothermal				
30. Heated floor tiles				
31. Ion blasting air cleaning				
32. Irrigation pump				
33. Kitchen fax				
34. Ladle preheating, electric resistance				
35. Lawn leaf mulching, electric vacuum				
36. Magazine ink drying, uv				
37. Medical waste, electron beam				
38. Medical waste, Medaway-1				
39. Medical waste, microwave				
40. Meglev train				
41. Microwave oven				
42. Mower, cordless electric				
43. Noise cancellation muffler				
44. Outdoor lighting versus gas light				
45. Paint curing, infrared				
46. Paint spraying, supercritical CO_2				
47. Parboiling rice, microwave				
48. Pasta drying, microwave				

Title of LCA case study or related study	Category	Performed for	Performed by	Date
Electrotechnology Case Studies	See first column	The Edison Electric Institute	Mills, McCarthy & Associates/Chem Systems	Published 1994
49. Powdered coating curing, ir				
50. Powdered coating curing, uv				
51. Powdered plastic coating curing, ir				
52. Pressure washing, electric				
53. Riding lawn mower				
54. Sand reclamation, ir				
55. Silk-screen curing, uv				
56. Telecommuting				
57. Trash compactor				
58. Wastewater treatment, reverse osmosis				
59. Water heater, heat pump				
60. Water-jet paint stripping				
61. Welding of tube, resistance				
62. Yarn drying, radio frequency				
Technical "Audits" of 17 Selected Electrotechnologies				
1. Active acoustic muffler				
2. Cooling tower water ozonation				
3. Continuous electromembrane deionization				
4. Corona discharge VOC/air toxics destruction				
5. Electroreactivated carbon bed absorption				
6. Electrostatic coating				
7. Ion blast indoor air cleaning				
8. IR paint coating				
9. Microwave clothes drying				

Title of LCA case study or related study	Category	Performed for	Performed by	Date
Technical "Audits" of 17 Selected Electrotechnologies 10. Pressurized water cutting 11. Supercritical CO_2 paint spraying 12. Toxic waste vitrification 13. Ultrasonic commercial dish washing 14. UV/EB cured paints and coatings 15. UV irradiation water treatment 16. UV setting of offset printing inks 17. Water-jet-spray paint stripping	See first column	The Edison Electric Institute	Mills, McCarthy & Associates/Chem Systems	Published 1994
Electric Vehicle Total Energy Cycle Assessment (a.k.a. Life-Cycle Assessment of Electric and Reformulated Gasoline Vehicles)	Electric and reformulated gasoline vehicles	DoE	Battelle, Pacific Northwest Labs, and DoE	1994 (draft version)
Life Cycle Assessment of Ethylene Glycol and Propylene Glycol Based Antifreeze	Antifreeze	Union Carbide Corp.	Franklin Associates	1994
Energy Implications of Glass-Container Recycling	Glass containers		Argonne National Laboratory	March 1994
ERG—Wallcoverings and Plastic Laminates	Wall coverings and plastic laminates			Summer 1994
Environmental Resource Guide—Building Materials: [life-cycle analysis on] Gypsum Board Systems: Technical Report	Gypsum board systems	American Institute of Architects, EPA	SCG	Winter 1994

A.14

Title of LCA case study or related study	Category	Performed for	Performed by	Date
Environmental Resource Guide—Building Materials: [life-cycle analysis on] Acoustical Ceiling Panels and Tiles and Suspension Systems: Technical Report	Acoustical ceiling panels and tiles and suspension systems	American Institute of Architects, EPA	SCG	Winter 1994
PVC Pipe Life-Cycle Assessment	PVC pipes			Sometime in the last 5 years
Phosphates LCA	Phosphates	Tenneco		Unknown
Life-Cycle Energy Assessment of Lightweight Vehicles	Lightweight vehicles	DoE	Argonne National Laboratory	In progress
Tellus-EPA study using degreasing as a case study	Degreasing	EPA Pollution Prevention Division	Tellus Institute	In progress
LCA on Industrial Laundries	Shop towels and disposable paper towels	EPA	EPA	In progress
Energy Lifecycle Analysis of Newspaper	Newspaper		Argonne National Laboratory	In progress
Kraft Bag versus Plastic Bag Life-Cycle Assessment	Bags	American Forest & Paper Association (AFPA)§	Roy F. Weston, Inc.	In progress
LCA on Municipal Solid Waste Options	Municipal solid waste	EPA	EPA	In progress
Reformulated Gasoline Life-Cycle (this LCA is included as a part of the LCA on recycled office paper)	Gasoline	DoE	DoE	In progress
Fuel Cycle Assessments of 8 Fuel Cycles Including Coal, Biomass, Oil, Natural Gas, and Small Hydroelectric Cycles¶	8 different fuels	DoE and Commission of European Communities	DoE and EC	In progress

A.15

Title of LCA case study or related study	Category	Performed for	Performed by	Date
Aluminum LCA (not exact title)	Aluminum	Alcoa, Reynolds Aluminum, others		In progress
Life-Cycle Analysis on the Effects on the Environment of the Manufacture, Use, and Eventual Decommissioning of a Gas Storage and Transfer System for a Weapon Component	Gas storage and transfer system for a weapon component	DoE, Office of Waste Management	Sandia National Laboratories	In progress
Urethane LCA	Urethane	ARCO and The American Plastics Council		In progress
Life Cycle Design Case Study	Business phones	EPA	NPPC, AT&T, University of Michigan	1995
Life Cycle Design Case Study	Heavy-duty oil filter	EPA	University of Michigan, NPPC, Allied-Signal	1995

Resource and environmental profile analysis (REPA) is a term used by Franklin Associates for a life-cycle inventory as described by the Environmental Protection Agency and SETAC.

†The source for this information is the bibliography section of "Industrial Pollution Prevention: A Critical Review," prepared by Harry Freeman et al. Another source, the bibliography section of "Resource and Environmental Profile Analysis: A Life Cycle Environmental Analysis for Products and Procedures," by Franklin Associates, states that this life-cycle assessment was completed in 1977 by Midwest Research Institute and Franklin Associates.

‡This life-cycle assessment may be the same LCA as "Total Energy Impacts of the Use of Plastics Products in the United States."

§According to AFPA, it is considering having LCAs performed on bleached paperboard, recycled paperboard, and tissue paper in the near future. AFPA is currently accepting proposals for such LCAs.

¶DoE is conducting this project in cooperation with the Commission of European Communities. The U.S. and EC research teams are both undertaking the coal fuel cycle assessment. The U.S. team is leading the efforts on biomass, oil, natural gas, and small hydroelectric cycles.

INDEX

Index note: The *f.* after a page number refers to a figure; the *t.* to a table.

ABOUT THE EDITOR

Mary Ann Curran is a project officer in the Systems Analysis Branch of the United States Environmental Protection Agency, where she manages the Branch's growing Life Cycle Assessment Research Program. She is the EPA representative to the ISO 14000 subcommittee on LCA, a member of the ASTM subcommittee on Green Buildings, and chairs the SETAC committee on Streamlining LCA. She is the author or coauthor of numerous papers on life-cycle assessment and life-cycle design, and is well-known internationally for her research on these topics. She resides in Cincinnati, Ohio.